The GIANT Encyclopedia of Lesson Plans

The GIANT Encyclopedia of Lesson Plans

For Children 3 to 6

More Than 250 Lesson Plans Created by Teachers for Teachers

Edited by Kathy Charner, Maureen Murphy, and Charlie Clark

Gryphon House, Inc.
Silver Spring, Maryland

© 2008 Gryphon House
Published by Gryphon House, Inc.
10770 Columbia Pike, Suite 201, Silver Spring, MD 20901
800.638.0928; 301.595.9500; 301.595.0051 (fax)

Visit us on the web at www.gryphonhouse.com

Illustrations: Kathi Whelan Dery
Cover Art: Beverly Hightshoe

Reprinted August 2010

Library of Congress Cataloging-in-Publication Data
The giant encyclopedia of lesson plans / edited by Kathy Charner, Maureen Murphy, and Charlie Clark.
    p. cm.
 Includes indexes.
 ISBN 978-0-87659-068-3
 1. Education, Preschool—Curricula—United States. 2. Lesson plans—United States. 3. Curriculum planning—United States. I. Charner, Kathy. II. Murphy, Maureen. III. Clark, Charlie.
 LB1140.4.G53 2008
 371.3028—dc22
                              2008010074

Bulk purchase
Gryphon House books are available for special premiums and sales promotions as well as for fund-raising use. Special editions or book excerpts also can be created to specification. For details, contact the Director of Marketing at Gryphon House.

Disclaimer
Gryphon House, Inc. and the authors cannot be held responsible for damage, mishap, or injury incurred during the use of or because of activities in this book. Appropriate and reasonable caution and adult supervision of children involved in activities and corresponding to the age and capability of each child involved, is recommended at all times. Do not leave children unattended at any time. Observe safety and caution at all times.

Table of Contents

Table of Contents

THE GIANT ENCYCLOPEDIA OF LESSON PLANS

Table of Contents

Table of Contents

"What is my child doing all day long?" asks a concerned family member as she drops off her four-year-old one morning, *"When I ask my child what he does each day, he says he plays. Is he playing all day long? When does he learn? What are you teaching him?"*

Most teachers hear these questions often. Family members want to know what their children are learning and how it is being taught. One way to ensure you have an answer to these questions is to structure the children's days using a well-written and understandable lesson plan. If a family member asks what her child is learning, showing her a lesson plan gives her a better sense of how you structure each day to give young children opportunities to learn.

The lesson plan, which is an outline of how you intend to cover a certain topic in the classroom, helps you concentrate on the concepts you want the children to learn. A lesson plan includes children's books and songs or poems you will need to help the children learn, as well a description of how you will assess the children's understanding of the material covered in the lesson plan. A well-written lesson plan will help you stay on track throughout the day and make sure the children understand the concept you are teaching them. It is also an effective tool to communicate with family members so they know what to expect from their child's learning experiences.

It is important to have a lesson plan in a preschool classroom because preschool children are developing social, emotional, cognitive, physical, and literacy skills, all of which prepare them to be ready to learn in kindergarten. A well thought-out and effectively implemented lesson plan helps you keep the children on track toward accomplishing their educational goals.

Teaching Preschoolers

Lesson plans must be flexible so you may cater to the needs and learning styles of individual children. There is no room for rigid lesson plans and worksheets in a supportive educational environment that engages young children in problem solving and inquiry learning. Fill a preschooler's day with opportunities for the child to engage and interact with the environment. Children should experience art, engage in construction, have opportunities to play music and to dance, experiment with science, and have the chance to participate in a myriad of other learning activities in a variety of centers. During this time, when to the untrained eye it might appear the children are "just playing," you should travel among learning centers, offering opportunities for the children to expand on their own ideas and giving them a chance to take on new experiences.

Following the Lesson Plan

Before following a lesson plan from this book, it is important to assess the needs and abilities of the children in your care. While each idea in this book certainly provides an enjoyable and educational experience, you are the best judge of how well it will work for the children in your class and whether you need to adapt it for your class.

The Components of Each Lesson Plan
The lesson plans in this book are well organized and easy to follow. The learning objectives are clear and concise, and each lesson plan covers all parts of the daily curriculum, including circle and group time activities, suggested book lists, activities for a variety of learning centers, ideas for curriculum-related snacks, reviews of the information each plan presents, and ways to assess how well the children are learning the material.

Circle or Group Time
Circle or Group Time is an integral part of the early-childhood experience and each plan in this book provides a fun and developmentally appropriate circle time activity that matches the unit of study and helps to achieve the stated objectives. When planning Circle or Group Time, remember to minimize the amount of time children spend sitting and listening. Circle Time for preschoolers should be a good mix of active and passive engagement. Sing a song, do a fingerplay, or engage in a movement activity in between those parts of a Circle or Group Time activity when the children are sitting and listening. This balance helps the children to stay engaged and makes it a pleasurable experience for all.

Center Time
Center Time is usually the time during which the children are actively learning. Each plan in this book contains activities across the curriculum that are meant for use in many different learning centers. Providing interesting and developmentally appropriate activities in different learning centers gives the children more opportunities to engage in active inquiry and support their own learning. It is your responsibility during this time to monitor the children carefully, intervening as necessary and offering insight or help in finding the answers to questions. For example, suppose your unit of study that day is on the transition from preschool to kindergarten. At Circle or Group Time, you read *Danny's First Day in Kindergarten* to the children and talk with the children about what they think it will be like when they go to a new and different school. At Center Time, some of the children go to the Dramatic Play Center you set up to resemble a typical kindergarten classroom by setting out a flannel board graph story, several books, some manipulatives, and a table with two chairs. You observe a little girl playing in the center as she places several dolls at the table, and begins yelling at the dolls, telling them to stop moving and be quiet. You approach and offer insight on her play.

"I can see that you are pretending to be the teacher," you might say, "can you tell me why you sound so angry?"

"They won't sit still. They are supposed to be learning their ABCs but they won't sit still."

"Do you remember the book we just read?"

"Yes, *Danny's First Day in Kindergarten.*"

"In the book, Danny was afraid to go to kindergarten. Do you remember why?"

"Yes, Danny was afraid he would not be allowed to play."

"Do you remember what the teacher did?"

"Yes, she let Danny play."

From there you can lead the child to the conclusion that while children do have to listen to the teacher in kindergarten, they will not be expected to sit quietly all day. This is a non-threatening, positive way to help a child better understand what kindergarten will be like.

Lesson Plans

Lesson planning does not come naturally to many teachers. There is no "lesson planning" gene. However, successful teachers do possess certain intrinsic traits: they enjoy teaching and being with children. Other skills teachers acquire through training and practice. As you learn to plan, organize, and present effective activities, your ability to produce quality lesson plans will also increase. These lesson plans provide direction to your teaching and learning that happens in your classroom. Teaching and learning are complex processes that cannot be left to chance.

Organization and Use

First, think about the reason for the lesson plan. A lesson plan is not just proof that you are doing your job; it is also a great way to help organize the curriculum. Lesson plans serve as records of the activities that children engage in. Lesson plans are instrumental in tracking successful ways of presenting concepts to young children. In addition, it is crucial to have written lesson plans available in the event you need a substitute teacher.

Second, allow adequate time to develop a lesson plan. You cannot write an effective plan on the run. It takes time and thought to prepare a lesson plan of activities that actively engage children. Ideally, give yourself 48 hours to prepare an effective lesson plan.

Third, develop your plan with care. Decide what the children will learn. Look at the current concept you are teaching and determine the next logical sequence. What new skills should you expand the lesson plan to include? What new knowledge should the children gain? When thinking about these things, try to include reference notes and materials so you can have them ready if you need them. Next, reflect on what the children already know. Is there new information they need to have before they can move on to what you want them to learn? How will today's activities build on yesterday's? Keep copies of any materials you may need to refer to with your lesson plan.

Ideas for Lesson Plans

The best source for inspiration on what to teach in the early-childhood classroom is the children. Listen to them, observe them, and talk to them, and you will quickly find out what interests them. For example, you might see a few children in the Dramatic Play area wearing hardhats and work vests. They then march across to the Block Center where they proceed to build large structures with the biggest blocks they can find. Observe this behavior and you will undoubtedly realize it is time for a unit on construction!

When planning, many teachers use the KWL chart. To do this, the teacher asks the children two questions about the unit of study: What do the children already know (K) and what do they want (W) to know. The third aspect (L) outlines what the children learned through the unit of study. To make a KWL chart, create a large three-column chart with appropriate headings that you can refer to as the unit progresses. A sample KWL chart looks like this:

All About Dinosaurs KWL Chart		
K—What we already know	W—What we want to know	L—What we have learned
Dinosaurs lived a long time ago.	Exactly how long ago did dinosaurs live?	We looked up dinosaurs on the computer and learned that they lived millions of years ago.
There are lots of different kinds of dinosaurs.	How many different types of dinosaurs are there and what are they?	We found out through research that there were more than 300 different kinds of dinosaurs. Since we could not study that many, we decided to concentrate on the tyrannosaurus rex, the pterodactyl, and the plesiosaur.
Some dinosaurs were mean and they ate other dinosaurs, but some were nice and only ate plants.	Which dinosaurs ate plants? Which dinosaurs ate other dinosaurs?	Currently researching
Some dinosaurs lived in the United States but we do not know where the others lived.	Where did dinosaurs live? How do we know where they lived?	We read a book that told us that dinosaurs lived all over the whole world. We know this because people find dinosaur fossils all over the world.

When planning for young children, limit the learning objectives to three or four so you can successfully complete the unit of study and meet all of your objectives.

Review

As the end of the day approaches, take some time to review with the children the ideas and activities they have been working with all day. This process is as simple as gathering the children in small groups and playing a quick game to assess how well the children are learning. For example, if you were studying dinosaurs, as cited above, consider presenting two or three dinosaur models to a group of children and ask them to show you the ones that ate plants and the ones that ate meat.

Assessment

A lesson plan is not complete without this final step to help you determine how well the children successfully completed the learning objectives. To assess the children's learning, present a fun and engaging activity from which you can ascertain how well the children understand the day's concepts. This can be as simple as asking children to point out red items in the room if you were learning about the color red. Or, ask yourself a question such as, "Do the children use the word *red* when talking to each other?" Listen carefully to classroom conversations to find the answer. If you find that the children did not adequately achieve the learning objectives, you may need to repeat the lesson plan at another time or in another manner. How well the children gain knowledge helps you determine which lesson plans to use in the future.

 *Virginia Jean Herrod, Columbia, South Carolina*

All About Us: Me and My Classmates

Learning Objectives The children will:
1. Experience self-discovery and build self-esteem.
2. Learn about each other.

Circle or Group Time Activity
- Sing the following song with the children.

  What Can You Do? (author unknown)
  (Tune: "Skip to My Lou")
  What can you do all by yourself?
  What can you do all by yourself?
  What can you do all by yourself?
  How about you, _____?

- The children take turns holding a microphone or tape recorder and answering the question in the song. Answers might include "dress myself," "put on my shoes," "write my name," "brush my teeth," and so on.

Learning Centers **Note:** In many of the following activities, children need to use photographs of themselves. Have family members send in photos of their children, or take photos of the children using a digital camera. Make copies of the photos so that you have several of each child.

Art
Provide drawing paper, markers, crayons, yarn, and tissue paper. Invite the children to look at their faces in the mirror and draw self-portraits. Make sure they use the appropriate colors marker or crayons for eyes and yarn for hair. Ask them to describe their hair color and eyes. Underneath each portrait, help them write their names, ages, and hair and eye colors.

Dramatic Play
Encourage the children to talk about themselves to each other while playing; they may use dolls or puppets to talk for them.

Math
Create a graph to determine the children's favorite centers. Glue four photos of different centers on the left side of the graph. Invite the children to put their photos on the row of the graph marked for their favorite centers. When complete, have them count the photos in each row and write the totals at the end of the rows. Count the photos aloud with those children who need help.

Literacy
Use the pages from the Art Center activity to make an "All About Me" book for each child (using a hole punch and yarn or a stapler). On another piece of

paper, the children glue photos or draw pictures of themselves as babies or toddlers. Provide glitter, glue, and other to make covers for their books.

Writing

Write "I Can Do It Myself" on top of a piece of chart paper. Each child places a photo of himself on a line of the chart paper and tells you what to write next to his photo. Older children can write the words themselves. Give each child a piece of paper divided into four sections (My Favorite Color, My Favorite Food, My Favorite Activity, and What I Can Do Myself). Ask the children to draw pictures in each box related to the subject. If possible, the child can also write about each category. Add this to the "All About Me" books the children make in the Art Center.

Book Suggestions

All By Myself by Mercer Mayer
I Can Do It Myself by Emily Kingsley

Snack

Send a note home to the children's families, asking each family to send in their child's favorite snack to share with the children in the class on a designated day.

Review

During Circle or Group Time, read the "I Can Do It Myself" chart with the children's help and review the graph that shows the children's favorite centers. Ask the children to count the photos for each center. Have them share their "All About Me" books with the class.

Assessment

Can the children say what color their hair and eyes are? Can the children describe what they can do by themselves?

Related Song

I Am Special by Deborah Hannes Litfin
(Tune: "Twinkle, Twinkle, Little Star")
I am special, you are too.
We are friends, here at school.
We play together and learn too.
We are friends, here at school.

 Deborah Hannes Litfin, Forest Hills, NY

Differences

Learning Objectives The children will:
1. Learn about themselves.
2. Talk about the likenesses and differences of people.
3. Understand that they are special in their own ways.

Circle or Group Time Activity
- Attach an unbreakable mirror to the bottom of the inside of a box. Gather the children and show them the box with the lid on.
- Do not open the box. Instead, engage the children's interest by telling them there is something in the box. Start by saying: "I have something very special in my box. Can you guess what it might be?" Allow time for the children to guess.
- After the children offer several suggestions, tell them there is a picture of someone very special in the box, and you are going to let them see who it is one at a time. Ask them not to say anything after they have looked in the box so all the children can be surprised.
- The first child opens the box, looks inside, and then passes it to the next child.
- When all the children have seen themselves in the mirror, ask them who they saw. Ask them if they noticed the color of their hair, skin, or eyes and talk about different physical attributes. You might even want to make a class graph of hair colors or eye colors.
- Remind them that you said the person in the box was very special. Tell them everyone is special.

Learning Centers

Art
Provide multicultural skin-toned paints, paper, playdough, crayons, markers, wiggle eyes, and yarn for the children to make self-portraits. Have them use cotton swabs to dab paint on their wrists to find the color that most closely matches their skin color. Talk about how people have a variety of skin colors, which is one thing that makes everyone unique.

Dramatic Play
Make a stage out of large hollow blocks, or mark an area on the floor. Add different costumes or stage clothing, props, and a microphone and let the children put on a show. They can dress up and sing and dance to show how special they are.

Sand and Water
Line the bottom of the water table with aluminum foil. Be sure it lies flat and smooth. Invite the children to look at their reflections in the aluminum foil and talk about their features.

Science

Add unbreakable mirrors of different sizes and other reflective objects to the Science Center. As the children look in the mirrors, talk about their hair, eye, and skin colors.

Snack and Cooking

Use people-shaped cookie cutters to cut pieces of bread into people shapes. Provide watercolor brushes and food coloring for the children to use to paint them. If possible, use colors that represent skin colors, or let the children paint their pieces whatever color they want for a crazy, unique snack!

Book Suggestions

Here Are My Hands by Bill Martin Jr.
The Skin I'm In by Pat Thomas
We're Different, We're the Same by Bobbi Cates
Whoever You Are by Mem Fox

Snack

Provide food options that have both similarities and differences, such as bananas and oranges (both fruits but with different colors and tastes), or crackers and noodles (both starches but with different textures). Encourage the children to discuss the ways in which they differ and the ways in which they are the same.

Review

Have the children look in the mirror in the box again and name something that makes them special (their hair, eyes, something they like to do, or their clothes).

Assessment

Can the children recognize their own features, including hair, skin, and eyes when the feature is called out during class? ("If you have brown hair, stand up.") Can they find someone who has a similar feature or a different feature? Can they name something that makes them unique?

Related Song

You Are Special by Shelley Hoster
(Tune: "Twinkle, Twinkle, Little Star")
You are special, yes it's true.
There is no one just like you.
You have your own beautiful smile,
And your own special style.
Come on, everybody, can't you see,
You're as special as can be!

 *Shelley Hoster, Lawrenceville, GA*

Hands

Learning Objectives The children will:
1. Discuss what fingers and hands do.
2. Practice following directions.
3. Refine small motor skills.

Circle or Group Time Activity
■ Read *Here Are My Hands* by Bill Martin, Jr. and John Archambault to the children, or teach them the following song:

My Hands Can Wave by Margery Kranyik Fermino
My hands can wave,
My hands can clap.
Then I lay them in my lap.
My fingers wiggle fast and slow,
Then back into my lap they go.
My thumb can circle 'round and 'round,
Pointing up and then straight down.

■ Repeat the verse with the children, inviting them to mimic the motions the verse describes.
■ Invite children to look at their hands. Ask them questions such as, "How many fingers and thumbs do you have?" "Can you twirl your thumbs in a circle?" Ask them to touch their fingers to their palms, wiggle their fingers fast and slow, and so on.

Learning Centers ### Art
Provide magazines, construction paper, child-safe scissors, and glue. Invite the children to cut or tear out pictures of people doing things with their hands. As the children glue the pictures to construction paper, talk with them about the pictures.

Dramatic Play
Encourage the children to think about ways they communicate with others using only their hands and fingers and no words. For example, they can wave hello or goodbye, use their hands to say "come here" or "stop," and give a thumbs up to say "good job." If possible, teach the children some simple signs using sign language.

Math
Provide children with markers and paper or counting chips, and pictures of a triangle, circle, oval, square, and rectangle. Ask them

to use the chips or make marks on paper to count the different ways their fingers and hands can make shapes (finger-to-thumb circles, two fingers and two thumbs for a triangle, and so on). Children can increase their possibilities with partners.

OVAL   **SQUARE**   **RECTANGLE**

Science
The children place a fingertip on a stamp pad and then press it onto paper to make a fingerprint. Invite them to look at their fingerprints using a magnifying glass. Have them compare their fingerprints with friends.

Writing
Provide drawing paper, lined paper, and markers. Help the children trace their hands on the drawing paper. This will be the cover sheet. Have them dictate what their hands can do as you write their words on lined paper. Staple their cover sheets to their lined papers.

Book Suggestions
Finger Rhymes by Marc Brown
Head, Shoulders, Knees, and Toes by Zita Newcome
Here Are My Hands by Bill Martin, Jr. and John Archambault

Snack
Make thumbprint cookies with the children. Use a favorite sugar-cookie recipe, or buy refrigerated sugar-cookie dough. Let children place spoonfuls of cookie dough on cookie sheets. Have them make thumbprints in the center of each cookie. Fill the center of each cookie with jam, if desired. Bake and enjoy.

Review
Review the songs and incorporate them into classroom favorites during Circle or Group Time. Discuss the different ways the children use their hands at home, at school, and at play.

Assessment
Observe children making connections between their hands and fingers and the songs and verses. Can they follow directions given in the songs and verses? Did they appear to enjoy participating? Were they able to complete the activities?

 Margery Kranyik Fermino, West Roxbury, MA

Happy Birthday to Me!

Learning Objectives
The children will:
1. Learn the dates of their births.
2. Learn what a birth certificate is.

Circle or Group Time Activity
- Ahead of time, wrap a birth certificate (create a facsimile) in a box and tie it with a bow.
- Ask the children to guess what is inside. After a few guesses, open the box and show them the birth certificate.
- Explain that everyone gets one of these special papers when they are born, telling the name of the person born and the parents' names.
- Tell the children when your birthday is, then show the children the picture for the month of your birth on a calendar.
- Show the children every month and ask them to stand when you show the months in which they were born.
- Recite the following poem with the children:

Poem of the Months by Susan Oldham Hill

January snowflakes,	*July has the Fourth,*
February hearts,	*And August has the rays!*
March has shamrocks,	*September gets much cooler,*
April's raindrops start.	*And October's leaves do fall,*
May has sunshine,	*November is so thankful,*
June has summer days,	*December's last of all.*

- Go back over the calendar pictures and say the poem again. See how many children have birthdays in each month. Practice saying their birthdays.
- Explain to them that even our country has a birthday. Tell them about July 4, fireworks, and show them the copy of the Declaration of Independence. Display the pictures of the nation's birthday celebrations.

Learning Centers

Art
Make birthday books with the children. Provide 9" x 12" construction paper in light colors and markers for the children to make self-portraits. When the drawings are finished, take dictation from the children about the dates of their birth and a sentence about why they like birthdays, or a special birthday they remember. Staple the drawings together to make a classroom book. **Safety note:** Adult-only step.

Dramatic Play
Make a party store. Provide a cash box, play money, and party items to buy, such as hats, banners, wrapped boxes, table decorations, and favors. Have on hand shopping bags and store receipts.

Small Motor
Provide headbands, folded for strength, with each child's name and birthday written across the front. Encourage the children to decorate the headbands with birthday stickers.

Math

Make a birthday bar graph. Ahead of time, prepare a large chart paper with a grid of boxes 7" x 4", marked in 12 columns and 10 rows, with the names of the months in the bottom row. Make a 6" x 3" name card for each child to fit in the grid boxes. Ask the children to tell which month they were born in, checking the list for those who are not sure. Show them how to tape or glue their name cards

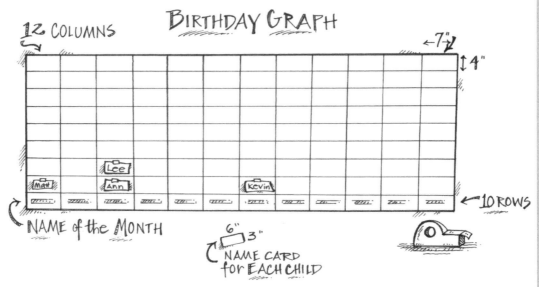

in the grid, starting at the bottom box nearest the name of the month. Ask the children which month has the most birthdays and which has the fewest.

Music

Provide rhythm instruments the children can use to play songs, such as "Happy Birthday" and "Yankee Doodle Dandy."

Book Suggestions

Happy Birthday, Dear Duck by Eve Bunting
Happy Birthday, Moon by Frank Asch
Hooray for the Fourth of July by Wendy Watson
Over and Over by Charlotte Zolotow

Snack

Bake apple or carrot muffins. Serve each with a birthday candle for children to blow out after they sing "Happy Birthday" together.

Review

Recite "Poem of the Months" with the children several times. Display the birthday graph and ask the children to explain what it shows. Name each month and ask the children to stand if their birthday falls in that month. Read the birthday book and enjoy each child's thoughts about his special day. Wear the birthday headbands and discuss birthdays coming soon.

Assessment

Ask the children to tell their birthdates. If necessary, tell them the month to help them remember.

Susan Oldham Hill, Lakeland, FL

I Am Special

Learning Objectives The children will:
1. Feel good about themselves.
2. Learn that they are all unique and different.
3. Find their own special talents.

Circle or Group Time Activity
- Pass an unbreakable mirror around and let each child find one or more thing that they like about themselves.
- Let each of them take a turn describing to you what they like. For example, "I like my hair," "I like my eyes," and so on.
- Write the children's names and their descriptions of their features that they like on paper and then hang them up in the classroom for all to see.

Learning Centers

Art
Set out wiggle eyes and collage materials beside several face shapes cut out of construction paper. Encourage the children to decorate face shapes to look like themselves.

Blocks
Tape individual photos of each child on blocks for use in the Blocks Center.

Dramatic Play
Set out a prop box containing old hairstyling materials that have their cords cut off, like curling irons, hair dryers, and so on. Add unbreakable mirrors, combs/brushes (disinfect after each use), pretend nail polish, rollers, hairnets, and salon aprons. Let children have fun creating hairstyles for each other and pretending to be salon stylists.

Literacy
Take full-body photos of each child, develop, cut out their body shapes, laminate them, and add magnets to the backs of each child shape. Write each child's name on construction paper and laminate it, adding a small magnet to the back. Set out the photos and names so the children can match them.

Library

Set out paper, crayons, and markers and encourage the children to draw self-portraits. Collect the portraits and staple them into a book. Title the book "I Like Me." Laminate the pages and set it out for the children to look through.

Book Suggestions

ABC I Like Me! by Nancy Carlson
I Like Me! by Nancy Carlson
I'm Gonna Like Me: Letting Off a Little Self-Esteem by Jamie Lee Curtis

Snack

Have children bring in their favorite snack to share with everyone. Let them each have a day that is just for them to bring a special snack. Have a sign-up sheet for families to choose a date for that month.

Review

Play games that have to do with acting, using a favorite talent like clapping, jumping, balancing on one foot, and so on.

Assessment

Ask the children to describe their favorite things about themselves.

 *Sue Myhre, Bremerton, WA*

I Like Me

Learning Objectives The children will:
1. Get to know each other.
2. Learn body-parts awareness and self-awareness.
3. Learn to develop cooperative behavior.

Circle or Group Time Activity
■ With the children, sing "The Hokey Pokey," performing the actions that the song describes. Sing several verses, including various body parts in each verse.

Learning Centers

Art
Set out paper towel rolls, scissors, tape, markers, yarn, and felt. Show the children how to draw faces on the paper towel rolls and then use the other materials to create characters or models of themselves.

Large Motor
Play "Simon Says" using body parts. Example: "Simon says hop on one foot," "Simon says jump on two feet," "swing your arms," "bend your elbows," and so on.

Literacy
Set out several pictures of people, cutouts from magazines, or photos of the children with one body part cut out of each photo. Ask the children to name the body parts that are missing, or to match the cutouts of the body parts to their photos. Also consider using images of animals as a variation on this center.

Math

Put cutouts of the letters of each child's name in baggies, and then write the children's names on the fronts of their baggies. Set out the baggies so the children can compare how many letters are in each of their names.

Music

Sing the song "Head, Shoulders, Knees, and Toes," and have children touch the body parts the song describes.

Book Suggestions

I Like Me! by Nancy Carlson
The Kissing Hand by Audrey Penn
My Hands by Aliki

Snack

Set out round crackers, cheese, jelly, raisins, carrots, and other small food items, encouraging the children to use the ingredients to make edible faces.

Review

Just before going home for the day, ask the children to sit in a circle. One child rolls a beach ball to another child in the circle, says the child's name, and says one positive thing about that child. The child responds by saying "thank you" and rolls the ball to the next child.

Assessment

Play a hand game with the children, asking them to pat a different body part to see how many body parts they can identify.

 Eileen Lucas, Fort McMurray, Alberta, Canada

I'll Find Myself

Learning Objectives   The children will:
1. Recognize their noses, eyes, and mouths.
2. Develop their small and large motor skills.

Circle or Group Time Activity
- Collect photographs of all children.
- Change the children's appearance in the photographs by drawing hats, moustaches, earrings, necklaces, ribbons, or different hair on them. Be sure to not to alter their eyes, noses, and mouths.
- Pin all the photographs on the tagboard.
- Challenge the children to pick out their photographs, and then ask them to explain how they knew which photos were theirs.
- If they are having trouble, encourage the children to help one another find their photos.

Learning Centers   **Art**

Fold a 10" x 2" card paper strip in half so each half is 1" wide. Help the children write their names on both sides of the card, with the crease at the top. Open the folded card slightly and display the creation on their desks as a nameplate.

Blocks

Challenge the children to stack the blocks as tall as themselves to measure their heights.

Listening

Tape the voice of every child in the classroom. Play the tape in the classroom, explaining that every person has a unique voice. Ask the children to guess whose voices they hear in the tape.

Math

Ask the children to wash their hands. Ask them to count the number of teeth they have by touching each one in their mouths.

Science

Tell the children how their bodies grow all the time. Paint their little fingernails with nail polish. Observe these nails daily for two weeks. Tell the children the plain area between their skin and the nail polish shows how much the nails have grown.

Book Suggestions

Eyes, Nose, Finger, and Toes by Judy Hindley
Look What I Can Do by Jose Aruego

Snack

Declare a month of favorite foods. Tell the children that every day they try a food that one of their classmates suggests. Ask the children to talk about favorite snacks their families prepare for them at home. Consult with the children's families about how to prepare the various snacks, and then serve a new one each day to the children.

Review

Ask the children to point out multiple things they have in common with the other children in the classroom.

Assessment

Ask the children to describe the objects in the classroom that belong to them.

Related Song

Do Your Ears Hang Low? (Traditional)

Do your ears hang low?
Do they wobble to and fro?
Can you tie 'em in a knot?
Can you tie 'em in a bow?
Can you throw 'em over your shoulder
*   like a continental soldier?*
Do your ears hang low?

(additional verses)
Do your eyes hang low?
Does your nose hang low?
Does your neck hang low?

 Shyamala Shanmugasundaram, Nerul, Navi Mumbai, India

Me

. . . .

Learning Objectives

The children will:
1. Talk about what makes them special.
2. Develop their self-esteem.
3. Improve their oral language skills.

Circle or Group Time Activity

- Bring in a photo of your family. Collect items that represent you and place them in a bag.
- Wear a lei around your neck as you display your family photo.
- Talk about your family, hobbies, talents, and so on as you hold up each item from the bag.
- Explain to the children that each one of them is very special and unique.
- Take the lei off your neck and place it around a child's neck. Invite that child to stand up as the class chants, "One, two, three…." The child then replies with "…all about me," and shares one or more things that make him special.
- Provide the child with the following sentence prompts if he needs help with what to say. For instance, "I am good at…," "I like…," "My family…," and so on.
- Give the child a round of applause and continue the activity as that child puts the lei around another child's neck.

Learning Centers

Art
Invite children to create a brightly colored "All About Me" quilt by following the steps below.
- Give each child a piece of bright yellow art paper divided into nine sections.
- In the center space, each child writes his name and uses collage materials to decorate the center square. If available, invite each child to glue a picture of himself in the center square.
- The children use oil crayons to draw pictures depicting the special things about them in each of the eight spaces of the quilt. For example, the children can draw pictures of sports equipment, pets, family outings, hobbies, and toys.
  Invite the children to show their quilts and talk about them to their classmates before they take them home.

Math
Invite children to weigh themselves and measure various parts of their bodies. Help the children write their findings on "people-shaped" pieces of paper.

Music
Have the children play the first three keys on the xylophone as they sing, "One, two, three, I like me." Have them play three notes up the scale and then the same three notes back down the scale, as they sing the tune over and over.

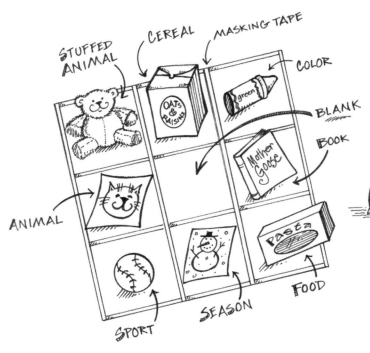

STUFFED ANIMAL · CEREAL · MASKING TAPE · COLOR · BLANK · BOOK · ANIMAL · FOOD · SEASON · SPORT

FAVORITE THINGS

Large Motor

Prepare a tic-tac-toe grid and a tossing line on the floor with masking tape. Place an item (such as a toy, book, or crayon) in each square, leaving the center square empty. Invite pairs of children to stand behind the tossing line. Each player takes turns tossing five beanbags onto the grid and talking about his favorite color, cereal, book, and so on, according to where the beanbags land.

BEANBAGS

Science

Place several objects that relate to healthy habits on the table and discuss how people use the items to take care of their bodies. Talk about the importance of eating right, getting enough sleep, exercising, keeping our bodies clean, and so on.

Book Suggestions

ABC I Like Me! by Nancy Carlson
I Like Me! by Nancy Carlson

Snack

Serve up a platter of crunchy "Me Cakes." Have the children spread peanut butter or cream cheese on a rice cake and top it with small pieces of fruit, cheese, nuts, or other toppings to create their own faces.

Review

Place each child's name card or picture card in a "Me Box" and pass the box around the circle. Each child removes a classmate's card and says something special about that child.

Assessment

Ask the child three questions about himself, such as "What do you like to do?" "What are you good at?" and "What is your family like?"

 *Mary J. Murray, Mazomanie, WI*

Move Me

Learning Objectives The children will:

1. Learn how we use our bodies to move.
2. Identify sounds our movement makes.
3. Learn to identify body parts.
4. Develop large motor skills.

Circle or Group Time Activity

- Recite "Head, Shoulders, Knees, and Toes" with the children, asking that they touch the body parts they mention as they sing.
- Tell the children that they will be learning about body movements today.

Learning Centers

Art

Tape two long sheets of white mural paper on the floor. Place four different tempera paint colors in flat, disposable aluminum pans. Have children place their feet in the two colors of their choice. Play some danceable music and encourage children to move with the music on the paper. Have an easy accessible wash area for children to wash off their feet and dry them with paper towels.

Dramatic Play

Create an exercise room. Provide mats, water bottles, hula-hoops, towels, jump ropes and exercise charts for children to use in the pretend gym.

Literacy

Set out markers, crayons, and several sheets of paper with the following phrase written on them: "I like to _____ it, _____ it." Ask each child to pick an action word to place in the blanks. For example, a child might say, "I like to jump it, jump it." Use a colored marker to copy each child's response on a sheet of paper, and then give the children the sheets with their responses and encourage them to illustrate their pages.

Math

Place cards with the numerals 0–20 on them on the floor. Play music and invite the children to dance and move to the beat. Occasionally stop the music and encourage the children to find a number to stand on. Once the children all find numbers, have them say which number they are standing on.

Science

Provide a poster of a child's body. Point out the parts of the body and name them. Discuss with the children what each part can do. Ask the children to name things that their hands, feet, legs, arms, and fingers help them do. Have children stand up and tell them to move the parts mentioned.

Writing

Draw or cut out a small picture of a foot, leg, arm, and hand. Make a copy of the pictures for each child. Help the children make flipbooks by folding a 18" x 24" piece of construction paper in half lengthwise. Unfold the paper and measure four equal sections from the top of page to the fold and cut along each line to make four flaps. Fold the paper and glue the pictures of the foot, leg, arm, and hand (one of each) on front flaps. Encourage the children to use magazines to find things they can do with their feet, legs, arms, and hands. Glue one picture under each flap on the uncut folded paper.

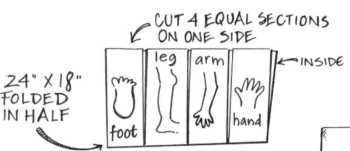

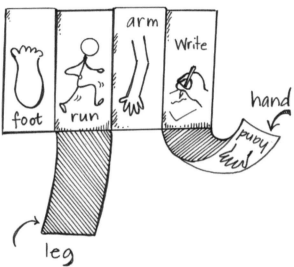

Book Suggestions

Clap Your Hands by Lorinda Bryan Cauley
Hello Toes! Hello Feet! by Ann Whitford Paul
Here Are My Hands by Bill Martin, Jr. and John Archambault
Tumble Bumble by Felicia Bond

Snack

Serve health bars, granola bars, milk, and water.

Review

Ask the children to name parts of the body that move.

Assessment

Ask children to name things that they can do with their bodies and to demonstrate one movement.

— Quazonia Quarles, Newark, DE

My Special Letter

Learning Objectives The children will:

1. Identify the first letter in their names.
2. Recognize their written names.
3. Make verbal greetings and respond to verbal greetings.

Circle or Group Time Activity

- Make nametags for each child. Tell the children that each child is going to have a special letter for the day (letters can be repeated, since many children's names may start with the same letter). Show the first nametag and point out the first letter. "The first letter in this name is K, which makes the sound /k/. Whose name could that be?" If children need more clues, focus on hints about child's gender or hair color or what they are wearing.
- When the child is identified, draw a highlight line under the first initial and say, "Your name starts with 'K,' and that's going to be your special letter for today."
- Give the child her nametag and ask the children to say, "Hello, Katy." The child can reply, "Hello, friends."

Learning Centers

Art
Provide alphabet stencils, sponges, paint, and paper. Encourage children to paint their "special letters."

Literacy
Provide a photograph of each child, paper, glue, and a set of alphabet stamps and inkpads. Have each child glue her photo to a page and then stamp her "special letter" around the picture. The pictures can then be laminated and bound together to create an alphabet book of classmates for the class library.

Sand and Water
Encourage children to draw their special letters in the sand.

Science
Provide water and small chalkboards. Encourage children to paint their "special letters" on chalkboards with water. Place boards in the sun. Ask the children what they observe.

Snack and Cooking
Encourage each child to roll a small ball of premade bread dough into a snake, and then make the dough into the first letter of her name. Bake per bread dough directions but check oven after 10 minutes because the small portions of dough will cook quickly.

Book Suggestions *A, My Name Is Andrew* by Mary McManus Burke
Chrysanthemum by Kevin Henkes
Mommy Doesn't Know My Name by Suzanne Williams

Snack Write the phrase, "_____ likes" on the top of a paper plate. Provide a small buffet of sliced fruit or vegetables and let children put things on their plate that they like. Serve with the alphabet bread letters.

Review Ask each child to say, "My name is _____ and my special letter is _____." As children leave for the day, ask the other children to say goodbye to them by name. For example, "Goodbye, Katy." Encourage the child to respond by saying, "Goodbye, friends."

Assessment If given an assortment of capital letters, can the children identify the first letters of their names?

Related Songs **Hello, How Are You?** by Cassandra Reigel Whetstone
(Tune: "Twinkle, Twinkle, Little Star")
Hello, (child's name), how are you?
It's nice to see you at our school.

ABC Song (Traditional)
Challenge the children to sing the "ABC Song" (slowly at first) and jump up when they sing the first letters of their names.

Cassandra Reigel Whetstone, Folsom, CA

Self-Awareness and Acceptance

Learning Objectives
The children will:
1. Become aware of specific qualities in their physical appearances and personalities.
2. Compare and contrast their specific qualities with those of others.
3. Appreciate what it means to be a unique and special individual.

Circle or Group Time Activity
- Play the Choosing Sides game with the children.
- Place a jump rope on the floor with the children standing on either side of it.
- Name a pair from the list below, designate one side of the rope for each item, and invite the children to stand on the side of the thing they prefer. Children who have no preferences can stand on the rope itself.

Sample Pairs
- apples and oranges
- salt and pepper
- chocolate and vanilla
- hot dogs and hamburgers
- peanut butter and jelly
- ketchup and mustard
- macaroni and spaghetti
- ice cream and cake
- carrots and cucumbers
- pancakes and waffles
- grapes and bananas
- potato chips and pretzels

Learning Centers

Art
On large sheets of butcher paper, make outlines of each child's body. Give the children child-safe scissors so they can cut out their outlines. Provide markers, yarn, and glue for the children to use to make self-portraits.

Language
Provide an unbreakable full-length mirror. Attach a sign at the top that reads, "This is me. I like who I am." Ask the children to describe themselves while looking in the mirror.

Library
Read *Dumpling Soup* by Jama Kim Rattigan to the children. Make a recording of the book, and put the recording and the book in the center for the children to listen to and explore.

Science

Provide a height measurement chart and weight scale. Place a label for each child's name, height, and weight on the wall. Encourage the children to take turns measuring themselves, and then help the children copy the information onto their labels.

Writing

Design a bulletin board entitled "Our Favorites." Type and print a survey form for each child, asking that the children to list their favorite colors, foods, animals, games, songs, books, toys, movies, places to visit, and so on. The children may print, dictate, or make drawings of their answers. Post the surveys on the board with a photo of each child above his survey.

Book Suggestions
I'm Gonna Like Me: Letting Off a Little Self-Esteem by Jamie Lee Curtis
It's OK to Be Different by Todd Parr
Just Dog by Hiawyn Oram
Just the Way You Are by Marcus Pfister
Stand Tall Molly Lou Melon by Patty Lovell

Snack
Reread *Dumpling Soup* by Jama Kim Rattigan to the children, and then serve the children dumplings (available in the frozen food section of most major grocery stores). Make chopsticks available to the children and challenge them to eat the dumplings with the chopsticks.

Review
Ask the children to take turns standing in front of the unbreakable full-length mirror and describing what they see. Ask the children to talk on play telephones and introduce themselves to imaginary friends.

Assessment
Can the children name at least five qualities that accurately describe themselves?

 Susan Arentson Sharkey, La Mesa, CA

Use Your Imagination!

Learning Objectives   The children will:

1. Be introduced to imaginary characters and situations in literature.
2. Experience role-playing and pretending.
3. Gain an understanding that pretend play means using our imagination.
4. Develop large and small motor skills.

Circle or Group Time Activity

- Ask the children questions like, "Who likes to pretend? Who or what do you pretend to be? What do you like to pretend to do?" Listen to their responses.
- Play a short impromptu game of charades. Pick a child to act out a role, an animal, or an action, and challenge the other children to guess what the child is mimicking.
- Explain to the children that they will spend the day pretending and using their imaginations.

Learning Centers   **Art**

Read *There's a Wocket in My Pocket!* by Dr. Seuss. Look at each illustration and discuss what Dr. Seuss did to create his silly imaginary creatures. Tell the children they will each create a "wocket" for their own pockets! Give each child a 9" x 12" piece of construction paper and a 4" x 4 ½" piece of the same color construction

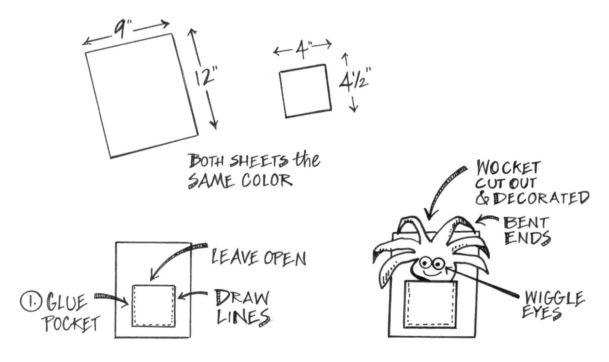

paper. Demonstrate how to glue the sides and bottom of the small sheet onto the larger piece of paper, leaving the top open to create a pocket. Invite the children to decorate their pockets by drawing patches or stitches. Have the children draw the outlines of their wockets on paper and cut them out. Invite them to decorate their wockets as desired. Encourage creativity, such as using 3-D effects (pop-up accordion folds or curled paper). Provide wiggle eyes to glue on.

Blocks

Encourage groups of children to use their imagination to build something together as a team for the other children to identify.

Dramatic Play

Provide a container full of "new" and unusual dress-up items and accessories. Allow the children plenty of time to try on or use the various items for dress-up and pretend play.

Library

Read *Harold and the Purple Crayon* by Crockett Johnson. Make sure the children are all able see and examine the illustrations before you turn each page. Ask the children to think about what Harold drew with his purple crayon and why. If they had a magic purple crayon, what would they draw? Give each child a large piece of story paper and a purple crayon or marker. Encourage them to draw a picture of something or somewhere that that could become real with a magic crayon (or marker). Ask the children to describe for you what they drew. Write each of their stories below their artwork, and compile them into a class book.

Snack and Cooking

Let the children pretend to be cooks, chefs, and bakers in a restaurant. Provide chefs' or bakers' hats or "uniforms" for them to wear. After washing their hands, give them a variety of simple, fun, healthy finger foods to prepare any way they like for their "customers." Let them take turns serving the treats on paper plates.

Book Suggestions

Cloudy with a Chance of Meatballs by Judi Barrett
The Giant Jam Sandwich by John Vernon Lord and Janet Burroway
Harold and the Purple Crayon by Crockett Johnson
There's a Wocket in My Pocket! by Dr. Suess

Snack

Serve child-prepared treats as described in the Snack and Cooking Center.

Review

Have the children share their wockets with the group. Encourage them to describe their wockets and what makes them special by letting the other children ask questions: "Is your wocket a boy or a girl? Where did it come from? How old is it? What can it do? What does it eat?"

Assessment

Have a short discussion about the differences between "real" and "imaginary." Let the children define or describe each and give examples of real things and imaginary things.

 *Sandra Bynum, Blackfoot, ID*

We're All Special

Learning Objectives   The children will:
1. Develop self-esteem and self-confidence.
2. Create original artwork.
3. Sort pictures by one criteria.
4. Follow and finish a simple A-B or A-A-B pattern.

Circle or Group Time Activity

■ With the children, read and discuss *We're All Special* by Arlene Maguire. This book emphasizes the diversity of children's backgrounds. The author reminds us that every child has different interests and strengths.

Learning Centers   ### Art

The children use markers, crayons, or watercolors to illustrate the things they say they can do in the Literacy Center activity below. (**Note:** The children start this activity in the Literacy Center, move to the Art Center, then go back to the Literacy Center to finish.) Have them create a front cover for their "I Am Special" books by drawing a self-portrait on a piece of paper, leaving room above and below their drawing for the book title and their name. Have them take their drawings to the Literacy Center to finish their booklets.

Blocks

Add small plastic people that represent the children to the center. Invite the children to create places for the pretend children to play and have fun.

Literacy

Ask each child to dictate things he can do, such as tie shoes, kick a ball, run, write, or read. Print the dictations on sentence strips, and have them visit the Art Center to draw themselves doing what they said they can do. Each child should have at least four pages. When they come back to the Literacy Center, help them write "I Am Special" above the portrait and their name under the portrait. Place the cover, the drawings, and a piece of paper (back cover) together and use a three-hole punch to punch holes in them. Bind together with heavy yarn.

Math

Divide the class into equal groups and have each group wear a specific color of shirt to school on the same day. For example, if you have 20 children, ask five children to wear red shirts, five to wear green shirts, five to wear blue shirts, and five to wear yellow shirts on the same day. Take a full-length photo of each child. Print the photos and cut around the outline of each child. Tape the cutouts to heavy 4" x 6" card-stock paper and laminate. To play the game, the children sort the cards by a certain criteria. Along with sorting by shirt color, they might sort by hair color, type of clothing (shorts, long pants, skirts), or by types of shoes. You can also start a pattern by arranging a few cards in a simple pattern and asking the children to continue it (for example, red shirt, red shirt, blue shirt, red shirt, red shirt, blue shirt). Children can also make their own patterns.

Music

Provide diversity-themed music for the children to listen to. Suggestions include "We are America's Children" from Ella Jenkins' *We Are America's Children* CD and "The More We Get Together" from Lauri Berkner's *Buzz Buzz* CD.

Book Suggestions

Annie's Gift by Angela Shelf Medearis
Another Important Book by Margaret Wise Brown
Happy to Be Nappy by bell hooks

Snack

Make a Funny Faces snack. Give each child a rice cake, a spoonful of cream cheese, a green pepper strip, two black olives, shredded cheddar cheese, and a few slices of banana. The children spread a thin layer of cream cheese on the rice cake and use other food items to create a funny face.

Review

Ask the children to read their "I Am Special" books to you. Discuss the things they are able to do. Point out patterns that occur naturally in the room (blocks, table toys, and so on). Ask the children to find some patterns for you.

Assessment

Using the sorting photo cards from the Math Center, place several cards on the table and ask the children pick out cards according to a certain criteria (shirt color, hair color, eye color). Create a pattern with manipulatives for the children to finish.

 *Virginia Jean Herrod, Columbia, SC*

What Are Our Feelings?

Learning Objectives The children will:
1. Develop their language and communication skills.
2. Learn about how to classify and compare objects.
3. Develop their small and large motor skills.

Circle or Group Time Activity

- Before the children arrive, cut pictures from magazines of several faces whose expressions depict various emotions. Find representations of happy, sad, angry, scared, and excited.
- Explain to the children that they will be learning about and talking about their feelings today.
- Give each child a cutout face and ask each child to describe the emotions the face exhibits.

Learning Centers ### Art

Provide paper, paint, and brushes, and invite the children to paint faces that express different emotions.

Dramatic Play

Have the children gather in a circle. One child calls out an emotion (happy, sad, angry, scared, excited, and so on). The rest of the children change their facial expressions to show the feeling. The child to the first child's right then calls out another emotion, and the children change their faces to express that feeling. Continue until everyone has had a turn.

Literacy
Ask each child to finish this sentence: "Today I feel _____." Write the children's responses on white paper, and then provide crayons and markers so the children can draw pictures of themselves illustrating how they feel.

Math
Put the face cutouts from circle time into a basket. Ask children to sort the faces into groups by emotion. Then ask them to compare groups. Which group has the most faces? Which has the fewest?

Music
Play several pieces of instrumental music. Play fast and slow music with different beats and tempos. Ask the children to describe how each piece of music makes them feel: happy, sad, angry, excited, scared, and so on.

Book Suggestions

The Feelings Book by Todd Parr
Fun Is a Feeling by Chara M. Curtis and Cynthia Aldrich
Story of My Feelings by Laurie Berkner
Today I Feel Silly: And Other Moods That Make My Day by Jamie Lee Curtis

Snack

Provide whole-wheat crackers and a can of spray cheese so each child can draw happy and sad faces on their crackers before they eat them.

Review

Ask the children to describe times they felt different emotions, and talk about appropriate ways to handle feelings.

Assessment

Display the magazine faces from the Circle or Group Time activity and ask each child to identify the feeling each picture illustrates.

 Kimberly Hutmacher, Illiopolis, IL

What Is a Family?

Learning Objectives The children will:
1. Learn what a family is.
2. Learn who is in their families.
3. Find out how families are different.

Circle or Group Time Activity
- To prepare for this activity, ask parents to send in photographs of their families for a "Show and Tell" day.
- On the designated day, gather the children at circle time. Let each child have a turn to hold up the photo of their family or caretaker and describe who they are and what makes them special.
- Tell the children that they are going to learn about families today.
- Talk to them about the different types of families. Explain that children's families can consist of a mom and a dad, one parent, step parents, grandparents, aunts, uncles, or other people raising the children.

Learning Centers

Art
Make family trees with the children. Show the children how to draw trees with branches on construction paper. Provide cutout leaves from green construction paper. Help them write the names of everyone in their families on the leaves. Children glue the leaves onto their family trees.

Blocks
Encourage the children to use blocks to build houses that look like those in which their families live.

Dramatic Play
Provide the children with baby dolls, plastic dishes, plastic food, and other materials with which they can play house. They can feed a baby, set the table, wash the dishes, and buy groceries.

Literacy
Give the children several sheets of paper and ask them each to draw a picture of each of their family members on a different sheet. Help them write the names of each person underneath the pictures, and then staple the pages together, making a "Family Book" for each child.

Small Motor

Glue cardboard to the backs of photocopies of the children's family pictures. The children cut the pictures into 10 pieces to make "family puzzles." See if they can put one another's puzzles together.

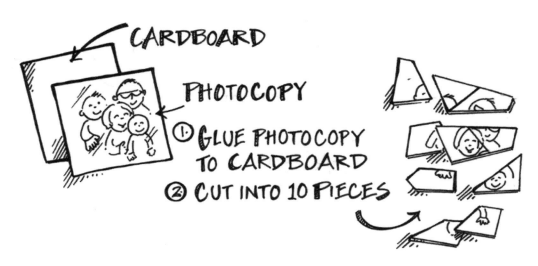

Book Suggestions

Are You My Mother? by P.D. Eastman
Daddy's Girl by Garrison Keillor
The Family Book by Todd Parr
The Relatives Came by Cynthia Rylant

Snack

The day before doing this lesson, ask families to send in their child's favorite healthy snack foods from home. Combine the snacks into a large bowl for the children to enjoy.

Review

Ask the children to draw a picture of their families and talk about the picture.

Assessment

Can the children name all of the members of their families?

Renee Kirchner, Carrollton, TX

All About Eggs

Learning Objectives The children will:
1. Identify and become familiar with animals that lay eggs.
2. Recognize number words.
3. Name and identify colors.
4. Understand one-to-one correspondence.
5. Develop an understanding of the numbers 1–10.

Circle or Group Time Activity
- Inside several plastic eggs, place a picture of something that hatches from an egg, then show the eggs to the children.
- Ask the children to name animals that hatch from eggs.
- Make a list of their correct responses on chart paper.
- Ask the children to open the eggs and see if there are any animals inside the eggs that they do not already have on the list.

Learning Centers

Art
Ask children to decorate coffee filters with washable markers and use eyedroppers to drop small amounts of water onto the filters, making the marker colors spread. After the filters dry, provide child-safe scissors and an egg-shaped template so the children can cut egg shapes out of the filters. Help the children punch holes in the filters, and then string yarn through them, so the children can hang them.

Listening
Put a recording of Tom Ross's *Eggbert, the Slightly Cracked Egg* in the center for the children to listen to. Add markers, crayons, and several precut egg shapes so the children can draw their own Eggberts. Help the children glue their Eggberts onto sheets of cardboard, and then draw arms and legs.

1. PRECUT EGG SHAPE
2. CRACK CUT OUT
3. DRAW FACE
4. GLUE DOWN EGG
5. ADD ARMS and LEGS

Math
Set out several numbered construction-paper egg shapes of various sizes along with the same number of construction-paper nests, each with a number matching the eggs, and challenge the children to lay the eggs in the nests that have the same numbers. Also consider challenging the children to put the eggs in order from largest to smallest.

Sand and Water
In the sand, bury plastic eggs along with small plastic egg-hatching creatures for the children to find.

Small Motor
Provide several laminated cardboard cutouts of Humpty Dumpty with holes punched around the edges. Let the children use a shoelace to lace around the egg shapes.

Writing
On various sheets of paper, make dotted outlines of the numbers 1–10 as well as a corresponding number of egg shapes. Provide markers and crayons so the children can connect the dots to see the number of egg shapes on the page, and to fill in the different egg shapes as well.

Book Suggestions

Big Fat Hen by Keith Baker
Chickens Aren't the Only Ones by Ruth Heller
The Easter Egg Farm by Mary Jane Auch
Eggbert, the Slightly Cracked Egg by Tom Ross
An Extraordinary Egg by Leo Lionni

Snack

Make egg salad with the children and serve egg-salad sandwiches for the children's snack.

Review

Give clues that describe different animals that hatch from eggs, and then ask the children to guess which you are describing.

Assessment

Can the child roll playdough into the shape of an egg and then use the remaining playdough to make a nest for the egg?

 *Jackie Wright, Enid, OK*

All Kinds of Fish

Learning Objectives
The children will:
1. Learn about fish.
2. Share what they already know about fish.
3. Develop small motor skills.

Circle or Group Time Activity
■ Teach the children the following song:

Little Fish, Little Fish by Sandra Bynum
(Tune: "Twinkle, Twinkle, Little Star")
Little fish, little fish,
Swimming along.
I am a little fish,
Singing this song!

Little fish, little fish,
Swimming in my pool.
I am a little fish,
And this is my school!

Little fish, little fish,
Swimming along.
I am a little fish,
Singing this song!

■ While singing the song, the children may sit or stand while swaying and waving their hands up and down at their sides as though swimming.
■ Tell the children that they will be learning all about fish today.

Learning Centers

Art
Give each child a piece of white paper cut in a fishbowl shape. Provide glue and several variously colored construction-paper cutouts of fish for the children to attach to their fish bowls, as well as markers and crayons with which the children can draw faces on their fish, or draw additional fish in their fish bowls.

Literacy
It is likely that some of the children in your class have "fish stories" to tell. Many have gone fishing with their families, and some may have even fished themselves. Others may have a fish aquarium at home. Invite the children to share their fish stories as you write them on story paper. When you finish copying down the children's stories, give them the papers and set out markers and crayons that they

can use to illustrate their stories. Consider displaying these stories on the wall or collecting them into a book called, "Our Fish Stories," and place it in the library for the children to read.

Math

Read *Fish Eyes: A Book You Can Count On* by Lois Ehlert to the children, several times. Each time, ask the children to focus on one of the different numerical concepts that are present in the book, especially numbers, counting, and shapes.

Sand and Water

At the sand and water table, set out several small toy fish and encourage the children to use the sand to shape ponds, streams, and rivers for the fish to swim in.

Science

Introduce one or more goldfish or other easy-to-care-for fish to the classroom. Invite the children to examine the fish closely (they can take turns using a magnifying glass) and encourage them to talk about their observations. Ask the children questions, such as, "Do the fish try to hide from you? How do the fish move around in the water? How do the fish breathe? What kind of fish are these? What do the fish need so that they can stay healthy and happy in their new home? How can we take care of them? How can we keep the water clear and clean? How much and how often will the fish need to be fed?" Consider creating a schedule for when the children get to feed the fish or help clean out the fish bowl.

Book Suggestions

A Fish Out of Water by Helen Palmer
Fish Eyes: A Book You Can Count On by Lois Ehlert
One Fish, Two Fish, Red Fish, Blue Fish by Dr. Seuss
Swimmy by Leo Lionni
What's It Like to Be a Fish? by Wendy Pfeffer

Snack

Serve fish-shaped crackers, and possibly "fish food" treats, such as gummy worms.

Review

Ask the children questions, such as, "Who has pet fish in their home? What kind of fish are they? How does your family care for them? How do you help? What kind of fish do we have in our classroom? What do our fish need to live?"

Assessment

Encourage the children to take turns telling fish stories or describing how to take care of the new classroom fish.

 *Sandra Bynum, Blackfoot, ID*

Animal Antics

Learning Objectives The children will:
1. Identify various animals.
2. Role-play various animals.
3. Improve large-motor and small-motor skills.
4. Use their five senses to explore the topic of animals.
5. Improve their oral language skills.

Circle or Group Time Activity
- Cut a hole in both side panels of a paper grocery bag, near the bottom, large enough for children to place their hands through the holes and into the bag. Prepare enough bags for all the children in the class.
- Place a toy animal (stuffed or plastic) inside each bag and staple the bags shut.
- Number the bags from 1–10 (or however many bags you have) and display them randomly around the room.
- Tell the children that the topic for today's lesson is animals.
- Invite children to walk around the room to find each bag. When they find a bag, they place their hands inside and feel the animal.
- Encourage them to try and identify the animal as they feel its shape. After children have had an opportunity to "feel and guess" all the animals, invite each child to bring one bag to the circle area.
- Have each child open a bag and look inside without naming the animal. Each child describes the animal as the rest of the children raise their hands to identify it.
- After all the animals are revealed, invite the children to carry their animals up in the air as you lead them in marching around the room in an "animal parade."

Learning Centers **Art**
Invite children to cut out and paste pictures of animals on a giant sheet or mural paper to create a class "animal collage." Help the children sign their names next to each animal they cut out and paste onto the mural.

Blocks
Set out several small toy animals and blocks, encouraging the children to use the blocks to create a zoo for the animals. Alternatively, put out various patterns of imitation animal fur beside the blocks and challenge the children to make large animal shapes with the blocks and then drape the animal patterns over them.

Dramatic Play
Display the various animal masks and invite children to role-play a variety of animals. Display the assorted animal puppets. Invite children to create short puppet shows using the various animal characters.

Large Motor
Set out several beanbag animals and boxes, encouraging the children to toss each animal into a separate box. Afterwards, the children can display each animal in its "cage" and describe its characteristics and habits.

Math
Suggest that the children use pieces of various imitation animal furs to make a pattern of textures. Also, encourage the children to create "animal noise" patterns by displaying a pattern of animals and then sounding off with the noisy pattern. For example, *oink, oink, neigh; oink, oink, neigh.*

Book Suggestions

Brown Bear, Brown Bear, What Do You See? by Bill Martin
Polar Bear, Polar Bear, What Do You Hear? by Bill Martin

Snack

Animal crackers and animal fruit snacks make a perfect animal snack.

Review

Display six plastic hoops in the center of the circle area. Display a different animal inside each hoop. Invite children to volunteer to stand in a hoop, describe the animal, and then move about the area as they role-play as that animal.

Assessment

Display an assortment of small toy animals and other objects inside a shoe box. Invite the child to remove the items that are not animals.

 *Mary J. Murray, Mazomanie, WI*

Animal Body Coverings

Learning Objectives The children will:
1. Learn the importance of the animal body coverings.
2. Learn what hides and coverings the different animals have.

Circle or Group Time Activity
- Give each child a feather. Ask her to blow it in the air and see how long she can keep it floating.
- As a variation, separate the children into pairs and have the pairs lie on the floor on their sides and blow the feather back and forth across the floor.

Learning Centers

Art
Provide fake fur, scales made from paper or sequins, feathers, and other materials for the children to use to create animals.

Blocks
Place some stuffed animals with different body coverings in the Block Center and engage the children in discussions about what animals to put in the different block buildings they are making. They can pretend they have farms, a zoo, a fish pond, and so on.

Dramatic Play
Tell the children several animal-based riddles, and invite them to act out the clues in each until they guess what animal the clues describe. For example: "I am long, I slither, and I shed my skin. I am a _____."

Music
Set out several fake animal hides or images of different animals. Have the children sit in a circle, pick one hide or picture from the set, and pass it around as they sing the following song:

'Round and 'Round (author unknown)
(Tune: "Pop Goes the Weasel")
'Round and 'round the _____ goes.
Pass it to your neighbor.
Where it stops, nobody knows.
Stop! Where's the _____?

Ask the child who is holding the hide or picture to imitate the sound or an action that animal would make, then select another and repeat the process.

Science
Set out several animal coverings, and encourage the children to take turns feeling the skins and discussing what animals the coverings come from. After the children are familiar with the various types of animal body coverings, show them a chart

divided into four sections, each labeled as follows: *fur/hair, feathers, dry scales,* and *shells.* Set out cards with different animals on them and challenge the children to group the animals based on their body coverings.

Book Suggestions   *Animals Should Definitely Not Wear Clothing* by Judi Barrett
Animal Skin and Fur (Why Animals Look Different) by Jonathan A. Brown

Snack   Cut slices of banana bread into fish shapes. Show the children how to use cream cheese to attach cornflakes to the fish shapes as though they are scales, and then add raisins or nuts as eyes.

Review   Make two sets of cards, one with animals on them, and the other set with images of the same animals' body coverings. Give each child one card. Have the children all move around, making the sound of their animals or imitating the way they move, until they find the person in the class with the card that matches theirs.

Assessment   Provide several magazines and child-safe scissors and invite the children to cut out pictures of animals and paste them in groups based on their types of hide.

Related Song   **Animals Have Many Coats** by Eileen Lucas
Some animals have coats of fur.
Some have coats of hair,
Still others have coats of scales,
And for this I do not care,
'Cause I also have a coat
That I wear each single day.
And if I didn't have a coat
I couldn't live, no way!

 Eileen Lucas, Fort McMurray, Alberta, Canada

Animal Habitats

Learning Objectives The children will:
1. Learn where animals live and why they live there.
2. Learn that animals live in many places.
3. Start to recognize different types of animal habitats.

Circle or Group Time Activity

- Put pictures of habitats where animals live in four corners of the room.
- Give each child a plastic animal or a picture of an animal.
- Ask the children, "What kind of animal lives on (in, at) the _____?" (farm, zoo, Arctic, and so on).
- Ask the children to look at the animal they are holding and raise their hands if they think it lives in the habitat you named. If the animal does live there, the child takes the animal to the corner of the room that has the image of that habitat.
- Ask the children if there are animals that could fit into more than one category. For example, explain that a cat could live on a farm, in a home, or in the wild.
- Have them decide which of the habitats they would like to live in, and go to those habitats. Talk with the children in each of the habitats about why they picked one over another.
- Finally, let the children swap animals with children in different habitats, and to describe something about the animals and their habitats as they do so.

Learning Centers

Art
Provide construction paper, paints, and paintbrushes for the children to design and paint real or imaginary homes for animals.

Dramatic Play
Set out a few blankets or large sheets that have animal-hide patterns on them and invite the children to wrap themselves up in them. Then have the children jump, hop, or crawl, imitating a creature of their choice.

Literacy
Set out pencils, markers, paper, letter stencils, and written samples of various animals' names. Invite the children to practice writing the letters in different creatures' names.

Sand and Water
Add plastic animals of all kinds to the sand and water table for the children to explore. Encourage them to separate the desert-dwelling creatures from those that live in other habitats.

Blocks

Provide various materials (cereal boxes, empty paper-towel tubes, fabric with animal patterns, tape, markers, and so on) for the children to use to create animal habitats. Encourage them to think about and discuss the creatures that would live in the habitats they create, and explain why those creatures would prefer these habitats.

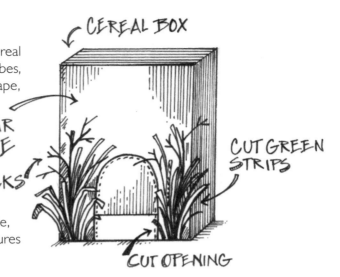

CEREAL BOX

BEAR CAVE

STICKS

CUT GREEN STRIPS

CUT OPENING

STRIPS of TORN PAPER

CEREAL BOX WITH BACK REMOVED

MOUSE or BIRD NEST

BROWN PAPER

PRAIRIE DOG TUNNEL or SNAKE BURROW

PAPER TOWEL TUBE

Book Suggestions
Animal Homes by Angela Wilkes
My Very First Book of Animal Homes by Eric Carle
Moose Tracks! by Karma Wilson

Snack
Serve the children animal crackers and pretzels, along with some cream cheese or icing for glue. Show the children how to make fences or cages, and then put animal crackers in the homes before eating them.

Review
Sing the following song with the children, having them fill in the appropriate habitats and sounds of the different animals you name in the first line.

Where Do You Live? by Eileen Lucas
Oh, _____, oh, _____. Oh where do you live?
I live on a _____, and say _____ to you!

Assessment
Show the children several images of animals and challenge them to name the correct habitat for each.

 Eileen Lucas, Fort McMurray, Alberta, Canada

Animals All Around

Learning Objectives   The children will:
1. Discuss the nature of animals and their habitats.
2. Develop their motor skills.
3. Engage in creative dramatics.
4. Strengthen emergent literacy skills through writing and stories.

Circle or Group Time Activity

- Sing "Old MacDonald Had a Farm" with the children.
- After singing the song, ask children to imagine that Old MacDonald had a zoo. What kind of animals would he have? What sounds would these animals make?
- Sing the song again substituting zoo animals and their sounds.
- Ask children to talk about pets they have at home. Are they like farm and zoo animals?
- Tell children that they will learn about different animals, how they move, and where they live.

Learning Centers   ### Art

Provide drawing paper, crayons, markers, and fabric glue or paste. Let children create their own make-believe animal out of anything in the center. Encourage them to think about how they want their animal to look. Ask, "Will it have wings or legs? Will it crawl? What color or colors will it be?" Ask the children to name their creations and introduce them to the rest of the group.

Blocks

Provide animal figurines or stuffed animals. Add materials for grass and trees. If appropriate, include sand and leaves. Have children create an environment for the animals using wooden and plastic blocks and other materials.

Dramatic Play

Provide children with animal paper plates, paper punches and yarn or string. Cut the string to fit around child's neck to form an animal necklace. Ask them to punch a hole in each side of the paper plate and tie the string through the hole. Invite them to wear their necklace and pretend they are animals making the appropriate sounds and imitating their animal's movement.

Math

Assemble animal plates or pictures. Provide sheets of paper labeled *Zoo, Jungle, Farm,* and *Our Home.* Have children categorize animals according to where they usually live. Ask questions: "How many were in each pile? Could some animals live in more than one place?" You may also create a graph with pictures of animals that children are likely to have for pets. Have children place a sticker or color in a block in the column indicating their pet. Ask them to count the number of pets in each category to see which kind of pet "wins."

Small Motor

Collect animal cookie cutters, tagboard or heavy construction paper, markers, glue or paste, yarn, feathers, and tongue depressors or florist card sticks. Encourage children to trace, cut out, and decorate an animal of their choice. Glue to a tongue depressor or slip onto the floral stick. Use these as props for "Old MacDonald" and other songs about animals.

Snack and Cooking

Provide ingredients for cookie dough and animal-shaped cookie cutters. Invite children to help prepare the dough, select an animal cutter, and cut out the shape from the dough. Bake cookies and enjoy for snack.

Book Suggestions

The Animal Boogie by Debbie Harter
From Head to Toe by Eric Carle
Hillside Lullaby by Hope Vestergaard
In the Tall, Tall Grass by Denise Fleming

Snack

Provide appropriate animal-shaped cookies or crackers for children to identify.

Review

Ask children to name an animal you have discussed, and then ask them to say where it lives, how it moves, what sound it makes, and whether or not it would be an appropriate pet to have at home.

Assessment

Given an assortment of pictures of animals, can children identify them by name and usual habitat (farm, jungle, house)? Shown a picture of an animal, can children move their bodies as if they were that animal?

Related Song

The Bear Went Over the Mountain (Traditional)
The bear went over the mountain,
The bear went over the mountain,
The bear went over the mountain,
To see what he could see.

 Margery Kranyik Fermino, West Roxbury, MA

The Elephant

Learning Objectives The children will:
1. Learn about elephants.
2. Use their imaginations.

Circle or Group Time Activity

- Play a guessing game with the children by reciting the lines below. After saying each of the lines below, pause and see whether the children can guess the animal you are describing.

  I'm thinking of a very, very big animal.
  I'm thinking of a very, very big animal with gray skin.
  I'm thinking of a very, very big animal with gray skin and big floppy ears.
  I'm thinking of a very, very big animal with gray skin and big floppy ears that makes a loud trumpeting noise. (demonstrate)
  I'm thinking of a very, very big animal with gray skin and big floppy ears that makes a loud trumpeting noise and has a long trunk.

- Show the children the picture of an elephant.
- Point to its gray skin, floppy ears, and trunk.
- Show the children how to pretend to be elephants by clasping their hands in front and swinging their arms, then lifting their arms to trumpet.

Learning Centers

Art
Prior to the activity, draw a simple profile of an elephant head using a white crayon on white paper. Prepare one per child. (Don't tell the children you've drawn anything.) Invite children to use watercolors to paint their sheets of paper and then name the mystery animal.

Large Motor
Make an elephant parade. Have children stand in line, a couple feet apart. Show children how to stretch one arm to the front and the other to the back, and then link hands with the person in front of and behind them. Encourage the children to walk together slowly, swinging their "trunks and tails."

Listening
Provide a tape or CD of animal sounds and challenge the children to identify the elephant sounds.

Math
On the playground, draw a life-sized chalk elephant. Invite children to sit "inside" the elephant. Count how many children will fit the space. Talk with the children about how big the elephant is, and ask them what else they think could fit in a space that large.

Sand and Water
Create an elephant watering hole with a children's pool. In the center of the pool, place the shallow dish filled with water. Place sand in the remainder of the pool. Set plastic elephants around the water. Encourage the children to play.

Snack
Provide peanuts and circus popcorn for the children to enjoy. **Safety note:** Be sure none of the children has a nut allergy before serving peanuts.

Review
Ask the children to talk about all things they now know about elephants.

Assessment
Ask the children to find either an elephant toy or a picture of an elephant in the classroom and bring it to you.

Related Song

The Elephant Goes Like This and That (Traditional)
The elephant goes like this and that. (sway from side to side)
He's terribly big and terribly fat. (hold out arms in a circle and puff up cheeks)
He has no fingers; he has no nose. (make hands into fists and cover nose
   with them)
But goodness gracious, what a hose! (dangle arm like an elephant's trunk)

 *Karyn F. Everham, Fort Myers, FL*

Elephants

Learning Objectives   The children will:
1. Learn about elephants.
2. Learn that black and white mix to create the color gray.
3. Brainstorm words that begin with the /e/ sound.
4. Identify the smallest and largest object in a group.
5. Trace the letters E, L, E, P, H, A, N, and T.

Circle or Group Time Activity
■ Teach the children the following song:

Ten Little Elephants by Laura Wynkoop
(Tune: "Bumping Up and Down in My Little Red Wagon")
One little, two little, three little elephants,
Four little, five little, six little elephants,
Seven little, eight little, nine little elephants,
Ten little elephant calves!

Learning Centers   **Art**
Provide construction paper, sponges, trays, and black and white tempera paint.
Encourage the children to mix gray paint, and then have them dip their sponges
into the paint and sponge-paint an elephant.

Dramatic Play
Provide khaki-colored clothes, hats, cameras, binoculars, and stuffed animals.
Encourage the children to pretend they are on a safari to see elephants.

Literacy
Set out several die-cut copies of the letter E. Ask the children to think of other
words that begin with the /e/ sound. Record their words on a sheet of chart paper.

Math
Display three paper elephants, each a different size. Ask the children to identify the
smallest and largest elephants.

Science
Supply photographs of elephants in their natural environments. Point out the
elephant's trunk, and ask the children how they think elephants use their trunks.
Explain that the trunk is both a nose and an upper lip. Elephants can use it to pick
up food, to suck up water, and to smell. An elephant's trunk is strong enough to
push down trees, and gentle enough to pick up a single piece of hay.

Writing
Provide several copies of dot-to-dot letters E, L, E, P, H, A, N, and T for the children
to trace.

Book Suggestions   *Baby Elephant* by Julie D. Shively
Ella the Elegant Elephant by Carmela and Steven D'amico
Ellison the Elephant by Eric Drachman
Grandma Elephant's in Charge: Read and Wonder by Martin Jenkins
Miss Mary Mack: A Hand-Clapping Rhyme by Mary Ann Hoberman

Snack   Explain that elephants love to eat fresh fruit such as berries, plums, and bananas. Tell the children they will be eating like elephants today, and provide them with fresh fruit. Also consider offering the children peanuts since elephants enjoy eating peanuts. **Safety note:** Make sure none of the children have nut allergies.

Review   Hold up a picture of an elephant and ask the children to tell you what they like best about elephants.

Assessment   Show a child several pictures of a hippopotamus, an elephant, and a rhinoceros. Ask the child to pick out the elephant. Ask the child to name one fact about elephants.

 Laura Wynkoop, San Dimas, CA

Fabulous Frogs

Learning Objectives   The children will:

1. Learn about a frog's development.
2. Listen to stories about frogs.
3. Practice hopping like a frog.
4. Learn what a frog eats.

Circle or Group Time Activity

■ After reading a book about frogs, invite the children to move and hop as if they are frogs.

Learning Centers   **Art**

Cut out simple frog patterns and give one to each child. Provide a 3" x 3" sheet of small bubble wrap and have the child paint the bubbles green. Invite them to use a clothespin to pick up the bubble wrap and rub it gently on the frog to make interesting designs.

Blocks

Add plastic frogs to the Block Center for the children to explore.

Dramatic Play

Provide frog and tadpole puppets for the children to play with.

Sand and Water

Cut out lily pads from sponges. Add the lily pads and plastic frogs to the water table for the children to play with.

Small Motor

Make frog patterns out of several small portions of different wallpaper, making two from each design. Put all the frogs in a bucket with blue crepe paper and challenge the children to find the frogs with the matching patterns.

Snack and Cooking

Make frog-shaped sugar cookies with green food coloring and serve them with raisin "bugs."

Science

Introduce the children to the life cycle of the frog, showing and discussing images of eggs, tadpoles, and frogs. Draw, cut out, and laminate each of the five images and set them out for the children to arrange in order. Add paper and crayons so the children can draw their own life-cycle charts.

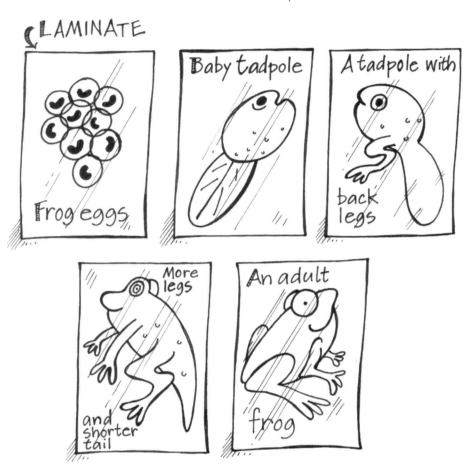

Book Suggestions *All About Frogs* by Jim Arnosky
Froggy's Sleepover by Jonathan London
It's Mine! by Leo Lionni

Review Set out the images of the different stages of the frog's life cycle and challenge the children to put them in the correct order.

Assessment Listen to the children while they work with frog puppets.

 *Sandy Scott, Meridian, ID*

Frog Follies

Learning Objectives The children will:
1. Gain an appreciation for frogs.
2. Learn how to spell *frog*.
3. Learn about the life cycle of frogs.

Circle or Group Time Activity
- Before the children arrive, create a frog puppet out of felt and cloth, or purchase a frog puppet.
- Show the frog puppet to the children ("Friendly Frog"), and explain that Friendly Frog is here to introduce the sound of the letter F.
- Using the puppet, talk with the children about frogs, as well as other things that start with the letter F.
- Use the puppet to introduce a frog poem to the children, such as "Five Little Froggies" or "Froggy Went A-Courtin'." It may help the children if you write the words of the poem or song you use on chart paper and display it.

Learning Centers

Art
Provide crayons, markers, and sheets of paper with a frog outline on them and invite the children to create drawings of their own Friendly Frogs. Consider cutting out the frog shapes and taping straws to the backs of them so the children can wave them when participating in frog-related songs.

Listening
Put a copy of *Green Wilma* by Tedd Arnold, along with a recording of the book, in the Listening Center.

Literacy
Provide magnetic letters and a picture of a frog. With the word printed below the picture, encourage the children to spell out *frog* using four lower-case magnetic letters on a magnetic board.

Math
Put a recording of "Ten Speckled Frogs" in a center along with 10 frog cutouts (numbered 1–10) next to a flannel board and tape player, so the children can match the cards to the numbers as they are mentioned in the song.

Science
Collect tadpoles from a pond. Put them in an aquarium with the original water and allow the children to watch them turn into frogs. Set out pictures of frogs in all phases of development so the children can compare these images to how the

frogs are developing in the tank. Empty out the water and replace it with fresh pond water every other day. (Tadpoles should be fed fish flakes or tadpole pellets, which can be purchased at a local pet store.)

Writing

Put out crayons, colored pencils, and several sheets of paper with the word *frog* written in dots, and invite the children to connect the dots to write the word.

Book Suggestions

Days with Frog and Toad by Arnold Lobel
The Frog Prince by Edith H. Tarcov
Frog Went A-Courtin' by John Langstaff
Froggy Goes to School by Jonathan London
Frogs, Toads, Lizards, and Salamanders by Nancy Winslow Parker
Green Wilma by Tedd Arnold

Snack

Let the children play leapfrog while finding their places at snack. Serve raisin "bugs," or set out crackers and other snacks that the children can use to create edible frog faces.

Review

Repeat the "Ten Speckled Frogs" poem from the Math Center at both circle times during the day and again before going home.

Assessment

Observe the children's comments and participation in center activities. Is each child engaged in the activity? How so?

 Jackie Wright, Enid, OK

Frog Jump

Learning Objectives The children will:
1. Learn how frogs move.
2. Learn some sounds frogs make.
3. Learn the names of some things that frogs eat.
4. Develop large motor skills.

Circle or Group Time Activity
- Teach the children the following action rhyme:

    Three Little Frogs by Christina Chilcote
    Three little frogs (show three fingers)
    Asleep in the sun (close eyes, head on palm of hand)
    We'll wake them up (eyes open wide)
    And then we'll run. (run in place)
    Find a foot (point to one foot)
    And hop, hop, hop. (hop three times)
    When we're tired, (wipe back of hand on forehead)
    We'll stop, stop, stop. (arm out, palm forward, no hopping)
    Turn around (turn around one time)
    And count to ten (count aloud to 10, showing fingers)
    Find a foot (point to one foot)
    And hop again. (hop three more times)

- Once the children learn the rhyme and motion, repeat the rhyme two more times.
- Tell the children that they will learn about frogs today.

Learning Centers **Art**
Let children color a simple outline of a frog with iron-on transfer crayons.
(**Note:** Keep in mind that not all frogs are green. Some that live in rain forests are very brightly colored.) Send the frog home along with iron-on directions, or ask an aide to iron the frogs onto inexpensive cotton T-shirts. **Hint:** Cut out the frog before ironing.
Dramatic Play
Provide adult (small size) T-shirts with large frogs drawn on them. Children wearing them can pretend to be frogs.
Large Motor
Up to four children at a time can take two beanbags and, standing 2' or 3' away, try to "feed the frog" by tossing the beanbags into a large basket with cutout frogs on it.

Music

Set out a poster with the images of various animals (duck, a little black bug, a snake, and a frog), as well as a recording of the song "Little White Duck." As the children listen to the song, encourage them to imitate the animal sounds they hear and to point to the same animals on the poster.

Sand and Water

Place several plastic frogs, fish, snakes, and turtles in the water. Invite the children to re-enact their version of the story, *Jump, Frog, Jump* by Robert Kalan.

Snack and Cooking

Write each child's name on a 9-oz. cup. Each child spoons in a ½ cup of chocolate pudding, then one crushed Oreo, then one Gummy worm or Gummy insect on top of the crushed cookie "dirt." Chill until snack time.

Book Suggestions

From Tadpole to Frog by Wendy Pfeffer
Jump, Frog, Jump by Robert Kalan
Red-Eyed Tree Frog by Joy Cowley
Some Frog! by Eve Bunting

Snack

Serve the "gummy worm in dirt" pudding cup that the children made. Add some green grapes on a plate.

Review

Ask children what sound a frog makes. Ask children to choose what a frog would eat. (Give obvious choices, such as "A fly or a pie?" or "A worm or a hot dog?") Ask the children (if outside or in a large area) to move from one place to another while jumping like a frog.

Assessment

Can the children pick out the frog from a poster of animals or a small group of animal cards?

 Christina Chilcote, New Freedom, PA

Frog Life Cycle

Learning Objectives The children will:
1. Increase knowledge of the life cycle of the frog.
2. Practice counting skills.
3. Develop motor skills.

Circle or Group Time Activity
- Read *Five Green and Speckled Frogs* to the children.
- Engage the children in a discussion about frogs.
- Set out a poster or flannel-board pieces that illustrate the life cycle of a frog.
- Teach the children the following song, using motions and movements. Point to the corresponding images on the poster to help the children understand the different phases of the frog's life cycle.

Metamorphosis by Sandra Nagel
Metamorphosis, (tap hands on legs with every syllable)
Metamorphosis, (tap hands on legs with every syllable)
Metamorphosis, (tap hands on legs with every syllable)
See me change. (clap the syllables)
Started as an egg, (curl hand up into a ball)
Then a hungry tadpole, (wiggle pointer finger)
Grew some legs, (move arms)
Now I can hop. (jump up)
Metamorphosis, (tap hands on legs with every syllable)
Metamorphosis, (tap hands on legs with every syllable)
Metamorphosis, (tap hands on legs with every syllable)
See me change. (clap the syllables)

Learning Centers

Art
Provide a few containers of blue, white, and black paint and several additional containers of green paint. Invite the children to mix a bit of each color with the green paint to create various shades of green. Have them paint pictures using the different shades of green they create.

Large Motor
Place several foam or rubber circles a few inches apart on the ground, and have the children squat and jump between them, like frogs on lily pads.

Math
Give the children several plastic frogs and paper plates and challenge them to group the frogs on the paper plates based on different characteristics, such as size and color. Ask them to count how many are in each group, and compare which group has more and which has fewer. Also, consider taking some of the pipe cleaner flies from the Small Motor center and asking the children to give a certain

number of them to each plastic frog to eat. Ask the children whether there are enough flies to go around.

Science

Make several cards with images of frogs, as well as images of things that frogs will and will not eat. Invite the children to match the pictures of things that frogs will eat to the pictures of frogs, and to set the other cards aside.

Small Motor

Provide various colors of playdough and pipe cleaners, inviting the children to create frogs out of the playdough, and use the pipe cleaners to create flies for the frogs to catch. Children may want to make playdough lily pads, too.

PLAYDOUGH

PIPE CLEANERS

PLAYDOUGH FROG

PIPE CLEANER FLIES

PLAYDOUGH LILY PAD

Book Suggestions

Five Green and Speckled Frogs: Handprint Books by Kelly Martin
Frog on a Log by Phil Roxbee Cox
A Frog Thing by Eric Drachman
Icky Sticky Frog by Dawn Bentley
See How They Grow: Frog by Angela Royston and Mary Ling
A Wood Frog's Life by John Himmelman

Snack

Provide celery or pretzel sticks, peanut butter or cream cheese, plastic knives, and green jelly beans so each child can make a Frog-on-a-Log snack. Show the children how to spread the peanut butter or cream cheese on their celery or pretzel sticks and place jelly bean frogs on top. Encourage the children to sing "Five Little Speckled Frogs" as they prepare their snacks.

Review

Use the flannel board to review the life stages of the frog. Sing "Metamorphosis" with the children again, reviewing the life stages of the frog.

Assessment

Given playdough, can the child demonstrate the life cycle of the frog by forming the stages: the egg, a tadpole without legs, with beginning legs, and then a frog? Can the child count plastic frogs? Can the child leap and jump like a frog?

 Sandra Nagel, White Lake, MI

Fun with Frogs

Learning Objectives The children will:
1. Learn general information about frogs.
2. Improve large motor skills.
3. Practice telling simple story problems for addition and subtraction.
4. Practice rhyming words.

Circle or Group Time Activity
- Display two rows of "lily pads" (paper cutouts) on opposite sides of a large area.
- Split the children into two groups, and ask each child to squat down on a lily pad and prepare to hop across the game area.
- Start to play the frog sounds, say "1, 2, 3, hop, frog, hop," and signal to the children to hop across the room to the other side.
- Warn the frogs to be careful of each other as the two rows of frogs pass each other in the middle of the game area.
- When the frogs reach the other sides of the room, they should find lily pads to sit on.
- Once the children sit on lily pads, share one of the frog facts below with them, and then ask the frogs to recite the "frog fact" aloud after you.
- Next, have the frogs hop across the room again.
- Repeat this activity several times until you finish sharing all the frog facts with the children.

Frog Facts
Frogs croak.
Frogs have slippery skin.
Frogs live on water and on land.
Frogs have long strong legs.
Frogs leap.
Frogs have a long tongue used to catch insects.
Frogs lay eggs in the water.

Learning Centers

Art
Invite children to paint large frog shapes and sprinkle green glitter on their frogs before the paint dries. Display the creatures at the Science Center on a backdrop of trees, pond, rocks, and so on. **Note:** Teachers or children can create the backdrop.

Blocks
Invite children to create a frog pond at the Block Center using a blue sheet of pond-shaped mural paper. Have them create a border of rocks and boulders (blocks) around the pond, and arrange several lily pads and frogs in the pond.

Large Motor
Invite pairs of children to place cutout lily pads in order from 1–10, leaving 3'–4' of space between numbers. Invite the children to play leapfrog along the trail of lily pads, pretending to be two playful frogs.

Literacy
Provide frog-related rhyming picture word cards so the children can explore them and practice identifying and reciting the words.

Science
Display a real frog at the center. Stock the center with an assortment of books, toy frogs, and pictures of various kinds of frogs. Play the CD of "frog sounds" as the children observe the class pet and gather information about frogs.

Water Table
Display the frogs and marbles at the center. Encourage the children to pretend a frog has laid its eggs, as they place groups of marbles underneath the water and set the plastic toy frog on top of the eggs.

Book Suggestions

Frogs by Peter Murray
From Tadpole to Frog by Wendy Pfeffer
A Tadpole Grows Up by Pam Zollman
Watch Me Grow: Frog by Lisa Magloff

Snack

Give each child several lettuce leaves to represent lily pads. Set out several pieces of green pepper and celery "frogs" the children can hop from the lily pads to a container of ranch dressing before they eat them.

Review

Pass a collection of toy frogs around the circle while playing a CD of frog sounds. Pause the CD from time to time, and ask the children holding the frogs to repeat one of the "frog facts" from the day's Circle or Group Time Activity.

Assessment

Display an assortment of pictures of frogs and other animals. Ask the children to select the frogs from the group of animals, describe the frog, and share what they know about its habitat, young, food, and life cycle.

 *Mary J. Murray, Mazomanie, WI*

Giddy-Up

Learning Objectives The children will:
1. Learn about horses.
2. Learn about different jobs for horses.
3. Use their imaginations.

Circle or Group Time Activity
- Hit two blocks together, imitating the "clip-clop" of a horse, and at the same time, imitate the whinny and neigh of a horse.
- Ask children what you are pretending to be.
- Show the children pictures of horses, and talk about what is happening in the pictures. Invite them to make horse sounds.
- Give each child two blocks to imitate the movement and sounds of horses.
- Demonstrate how to vary the speed of the sound by hitting the blocks together more slowly, and talk with the children about how horses run sometimes, and walk slowly at other times.
- Ask the children to vary the speed at which they hit their blocks together, and to run in place in time with the rhythm that they make.

Learning Centers

Art
Draw the outline of a life-size horse on a sheet (or several taped sheets) of paper. Encourage all the children to help paint the horse with the poster paint. After the paint is dry, cut out the horse and hang it in the hallway, so the children can stand next to it to appreciate the size of a horse.

Dramatic Play

Hang the pictures used in the Circle or Group Time Activity. Provide clothing for children to act out the various roles of the people in the images with the horses.

Literacy

Ask children to complete the following sentence: "If I were a horse I would _____." Write each child's response on a sheet of drawing paper and encourage all the children to illustrate their pages.

Math

Encourage children to play with plastic farm animals. Challenge them to sort the horses. Ask the children to count the number of horses.

Small Motor

Set out glue, precut lengths of yarn, and sheets of paper cut into the shapes of a horse's head. Invite children to glue yarn to create manes.

GLUE

YARN

Book Suggestions　　*Barn Sneeze* by Karen B. Winnick
　　　　　　　　　　　　　Clip-Clop by Nicola Smee

Snack　　Provide apple and carrot slices for the children to eat.

Review　　Take the children outside and pretend to be horses and horseback riders. Encourage children to try a variety of roles. Show them how to gallop, trot, and race.

Assessment　　Play a guessing game with the children by asking questions such as, "I say neigh. What am I?" and, "Cowboys ride on my back. What am I?" Ask a variety of questions, including those to which the answer is not "horse."

Karyn F. Everham, Fort Myers, FL

Learn About Chipmunks

Learning Objectives The children will:
1. Learn about chipmunks.
2. Develop small motor skills.
3. Develop color concepts.
4. Increase vocabulary and attention span.
5. Learn the letters C, H, I, P, M, U, N, and K.

Circle or Group Time Activity

■ Teach the children this fingerplay:

The Little Chipmunk (author unknown)
Watch the little chipmunk (hold one hand up)
Run right up the tree. (with other hand, run fingers up the arm to the wrist)
He finds a hole and then hides from me. (run fingers behind the wrist)
If you watch closely, you'll see him turn around. ("peek" fingers around the wrist)
Now be very still and watch him come back down. (run fingers back down arm)

■ Tell the children they will learn about chipmunks today. Explain the difference between chipmunks and squirrels (chipmunks are smaller and their stripes extend to their faces).

■ Ask the children if they have seen chipmunks. Encourage them to talk about their experience. Explain that even though chipmunks are cute and furry, we should not touch them because they are wild creatures.

Learning Centers

Art
Provide children with pictures of chipmunks to paint (pictures from a coloring book, for example). Encourage them to use the correct colors. Have a color picture or photograph available for the children to refer to when painting.

Dramatic Play
Provide brown, black, and tan shirts, hat, and caps for pretend play. Encourage the children to act like chipmunks.

Literacy
As the children to finish the following sentence: "When I think of a chipmunk, I feel_____." Write their answers on paper. Encourage them to draw their feelings. Post them for all to see.

Science
Provide the children with pictures of chipmunks, squirrels, other small rodents, and other small animals. Ask them to pick out the pictures of the chipmunks. Ask them to tell you why the pictures they choose are ones of chipmunks.

Writing
Set out paper, pencils, markers, stencils, and plastic letters C, H, I, P, M, U, N, and K so the children can practice writing the letters.

Book Suggestions

Baby Chipmunks and Backyard Friends by Nancy Lee
The Berenstain Bears and the Baby Chipmunk by Stan and Jan Berenstain
Chattering Chipmunks by Janet Piehl
Richard Scarry's Chipmunk ABC by Roberta Miller and Richard Scarry
The Tale of Sandy Chipmunk by Arthur Scott Bailey

Snack

Serve soft nuts, sunflower seeds, raisins, and sliced apples. Tell the children that chipmunks also eat these foods.

Review

Ask the children to look around the room. Have them point out objects that are "chipmunk colors."
Encourage them to talk about chipmunks.

Assessment

Show the children pictures of chipmunks, squirrels, other small rodents, and other small animals. Can they pick out those that are chipmunks?

 Shirley Anne Ramaley, Sun City, AZ

Mice Are Nice

Learning Objectives The children will:
1. Count to 10.
2. Learn how to make larger items smaller.
3. Develop large motor skills.

Circle or Group Time Activity
- Read *Mouse Count* and act it out with the children.
- Cut one side off a large box and use the box as a pretend cage.
- Choose several children to be mice scampering around on their hands and knees on a blanket. The mice must stay on the blanket.
- Choose one child to be the snake. The snake tags the mice and sends them into the cage. Mice may escape when the snake is not watching. Keep count with the children of how many mice are in the cage.

Learning Centers **Art**

Make mice with the children. Fold a piece of paper in half, and draw half of a heart on it. Show the children how to cut on the line and open up the fold. Glue on two half circles for ears. Add a yarn tail. The children can draw eyes, noses, and mouths to finish their mice.

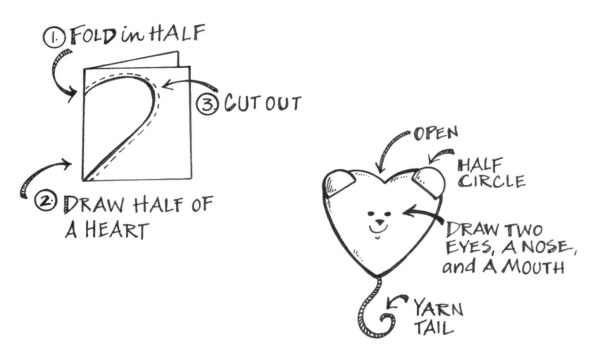

① FOLD in HALF

② DRAW HALF OF A HEART

③ CUT OUT

OPEN

HALF CIRCLE

DRAW TWO EYES, A NOSE, and A MOUTH

YARN TAIL

Dramatic Play

Read *Town Mouse, Country Mouse* by Jan Brett to the children. Use two big boxes that are large enough for several children to fit inside. Turn the boxes on their sides and use them as mouse holes. Label one hole "country mouse" and the other one "city mouse." Have the children find things for their mice holes that they think a country mouse would need and other items a city mouse would own.

Large Motor

Set up an obstacle course to help the little mouse find the way to some tasty cheese. Use pillows, blankets, chairs, balance beams, tunnels, and so on. Set out yellow wooden blocks (the "cheese") at the end of the course. Encourage each "mouse" to move through the course and find the cheese.

Literacy

Tell mouse tales with the children. Sit the children in a circle, and start telling a story about a mouse getting lost or scared of a cat. Encourage the children to add to the story as you go around the circle. Write the children's dictation on a large piece of paper. When the story is finished, read it back to them, pointing to the words as you go, so they can follow along.

Math

The children sit in a circle on the edges of a blanket. Spread yellow blocks around on the blanket for cheese. Most of the children are mice and one child is a cat. When you call "cheese" the mice grab as many pieces of cheese as they can. When the cat calls "scat" all the mice run back to their spot in the circle. Now the mice count how many pieces of cheese they grabbed. To make the game more challenging, a mouse has to drop her blocks and start over if the cat tags her.

Book Suggestions

Frederick by Leo Lionni
If You Give a Mouse a Cookie by Laura Numeroff
The Little Mouse, the Red Ripe Strawberry, and the Hungry Bear
　　by Don Wood and Audrey Wood
Little Mouse's Trail Tale by JoAnn Vandine
A Mouse Called Wolf by Dick King-Smith
Mouse Count by Ellen Stoll Walsh
Mouse Mess by Linnea Riley
Mouse Paint by Ellen Stoll Walsh
One Little Mouse by Dori Chaconas
Town Mouse Country Mouse by Jan Brett

Snack

Make mouse snacks: Have the children crumble cookies or crackers into smaller pieces. Give the children small bites of cheese. Use small cups for a drink of milk.

Review

Show the children groups of various objects so they can practice counting to 10.

Assessment

Given a group of objects, can the child count out 10 of them?

 Monica Hay Cook, Tucson, AZ

Mouse in the House

Learning Objectives The children will:
1. Learn about mice, particularly about how they sleep.
2. Sing songs and read stories about mice.
3. Taste different types of cheeses.
4. Practice counting skills.

Circle or Group Time Activity
- Set out a sheet of paper so all the children can see it.
- Recite the following song. On the sheet of paper, draw the marks described in the parentheses, and ask the children to guess what you are drawing after you complete each new line:

My Mouse (author unknown)
I am small and have some fur. (draw an oval)
I have eyes, a nose, and whiskers. (draw eyes, a nose, and whiskers)
I squeak, but I don't purr. (draw a mouth)
I have a long, thin tail. (draw a mouse tail)
I might live in your house! (draw a house shape around the mouse)
I have two little ears. (draw ears)
I'm a small and furry…mouse!

Learning Centers   ### Art
Set out craft materials (craft foam in yellow, brown, white, pink, and tan; wiggle eyes; chenille sticks; pompoms; and glue) for the children to use to make their own mice. Make a model using craft foam and materials such as a chenille stick for the tail, wiggle eyes, mini pompoms for the nose, and foam pieces for ears. Encourage the children to be creative and compare the differences between the individual mice.

Blocks
Cover blocks with yellow cellophane and add circles with a permanent marker to represent the holes in Swiss cheese. Set out for the children to explore.

Library
Set out watercolors, brushes, and paper, inviting the children to paint images of mice

PIPE CLEANER

OVAL FOAM PIECE

FOAM EARS

WIGGLE EYES

MINI POMPOM

and foods they might eat. Write down their dictations about the pictures. Collect the paintings and bind them into a book.

Sand and Water
Fill the sensory table with cotton balls, cotton batting, and poly-fil so the children can hold the objects exploring how they feel. Explain that mice love to have soft and comfortable places to sleep.

Small Motor
Cut yellow craft foam into 4" squares. Put a pair of squares together and punch matching "Swiss cheese" holes in them using a hole punch. Make several different pairs. Invite the children to match the pairs of cheese squares.

Snack and Cooking
Provide a variety of cheeses and crackers the children can taste. Ask them to determine which type of cheese they would eat if they were a mouse. Tally the results.

Book Suggestions
Eek! There's a Mouse in the House by Wong Herbert Yee
If You Take a Mouse to School by Laura Numeroff
Lunch by Denise Fleming
Seven Blind Mice by Ed Young

Snack
Provide carrots, apples, cheese, and small grains, explaining that mice will eat whatever food is available. Ask the children how a little mouse might bite into an apple.

Review
Take a poll to determine which cheese is the children's favorite.

Assessment
When you ask the children what they know about mice, can they name three things they learned through the day?

 Sandy Scott, Meridian, ID

Sharks

Learning Objectives The children will:
1. Identify rough textures.
2. Learn about sharks.
3. Count backwards from five to one.

Circle or Group Time Activity
- Show children the pictures of sharks. Say, "What can you tell me about this animal? Where does it live? How does it move?"
- Tell children that sharks have a very thick skin that is rough like sandpaper. Pass around the sandpaper and ask children to describe what it feels like.
- Discuss a shark's diet. Different types of sharks eat different things; for example, some eat fish, squid, clams, crabs, or plankton.
- Have children help count to five as you put five pre-cut felt fish on a flannel board.
- Put a cutout felt shark onto the board and have it "eat" one fish. Say, "We have five fish. Here comes a shark. Gobble-gobble. Now how many are left?"
- Repeat with the remaining four fish.

Learning Centers

Art
Cut out shark shapes from sandpaper. Have the children glue the sharks onto construction paper and use crayons to draw fish, seaweed, and rocks. They can also use blue watercolor paint to paint over the scene.

Math
Provide strips of paper, a die, shark or fish stamp, and an inkpad. Have a child roll dice and stamp the shark or fish on the paper the number of times indicated on the die.

Sand and Water
Add plastic sharks and fish to the water table for children to play with.

Science
Tell children that sharks have a strong sense of smell that they use to help find food. Blindfold a child (or ask her to close her eyes) and have her smell various foods, such as cocoa powder, fresh mint, cut lemon, hardboiled egg, and so on. Can she guess what each one is?

Sensory
Provide items with various textures, such as sandpaper, play silk, marbles (if age appropriate), bark, pebbles, pinecones, and so on. While children explore the different textures, ask them to describe what the items feel like.

Book Suggestion   *Surprising Sharks: Read and Wonder* by Nicola Davies

Snack   Serve fish-shaped pretzels and blue gelatin. While the children are eating, ask which snack is rough and which is smooth.

Review   Give each child a cup with five fish crackers or fish candies. Say, "We have five fish in our cup. Here's comes the shark to gobble one up." The children eat one fish. Ask, "Now how many are left?" Repeat until the children eat all the fish.

Assessment   If given a collection of objects of that are either rough or smooth, can the child identify one that is rough?

Related Fingerplay   **Five Little Sharks** by Cassandra Reigel Whetstone
(Hold up five fingers and put one down as the rhyme subtracts each shark.)
Five little sharks, hunting by the shore,
One swam away and then there were four.
Four little sharks, swimming in the sea,
One swam away and then there were three.
Three little sharks, in the ocean blue,
One swam away and then there were two.
Two little sharks, looking for some fun,
One swam away and then there was one.
One last little shark finally gets her wish,
She swims and swims and gobbles up a fish!

 Cassandra Reigel Whetstone, Folsom, CA

This Little Piggy

Learning Objectives The children will:
1. Learn about pigs.
2. Brainstorm words that begin with the /p/ sound.
3. Identify and continue a pattern.
4. Practice writing the letters P, I, and G.

Circle or Group Time Activity
- Hide a toy pig in a brown paper bag.
- Give the children clues and have them use their reasoning and deduction skills to figure out what is in the bag.
- Once they guess correctly, show them the pig and tell them they are going to be learning about pigs.

Learning Centers

Art
Provide precut pig shapes, glue, and tissue paper in various shades of pink. Have the children cover their pig shapes with bits of tissue paper.

Literacy
Give each child a die-cut letter P, and ask them to think of other words that begin with the /p/ sound. Record their words on a sheet of chart paper.

Math
Provide pink, white, and brown die-cut pigs. Display an ABAB pattern with two of the colors and have the children continue the pattern. Encourage the children to invent their own patterns and challenge one another to continue them.

Snack and Cooking
Provide pig-shaped cookie cutters and slices of American or Swiss cheese. Have the children use cookie cutters to stamp out pig shapes in the cheese. Eat.

Writing
Set out markers, pencils, sheets of paper, and models of the letters P, I, and G so the children can practice copying and writing the letters.

Book Suggestions *All Pigs Are Beautiful: Read and Wonder* by Dick King-Smith
If You Give a Pig a Pancake by Laura Numeroff
Olivia by Ian Falconer
The Pig in the Pond by Martin Waddell
The Three Pigs by David Wiesner

Snack Serve the children "Pigs in a Blanket." For each child, wrap half of a hot dog in a triangle of refrigerated crescent roll dough. Bake at 350 degrees for 12–14 minutes, and serve with ketchup or mustard.

Review

Have the children look around the room and point out all the pigs they see.
Ask the children to tell you their favorite thing about pigs.

Assessment

Have each child tell you one fact about pigs.
Ask what letter the word *pig* begins with.

Related Fingerplay

This Little Piggy (Traditional)
(hold up hand with all five fingers out)
This little piggy went to market. (point to and close pinky)
This little piggy stayed home. (point to and close ring finger)
This little piggy had roast beef. (point to and close middle finger)
This little piggy had none. (point to and close pointer finger)
This little piggy cried, "Wee, wee, wee, wee." all the way home. (point to and close thumb)

 Laura Wynkoop, San Dimas, CA

Turtle Time

Learning Objectives The children will:
1. Learn basic facts about turtles.
2. Read simple sight words.
3. Enhance their vocabularies development and oral language skills.

Circle or Group Time Activity
- Recite the following poem to the children:

  Turtle, Turtle by Mary J. Murray
  Turtle, turtle, on the go.
  Turtle, turtle, oh so slow.
  Turtle, turtle, getting wet.
  Turtle, turtle, perfect pet.
  Turtle, turtle, in its shell.
  Turtle, come for "Show and Tell."
  Turtle, turtle, asleep in the sun.
  Turtle, turtle, having fun.
  Swim in water, crawl on land.
  Turtle, turtle, in my hand.

- Recite the poem a second time, inviting children to crawl around on the floor quietly like turtles as they listen.
- Place a stuffed or toy turtle on each child's back for them to carry on their backs as they crawl.
- Invite children to help you create a large diorama of a turtle habitat inside a large cardboard box. Use various art supplies of your choosing to create sand, water, grass, trees, sun, clouds, and so on.
- Put rocks, sticks, and small tree branches on the floor of the box.
- Place several plastic or stuffed toy turtles inside the box. As you build the diorama, share some basic facts about turtles with the children.

Learning Centers **Art**
Provide 4" light green paper circles. Invite children to add patterns to the green "turtle shells" (4" circles) by placing the circle on top of a plastic toy turtle (or other textured material) and rubbing with a crayon, pressing hard. Have children cut a rock shape from gray paper and glue their turtles to the rock. Children can add legs, head, and tail, using crayons.

Large Motor
Use masking tape to mark off a 4-foot wide turtle runway on the floor. Invite two children at a time to race down the runway on hands and knees, with a chair pad (turtle shell) balanced on their backs. The goal is to get to the end of the runway before the other turtle with out losing the shell.

Literacy

Display the American Sign Language sign for "turtle" at the center. Have the children sign the word *turtle* as they recite sentences using the words in the diorama in their sentences.

ASL sign for "Turtle"

- Close the right hand with the thumb pointing upward.
- Place the left hand over the right, leaving the thumb out as the turtle's head gently wagging beneath its shell.

Math

Display several small plastic toy turtles and several numeral cards at the math center. Invite children to trace numbers from 1–10 by having the turtle crawl in the formation of each numeral.

Sand and Water

Print a shape, number, or letter on the bottom of each plastic turtle and place the turtles at the sand and water table. As children explore with the turtles in sand or water, invite them to pick each one up and identify what is on its tummy.

Book Suggestion

A Turtle Hatchling Grows Up by Pam Zollman

Snack

Invite children to create their own turtle snack. Spread cream cheese on a round cracker. Add slices of green or black olives to add detail to the shell and use a whole olive for the head. Set the "turtle shell" across two thin celery sticks to create four feet sticking out from beneath the shell. Enjoy the turtle snack.

Review

Toss a stuffed or beanbag toy turtle to a variety of children as you start the sentence, "Turtle, turtle_____." Invite each child who receives the turtle beanbag to complete the sentence as desired.

Assessment

Display an assortment of plastic or stuffed animals, including turtles, on the table. Invite the child to pick up the turtles, put them on a paper rock, and tell you some of the things he knows about turtles.

Mary J. Murray, Mazomanie, WI

Backyard Birds

Learning Objectives   The children will:
1. Recognize common backyard birds.
2. Feed the birds.

Circle or Group Time Activity
■ Teach the children the following song:

Five Little Birds by Donna Alice Patton
(Tune "Five Little Monkeys")
*Five little birds hopping in the nest
One fell out and left the rest.
Mama called Papa and said with a cry,
"Look, our baby learned to fly!"
Four little birds hopping in the nest
One fell out and left the rest.
Mama called Papa and said with a cry,
"Look, our baby learned to fly!"*

(Go until all birds have gone and end with the following)

*No little birds hopping in the nest
They all fell out and it's an empty nest.
Mama called Papa and said with a cry,
"All our children learned to fly!"*

■ Sing the song again, while the children hop, tweet, and flap like birds.
■ Show the children pictures of common or local birds, such as robins, blue jays, sparrows, and woodpeckers and engage them in discussion about each.

Learning Centers   **Listening**
Play a recording of birdcalls and challenge the children to identify some of the calls. Give hints based on other information you provided about birds earlier in the day. As a follow-up activity, bring the children outside and challenge them to recognize the local birdcalls.

Math
Count real birds with the children. If possible, have children stand outside or beside a window, looking in different directions. Each child should count the number of robins, sparrows, and other birds he sees in 10 minutes. Compare the children's totals. Ask, "Were there more birds in certain locations?"

Art
Provide paper and drawing utensils. Have children draw one of the birds you've discussed or create an imaginative bird of their own. Older children can make

"nests" from strips of construction paper or found objects, formed inside paper bowls. Roll bird eggs from playdough and put them inside the nests.

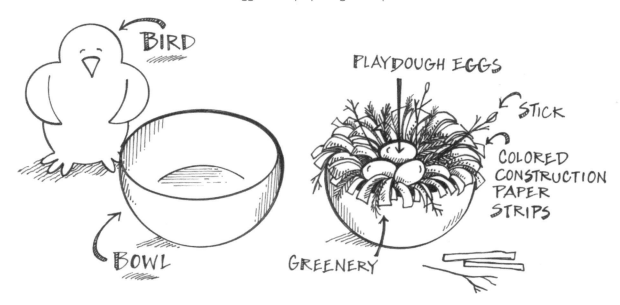

Science

Make pinecone bird feeders with the children by rolling pinecones in peanut butter and dipping them in birdseed to coat. Tie yarn to the tops of the cones and hang them outside the window so the children can observe birds feeding at them. **Note:** Do not do this activity if any of the children have peanut allergies.

Writing

Using the information they learned about birds, the children write or dictate two sentences about the bird of their choice (each child does this). Provide markers and crayons for the children to draw the descriptions of the birds of their choice. Consider binding these pages into a book and putting it in the classroom library for the children to explore.

Book Suggestions	*Birdsongs* by Betsy Franco *Grumpy Bird* by Jeremy Tankard *Today at the Bluebird Café: A Branchful of Birds* by Deborah Ruddell
Snack	Provide sunflower seeds, berries, and other foods birds commonly eat.
Review	Ask each child to relate to you a fact about birds.
Assessment	Show the children pictures of birds and ask them to call out the birds' names or try to imitate the birdcalls.

 Donna Alice Patton, Hillsboro, OH

Beautiful Birds

Learning Objectives   The children will:
1. Learn that there are many kinds of birds.
2. Learn facts and information about birds.
3. Practice gross motor skills.
4. Improve their oral-language skills.

Circle or Group Time Activity
- Before children arrive, hide a collection of stuffed or beanbag birds randomly around the room but within the children's reach.
- When the children arrive, invite them to close their eyes and lie on the floor.
- Ask the children to listen as you play a bird sounds CD. After a minute or two of listening, invite children to stand up and "fly" around the room like a bird as they move to the bird sounds and look for a stuffed bird to bring back to the circle area.
- Once a child finds a bird, have the child fly the bird back to the circle area and set it in the center of the circle.
- Once all the children are back together, invite them to stand up one at a time and flap their wings, fly around the circle, and then tell about the bird they found as they pick it up and display it to the other children.
- Finally, show the children pictures of various birds, and talk with them about the general characteristics that birds share, such as having wings, feathers, beaks, and tails; living in nests; laying eggs; and so on.

Learning Centers   ### Art
Place a stamp pad and a collection of bird rubber stamps (if available) at the Art Center. Invite the children to use art supplies to create an outdoor scene, and then draw or stamp birds on the illustration.

Blocks
Display an assortment of beanbag birds at the block center. Invite children to build birdhouses using blocks and place birds on or inside the houses.

Dramatic Play
Display an assortment of birds randomly around the room. Provide binoculars, a bird book, and an outdoor "bird watching" hat. Invite children to go on a bird-watching excursion as they look through the binoculars and move about the room trying to spot the various birds on display.

Math
Invite children to sort a variety of feathers by size, type, or color. Have children compare the lengths and sizes of pairs of feathers. Invite children to place the feathers end to end to see how long a train of feathers they can make.

Music

Invite children to make "bird songs" using hand bells or xylophone. Ask them to mimic or create their own bird sounds as they gently play the notes.

Sand Table

Fill the sand table with birdseed. Provide an assortment of plastic or toy birds for the children to explore with. Then spread birdseed outside for birds to eat.

Science

Display one or more bird's nests, birdhouses, and empty bird eggs at the center. If possible, bring in a real pet bird (from someone you know or a local pet store) and set it at the Science Center. Invite children to observe the bird and record their observations by drawing on paper. Take the children on a "bird-watching" walk through the neighborhood to observe live birds in nature. Display two or more bird photos. Invite children to compare and contrast the two birds and tell someone else what they observe.

Book Suggestions *About Birds: A Guide for Children* by Catherine Sill
Birds, Nests and Eggs by Mel Boring
Grumpy Bird by Jeremy Tankard

Snack Give the children cream cheese or peanut butter to spread on crackers, and then sprinkle with various seeds, nut pieces, or tiny bits of dried fruit. **Safety note:** Make sure that no children have nut allergies before serving them to the children.

Review Gather 10 or more brown lunch bags. Shape each bag into a "nest" by rolling and crumbling the sides of the bag downward until it is bowl-shaped. Hand each child a bird. Ask each child to set a bird on a nest as and say one thing she or he has learned about birds.

Assessment Display several beanbag pals on a tray, including birds and other animals. Invite the child to pick up the birds and identify the main characteristics of each bird, beak, wings, feathers, tail, and so on.

 Mary J. Murray, Mazomanie, WI

Feathered Friends: Chicken and Ducks

Learning Objectives The children will:

1. Learn characteristics of ducks and chickens, what they look like, how they move, where they live, and the sounds they make.
2. Distinguish the difference between facts and silly duck and chicken phrases.
3. Develop motor and movement skills.
4. Participate in sensory activities.

Circle or Group Time Activity

■ On butcher paper, draw and color a large pond and a chicken coop.

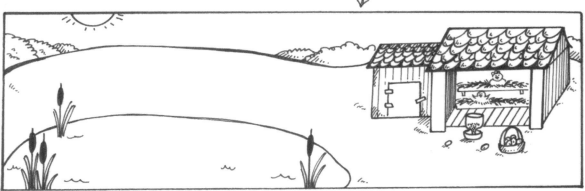

■ Make chicken and duck footprint cutouts from paper. Tape them to the floor.
■ Create two paths, one of chicken prints for the chickens to follow and the other of duck prints for the ducks to follow. At the end of the chicken path, tape the chicken coop in place and at the end of the duck trail, the pond.
■ Bring the children together and engage them in a discussion about chickens and ducks. Ask the children to describe how both types of birds walk.
■ Ask the children to stand up and practice moving like chickens and ducks. Explain that chickens bob their heads, cluck, and strut, and ducks quack, waddle and shake their tails. Talk about the fact that chickens and ducks both lay eggs.
■ Divide the children into the two bird groups, chickens and ducks, and ask them to follow their footprints in single file.
■ As the children follow their paths, they cluck, quack, strut, and waddle. The chickens follow their paths to the chicken coops, and the ducks for theirs to the pond. Encourage the children to trade places if desired.

Learning Centers

Art
Give the children paper and paint, and ask them to paint using feathers.

Dramatic Play
Create a chicken coop the children can play in. With an X-acto knife, cut the holes for doors and windows into large boxes (adult-only step). Provide the children with paint and brushes and invite them to decorate the chicken coop as they like. Set out plastic eggs and baskets, and encourage the children to pretend they are chickens laying eggs. Consider providing a set of overalls and a straw hat that a child can wear to play the farmer.

Library
Read several books about chickens and ducks. Talk with the children about what they have learned or know about chickens and ducks. Discuss similarities and differences; for example, they both have feathers and lay eggs, but they live in different places, eat different foods, and make different sounds.

Math
Read Doreen Cronin's book, *Duck for President,* to the children. Engage the children in a discussion about voting and what a president does. Use the stuffed animals to stage a pretend election. Invite the children to take turns presenting the animals to the class and then vote on their favorite animal. Record the children's votes on a chart and count them to elect your president.

Sand and Water
Put sand in the sand and water table. Pour water in a bowl and place it in a corner to make a duck pond, and add small plastic ducks to it. The children will have a great time playing with the ducks in the sand and pond.

Sensory
Invite children to drop feathers onto the floor and then sit in chairs and pick up the feathers using their toes.

Book Suggestions

Click, Clack, Moo: Cows That Type by Doreen Cronin
Dora's Eggs by Julie Sykes
Duck, Duck, Goose by Tad Hills
Duck for President by Doreen Cronin

Snack

The children make chicken feed they can eat. The children can choose their own mix from bowls of nuts, cereal, raisins, dried fruits, yogurt pieces, and chocolate candies. The children spoon their choices in a bowl.

Review

Have the children talk about what they learned about chickens and ducks.

Assessment

Play a questioning game asking the children questions about ducks and chickens. Some questions are factual and some are silly sayings. See if the children can answer correctly. Here are some sample questions: Do chickens swim? Do ducks fly? What sound does a chicken make? Do ducks live in a coop? Which one waddles, a chicken or a duck? Do ducks cluck?

 *Monica Hay Cook, Tucson, AZ*

Owls

Learning Objectives The children will:
1. Learn about owls.
2. Form the letter O.
3. Practice listening skills.

Circle or Group Time Activity

- Show pictures of owls. Discuss the shape of the owls' faces. Ask the children what they know about owls, such as, "How do owls get their food?" "What sound do they make?"
- Explain that they use their hearing to help them hunt.
- Play "Whoooo has the mouse?" Instruct children to sit in a circle and to put their hands behind their backs. Tell them that one child will play the owl and one will be the mouse.
- Choose someone to be the owl, and tell him to close his eyes.
- Put the mouse in someone's hands and tell him to squeak the toy when the owl opens his eyes.
- The Owl opens his eyes and uses hearing to guess who has the mouse.
- Repeat with a new owl and mouse.

Learning Centers   **Art**

Provide clay, buttons, and natural colored feathers. Encourage the children to make owls out of clay and then add buttons for eyes and feathers for the body.

Blocks

Add toy owls and other toy birds to the block area. Encourage children to build "nests" for the owls.

Math

Provide various sizes of circles, triangles, wiggle eyes, and glue. Have children put the triangles and the eyes onto the circles to make owl faces.

Snack and Cooking

Have children spread peanut butter (or cream cheese) on an English muffin half. Use a teaspoon of jelly for each eye and put a piece of O-shaped cereal on each eye. Finish the owl with a triangle wedge of orange.

Writing

Set out yarn and glue so the children can make O shapes and glue them to construction paper.

Book Suggestions

The Barn Owls by Tony Johnston
The Owl and the Pussycat illustrated by Jan Brett
Owl Babies by Martin Waddell

Snack

Serve peanut butter owls from snack center and orange slices.

Review

Ask the child this riddle: "I'm a bird with quiet wings. I have big eyes and very good hearing. I hunt at night for my favorite foods. Who am I?"

Assessment

If shown a picture of several different types of birds including an owl, can the child correctly identify the owl?

Related Poem

Two Great Owls by Cassandra Reigel Whetstone
Two great owls, sitting in the night.
One was dark and the other was light.
Whoo said the dark,
Whoo-whoo said the light.
And they flew off to hunt in the dark of the night.

 Cassandra Reigel Whetstone, Folsom, CA

Penguins

Learning Objectives   The children will:
1. Learn about penguins and how they move.
2. Develop basic motor skills.
3. Identify the colors black and white.

Circle or Group Time Activity
- Show pictures of penguins.
- Ask children what they know about penguins. What do they look like? Is a penguin a mammal, a reptile, or a bird? Do penguins fly? How do they move? (They walk, hop, slide, and swim.)
- Lead the children on a penguin march. Walk/waddle, hop, swim, and if possible, use a slide while on the march.

Learning Centers   **Dramatic Play**
Put blocks of ice in a dishpan and fill it halfway with water. Put plastic penguins (or objects representing penguins) in the tub. Encourage the children to make the penguins slide on the ice and swim in the water.
Snack and Cooking
Have children spread white icing on a chocolate cookie and use chocolate candies for eyes and a piece of orange gummy candy for the beak.

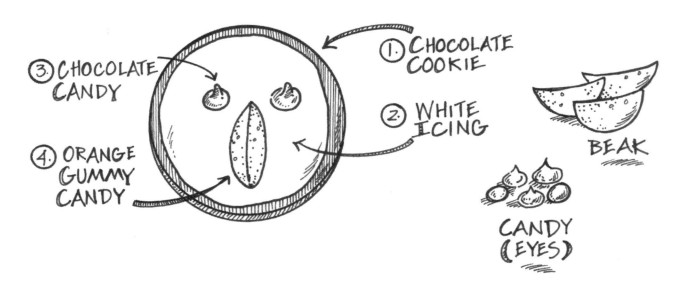

③ CHOCOLATE CANDY

④ ORANGE GUMMY CANDY

①. CHOCOLATE COOKIE

②. WHITE ICING

BEAK

CANDY (EYES)

Large Motor

Let children lie on their stomach on a skateboard and scoot around like a penguin sliding on the ice.

Math

Put black and white objects on a table with sorting boards. Encourage children to sort the objects into groups by color. Ask which side has more or fewer objects.

Science

Tell children that penguins are able to keep warm because they have a layer of blubber. Have a child put a plastic glove on one hand. Put a thick layer of shortening and a glove onto the other hand. Have the child put both hands into a tub of ice water. Which hand gets cold faster?

Book Suggestions

Antarctic Antics: a Book of Penguin Poems by Judy Sierra
Busy Penguins by John Schindel
Tacky the Penguin by Helen Lester

Snack

Serve penguin faces from the Snack and Cooking Center with fish crackers and ice water.

Review

Ask each child to say one thing he knows about penguins.

Assessment

If asked to move like a penguin, can the child waddle or hop?

Related Song

Being a Penguin by Cassandra Reigel Whetstone
(Tune: "Row, Row, Row Your Boat")
Walk, hop, on the ice
Swim fast in the sea.
Hunt for fish, your favorite dish,
A penguin you must be.

 Cassandra Reigel Whetstone, Folsom, CA

Penguins Are Birds

Learning Objectives The children will:
1. Learn that penguins are flightless birds that swim.
2. Become familiar with the characteristics of a penguin.
3. Learn about the habitat where penguins live.
4. Learn about the male and female penguin's roles in taking care of their egg and the chick.
5. Become familiar with the life cycle of the penguin.

Circle or Group Time Activity

■ Show the children pictures of penguins and talk about their colors and their body parts (two feet, a beak, two eyes, flippers).

■ Explain that penguins live in Antarctica, and discuss the cold environment.

■ Talk about how penguins are hatched from an egg and how the males take care of the eggs.

■ Encourage the children to try to be like daddy emperor penguins by trying to hold balloons on their feet and not move.

■ Talk about what a baby penguin is called once it hatches from the egg. Also discuss the color of the chick and how chicks' feathers are not yet ready for swimming.

Learning Centers

Art

Let children paint their favorite penguin at the easel. Children paint an oval shape with black and white paint, and then glue on a beak, eyes, and feet. Sprinkle dry tempera paint onto sheet of paper and let children paint with an ice cube and talk about how this feels on their hands. The children then glue pieces of torn-up white construction paper onto a small egg shape for a baby penguin egg.

Math

Cut a life-sized emperor penguin out of large black mural or bulletin board paper and put face, feet, beak, and eyes on it. Show children with a tape measure that the emperor penguin is 5' tall.

BLOCKS

EMPEROR PENGUIN TAPED to WALL

MEASURING TAPE

Let children stand against the penguin and measure where they come to on the penguin. Encourage the children to stack blocks beside the penguin. Once the stack of blocks is as tall as the penguin, challenge the children to count the blocks.

Blocks

Cover blocks with white copier paper and put Styrofoam pieces and white Duplo blocks in the Block Center, along with plastic or stuffed penguins. The children can use these to make icebergs or homes for the penguins.

Sensory

Fill a tub with water and add ice cubes or Styrofoam pieces to represent icebergs. Let the children catch the ice with tongs.

Small Motor

Make puzzles out of penguin pictures and let children put them back together. Write the numbers 1–10 on penguin die cuts, and then let children count out that many fish to go on each penguin. Let children sort the plastic fish by colors.

Writing Center

Ask each child to dictate a story about what he would do if he were a penguin. Let them illustrate the pages on which you copied their stories and then bind them together for a class book. Let each child take the book home to share with their families and bring back the next day.

Book Suggestions

Counting Penguins by Betsey Chessen
The Emperor's Egg by Martin Jenkins
Penguin Pete and Pat by Marcus Pfister
The Penguin Who Wanted to Fly by Catherine Vase
Penguins by Kathleen Weidner Zoehfeld
Penguins Through the Year by Robin Bernard
Plenty of Penguins by Sonia W. Black

Review

At the end of the week, have the children dictate to you what they learned about penguins. Post the dictations outside the door so family members can read what their children learned during the week.

Assessment

Tell the children that if you say something that is true about penguins, they should flap their arms like a penguin flippers. For example, if you say, "Penguins can swim in the water," the children should flap their arms like penguins. Make some statements to the children, such as, "Penguins can fly like other birds," and see how the children react. This is a great way to make transition times easier. It also helps build listening and large motor skills.

 *Holly Dzierzanowski, Brenham, TX*

Birthday Celebration

Learning Objectives   The children will:
1. Learn how birthdays are celebrated.
2. Discuss each other's birthdays.
3. Plan a class birthday celebration.
4. Play games we play at birthday parties.

Circle or Group Time Activity
- With the children, sing "Happy Birthday."
- Give each child a party hat.
- After you sing the song, talk about what a birthday means.
- Tell children they will learn about the celebration of birthdays by having a class birthday party today.

Learning Centers   **Art**
Prepare crown patterns on an assortment of colored paper. Provide, glitter, confetti, stickers, and other bits of sparkle for children to decorate birthday crowns.
Dramatic Play
Set up the area with a "Happy Birthday" banner, balloons, a tablecloth, small table, chairs, paper plates, cups, hats, streamers, sequins, confetti, pin the tail on the donkey, play food cakes, and cupcakes so the children can pretend to have a birthday party. For added fun, provide playdough and baking cups for children to make "cupcakes" and add birthday candles (with the wicks cut off).
Games
Set up several chairs and a small stereo so the children can play musical chairs.
Literacy
Provide each child with a 3" x 6" strip of colored paper with the following sentence copied onto it: "The best gift I could ever receive would be a _____ for me." In advance, decorate a box with a lid. Encourage the children to describe their perfect dream presents, and copy the children's responses onto their sheets of paper, then have them write their names at the bottoms of their sheets.
Writing
Provide markers, crayons, and 24" x 12" strips of white paper (one per child) for children to make a birthday banner.

Math

Draw or find a picture of a cake and write "There are _____ candles on my cake" underneath the picture. Make a copy for each child. Invite the children to draw candles on the cakes, and then count the number of candles on the cake and write the number in the blank.

There are ___ candles on my cake.

Book Suggestions	*Happy Birthday, Moon* by Frank Asch *It's Hard to Be Five* by Jamie Lee Curtis *Just Like Jasper!* by Nick Butterworth *Tell Me Again About the Night I Was Born* by Jamie Lee Curtis
Snack	Provide premade undecorated chocolate and vanilla cupcakes. Allow children to choose a flavor. Provide containers of chocolate, vanilla, and strawberry icing and plastic knives for children to spread icing on. Let them decorate their cupcakes with colorful sprinkles. Sing "Happy Birthday" before eating!
Review	Ask the children to describe their ideal birthday gifts and parties.
Assessment	Ask the child about her birthday. For example, ask, "What do people do and have on their birthdays?" "What is a birthday and why do we celebrate birthdays?" Have the child name five things that we associate with birthdays. For example, presents, candles, cakes, party hats, cupcakes, parties, or birthday cards.

 *Quazonia Quarles, Newark, DE*

Chinese New Year

Learning Objectives   The children will:
1. Learn about Chinese New Year.
2. Develop their large and small motor skills.

Circle or Group Time Activity
- Ask the children what they know about Chinese New Year. Explain that it is an important holiday in East Asia.
- Show the children where they live on a world map and then show them where East Asia is located. Tell them Chinese New Year is a festival to celebrate the New Year. Note that while the festival originated in Asia, people now celebrate it in many other places.
- Read one of the suggested books to give children an overview of the holiday.
- Tell children that one of the highlights of the Chinese New Year is the dragon dance. Arrange the children into one or two "dragon trains."
- The children hold the waist of the person in front in them. The front of the line is the head and should make a dragon face.
- Tell children when you play the drum, they will make their dragon dance around the room. When the drumming stops, they must freeze.
- While the dragon dances to the drum, occasionally stop drumming and remind the children to freeze. Tell the front of the dragon to move to the back and let the next child lead the dance.
- Repeat until all children have a turn as the leader.

Learning Centers   **Art**
Provide paper, thinned glue, straws, and glitter. Set up some sample pieces of firework art, so the children can see how to put a squirt of glue onto the paper, blow it along using the straw, and then sprinkle glitter onto the glue.

Dramatic Play
Tell children that before Chinese New Year many people clean their homes in order to sweep away bad luck. Provide brooms, dustpans, sponges, and mops and encourage children to sweep away any bad luck left from the old year.

Small Motor
Put out bowls of cotton balls, uncooked chunky pasta shapes, and sets of chopsticks. Encourage children to try to pick up objects with the chopsticks.

Science
Set out several pennies, containers of vinegar, and pie pans filled with salt. Show the children how they can clean pennies by dipping them into the vinegar, pulling them out, setting them in the pie pans, and then using toothbrushes to scrub the pennies. Also provide a cup of water in which the children can rinse their pennies and several towels to dry them.

Construction

Have children string four egg-carton segments together to make a dragon. Help children tie a knot around the hole at the front and back of the dragon. Poke a craft stick in the center of the head and the back. They can paint a face and decorate the body. Children can use the craft sticks to make the dragon dance.

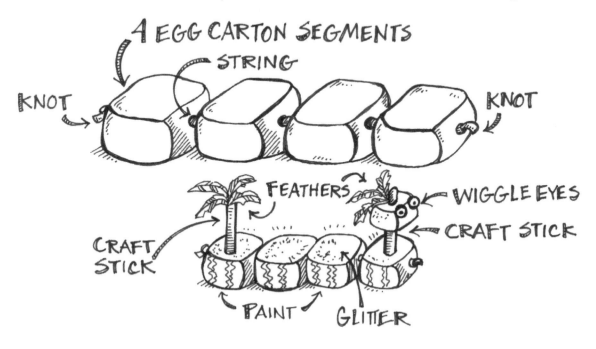

Book Suggestions   *Lanterns and Firecrackers: A Chinese New Year Story* by Jonny Zucker
Lion Dancer: Ernie Wan's Chinese New Year by Kate Waters and
   Madeline Slovenz-Low
Sam and the Lucky Money by Karen Chinn

Snack   Cook several packages of ramen noodles and a bag of frozen mixed vegetables in a crock pot. Ladle noodles into bowls at least five minutes before snack time so it will have time to cool. Serve with chopsticks and spoons. (If children need help with chopsticks, fold a small square of paper and put it between the ends of the chopsticks. Secure with a rubber band.)

Review   Ask children to share what their favorite part of Chinese New Year celebration might be.

Assessment   Ask the children to respond to the following statement: "On Chinese New Year, I might see _____." Can the child give a reasonable answer?

Cassandra Reigel Whetstone, Folsom, CA

Flag Day Fun

Learning Objectives   The children will:
1. Learn about Flag Day.
2. Develop their small motor skills.
3. Identify and continue a pattern.
4. Practice writing the letters F, L, A, and G.

Circle or Group Time Activity
- Hide a small American flag in a brown paper bag.
- Provide clues for the children to use their reasoning and deduction skills to figure out what is in the bag.
- Once they guess correctly (with your help, if needed), show them the flag.
- Explain that on Flag Day, people display and celebrate the American flag.

Learning Centers   **Art**

Provide white construction paper, paintbrushes, and trays of red, white, and blue tempera paint. Have the children design and paint flags.

Dramatic Play
Provide red, white, and blue clothes, shoes, hats, and flags for children to use in their pretend play.

Library

Have each child finish the following sentence: "When I see our country's flag, I feel _____." Write the children's answers on white paper and have them illustrate their ideas. Punch holes in the papers and bind them together with yarn or silver rings to make a book for the classroom library.

Math

Provide red, white, and blue paper stars. Display an ABAB pattern with two of the colors and have the children continue the pattern. Then begin an ABCABC pattern with all three colors and have the children continue the pattern. Create different patterns for the children to continue, and encourage them to design their own patterns.

Small Motor

Set out shoelaces and red, white, and blue beads. Have the children practice stringing the beads on the shoelaces.

Writing

Have the children practice writing the letters F, L, A, G with red and blue crayons.

Book Suggestions

Flag Day by Mir Tamim Ansary
A Flag for All by Larry Dane Brimner
Keep on Sewing, Betsy Ross! A Fun Song about the First American Flag by Michael Dahl
What Freedom Means to Me: A Flag Day Story by Heather French Henry

Snack

Serve vanilla yogurt with strawberries and blueberries. You can also offer red and blue gelatin topped with whipped cream.

Review

Ask the children who made the first American flag. Have them look around the room and point out all the American flags they see.

Assessment

Ask each child to name the colors in the American flag. Can they tell you who made the first American flag?

Related Song

Sing "You're a Grand Old Flag" with the children.

 *Laura Wynkoop, San Dimas, CA*

Groundhog Day

Learning Objectives The children will:
1. Learn about shadows.
2. Identify things that are the same.
3. Recognize things that are different.
4. Develop their problem-solving skills.
5. Develop their large motor skills.

Circle or Group Time Activity

■ Teach the children the following song:

Little Groundhog (author unknown)
(Tune: "I'm a Little Teapot")
I'm a little groundhog,
small and round.
I sleep in a burrow
Deep in the ground.
I look to find my shadow
On groundhog day,
To tell you if spring is on its way!

■ After they learn the song, turn off one light and challenge the children to find each other's shadows.
■ If the child sees a sun, the child will most likely will see a shadow.
■ Explain that according to legend, bright light means the groundhog will stay out of sight for six more weeks, but if it sees a cloud, then spring is near.
■ Have the children pretend to be groundhogs. Make a tunnel out of a box and at one end, put a picture of a sun, and at the other end put a picture of a cloud. One child at a time crawls in the tunnel and chooses which side to pop out of.

Learning Centers **Art**
Provide black crayons and stencils for the children to use to draw shadows.
Blocks
Encourage children to make tunnels with building blocks and hide toy animals inside.
Math
Provide several matching pairs of images of animals. Mix them up and challenge the children to find the pairs.
Music
In advance, place different materials inside plastic eggs (rice, cotton, buttons), tape them closed and see if children can guess what objects are inside the eggs by shaking them.

Large Motor

Create an obstacle course. Children can crawl under a table, climb up stairs, jump over a rope, and so on.

Sand and Water

Hide pairs of small animal toys in the sand table. Ask children to find matching animals. The animals could be the same color, both have spots, both have stripes, both have the same size tail, and so on.

Book Suggestions   *Moonbear's Shadow* by Frank Asch   *My Shadow and I* by Patty Wolcott

Snack   Make or provide premade chocolate and vanilla pudding. Encourage children to draw pictures in the vanilla pudding using Popsicle sticks, and ask them to try making an identical "shadow" in the chocolate pudding.

Review   Ask the children to look around the room to see if they can find images of similar things, such as two animals with pointy ears.

Assessment   Use flashcards of animal silhouettes to see if children can identify the shape of animals. Give the children clues if they need them. For instance, if the animal is a cat, say "This animal likes milk."

 *Melissa Andre, West Warwick, RI*

Let's Camp Out!

Learning Objectives The children will:
1. Count to 10.
2. Engage in dramatic play with peers.
3. Combine materials in new ways.

Circle or Group Time Activity

■ To prepare, make a pretend campfire by taping three paper towels or wrapping paper tubes together to make a teepee shape. Crumple balls of orange and yellow paper or tissue and put them inside the "teepee." Put the "campfire" in the center of the circle time area.

■ When the children arrive, ask them to gather around the campfire. Sing the following song with the children:

A-Camping We Will Go by Cassandra Reigel Whetstone
(Tune: "Farmer in the Dell")
A-camping we will go,
A-camping we will go,
We'll pitch our tent and set up camp.
A-camping we will go.

■ Have each child say what they will bring and insert that information into the song. Examples include:

Matthew brings a book,
Matthew brings a book,
We'll pitch our tent and set up camp,
And Matthew brings a book.

■ Show the children how to warm their hands on the campfire. Say, "We're going to pretend to roast marshmallows. Does anyone know what we need?"

■ Pass out paper roasting sticks (twist a 3" x 18" strip of brown paper until it holds its shape). Give each child a pretend marshmallow and have them pretend to put it on their sticks. Say, "Our fire is very hot. We're going to roast these marshmallows for 10 seconds. Let's put our sticks by the fire and count to 10. When we get to 10, we need to pull our sticks back and blow on our marshmallows."

■ Count to 10 with the children. At 10, say "blow!" and encourage the children to pretend to blow on and then eat their marshmallows.

Learning Centers

Art
Give each child two toilet paper tubes. Put the tubes side by side and fasten them together by using a long strip of tape around the middle of the tubes to make binoculars. Encourage children to decorate with markers. When done, ask children to go on a nature walk in the classroom and to use binoculars to spy 10 interesting things.

Dramatic Play
Provide chairs and sheets. Encourage children to try to build tents.

Library
Set up one or two pop-up tents. Put books, pillows, and blankets inside the tent to create a reading area.

Science
Tape a large sheet of butcher paper or chart paper on the wall in a dark part of the classroom. Provide flashlights and encourage children to create shadow puppets using their hands.

Snack and Cooking
Provide bowls of pretzels, raisins, sunflower seeds, granola, dried fruit bits, and baggies. Have children assemble their own bags of trail mix.

Book Suggestions

S Is for S'mores: A Camping Alphabet by Helen Foster James
When We Go Camping by Margriet Ruurs

Snack

Distribute trail-mix bags from the Snack and Cooking Center. Put the children in a line and hike around the school until settling in a spot for snack.

Review

Gather around the campfire from circle time. Pass out Popsicle sticks and say "We're going to roast one more marshmallow. Let's practice how we do it." Practice counting to 10. Pass out a real marshmallow to each child. Tell them to put in on the end of their sticks. Count to 10, blow, and eat.

Assessment

Ask the child to count to 10 with you. Can the child do it a second time alone?

Related Fingerplay

Setting Up Camp by Cassandra Reigel Whetstone
First we pitch the tent. (put hands together to make a triangle)
Next we eat and eat. (move hands to mouth each time you say "eat")
Then we snuggle in our beds and sleep, sleep, sleep. (put hands together and rest head on hands)

 Cassandra Reigel Whetstone, Folsom, CA

Valentine's Day

Learning Objectives The children will:
1. Gain a basic understanding of Valentine's Day.
2. Develop their language and communication skills.
3. Develop their small motor skills.
4. Develop their reasoning and problem-solving skills through classification and ordering.
5. Enhance their creativity.

Circle or Group Time Activity

- Begin by asking the children if they are familiar with Valentine's Day, and ask them to describe it to you. Explain what it is if the children are not sure.
- Teach the children the following song:

Please Be Mine by Kimberly Hutmacher
(Tune: "Are You Sleeping?")
You are special,
You are special.
Please be mine,
Please be mine.
You're a special friend,
You're a special friend.
Please be mine,
Please be mine.

Learning Centers

Games
Gather children in a circle and give one of the children a wrapped valentine gift. Play music and have them pass the gift around the circle quickly. When the music stops, the child holding the gift gets to keep it. Repeat until each child has received a gift.

Literacy
Ask each child to finish this sentence "I love _____." Write each child's answer and ask them to draw a picture of who/what they love.

Math
Fill three baby food jars with varying amounts of conversation hearts. Ask each child to identify the jar with the fewest hearts and the jar with the most.

Small Motor
Provide wrapping materials and encourage children to wrap gifts to use in the Games Center activity.

Art

Provide construction paper (red, white, pink, purple, or black), crayons, markers, tissue paper, scissors, and glue. Have the children fold their paper in half. Show them how to draw half of a heart at the fold line, cut it out (leaving fold intact), and open it to make a heart-shaped card. Invite them to decorate the valentine card for their family members.

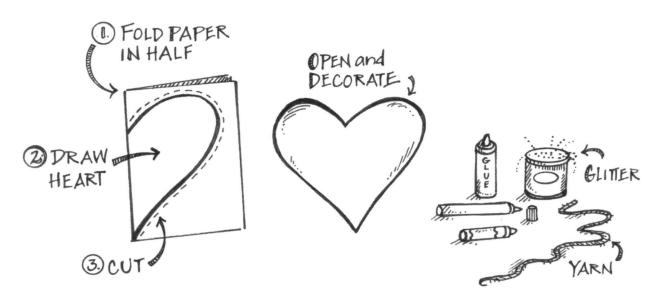

Book Suggestions

Be My Valentine Amelia Bedelia by Herman Parish
The Story of Valentine's Day by Clyde Robert Bulla
Valentine's Day by Anne F. Rockwell and Lizzy Rockwell
Valentine's Day by Trudi Strain Trueit

Snack

Make valentine sandwiches with the children using the following ingredients and materials:

- whole wheat bread
- strawberry jam
- heart-shaped cookie cutter

Guide each child in cutting heart shapes out of two slices of whole wheat bread. With a plastic knife, guide them in spreading strawberry jam on one slice. Top with the other slice and enjoy!

Review

Ask each child to share one word or phrase that makes them think of Valentine's Day.

Assessment

Ask the children to share, once again, what Valentine's Day means to them.

 *Kimberly Hutmacher, Illiopolis, IL*

Wind and Kites

Learning Objectives

The children will:
1. Develop motor skills.
2. Increase awareness of the wind.
3. Improve language skills.

Circle or Group Time Activity

■ Help the children learn the following poem:

A Kite by Sandra Nagel
I often sit and wish that I
Could be a kite up in the sky,
And ride upon the breeze and go
Whichever way I chanced to blow.

■ This activity can be tied with multicultural information or national heritage information at different times:
  ■ The Chinese New Year is in January or February. The kite is a Chinese invention.
  ■ April is National Kite Month. In April there is also a Cherry Blossom Festival in Japan, during which children fly colorful kites.
  ■ May 12th is Kite Day.
  ■ June 15th is Fly a Kite Day to commemorate the Benjamin Franklin experiment.
  ■ June 30th is Sky Day.

Learning Centers

Art
Provide diamond shapes of various sizes cut out of patterned paper (wallpaper, wrapping paper, or scrapbooking paper), pieces of yarn of various colors, glue, white paint, a kitchen or bath mesh sponge, and light blue paper. Encourage the children to use the mesh sponge to paint white clouds on the blue paper. They can glue on diamond kite shapes and a piece of yarn at the bottom of each diamond for the tail.

Construction
Children make a windsock by forming a cylinder out of construction paper. Help them to secure it with staples and tape. Staple streamers or fabric around the base of the cylinder. Punch three evenly spaced holes around the top of the cylinder. Tie a string to each hole and reinforce it with tape. Tie the three strings together to hang the windsock. The children can fly these outside or indoors next to a vent.

Outdoors
Go outside with the children and ask them to lie on the ground on their backs. Invite them to watch the clouds, observe their movement, and talk about how they change and what shapes they look like. Discuss what it might feel like to be a cloud, to fly with the clouds, or to be a kite in the sky.

Science

Children help tie one end of a 6' length of string to a craft stick and the other end to the handles of a plastic bag. The children take the bags outside, hold the craft stick in their hand, and run with the wind blowing into the bag, making it rise. Talk about the wind and how it makes the bag move. Experiment with the children using different lengths of string and different kinds of string and bags.

Small Motor

Give each child a piece of "cloud" (a cotton ball) and a straw. Encourage the children to be the wind by blowing through the straw to make their cloud move across the table. Children can also do this activity in pairs, taking turns blowing a cloud back and forth.

Book Suggestions

Cloud Counting by Dandi Daley Mackall
Curious George Flies a Kite by H. A. Rey and Margret Rey
Gilberto and the Wind by Marie Hall Ets
Kite Flying by Grace Lin
The Wind Blew by Pat Hutchins
Windy Days by Jennifer S. Burke

Snack

Have the children place half a graham cracker on a plate at an angle, put spreads on the cracker with the knife, and use pieces of pretzel sticks to make the frame of a kite. They can use fruit rope at the base to make a tail.

Review

When looking at books about clouds, wind, and kites, have the children talk about their experiences and what they see in the book. Ask them to recite " A Kite."

Assessment

Can the child hold one of the items made during the unit out in the wind and feel or see the kite or wind sock move about? Can the child blow on a cotton ball so that it moves? Can the child tell you three things about wind, clouds, or kites?

 *Sandra Nagel, White Lake, MI*

Under the Big Top

Learning Objectives The children will:
1. Learn about the circus.
2. Practice letter formation.
3. Develop their vocabulary skills.
4. Develop their small motor skills.
5. Practice color recognition.

Circle or Group Time Activity
- Help children stand evenly spaced around the edge of a parachute.
- Ask all the children to sit down, and then teach them the following rhyme:

> **Big Top Day** by Jennifer Galvin
> *It's going to be a big top day.*
> *We'll have some fun and play away.*
> *And when the circus comes today,*
> *We'll learn and read and laugh and play.*

- Once the children know the chant, ask them to stand up and chant it again while walking around in a circle and holding the parachute.
- After the children recite it a few times, ask them to walk toward the center of the room, creating a "big top" out of the parachute. If you like, you can have them sit on the edges, so they can remain under the "big top" for a minute while you explain that today they will learn about the circus and everything that happens in the big top tent.

Learning Centers **Art**
Set out glue, pompoms, sequins, markers, and other collage items, along with several sheets of paper with the outline of a head drawn on each, and invite the children to make clown faces out of the materials. Consider making a model for them to look at while they work, or encourage them to create their own designs.
Blocks
Provide toy circus animals in the Blocks Center. Encourage children to build three "rings" out of blocks and stage a pretend circus.
Dramatic Play
Provide oversize clothing, big shoes, and clown noses so the children can dress up like clowns.
Library
Draw a ring on a blank piece of paper for each child. Encourage the children to draw their favorite circus animals inside the ring. Ask each child to finish the sentence, "I like (my animal) because _____." Write this sentence under each child's picture and then bind the book together using silver rings or staples. Place the children's "Circus" book in the library for everyone to read.

Math

Draw a clown with arms outstretched on a piece of construction paper. Provide several colors of pompoms at the Math Center. Have children create a pattern of "juggled" balls between the clown's outstretched arms. Children can take turns creating several different patterns.

Sand and Water

Put a thin layer of white shaving cream in the sand table and let children take turns making clown faces in the shaving cream. Help the children write the names of their clowns in the shaving cream, and encourage them to practice making letters.

Small Motor

Provide three embroidery rings and three different colors of counters such as buttons, teddy bear counters, or large beads. Have the children sort the counters by color into the three different rings.

Book Suggestions

Circus Parade by Harriet Ziefert
Miss Bindergarten Plans a Circus with Ki by Joseph Slate
Olivia Saves the Circus by Ian Falconer
Sidewalk Circus by Paul Fleischman
Spot Goes to the Circus by Eric Hill

Snack

Serve animal crackers to the children.

Review

Ask the children what animals you can usually find at a circus and where a circus is performed.

Assessment

Given flash cards with pictures of animals, clowns, and other circus performers, mixed in with other animals and people, can the child pick out the circus animals, clowns, and circus performers?

 *Jennifer Galvin, Corvallis, OR*

Colors on My Clothing

Learning Objectives The children will:
1. Identify the colors of different articles of clothing.
2. Explore and try on clothing worn by people in different professions.
3. Compare clothing with the fur and skin on different animals.

Circle or Group Time Activity
- Create a chart similar to the one shown below and hang it on the wall.
- Have a volunteer come and stand near the chart. Ask the rest of the children to describe the colors of the various pieces of the child's outfit, and invite that child to put dots on the correct portions of the chart using markers in colors that match his clothes.
- Choose another child, and repeat the process, until all the children have marked the colors of their clothing on the chart.
- After everyone has had a chance to mark the chart, discuss the results.

	Dress	Shirt	Pants	Shorts	Jeans	Skirt	Socks or tights	Shoes	Jacket
Black									
Blue									
Brown									
Green									
Pink									
Orange									
Red									
White									
Yellow									

Learning Centers

Art
Cut out different articles of clothing (pants, shirt, dress, socks) from several colors of felt. Provide glitter, glue, markers, and other decorative materials. Encourage the children to glue the felt cutouts to construction paper and decorate as they wish.

Dramatic Play
Gather different articles of clothing that people in various professions (such as firefighter, police officer, nurse, doctor, and astronaut) would wear and place them in the center. Encourage the children to put them on. Talk about the color of each outfit and ask them why they think some of the clothing are that color.

Math
Provide construction paper circles in the same colors used on the chart from the Circle or Group Time Activity. Invite the children to tally the results from the chart by making piles of like-colored construction-paper circles.

Science
Explain that only humans wear clothes, and that animals have various hides and furs that cover their bodies. Provide pictures and examples of furs and hides for the children to look at and explore.

Writing
Set out several markers, pencils, and sheets of paper with the following sentence copied on them: "I love to wear my_____ _____." Encourage the children to write or draw the color and article of clothing they love to wear in the blank at the end of the sentence. For example, "I love to wear my green shirt."

Book Suggestions

Animals Should Definitely Not Wear Clothing by Judi Barrett
Color Zoo by Lois Ehlert
Joseph Had a Little Overcoat by Simms Taback

Snack

Serve a variety of colors of fruits that the children can peel easily, such as bananas and oranges. Talk about the color of the peel compared to the color inside.

Review

Show the children pictures of people from old magazines, and discuss the colors of the clothes the people are wearing.

Assessment

Distribute several crayons along with paper that has outlines of a pair of pants, a shirt, socks, shoes, and a jacket on them. Ask the children to color each article in a particular color. For example, "Color the shirt yellow and the shoes blue."

Related Song

Tailor, Tailor, Make Me a Dress by Shyamala Shanmugasundaram
(Tune: "Cobbler, Cobbler, Mend My Shoe")
Tailor, tailor, make me a dress,
I have to meet my empress.
Cotton, linen, silk or wool,
I want something in which I'll look cool.

Shyamala Shanmugasundaram
Nerul, Navi Mumbai, India

Crayons Add Color

Learning Objectives The children will:
1. Practice counting and making patterns.
2. Point out matching colors.
3. Recognize color words.
4. Use their five senses.
5. Develop their oral language skills.

Circle or Group Time Activity
- Tell the children that they will be talking about crayons today.
- Have them name different things they can do with crayons, such as color in a coloring book, make a card for someone, write their names, create a story, draw pictures, and count them.
- Give each child a crayon. Stack precut color squares on the floor.
- Point to the color square at the top of the stack and say "If I had a _____ (color word) crayon I could draw a _____." The children holding the color of crayon you mentioned stand up and name an object they would draw using that color.
- Put a new color square at the top of the stack and repeat the activity with children as volunteers.
- Continue until you or the children say all the colors. Have the children trade crayons, and repeat the activity.

Learning Centers ### Art
Invite the children to write their names or create patterns on white paper using white crayons, and then use watercolors to paint over their patterns or names. Invite them to describe the effect the watercolor has on the crayon as they paint.

Language
Separate the children into pairs. Ask one child in each pair to close his eyes, while the other children give the first child a crayon, and describes its color without naming it. Once the child guesses the color, they move on to another crayon, or they can switch positions are repeat the activity.

Math
Challenge the children to count how many crayons are in each box, then write the number on a self-stick note and stick it to the box. Provide pre-made color pattern cards for the children to duplicate by placing crayons in matching order.

Snack and Cooking
Provide foods that have shapes similar to crayons, and to pretend to write and draw with them before eating them. Foods that resemble crayons include:
- orange carrot sticks
- green pepper, pickles, or celery sticks
- yellow pepper sticks
- sticks of brown wheat bread,
- white sticks of peeled cucumber

Writing
Provide the children with a few crayons each, and ask them to hold all of them at once as they draw or write their names on large sheets of art paper. Have the children repeat the process, each time picking out a group of three crayons. After they finish drawing, talk about which group of colors they liked best.

Book Suggestions

The Colors of Us by Karen Katz
Harold and the Purple Crayon by Crockett Johnson
My Crayons Talk by Patricia Hubbard

Snack

Give each child a piece of construction paper to use as a placemat. Invite them to draw several circles on the paper. Place a piece of food from the Snack and Cooking activity in each circle for the children to enjoy.

Review

Give each child two crayons to hold. Hang several sheets of white poster paper randomly around the room, and have a crayon parade. Children can leave marks on each sheet as they pass them.

Assessment

Display an assortment of crayons, markers, chalk, and colored pencils. Invite the child to pick up the crayons, make a mark with each crayon on a sheet of paper, and name each color.

Related Song

I Like Crayons by Mary J. Murray
(Tune: "Are You Sleeping")
I like crayons; I like crayons.
Yes, I do; yes, I do.
Green and red and yellow,
Orange and brown and purple,
Black and blue, black and blue.

 *Mary J. Murray, Mazomanie, WI*

Crazy About Colors

Learning Objectives The children will:
1. Name and identify colors.
2. Demonstrate ability to sequence.
3. Develop small and large motor skills.
4. Compare sets to determine if they have more, less, or equal number of members.
5. Practice writing numerals 1–10.
6. Demonstrate and develop their rhyming skills.

Circle or Group Time Activity
- Prepare beforehand by cutting out appropriate colors of felt from the story, *Mr. Rabbit and the Lovely Present* by Charlotte Zolotow.
- As you read the book to the children, place the appropriate colored felt cutout on the flannel board.
- Make a large poster of the words to a song about colors and sing it with the children.

Learning Centers

Art
Fill resealable plastic bags ⅓ full of shaving cream (one per child). Ask the children to pick a color of tempera paint. Help them add a few drops of their chosen color to their bags, and then seal each bag. Encourage the children to rub and squeeze their bags gently, and observe the changes.

Construction
Provide colored interlocking cubes for the children to use to build creative constructions.

Math
Provide several teddy bear outlines precut from various colors of construction paper. Present the children with a few patterns of teddy bears, and challenge them to repeat the patterns, and then to invent their own.

Library
Make a recording of the book *Brown Bear, Brown Bear What Do You See?* by Bill Martin, Jr. Place the recording and a copy of the book in the center. Also add

BLACK SHEEP

RED BIRD

YELLOW DUCK

BLUE HORSE

several colored felt cutouts of the animals the brown bear sees in the book, so the children can hold them up when the story refers to them.

GOLDFISH   GREEN FROG   PURPLE CAT   WHITE DOG

Writing
Place yellow and blue highlighters next to sheets of paper with the numerals 1–10 written on them in dots. Have the children trace over the numerals with a yellow highlighter, then with a blue highlighter. Watch the new color emerge!

Book Suggestions

Brown Bear, Brown Bear, What Do You See? by Bill Martin, Jr.
A Million Chameleons by Jeanne Ann Macejko
Red Is Best by Kathy Stinson

Snack

Serve applesauce in a variety of colors (available at most grocery stores).

Review

Provide several pictures of foods, such as apples, bananas, carrots, and oranges, and challenge the children to name the color of each.

Assessment

Observe the children as they participate in the activities. Can they tell the difference between certain colors?

 *Jackie Wright, Enid, OK*

Discovering Blue

Learning Objectives The children will:
1. Learn about the color blue.
2. Mix together a blue tint.
3. Taste food that is blue.
4. Develop their small motor skills.

Circle or Group Time Activity
- Before the children arrive, make sure that there are several blue objects throughout the room.
- Play I Spy with the children.
- Look around the room and silently pick a blue object that all the children can see.
- Say "I spy with my little eye something blue."
- Ask the children to take turns guessing the blue object.
- When a child guesses the correct item, he picks something blue in the room, and the rest of the children try and guess the item.
- Tell the children that they will be learning about the color blue.

Learning Centers ### Art
Help the children put on paint smocks and stock the area with paper, blue paint, white paint, and paintbrushes. Explain that people make tints of a color by adding another color to it. For example, adding white to blue makes a new tint of blue. Invite the children to create different tints of blue and then paint with them.

Dramatic Play
Provide blue clothes in the dress-up area for children to use in their pretend play.

Literacy
Write the following statements on several sheets of paper:
When I see the color blue, it reminds me of _____.
When I see the color blue, it makes me feel _____.
Give the children blue markers and crayons and encourage them to draw or write their responses in the blanks on the pages. Help them write their responses, as needed.

Math
Place a piece of paper on a table and provide several blue crayons. Demonstrate how to add the crayons by making marks on paper to indicate the number of crayons they have. Challenge the children to make groups of marks that correspond to various numbers.

Writing
Provide paper, markers, crayons, and several samples of the letter B and encourage the children to practice writing the letter B. Consider providing a tray of blue sand in which the children can draw the letter B.

Book Suggestions *Blueberries for Sal* by Robert McCloskey
The Deep Blue Sea by Audrey Wood
Why Is Blue Dog Blue? by George Rodrique

Snack Serve blueberries, blue gelatin, blue yogurt, and any other blue food for the children to enjoy.

Review Ask the children to look around the room and point out something blue.
Point to some objects that are not blue, and ask the children what color they are.

Assessment Ask the children to bring you a blue object from the classroom, or to find a blue object at home that night and bring it in the following day.

Related Rhyme **Little Boy Blue** (Traditional)
Little boy blue,
Come blow your horn,
The sheep's in the meadow,
The cow's in the corn.
Where is that boy
Who looks after the sheep?
"Under the haystack
fast asleep."
Will you wake him?
"Oh no, not I
For if I do,
He will surely cry!"

 *Lynn Smaagaard, Minneapolis, MN*

Feeling Blue

Learning Objectives The children will:
1. Learn to identify the color blue.
2. Improve oral language skills.
3. Use their senses of touch to explore objects.
4. Develop their small and large motor skills.

Circle or Group Time Activity

■ Prepare for the activity beforehand by tracing around common classroom objects that are blue (ruler, pencil, block, ball, and so on). Trace around each common object using a blue marker on white paper, and then fold each paper and place it in a basket.

■ Place the blue objects on blue mural paper.

■ Explain to the children that they will be playing a game involving clues.

■ Each child takes a "clue" from the basket and opens it up.

■ The child then has to find the classroom object (on the mural paper) that matches the traced shape, identify it, and place on white paper.

■ Make sure everyone has a turn and continue until all the children have found an object to match their clue card.

■ Display the objects in a large circle. Invite the children to skip and sing "Skip to My Blue" (see the Related Songs section at the end of the lesson plan).

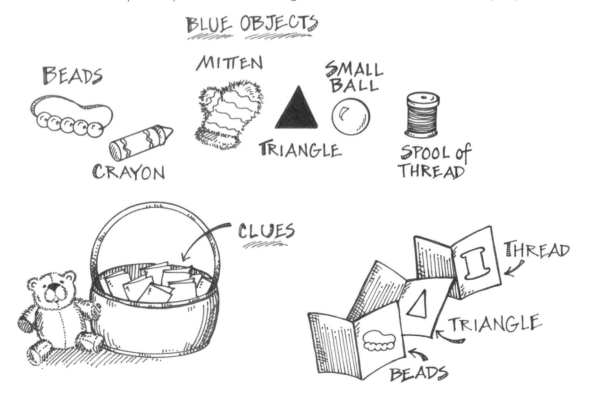

BLUE OBJECTS

BEADS

CRAYON

MITTEN

TRIANGLE

SMALL BALL

SPOOL of THREAD

CLUES

THREAD

TRIANGLE

BEADS

Learning Centers

Dramatic Play
Add articles of blue clothing to the center, including one or more sets of blue surgical "scrubs" for children to try on as they pretend to be surgeons or nurses. Provide yards of blue fabric and help the children wrap the fabric around themselves and then tie with a blue sash or belt. Encourage them to pretend they are wearing a sari (typically worn by women in southern Asia).

Large Motor
Create a tic-tac-toe grid on the floor with masking tape. Place a blue item in each space of the grid. Invite children to toss a blue tissue-paper ball or beanbag onto the grid, and whenever the beanbag lands in a space, the child describes the item.

Math
Display strands of yarn, fabric, and ribbon of different lengths. Have the children place the strands in order from shortest to longest. Provide blue rulers or yardsticks and have the children measure the various lengths of blue material.

Sensory
Stock the center with an assortment of blue objects with different textures, shapes, and surfaces (modeling dough, water, blocks, cotton, fleece, satin ribbon, wheels on a toy car, terry cloth, and so on). Invite the children to use their hands to feel each blue object and then verbalize what they feel.

Small Motor
Display a card with the word *blue* written on it. Invite the children to copy the word *blue* several times, using a different writing tool, such as a blue pen or blue marker, each time they print the word.

Book Suggestions

A Color of His Own by Leo Lionni
Is It Red? Is It Yellow? Is It Blue? by Tana Hoban

Snack

Serve blueberry bagel halves. Provide cream cheese mixed with blue food coloring and fresh blueberries for children to add to the tops of their bagels.

Review

Invite children to sit in small groups, each holding a blue item and the corresponding traced outline from the opening activity. Invite the children to trade objects amongst themselves and then place the objects on the correct paper. Encourage children to talk about the various blue objects.

Assessment

Display an assortment of colored objects on white paper. Invite the child to use a blue marker to circle the objects that are blue.

 *Mary J. Murray, Mazomanie, WI*

Fun with Red

Learning Objectives The children will:
1. Recognize the color red in different contexts.
2. Taste foods that are red.
3. Develop visual discrimination skills.

Circle or Group Time Activity
- Give each child two small scarves, one white and one red.
- Have the children stand in a circle and place the scarves at their feet.
- Sing the following song and ask the children to perform the motions as indicated:

Scarf Song by Virginia Jean Herrod
(Tune: "Head, Shoulders, Knees, and Toes")
Let's all pick up the red scarves, red scarves.
Let's all wave our red scarves, red scarves,
Up to the sky and down to our toes.
Let's all wave our red scarves, red scarves.

Learning Centers ### Art
Make red collages with the children. Supply the Art Center with a variety of materials in shades of red, such as tissue paper, construction paper, pompoms, sequins, and so on. Allow the children the freedom to create collages from their own imaginations. As they work, comment on the shades of red in the materials they are using.

Dramatic Play
Place a variety of things that are red in the Dramatic Play center. For example:
- pictures of red food, plastic play food, or actual red foods (beets, cherries, strawberries, radishes, red peppers, red apples, tomatoes, and so on)
- red clothes (shirts, pants, bandanas, boots, shoes, hats, and so on)
- red aprons
- red paper or plastic plates and matching plastic utensils

Put three paper grocery bags in the center. Label them "yellow," "blue," and "red." Paint a splotch of matching color on each bag (or use colored markers). Have the children sort the various items already in the Dramatic Play Center (as well as the red items) by color. For example, they can sort all of the play food, in addition to the added red food, by color.

Math
Visit a local paint-supply store and get a variety of paint-color chips or strips, all in shades of red. Place the chips on a low table and ask the children to line them up from lightest to darkest.

Sand and Water
Fill the sand table with red sand and provide red shovels, buckets, and other red tools for the children to use.

Science
Let the children help you mix two parts cornstarch and one part water (add ingredients gradually), alternating ingredients until the mixture is thick and smooth. Add a few drops of red food coloring. Let the children explore the red goop. As they play, comment on their activity. "How does the goop feel in your hands?" or "I noticed when you stretch the goop, it looks pink but when you ball it up it looks red. Why do you think that happens?"

Snack and Cooking
Make a red fruit salad with the children. Provide plastic knives for them to cut up strawberries, red grapes, cherries, and red apples to make a bright and festive red fruit salad. Add whipped cream on top for a tasty treat.

Writing
Provide red and pink markers, white copy paper, and sentence strips with the words "red" and "pink" written on them. Encourage the children to practice their printing skills by tracing and/or copying the words.

Book Suggestions
Big Red Barn by Margaret Wise Brown
The Lion and the Little Red Bird by Elisa Kleven
The Little Red Hen by Paul Galdone
Red Fox and His Canoe by Nathaniel Benchley
Red Wolf Country by Jonathan London

Snack
Enjoy your red fruit salad from the Snack and Cooking activity or serve strawberries with whipped topping.

Review
Ask the children to look around the room to find and name some red items.

Assessment
As the children participate in centers, ask them to point out red items.

 *Virginia Jean Herrod, Columbia, SC*

Green

Learning Objectives The children will:
1. Become familiar with the color green.
2. Increase their language and communication skills.
3. Develop their small motor skills.
4. Begin to understand the processes of scientific thinking and problem solving.

Circle or Group Time Activity

- Before the children arrive, draw the skeleton of a tree (trunk and branches) on white poster board.
- Cut out leaves from green construction paper and write each child's name on a leaf. Place the leaves around the circle.
- After the children arrive, gather them in a circle and explain that they will be talking about the color green today. Ask the children to name the seasons when leaves are green.
- Ask children to find the leaves with their names on them and then sit in the spots where they find them.
- After all the children find their leaves, ask them to come up to the tree, one at a time, and use a glue stick to attach their leaves to the tree.

TREE

GREEN LEAF

LEAF WITH CHILD'S NAME

Learning Centers

Art
Stock the area with paint, markers, crayons, colored pencils, and chalk in different shades of green, along with plenty of paper. Invite the children to draw pictures of things that are green.

Dramatic Play
Fill the dress-up area with green hats, shoes, jewelry, and clothes, as well as green blankets for dolls and green towels for the kitchen area.

Music
Tape the children singing the following song and add it to the Music Center for the children to listen to and sing along to:

Green by Kimberly M. Hutmacher
Speckled on frogs,
Sprinkled on trees,
Scribbled on grass,
Splattered on knees

Science
Let each child experiment with making his own shade of green. Provide yellow and blue food coloring, yellow and blue paint, yellow and blue sand, and so on. Demonstrate how to mix them to create the color green. Talk about why the blended colors turn green, and why the shades are different depending on how much blue or yellow is added.

Small Motor
Provide magazines, construction paper, scissors, and glue. Ask children to find pictures of green items and glue them on the construction paper to make a collage. Using scissors help children develop their small motor muscles.

Book Suggestions
Green as a Bean by Karla Kuskin
Green Eggs and Ham by Dr. Seuss
Go Away, Big Green Monster by Edward R. Emberley
Where Is the Green Sheep? by Mem Fox and Judy Horacek

Snack
Make lime gelatin with the children. For added fun, let them pour the gelatin into different shaped molds. Allow it to set and eat for snack.

Review
Ask each child to point to something in the room that is green.

Assessment
Provide a box of objects that are an assortment of colors. Ask each child to point out which objects are green.

 *Kimberly M. Hutmacher, Illiopolis, IL*

Mix It Up

Learning Objectives The children will:
1. Learn about the primary colors (red, blue, and yellow).
2. Combine primary colors to make orange, green, and purple.
3. Taste red, blue, and yellow foods.

Circle or Group Time Activity
■ Teach the children the following song:

The Crayons in My Hand by Renee Kirchner
(Tune: "The Wheels on the Bus")
The crayons in my hand are red, blue, and yellow,
Red, blue, and yellow,
Red, blue and yellow.
The crayons in my hand are red, blue and yellow.
These are the primary colors.

■ Show the children the three crayons in your hand.
■ Point out which one is red, which one is yellow, and which one is blue.
■ Pass the crayons around the circle while you sing the song again.
■ Explain that primary colors are the colors used to make all of the other colors in the rainbow.

Learning Centers **Art**
Provide containers of the three primary colors of paint for the children to mix together on paper, making secondary colors. Encourage the children to paint with all the colors. Talk about what they discover.

Blocks
Place red, yellow, and blue blocks in the center for the children to use with the other blocks.

Math
Cut out teddy bears from blue, yellow, and red construction paper. Have the children sort them by color. For an added challenge, use a variety of shades of each color and have the children sort them.

Writing
Give the children paper; stencils of the words *red, blue,* and *yellow;* and red, blue, and yellow crayons. Encourage the children to practice writing the names of the colors using crayons of the same colors.

Literacy
Provide red, blue, and yellow paper for the children to use to make primary color books. Help the children fold the sheets of paper together in book form, and staple

them together. Invite the children to draw pictures on the pages using crayons that match the colors of each page. For example, on the red pages, the children could color a red apple or a red fire truck.

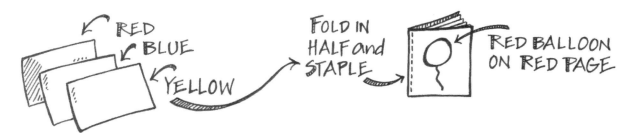

Book Suggestions

Brown Bear, Brown Bear, What Do You See? by Bill Martin, Jr.
Color Kittens by Margaret Wise Brown
How Do Dinosaurs Learn Their Colors? by Jane Yolen
Mouse Paint by Ellen Stoll Walsh

Snack

Serve red apple slices or strawberries, blueberries, and bananas for a snack.

Review

Ask the children to find objects in the room that are red, blue, or yellow.

Assessment

Place objects on a table and ask children to pick up the primary colors. See if the children can remember to pick up only red, blue, and yellow objects.

Related Song

Yellow Is a Daisy by Renee Kirchner

Yellow is a daisy.
Yellow is the sun.
Learning my colors
Is so much fun.

Blue is the rain.
Blue is the sky.
It is also the color
Of my favorite pie.

Red is a cherry.
Red is a beet.
It is also the color
Of my frozen feet.

 *Renee Kirchner, Carrollton, TX*

Primary and Secondary Colors

Learning Objectives The children will:
1. Learn about the primary and secondary colors.
2. Make secondary colors from primary colors.
3. Develop their small motor skills.

Circle or Group Time Activity
- Show the children a color wheel with primary and secondary colors.
- Explain to the children that red, blue, and yellow are the primary colors and that orange, green, and purple are the secondary colors.
- Discuss how red and yellow make orange, yellow and blue make green, and red and blue make purple.
- Cut squares of primary and secondary colors from colored construction paper and place the squares in a bag.
- Have each child reach into the bag, choose a color, and say if it is a primary or secondary color.
- After all the children have color cards, encourage them to organize themselves in a circle that matches the organization of the color wheel.

Learning Centers **Art**
Give each child crayons and two pieces of white construction paper. Ask them to draw a picture on one piece of paper using primary colors. On the other piece, have them draw a picture using secondary colors.

Math
Put several buttons painted in primary and secondary colors into bowls and ask the children to sort them by primary and secondary colors. After sorting, the children can count how many primary and secondary buttons there are, and then how many of each individual color there are.

Small Motor
Have children paint several buttons with primary and secondary colors. Help them to string the buttons onto a shoestring. Tie a knot at the end to make a necklace or doorknob ornament.

Snack and Cooking
Provide slice-and-bake sugar cookie dough. Bake according to package directions. Scoop vanilla frosting into six bowls. Let the children add red food coloring to the first bowl, blue food coloring to the second bowl, and yellow food coloring the third bowl for the primary colors. To make the secondary colors, add drops of red and blue food coloring to make purple, drops of red and yellow to make orange and drops of blue and yellow to make green. Spread the colored onto the cookies.

Science

Cut 3" circles out of thin cardboard. Bisect each circle using a pencil. With scissors, punch a hole in the center of each circle, large enough for a straw to fit through.

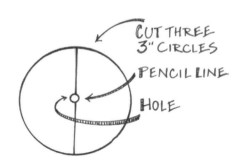

Give each child three circles and a red, blue, and yellow marker. Ask them to color half of the first circle red and the other half blue; half of the second circle red and the other half yellow; and half of the third circle blue and the other half yellow. Show them how to slide a circle onto a straw and then spin the circle. Watch the blue and yellow circle make green, the red and blue make purple, and the red and yellow make orange!

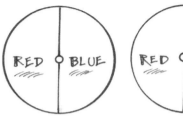

Book Suggestions   *Color Dance* by Ann Jonas
Mouse Paint by Ellen Stoll Walsh

Snack   Make a fruit salad. Ask the children's families to bring in fruit representing primary and secondary colors. Strawberries, blueberries, pineapple slices, kiwis, oranges, and grapes are good choices of fruit for this edible activity.

Review   Provide the children with a piece of construction paper cut into a circle and divided into six equal sections, like a pie. Invite the children to color the sections in the order of the color wheel. Remind them that the secondary colors lie in between the primary colors!

Assessment   Show the children color photocopies of famous paintings and challenge the children to identify the primary and secondary colors in them.

Randi Lynn Mrvos, Lexington, KY

Rainbow of Colors

Learning Objectives The children will:
1. Identify the basic colors that make up a rainbow.
2. Mix colors to discover new colors.

Circle or Group Time Activity
- Provide 3' lengths of crepe paper in the colors of the rainbow (red, orange, yellow, green, blue, indigo, and violet).
- Give the children dowel sticks and have them tape each color of crepe paper to their sticks to make Rainbow Wands.
- When they are finished making their rainbow wands, play a CD of rain sounds and encourage the children to make up a rain dance. When the rain sounds stop, have the children pick up their rainbow wands and wave them in the "sky."

Learning Centers

Art
Give each child a piece of heavy drawing paper, and set out red, yellow, and blue paint. Encourage the children to paint rainbows. Allow the paint to dry. Invite the children to use spray bottles of water (mist setting) to spray their rainbows. Watch the colors bleed and blend together, creating different shades of colors.

Blocks
Invite the children to help paint blocks with all the colors of the rainbow. When they are dry, add them to the Block Center.

Sensory
Help the children make bubbles by following this simple recipe:
- 4 cups water
- 1 cup mild dish soap
- ¼ cup clear corn syrup or glycerin

Mix the ingredients in a shallow container. Provide a variety of rings for bubble wands. Dip the wands and blow the bubbles. Watch for rainbows in the bubbles.

Small Motor
Give each child a resealable bag. Squirt whipped cream into the bags and let the children add a few drops of two colors of food coloring to their whipped cream. Zip the bags closed and invite the children to squish their bags to see what new colors appear. This whip cream is edible, so save it to add to the fruit salads the children make for their snack.

Science
Use a glass of water to create a prism. Put the glass of water in a place where the sun shines through it. Hold a piece of white paper on the other side of the glass so that the rainbow produced by the sun shining through the glass is more visible to the children. Explain that the rainbow appears because light is made up of the

colors yellow, green, blue, violet, red, indigo, and orange. When the light passes through the glass, the water disrupts it and separates it into its parts.

Book Suggestions
All the Colors of the Rainbow by Allan Fowler
The Colors of Us by Karen Katz
Little Blue and Little Yellow by Leo Lionni
Mouse Magic by Ellen Stoll Walsh
The Rainbow Fish by Marcus Pfister
A Rainbow of My Own by Don Freeman

Snack
Make a fruit cup rainbow. Begin with a purple food, such as dark red grapes. Place blueberries on top of the grapes, and add sliced kiwi or green grapes, a layer of sliced bananas, and finally, strawberries. Consider adding the rainbow whip cream the children made in the Small Motor activity as a topping.

Review
Show the children a rainbow with a color missing and ask them to identify the missing color.

Assessment
When shown a rainbow, can the children identify all the different colors?

Monica Hay Cook, Tucson, AZ

Warm and Cool Colors

Learning Objectives   The children will:
1. Explore "warm" and "cool" colors.
2. Create original artwork using warm and cool colors.
3. Practice visual discrimination.
4. Practice categorization skills.
5. Prepare and taste warm and cool colored foods.

Circle or Group Time Activity
- Explain to the children that there are "cool" colors, such as blue and green, and "warm" colors, such as red, yellow, and orange. Explain that cool colors make people think of cold things, while warm colors make people thing of hot things.
- Choose one category to focus on first, and switch to the other category later.
- Show the children a collection of colored items (scarves, fabric, toys, clothing) and ask them to identify each as a warm or cool color.
- With the children, decorate the room with either cool or warm colored items, depending on which you want to focus on initially.
- Talk about the kind of atmosphere the colors give the room. Does it feel soothing? Exciting?
- Talk with the children about expressions such as "seeing red" or "feeling blue." Ask them why people use colors in those descriptions.
- Encourage the children to make up their own color expressions. Copy them into a class book or onto a poster for the room.

Learning Centers   **Blocks**
Set out blocks in a variety of colors and encourage the children to build using only cool or warm colors. Discuss the effect of building with only one type of color.
Dramatic Play
Provide cool- and warm-colored dishes, play food, and dress-up clothes for the children to explore.
Literacy
Ask each child to finish the following sentence: "Cool (or warm) colors make me feel _____." Copy the children's responses onto paper and have them illustrate their sentences.

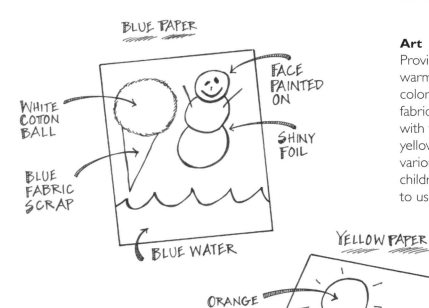

BLUE PAPER

WHITE COTTON BALL

FACE PAINTED ON

SHINY FOIL

BLUE FABRIC SCRAP

BLUE WATER

YELLOW PAPER

ORANGE

RED

FIRE

ORANGE and YELLOW TISSUE PAPER

Art

Provide materials for making cool or warm collages, including cool- or warm-colored paper, collage materials, and fabrics. Invite the children to fingerpaint with yellow and red (to make orange) or yellow and blue (to make green). Provide various images of famous paintings the children can look at for examples of ways to use warm and cool colors.

Small Motor

Give the children several lengths of string, along with containers of warm- and cool-colored buttons. Invite the children to create warm and cool patterns.

Book Suggestions

A Color of His Own by Leo Leonni
Color Zoo by Lois Elhert
Of Colors and Things by Tana Hoban

Snack

Prepare and serve appropriate snacks, such as sliced cucumbers and blueberries, red apples and oranges, cherry juice or grape juice, and so on.

Review

Place several warm- and cool-colored scarves, shirts, and other items of clothing in a large pile. Say, "warm colors" or "cool colors" and have the children pull something appropriate from the pile to hold up or wear.

Assessment

Given a familiar book about colors, such as *Brown Bear, Brown Bear, What Do You See* by Bill Martin, Jr., can a child identify a warm- or cool-colored animal?

 Elisheva Leah Nadler, Jerusalem, Israel

Dinosaur Romp

Learning Objectives The children will:
1. Create dazzle dinosaurs.
2. Improve their small motor skills by working dinosaur puzzles.
3. Walk, move, and dance like dinosaurs.
4. Make dinosaur fossils.

Circle or Group Time Activity

- Engage the children in a discussion about dinosaurs. Specifically, ask the children how they think dinosaurs would move when they dance.
- Read Dinosaurumpus! by Tony Mitton to the children.
- After finishing the book, ask the children if the dinosaurs moved the ways they thought they would.
- Turn on some upbeat music and invite the children to "dance like dinosaurs."

Learning Centers **Art**
Provide watercolors, brushes, and construction paper cutouts of dinosaurs for the children to paint and decorate. Consider adding small rolled strips of aluminum foil for children to create horns.

Blocks
Add large plastic dinosaurs to the Block Center, so the children can build homes and forests through which they can roam.

Math
Create a graph using images of several different species of dinosaurs. Take a poll of the children's favorite dinosaurs, and provide the children with nametags to attach to the appropriate section of the graph. Encourage the children to count the number of names next to each dinosaur, and to tell you which dinosaur has the most names and which has the least.

Science
Give the children playdough and several small plastic dinosaurs to make their own dinosaur "fossils." Show them how to push the dinosaurs' bodies into the playdough and then set the playdough aside to dry.

Small Motor
Gather several dinosaur puzzles for the children to work on. If you do not have any (or many) dinosaur puzzles, make your own. Glue dinosaur pictures to cardboard or sturdy paper and cut into simple puzzle pieces.

Construction
Give the children child-safe scissors and several green plastic or paper plates so they can make "dinosaur feet." Encourage their creativity as they shape their dinosaur feet. Tell them to give their feet as many toes as they like! Help the children punch two holes in the tops of the plates and thread yarn through

them to make straps the children can wrap around their feet.

Writing

Write the names of several dinosaurs, such as stegosaurus, tyrannosaurus rex, and so on, on a piece of poster board. Write the same dinosaur names on paper, but leave certain parts of the words blank (for example, "_____osaurus rex" or "_____ceratops"). Invite the children to write their names in the space, or help them write their names, if needed. Help them to punch two holes on the sides of the paper with their dinosaur names on them, and lace and knot yarn through the holes, making signs the children can wear.

Book Suggestions

Danny and the Dinosaur by Syd Hoff
Dazzle the Dinosaur by Marcus Pfister
Dinosaurumpus! by Tony Mitton
How Do Dinosaurs Clean Their Rooms? by Jane Yolen
How Do Dinosaurs Say Goodnight? by Jane Yolen

Snack

Make dinosaur cookies with the children. Let the children help roll out cookie dough and then stamp it with dinosaur-shaped cookie cutters. After baking the cookies, provide various toppings so they can decorate their cookies before enjoying them.

Review

The children take turns sharing their dinosaur nametags with the other children.

Assessment

Ask the children a few questions about the dinosaurs they learned about.

Related Song

Dinosaurs by Sandy Scott

Five little dinosaurs went out to play
Over the hills and far away.
Momma dinosaur said, "Roar, roar, roar,"
Only four little dinosaurs came back to her.

Four little dinosaurs went out to play...
Three little dinosaurs went out to play...
Two little dinosaurs went out to play...

One little dinosaur went out to play...
Over the hills and far away.
Momma dinosaur said, "Roar, roar, roar,"
No little dinosaurs came back to her.
So papa dinosaur gave a great big roar
And all the little dinosaurs reappeared!

 Sandy L. Scott, Meridian, ID

Dinosaur World

Learning Objectives The children will:
1. Learn about dinosaurs.
2. Create a dinosaur land.
3. Identify a dinosaur.

Circle or Group Time Activity

- Pass out a small plastic dinosaur to each child. (Note: Packages of these are often available at dollar stores or discount stores.)
- Teach the children a version of "The Hokey Pokey," substituting dinosaur-related words. Ask the children to move their dinosaurs as the song suggests.
- Create additional verses and invite the children to move the dinosaurs in different ways.
- Tell the children they will be learning about dinosaurs today.
- Talk about dinosaurs. Ask the children what they know about dinosaurs and record the children's answers on chart paper.

Learning Centers

Art

Put several containers of brown, green, and blue paint next to large pieces of cardboard so the children can make grassy, rocky, and aquatic terrains for dinosaurs. Help the children to add details to their landscapes, such as crumbled paper for rocks, tiny plastic trees, dirt from outside, real or fake leaves, and so on.

Dramatic Play

Prior to doing this activity, fill several small plastic eggs with toy dinosaurs and hide them throughout the room. Have the children make binoculars by taping two toilet paper rolls together. The children use their "binoculars" as they search for dinosaur eggs.

Math

Provide a variety of plastic dinosaurs for the children to sort according to color, size, type, and so on.

Sand and Water

Add a few plastic dinosaurs and a little water to the Sand and Water Table. Encourage the children to play and make dinosaur fossil prints.

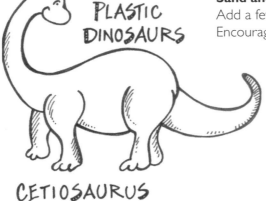

PLASTIC DINOSAURS

CETIOSAURUS

SECTION

Science

Provide several sheets of paper with one limb or section of a dinosaur drawn on each, along with several plastic dinosaurs. Have the children look at the single limb on paper and compare it to the characteristics of the toy dinosaurs, and match them together.

ALLOSAURUS

SECTION

Book Suggestions

Dinosaur! by Peter Sis
Dinosaur Hide and Seek
　　by Stu Smith
Dinosaur Stomp!
　　by Paul Stickland

Snack

Before the children arrive, paint a watermelon white and hide it in the room. When a child notices it, explain that it is a dinosaur egg. Later, when the children are out of the room, cut open the watermelon. When the children come back, tell them the dinosaur hatched. Show them a large toy dinosaur, and then enjoy the watermelon.

Review

Ask the children to list things they have learned about dinosaurs. Record their answers.

Assessment

Show the children pictures of different animals, including a dinosaur. Ask the children to identify the dinosaur.

Jodi Kelley, North Versailles, PA

Animals on the Farm

Learning Objectives The children will:
1. Identify farm animals.
2. Improve their large and small motor skills.
3. Improve their oral language skills.
4. Practice measuring and counting.

Circle or Group Time Activity
- To prepare for this activity, use masking tape or yarn to mark off several "animal pens" in the classroom "barnyard." Display a picture of a different farm animal in each pen (goat, cow, chicken, and so on) and a large word card to label each pen. Add pictures and objects related to a farm, such as toy tractors, toy tools, a play farm, and silo, if desired.
- Introduce the topic of "farm" to the children.
- Show the children the pictures and objects as you talk about farms, the different animals, and what farmers do.
- Remind the children of the various food products we receive from farm animals, such as wool, butter, milk, cheese, beef, pork, eggs, and so on.
- Invite the children to select favorite farm animals to role play and then go to the correct pen. The children role play the animals according to the pens in which they are standing.
- Play music and let the "animals" out. The children romp around the room, dancing to the music.
- When the music stops, the animals scurry back into their pens.
- Repeat the activity several times, so children can be different farm animals.

Learning Centers

Dramatic Play
Place the toy farm animals, tractors, barn, and so on in this center for children to manipulate as they practice the various jobs of a farmer. Invite children to put on the farmer clothes and use some of the tools as they pretend to be a farmer, planting and working on the farm. If possible, provide real ears of dry field corn and show the children how to "shuck" them. Explain that this corn would be used to feed farm animals. Be sure to donate the corn to a local farmer to feed the animals.

Large Motor
Display several sizes of empty cardboard boxes in a large open area of the room, leaving 5'–10' of space between each box. Invite the children to pretend they are horses and trot and jump over the boxes along the trail.

Literacy
Provide several word cards with animal names on them and challenge the children to read the names and then match each animal or farm picture with the correct word card. Have children play the "Who Am I?" guessing game as they take turns describing the animals and then identifying what their classmate describes.

Blocks

Invite the children to create various farm-animal pens using blocks, and display plastic animals or pictures of animals in each pen.

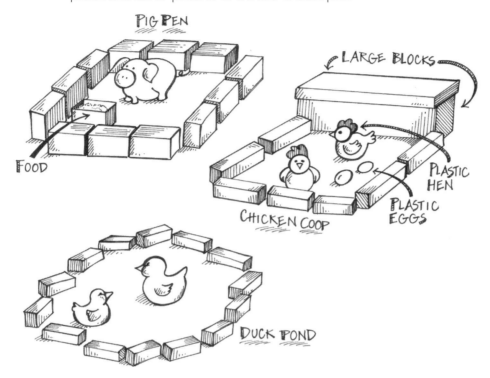

Small Motor

Have the children use tweezers or chopsticks to pick up cotton balls (sheep) and place each one in a compartment on an ice cube tray or muffin tin. Tell the children they are putting all the "sheep" in their "pens."

Book Suggestions

Farm Animals by Hans Helweg
On the Farm by Josette Blanco

Snack

Provide a variety of fresh farm products, such as fruits and vegetables, cheese and milk, butter and bread, or corn on the cob.

Review

Display several food containers of products that come from the farm, such as milk cartons, oatmeal boxes, butter tubs, and so on. Engage the children in a discussion about the containers and what they typically hold and how farmers produce these products.

Assessment

Display an assortment of farm and zoo animals. Ask the children to divide the pile of animals into two groups and to talk about each farm animal and what it provides for humans.

 *Mary J. Murray, Mazomanie, WI*

Down on the Farm

Learning Objectives   The children will:
1. Learn why farms are important.
2. Learn what type of animals live on farms.
3. Learn how to make butter.

Circle or Group Time Activity
- Ask the children to stand in a circle holding hands. Choose one child to be the farmer, and have that child stand in the middle of the circle.
- The children sing "The Farmer in the Dell" together. At the end of the first verse, the "farmer" in the center of circle chooses a "wife" by reaching out and taking another person's hand. The "wife" then enters the circle, and the song resumes with the two of them in the circle together.
- Repeat the process with every verse. At the end of the second verse, the wife chooses a child, and so on, until everyone is in the circle except for the cheese. Additional verses of "The Farmer in the Dell"
  The farmer takes a wife…
  The wife takes a child…
  The child takes a nurse…
  The nurse takes a cow…
  The cow takes a dog…
  The dog takes a cat…
  The cat takes a rat…
  The rat takes the cheese…
  The cheese stands alone…

Learning Centers   **Dramatic Play**
Provide hats, coveralls, and other things a farmer might wear. Invite the children to dress up in the clothes and pretend they are farmers. Encourage the children to use small toy farm animals as they play.

Literacy
Give each child a piece of paper with the following sentence on it: "On the farm I see _____." Encourage the children to draw or write an end to the sentence.

Math
Ask the children to name their favorite farm animals. Graph the favorite animals on a poster board and discuss the results with the children.

Science
Provide a container of potting soil. Give each child a small clay pot to fill with potting soil. Let them plant one or two bean seeds in the dirt of their pots, and then water them. Write the children's names on pieces of masking tape and wrap the tape around their pots. Place the pots in a windowsill so the children can observe the plants growing.

Art

Provide construction paper, markers, crayons, and child-safe scissors and ask the children to draw pictures of three farm animals and a barn and cut them out. Help the children punch holes in the tops of each picture and tie pieces of string through the holes. Tie the other ends of the string around paper towel rolls at equal distances. Be sure to use different lengths of string so the images hang at different heights.

Book Suggestions

Big Red Barn by Margaret Wise Brown
Down on the Farm by Merrily Kutner
Farm Alphabet Book by Jane Miller
Growing Vegetable Soup by Lois Ehlert
Maisy's Morning on the Farm by Lucy Cousins
Mrs. Wishy-Washy's Farm by Joy Cowley

Snack

Prepare a cornbread mix according to directions on the box. While it is baking, make homemade butter with the children. Pour a small amount of lukewarm cream into several clean, empty baby food jars. Put on lids, distribute them, and ask the children to shake the jars for about 20 minutes. They may get tired, or need to take turns shaking the butter. Explain that what they are doing is called "churning." After 20 minutes of churning, open the jars, spread the fresh butter on the hot cornbread, and enjoy!

Review

Ask the children to draw pictures of animals that live on a farm.

Assessment

Ask the children what farmers do. Can they name five animals that live on farms? Can they name some crops that grow on farms?

 *Renee Kirchner, Carrollton, TX*

Fun in the Mud with Pigs!

Learning Objectives The children will:
1. Identify pigs.
2. Learn about pigs.

Circle or Group Time Activity
- To prepare, make a pig puppet out of a pink or black glove. On each finger (and thumb) of the glove, glue a small pompom and two wiggle eyes above the pompom to represent pigs' eyes and snouts.
- Wear the pig glove puppet and ask the children if they know where pigs live.
- Show the children a picture of a farm. Ask if any of the children have ever been to a farm. What did they see? Record their responses on chart paper. Ask if any of the children have ever seen a pig while visiting a farm.
- Ask the children if they know what pigs eat. Record their responses.
- Teach the children the "This Little Piggy" fingerplay.

Learning Centers **Art**

Give each child a pink, black, or brown glove. The children glue wiggle eyes and paper or felt ears onto each finger of the gloves and felt or paper snouts on the palms (see illustration). After the glue is dry, encourage the children to wear their glove puppets and act out the fingerplay "This Little Piggy."

PINK GLOVE

EARS GLUED ON

WIGGLE EYES

PIPE CLEANER TAIL

SNOUT

Blocks
Encourage the children to think about what farms look like, and to try building farms out of the blocks. Add stuffed farm animals to the area for more fun.

Dramatic Play
Place cowboy hats and boots, stick horses (or small brooms), bandanas, and foam farm animal masks in the dramatic play area so the children can pretend to be farm animals or farm workers.

Sand and Water
Add dirt to a small amount of water in the water table to make a mud pit. Encourage the children to roll plastic pigs in the mud. Add small pieces of straw to the mud pit for a different texture.

Small Motor
Before doing this activity, make pig-shaped lacing cards for each child. Make copies of a picture of a pig, laminate, and cut them out. Punch holes around the perimeter of each card. Help the children tie a knot in a piece of yarn, thread the yarn through a hole in the card, and lace the yarn around the entire pig. (**Note:** Place a piece of tape around the top of the yarn to make threading easier.)

Book Suggestions

Everyone Hide from Wibbly Pig by Mick Inkpen
Pigs Aplenty, Pigs Galore! by David McPhail
The Three Little Wolves and the Big Bad Pig by Eugene Trivizas

Snack

Make "pig slop" with the children. The children help make chocolate pudding, and then mix in cereal, raisins, mini marshmallows, and so on.

Review

Ask the children to list things they have learned about pigs. Record their responses.

Assessment

Show the children different pictures of farm animals and ask them to pick out the pig. Next, show the children several different pictures of animals' homes and ask them to pick out where a pig lives.

Related Song

Milk, Milk, Milk Your Cow by Jodi Kelley
(Tune: "Row, Row, Row Your Boat")
Milk, milk, milk your cow while sitting on a stool.
Pulling, squirting, pulling, squirting 'til the bucket's full.

 *Jodi Kelley, North Versailles, PA*

Milk Cows

Learning Objectives The children will:
1. Discover where milk comes from.
2. Identify foods that are made from cow's milk.
3. Engage in cooperative pretend play.

Circle or Group Time Activity
- Fill a latex glove with water and tie it closed at the wrist. Use a pin to prick a tiny hole in each of the fingers of the glove before starting this activity.
- Tell the children that they will be learning about cows today.
- Show the children pictures of cows, and ask questions about cows, such as, "What can you tell me about cows?""Where to do they usually live?""What sound do they make?""What do they eat?"
- Explain that dairy cows are cows that give milk. Hold up pictures of cows and point out udders of the cows. Explain that udders are where cows store their milk and that people squeeze the udders to get milk.
- Set up a stool and bucket. Show the children the glove filled with water and ask them to pretend it is a cow's udders.
- Invite the children to sit on the stool and "milk" the glove while you hold it.
- While the children take turns milking the glove, engage the other children in a discussion about foods that people make from milk.

Learning Centers **Art**
Provide a large cardboard box, several containers of red paint, and many large paintbrushes. Cut two flaps on either side of the box to serve as doors. Encourage the children to paint the box to make a barn. When the paint on the box dries, the children can use the box in their pretend play.
Dramatic Play
Set out overalls, suspenders, boots, straw hats, stool, and a bucket for the children to use in their pretend play.
Literacy
Set out crayons, markers, and sheets of paper with the sentence "_____ comes from milk." written on it. Ask the children to finish the sentence, and copy down their responses. Then, give the children the sheets of paper with their responses on them and invite them to illustrate their responses.
Math
Provide a bag with several empty containers from various dairy products. Encourage the children to line up the containers based upon their preferences, from favorite dairy product to least favorite.

Snack and Cooking

For each child, fill an empty baby food jar ⅔ full with whipping cream and a pinch of salt, and then close it with a lid. Ask the children to shake the jars for several minutes until the cream turns into butter. Pour off the buttermilk. Spread the butter on crackers and taste it. Chill the rest until it is ready to serve at snack time.

Book Suggestions

Farmer McPeepers and His Missing Milk Cows by Katy S. Duffield
Milk: From Cow to Carton by Aliki
The Milk Makers by Gail Gibbons

Snack

Serve the butter the children made in the Snack and Cooking Center. Provide crackers, bread, yogurt, and milk to complete the snack.

Review

Sing the following song with the children:

First Comes Milk by Cassandra Reigel Whetstone
(Tune: "Are You Sleeping?")
(Teacher) *First comes milk.*
(Children) *First comes milk.*
(Teacher) *Then comes butter.*
(Children) *Then comes butter.*
(Teacher) *Or we can make yogurt.*
(Children) *Or we can make yogurt.*
(Teacher) *Ice cream, too.*
(Children) *Ice cream, too.*

Assessment

If given an assortment of food items, including five dairy foods from the class lesson, can the child correctly identify at least three dairy foods?

 Cassandra Reigel Whetstone, Folsom, CA

Who Lives on the Farm?

Learning Objectives The children will:
1. Identify the names of common farm animals.
2. Differentiate between farm and zoo animals.
3. Develop their small motor skills.

Circle or Group Time Activity

- Gather everyone into a circle. Hold up pictures of common farm animals (cow, pig, sheep, horse, and so on) and ask the children to name the animals.
- Hold up an image of a chicken last. After the children identify the chicken, explain to the children that chickens lay eggs and that eggs are very fragile and must be handled with care.
- Next, show the children several plastic eggs, and explain that they will have a relay race in which the children must cross the room while holding the eggs in spoons.
- Separate the children into two groups, and have the two groups stand on either side of the room. Break the two groups into equal subgroups, each facing each other across the room.
- Give the first child in each group an egg and a spoon, and have them walk across the room and hand off the egg and spoon to the first child in the next group.
- Encourage the children to cheer on the others in their groups.

Learning Centers

Art
Set out paper, markers, crayons, and several plastic farm animals so the children can draw pictures of the farm animals.

Blocks
Provide several blocks and plastic farm animals. Encourage the children to build a barn for the farm animals out of their blocks.

Dramatic Play
Set out various animal-print materials and various animal masks. Invite the children to dress up and have an animal parade, crawling around making animal noises.

Literacy
Ask each child to finish the following sentence: "A _____ lives _____."
Write down their answers on pieces of white paper and ask the children to illustrate the pages. Bind the pages together with a stapler. Place the "Farm Animal Book" in the library for the children to read.

Math
Ask the children to sort the farm animals and count how many there are of each type of animal.

Book Suggestions   *The Cow That Went Oink* by Bernard Most
The Little Red Hen by Jerry Pinkney
Rooster's Off to See the World by Eric Carle

Snack   Serve milk and animal crackers for the children.

Review   Make farm animal noises and ask the children to identify the animals that make those sounds.

Assessment   Place plastic zoo animals and farm animals on a table and challenge the children to pick out the farm animals.

Renee Kirchner, Carrollton, TX

A Is for Apple

Learning Objectives The children will:
1. Learn that apples come in different colors.
2. Taste raw apples and cooked apples.
3. Learn the meaning of the expression "the apple of my eye."

Circle or Group Time Activity
- Tell the children that they will learn about apples today.
- Show the children four different types of apples: a Red Delicious (red), a Granny Smith (green), a Golden Delicious (yellow), and a Gala or Fuji (striped).
- Ask what is different about each apple. Discuss the colors.
- Teach the children the following song:

Apples, Apples by Christina Chilcote
(Tune: "Baa, Baa, Black Sheep")
Apples, apples, red and green, (hold up red and green apples)
Yellow and striped can be seen.
Apples in an apple pie, (show an apple pie or a pie picture)
Be the apple of Mommy's eye. (point to your eye)
Apples, apples, red and green, (hold up red and green apples)
Yellow and striped can be seen.

- Ask the children what "the apple of Mommy's eye" means. Listen to their responses. Eventually, explain that the phrase means that their mothers love them very much.
- Once the children learn the song, have them sing it with you two more times.

Learning Centers **Art**
Provide each child with a drawing of a tree on light green paper. Provide either flat-end erasers or round sponge stencil brushes. Alternatively, the child may use her index finger to "stamp" apples onto the tree. There is no "wrong" place to stamp an apple. Apples do fall on the ground!

Blocks
Put red contact paper apples on about 10 blocks. Mix these blocks in with the other blocks. Encourage the children to find the blocks with the red apples on them and use them to make apple "towers" or apple pyramids (four on the bottom, three blocks on top of them, two blocks, and one block on the very top).

Math
Ask the child to draw four red apples, four green apples, and two yellow apples. Ask, "How many apples are on this paper?"

Small Motor

Mix 12 assorted 2" x 2" laminated pictures of apples, oranges, and bananas (one fruit per square) on a table in front of three baskets. Ask the child to put all the apple pictures in the apple basket, all the orange pictures in the orange basket and all the banana pictures into the banana basket.

Snack and Cooking

Under adult supervision, each child peels an apple with a hand-cranked apple peeler, if available. Otherwise, each child uses an apple corer/slicer on an apple. Use a knife to peel the apple slices. Put peeled, cored apple slices into a large metal saucepan or a large glass/plastic casserole, depending on cooking method. Add a quarter inch of water to the bottom of the pan or casserole. Cook apples until soft and then let them cool. The children take turns putting a teaspoon of sugar into the pot and stirring the applesauce. Add more sugar, if needed. Serve in small bowls at snack time.

Book Suggestions

An Apple a Day by Jennifer Gillis
Apples by Gail Gibbons
Ten Red Apples by Virginia Miller

Snack

Serve three apple slices (one red, one green, one yellow), a small bowl of homemade chunky applesauce, a tiny slice of apple pie, and a small cup of apple juice.

Review

Talk about the different apple snacks. Ask the children which snacks were raw and which snacks were cooked. "Were the apple slices raw or cooked?" Review the expression "the apple of my eye." "If you are the apple of someone's eye, do they like you or not like you?"

Assessment

Show the children five or six color cards (red, green, yellow, purple, and white, for example). Hold up a card and ask the children "Are apples (name the color)?"

 *Christina Chilcote, New Freedom, PA*

Dairy Products

Learning Objectives The children will:
1. Learn about dairy.
2. Make their own butter.
3. Learn through rhymes.

Circle or Group Time Activity
- Show the children pictures of dairy products (yogurt, butter, cheese, ice cream, milk, and so on) and engage the children in a discussion about each food.
- Talk about the different types of dairy. Ask, "What is your favorite dairy food?"
- Pour whipping cream into a jar and replace the lid. Pass the jar around so the children can take turns shaking it. Ask, "Is a solid forming?"
- The cream will turn into butter after about 20 minutes with vigorous shaking. Remove the butter from the jar, place it on a plate, and add salt.
- Have the children spread it on crackers and taste it.
- Recite the following original rhyme with the children:

One Big Butter by Lily Erlic
One big butter, (hold up one finger and extend arms wide)
Sitting on the table all day, (pretend to sit)
"Look over there!" said the butter, (point)
The sun is on its way!" (make a circle with arms)

"Oh my, oh me, oh dear,
I'll melt, I fear!" (shiver)
The sun said, "You know, it's hot today,
You're sure to melt anyway."

So the sun,
Stretching in the sky, (pretend to stretch)
Winked an eye, (wink eye)
Hid behind the cloud, (hide behind hands)
And said, "Goodbye!" (wave)

One big butter, (hold up one finger and extend arms widely)
Wondering about the sun, (make circle with arms)
The sun winked an eye, (wink eye)
He said, "I was only having fun!" (laugh)

Learning Centers **Art**
Give each child a small milk carton. Open the carton at the top. Ask them to glue cotton balls inside the carton and some on top to mimic milk pouring.

Dramatic Play
Make a sign that reads "Dairy Farm." Provide the children with clean, empty butter containers, yogurt containers, ice cream cartons, and milk containers. Ask them to pretend to collect milk from cows and churn the cream into butter.

Literacy
Give each child a piece of paper with the name and image of a dairy food outlined on it. Ask the children to color their pictures. Later, ask the children to say the names of the dairy foods they colored, and to identify the letters in their names as they appear on the sheets of paper.

Math
Provide cow cutouts in different colors. Ask the children to count them, and then separate them by color and count how many of each color there are.

Science
Talk about where milk comes from. Explain how cows are milked. Show the children pictures of cows and farmers milking them.

Book Suggestions

Dairy Plant by Angela Leeper
A Fairy in a Dairy by Lucy A. Nolan

Snack

Provide milkshakes for the children to enjoy. Serve it in cups with straws.

Review

Recite "One Big Butter" again. Show the children the dairy pictures and talk about dairy foods.

Assessment

Show the children a picture of the food groups and ask them to point to the dairy group, and then ask that they each name their favorite dairy foods.

Related Song

Are You Ice Cream? by Lily Erlic
(Tune: "Are You Sleeping?")
Are you ice cream?
Are you ice cream?
Yes I am.
Yes I am.
Morning bells are ringing.
Morning bells are ringing.
Ding, Dang, Dong.
Ding, Dang, Dong.

Additional verses:
Repeat song and replace "ice cream" with "yogurt," "butter," or "cream cheese."

 *Lily Erlic, Victoria, British Columbia, Canada*

Fall for Veggies

Learning Objectives The children will:

1. Learn about many types of vegetables.
2. Learn to tell the difference between healthy and unhealthy foods.
3. Discover what foods they need to have healthy bodies.
4. Make collages representing the food groups.

Circle or Group Time Activity

■ Teach the children the following song:

Vegetable Song by Sandy L. Scott
(Tune: "Skip to My Lou")
Corn on the cornstalks grows above ground.
Corn on the cornstalks grows above ground.
Corn on the cornstalks grows above ground.
Let's go harvest our garden.

Additional verses:
Potatoes in the dirt grow underground.
Squash on long vines grows above ground.
Carrots are roots: they grow underground.

Learning Centers

Blocks
Encourage the children to use the blocks to make rows and a border for a vegetable patch.

Dramatic Play
Set out plastic vegetables and baskets so the children can pretend to harvest and garden.

Large Motor
The children make several "potatoes" by crumbling newspaper into small wads and wrapping them in nylon. The children can then add "eyes" with a permanent marker. Once the children finish making their potatoes, set out a container and challenge the children to toss their potatoes into it from a specified distance.

Library
Ask the children to name their favorite vegetables, and copy down each child's response on a separate sheet of paper. Give the children their sheets and invite them to illustrate their responses. When they finish, collect their illustrations, let them help alphabetize them, and staple them into a book form.

Small Motor
Provide a variety of vegetable puzzles for the children to explore.

Snack and Cooking

Provide cooked potatoes, toothpicks, green and red pepper wedges, carrots, beans, peas, and so on for the children to use to make potato people. Then eat.

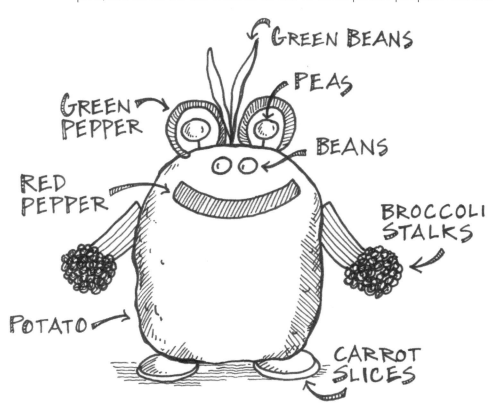

Book Suggestions   *The Carrot Seed* by Ruth Krauss
This Year's Garden by Cynthia Rylant

Snack   Serve a vegetable platter with ranch dip for the children.

Review   Ask the children to name some of the vegetables that grow in gardens. Can they distinguish between those that grow above ground and below ground?

Assessment   Can the child name at least four vegetables?

Sandy L. Scott, Meridian, ID

Fresh Fruit

Learning Objectives The children will:
1. Identify various fruits.
2. Understand that fruit is healthy.
3. Improve their large motor skills.
4. Identify simple fractions.
5. Weigh and measure fruit.
6. Use their five senses as they learn about fruit.

Circle or Group Time Activity

- Create a trail by winding a garden hose throughout the room.
- Display each type of fruit on a sheet of paper along the game trail.
- Introduce the topic of fruit as you draw the children's attention to the various fruits on display. Invite children to identify each type of fruit they see.
- Hand each child a foam bowl. Invite children to walk along the hose, like they would a tight rope, and carry the bowl on their head with both hands.
- When the teacher calls out "fruit bowl fun" children sit down near a fruit, two children per fruit. The children take turns setting the fruit in their own bowl and describing the fruit before them.
- After all the children have described a fruit, the class stands up and returns to walking on the garden hose. Children continue to walk along the hose until the teacher calls out "fruit bowl fun" once again.
- The game continues as children explore each of the various fruits.
- Record the 10 names of fruits on a sheet of chart paper and place it at the Writing Center.

Learning Centers **Art**
Display samples of various artists' work, including oil painting or watercolor paintings of fruit bowls as well, to give the children inspiration as they paint still-life pictures of a bowl of fruit.
Math
Set out several sheets of paper with images of halves of various fruits on them and invite the children to match the halves together, making wholes.
Snack and Cooking
Invite an adult to help children create a fruit smoothie. Have children add ice, fruit pieces, and ½ cup plain or vanilla yogurt then blend into a smooth and creamy treat.
Writing
Show the children sheets of paper with the outlines of fruits and the letters in the fruits' names on them. Ask the children to identify the names of the fruits, and then invite the children to color the images of the fruits and their names using appropriate colors.

Blocks
Invite children to use wooden blocks to cover a 12" × 18" sheet of paper with 10 images of different fruits on it. Invite pairs of children to take turns removing one block at a time. When a piece of fruit is showing completely, the child names the fruit. The game continues until the children reveal all the fruit on the page.

Book Suggestions

Eating the Alphabet by Lois Ehlert
Food for Thought by Joost Elffers
The Very Hungry Caterpillar by Eric Carle

Snack

Have children make fruit pizzas. Spread cream cheese on a rice cake. Sprinkle red decorative sugar on the cream cheese, then top with colorful fruit pieces.

Review

Invite children to roll a variety of colorful balls (representing fruits) back and forth across the circle. Ring a bell. The children holding pieces of fruit when the bell rings each recite something they learned about fruit or name their favorite fruits.

Assessment

Display an assortment of images of fruits and vegetables. Invite the child to identify which items are fruit.

Related Poem

Fruit Bowl by Mary J. Murray
Apples, bananas,
Oranges, plums.
Blueberries, cherries,
Coconuts are fun.
Watermelon, pineapple,
Peaches, and pears.
Fruit is a great snack anywhere.

Mary J. Murray, Mazomanie, WI

Green Foods

Learning Objectives The children will:
1. Learn that many of the healthiest foods are green.
2. Think about the different shapes of green fruits and vegetables.
3. Compare the flavors of green foods.

Circle or Group Time Activity

- Tell the children they will be learning about some of the healthiest foods they can eat, and that all of them are green. Explain that green fruits and vegetables are good for vision, help prevent some diseases (like cancer), and promote strong bones and teeth.
- Put out various green fruits and vegetables (celery, broccoli, green apples, green grapes, honeydew melon, for example). Engage the children in a conversation about the different shapes, sizes, and textures of each.
- Point out that some are dark green, some medium green, and some light green. Ask the children if they have an idea what each fruit or vegetable might taste like just from looking at them.
- Talk about how you might use each food. For example, lettuce in a salad, green apples in a pie or as a snack, and so on.
- Cut open and explore what is inside some of the various green fruits and vegetables that you assembled. Ask the children, "Isn't it a surprise that a bell pepper has so many seeds in it, or that a watermelon is green on the outside and pink inside?"

Learning Centers **Art**
Have the children draw pictures of their favorite green foods or their family eating a meal with lots of greens. Or, have them cut out pictures from magazines of green foods and glue them to their paper.

Blocks
Encourage the children to set up the blocks for a green fruit and vegetable stand. Talk about how some fruits and vegetables are sold from roadside stands or at farmer's markets.

Dramatic Play
Have the children take turns acting as customers and produce "salespeople," buying and selling green fruits and vegetables. The "salespeople" can tell the customers how good the green fruits and vegetables taste and how good they are for your health.

Literacy
Ask the children what words they would use to describe different aspects of the green fruits and vegetables (*round, long, short, good, tasty,* and so on). Have them watch while you write those words in big letters on white paper with green markers. Use only one word on each sheet of paper. Encourage the children to

look at the words when they have a chance and ask you what they are if they can't yet read them.

Music

Make up songs about your favorite green fruits and vegetables. For instance, sing the following original song to the tune of "Are You Sleeping?":

I like celery,
I like celery,
Yes I do!
Yes I do!
Celery, celery, celery.
Celery, celery, celery.
Good for you,
Good for you.

Snack and Cooking

Help the children make their own salad from the green foods that have been brought in. Use paper plates for the salad. You may want to chop up lettuce and provide some dressing for the small salads.

Book Suggestions

Eat Healthy, Feel Great by William Sears, Martha Sears, and Christie Watts Kelly
Eating the Alphabet by Lois Ehlert
Good Enough to Eat: A Kid's Guide to Food and Nutrition by Lizzy Rockwell
Green Eggs and Ham by Dr. Seuss
Growing Vegetable Soup by Lois Ehlert
The Terrible Eater by Mitchell Sharmat

Snack

Serve slices of green apples, or other green foods, such as those you cut open in the Circle or Group Time Activity.

Review

Ask the children what their favorite green fruit or vegetable is and why. Ask if they tried a new green fruit or vegetable today and if they liked it.

Assessment

Can the children give a reason why green fruits and vegetables might be a better food choice than green cookies or green cupcakes or green ice cream?

 *Jan Black, San Francisco, CA*

Healthy Food Fun

Learning Objectives The children will:
1. Discover healthy foods.
2. Taste healthy foods.
3. Talk about reasons to eat healthy food.

Circle or Group Time Activity

■ Teach the children the following song:

Good Food (author unknown)
(Tune: "London Bridge")
*Good food helps us grow up strong,
grow up strong, grow up strong.
Good food helps us grow up strong,
I like _____.*

■ Children take turns saying their favorite healthy foods, holding up plastic samples or pictures of the foods as they say them.

Learning Centers **Art**

Provide children with paper plates, markers, crayons, and magazine photos of healthy foods. Encourage the children to draw or cut out pictures of their favorite healthy foods and glue them onto the plates.

PICTURES
GLUED
ON
PLATE →

GLUE

MAGAZINES

Dramatic Play
Set out various plastic foods, a cash register, and play money and encourage the children to pretend they are shopping and working in a health-food market.
Library
Make a recording of one of the books from the Book Suggestions list, and put the recording and a copy of the book in the center for the children to listen to and explore.
Math
Set out a poster board and markers so the children can create a graph of favorite healthy foods. Put three or four photos of healthy foods on the left side of a piece of oak tag, along with photocopies of photographs of the children. The children place photos of themselves in the rows for their favorite healthy foods on the graph. After the children finish, encourage them to add up the totals and compare.
Sand and Water
Set plastic tuber vegetables (such as carrots and potatoes) in the table for the children to explore.

Book Suggestions

Growing Vegetable Soup by Lois Ehlert
Today Is Monday by Eric Carle
The Very Hungry Caterpillar by Eric Carle

Snack

Children help prepare fruits and mix them together to make a fruit salad to enjoy.

Review

Show the children images of various vegetables and ask them to say the names of their favorites when they see them.

Assessment

Give the children an assortment of healthy and nonhealthy toy foods or photos and ask the children to pick out healthy foods.

 Deborah Hannes Litfin, Forest Hills, NY

Pass the Pizza

Learning Objectives The children will:
1. Learn about the main ingredients of pizza.
2. Talk about nutrition.
3. Improve math skills in fractions and counting.
4. Develop their small motor skills.
5. Develop their oral language skills.

Circle or Group Time Activity

- Draw a large circle ("pizza") in the bottom of a pizza box. Use a black marker to divide the pizza into eight slices.
- Cut out eight matching slices of "pizza" from card stock. Attach a piece of Velcro to each card stock slice and a piece of Velcro to each "slice" on the pizza box.
- Attach the card stock slices of pizza to the spaces in the box.

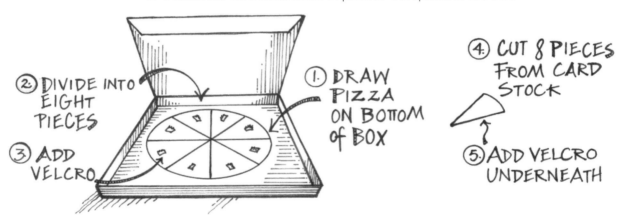

② DIVIDE INTO EIGHT PIECES

③ ADD VELCRO

① DRAW PIZZA ON BOTTOM OF BOX

④ CUT 8 PIECES FROM CARD STOCK

⑤ ADD VELCRO UNDERNEATH

- Invite the children to gather around as you display the pizza box.
- Have them comment on their favorite kinds of pizza or pizza restaurants.
- Talk about the main ingredients of pizza and how they relate to the food groups: sauce (vegetables), crust (grains), meat (protein), cheese (dairy), and other toppings (protein or vegetable).
- Begin the game by inviting children to pass the box around the circle as music plays.
- When the music stops, the person holding the box opens it up, takes a slice, and sits in the center of the circle.
- Continue the game, stopping the music every minute or so.
- Once all eight slices are gone, invite the children to piece the pizza together as they display it in the center of the circle.
- Play at least three times, allowing different children to choose a slice of pizza and put the whole pizza together.

Learning Centers

Blocks
Stock the center with several pizza boxes. Invite the children to include them in their block building to create unusual structures.

Dramatic Play
Provide several pizza boxes, nametags, paper pizzas, and a toy car so the children can pretend to deliver pizzas.

Literacy
Cut out five pieces of construction paper and decorate them to resemble slices of pizza. Put them together to form a pizza, and write the word "pizza" on them (one letter per slice) in a circle. Mix them up again and challenge the children to put them together again in the correct order. For older children, consider adding the names of ingredients on the tops of other cutout pizzas.

Math
Set out several number cards and construction-paper cutouts that resemble slices of pizza. Challenge the children to select a card, then use the pizza slices to count to the number listed on the card.

Small Motor
Invite the children to roll playdough into the shape of a pizza, and then use a pizza cutter to cut six or eight slices and serve them on paper plates.

Book Suggestions

The King of Pizza by Sylvester Sanzari
Pizza! by Teresa Martino
The Pizza That We Made by Joan Holub

Snack

Give the children toasted English muffin halves, and invite them to top them with sauce and cheese for a fun pizza snack.

Review

Ask the children to name toppings they might find on a pizza, and take a poll to see which toppings are the most popular.

Assessment

Can a child use lettered slices of pizza to spell the word "pizza?"

Related Song

I Like Pizza by Mary J. Murray
I like pizza.
I like it a lot
I like it cold.
I like it hot.
I like sausage.
I like cheese.
I like pepperoni.
Pass the pizza please.

 *Mary J. Murray, Mazomanie, WI*

Playing with the Food Pyramid

Learning Objectives The children will:
1. Learn about the food pyramid.
2. Taste foods from all groups of the food pyramid.
3. Develop their fine motor skills.

Circle or Group Time Activity
- Show children a food pyramid chart and talk about the foods in each group.
- Have the children sit in a circle. Pass around a few paper plates with photos of foods from each food group glued to them. Play lively music as the children pass the plates.
- Occasionally, stop the music and ask each child who is holding a plate to name the food group of the food on the plate.

Learning Centers **Art**
Have the children draw and color their own food pyramids, making sure to add their favorite foods in each group.

Math
Tape a large triangle outline on the floor. Use tape to mark off the six sections of the food groups. Write the six sections of the pyramid on construction paper and

tape them into the pyramid. Provide plastic play food. Have each child chose a food and match it to the correct section of the food pyramid.

Construction
Provide several construction paper cutouts of the different sections of the food pyramid, as well as black construction paper, and invite the children to pick the six different sections of the pyramid and paste them together properly on the black construction paper.

Literacy
Cut out 12–24 colored construction paper squares and write the names of foods on half of them, and their matching food group on the other half (for example, write "yogurt" on one card and "dairy group" on another card). Challenge the children to match the foods to the correct food group.

Snack and Cooking
The children make lunch using foods from the food pyramid. Make a beef stew with vegetables and rice or pasta. Ask each child to bring in one ingredient. Help them chop vegetables for the stew. Serve the stew with a piece of fruit and milk.

Book Suggestions

The Edible Pyramid by Loreen Leedy
Gregory the Terrible Eater by Mitchell Sharmat
Showdown at the Food Pyramid by Rex Barron

Snack

Serve one food from each of the food groups. From the meat, vegetable, milk, and grain groups, serve English muffins layered with a slice of turkey, steamed broccoli, and melted cheddar cheese. From the milk, fruit, sweets, and grain groups, serve cream cheese sweetened with powdered sugar on English muffins and top with sliced strawberries and grapes.

Review

Draw the food pyramid with the six food groups on a blackboard. Starting at the top and working downward, ask each child to name a food that belongs in each food group.

Assessment

Bring in pictures of foods from magazines. Can the children place the foods into their correct food groups?

 *Randi Lynn Mrvos, Lexington, KY*

Positively Pizza

Learning Objectives The children will:
1. Identify the ingredients in a pizza.
2. Develop their literacy skills.
3. Learn how to follow instructions.
4. Recognize number words.

Circle or Group Time Activity
- Create felt cutouts of pizza ingredients for the flannel board.
- With the children, sing a song about pizza. As you mention the various ingredients, ask the children to identify the felt cutout versions of them, and then add them to the flannel board.

Learning Centers **Art**

Cut out large circles ("pizzas") from painting paper. Provide several colors of paints and brushes, and invite the children to paint pizzas.

Dramatic Play

Fill the center with empty pizza boxes, red-and-white checked tablecloths, oven mitts, aprons, chef hats, dishes, eating utensils, rolling pins, pizza pans, plastic trays, clean plastic soda bottles, clock, play money, play cash register, and a play telephone so the children can pretend to work and visit a pizza parlor.

Literacy

Provide a cookie tray, magnetic letters, and sheets of paper with "pizza," "mush room," "pepperoni," and other pizza-related words on them. Challenge the children to recreate the words on the cards by ordering the magnetic letters on the cookie sheet.

Math

Number several cards from 1–10 and place them next to several construction-paper cutout slices of pizza. Challenge the children to pick a number card and then count the matching number of slices. Expand on this activity by providing several cutouts of toppings, such as mushrooms and pepperoni, and asking the children to pick the number cards again, and then add the correct number of the toppings to their slices.

Writing

Set out several stencils of the spellings of various pizza toppings, such as *pepperoni, mushroom,* and *onion,* as well as paper and markers, and invite the children to copy the words.

Book Suggestions *Hi, Pizza Man* by Virginia Walter
Pete's a Pizza by William Steig
Pizza Counting by Christina Dobson
The Pizza That We Made by Joan Holub

Snack Make Pizza Muffins using refrigerated biscuit dough pressed into muffin-tin sections. Let each child place a teaspoon of sauce over the dough and top it with a circle of pepperoni and a spoonful of shredded mozzarella cheese. Bake the muffins according to the directions on the biscuit tube.

Review Ask the children to spell "pizza." Send a few theme-related books home with the "Pizza Literacy Bag" to share with their families.

Assessment Can the children name their favorite pizza toppings?

Jackie Wright, Enid, OK

Spaghetti

Learning Objectives The children will:

1. Identify the letter S.
2. Learn how people make spaghetti sauce.
3. Recognize that print carries meaning.
4. Develop their small motor skills.

Circle or Group Time Activity

- Gather the children in a circle. Say, "I woke up so hungry today I ate spaghetti for breakfast. Isn't that silly? Slurping spaghetti is for supper, not for breakfast, isn't it?"
- Ask the children what letter spaghetti starts with. Give them hints by saying words that start with S.
- After the children say that spaghetti starts with the letter S, tell them that S has a *slithery, slippery,* and *silly* shape.
- Distribute paper, yarn, and crayons, and show the children how to make an S shape with the yarn on their paper. Help the children glue their yarn to their sheets of paper in S shapes. Once dry, encourage each child decorate it in any way they wish. As the children work, ask them if there are other slithery, slippery, and silly things that start with the letter S, such as snakes.

Learning Centers

Art
Give the children several sheets of paper, containers of paint, and lengths of yarn. Invite the children to paint with the yarn.

Dramatic Play
Put out a pot, bowl, strands of yarn, colander, and tongs, and encourage the children to pretend they are having a spaghetti feast together.

Library
Make a recording of *Strega Nona* and set it in the center along with a copy of the book and several lengths of yarn. Encourage the children to listen along to the recording as they look through the book and play with the yarn as though it were the growing ball of spaghetti.

Math
Give the children several numbered cards and pieces of yarn. Challenge the children to select a card, and then count out the corresponding number of pieces of yarn.

Small Motor
Set out tongs and strands of yarn and challenge the children to pick them up one at a time, moving them from one bowl to another.

Writing
Provide several pieces of yarn along with sheets of paper with one letter of the word "spaghetti" written on each. Encourage the children to use the yarn to make the shapes of the letters on top of the sheets of paper, and to put them in the correct order.

Book Suggestions

More Spaghetti, I Say! by Rita Golden Gelman
On Top of Spaghetti by Paul Brett Johnson
Strega Nona by Tomie dePaola

Snack

Prepare and serve spaghetti noodles with grated parmesan cheese and butter for those who don't want sauce.

Review

Recite the following song, asking the children to stress every S they hear:

Spaghetti Sauce Song by Cassandra Reigel Whetstone
(Tune: "Have You Ever Seen a Lassie?")
First, we cook tomatoes, tomatoes, tomatoes.
First we cook tomatoes and then we have sauce.
Next we add some veggies, some veggies, some veggies.
Next we add some veggies and we have thick sauce.
Last we add some spices, some spices, some spices.
Last we add some spices and eat spaghetti sauce.

Assessment

If shown three letters, can the child identify the letter S?

 Cassandra Reigel Whetstone, Folsom, CA

Tea Party Time

Learning Objectives   The children will:
1. Help to plan a tea party.
2. Learn the importance of helping each other.
3. Learn to express why they like and dislike certain foods.

Circle or Group Time Activity
- Play Hot Tea Cup with the children (a variation of Hot Potato).
- Sit the children in a circle, turn on lively music, and ask them to pass the tea cup around the circle. Explain that they should pass the cup around to try not to be holding it when the music stops.
- Occasionally, stop the music and see which child is holding the cup.
- Continue playing. No one has to sit in or out of the circle. Stress that the game is not a competition.

Learning Centers   **Dramatic Play**

Set out royal dress-up clothes for the children to put on. Encourage them to pretend to have a royal tea party.

Math

Provide table settings for four people (four cups, bowls, plates, cutlery, and placemats), and encourage the children to set the table for four with the appropriate number of items. Note: For younger children, consider laminating the placemats with outlines of the objects on them, so the children can see where things should go.

Music

Copy the words and movements of "I'm a Little Teapot" onto a sheet of poster board and put it up in the center, inviting the children to sing the song together and act out the movements as the poster board indicates.

Snack and Cooking

Prepare several cupcakes and other snacks that the children can enjoy at snack time. Set out toppings such as icing and sprinkles that the children can add to the cupcakes.

Writing

Set out several sheets of paper with "Foods I Like" and "Foods I Dislike" written on them. Ask the children to tell you foods they like and dislike, and copy them down onto the sheets, then give them to the children and encourage them to copy the words and illustrate the sheets.

Book Suggestions   *Let's Have a Tea Party* by Emilie Barnes
Miss Spider's Tea Party by David Kirk
My Very First Tea Party by Michal Sparks

Snack   Have a tea party. Serve the cupcakes the children prepared earlier, along with iced tea. Encourage the children to dress up for the tea party, and consider using plastic teacups and saucers to make the event feel more elegant.

Review   Discuss what children liked or disliked about the tea party. Did they like helping prepare the food? Did they have fun dressing up? Did they enjoy helping each other and serving the food?

Assessment   Give the children blank menus and writing tools and ask them to plan a menu for the next tea party. Encourage them to draw or write about what they would like to serve at the party and who they would like to invite.

Related Song   **Tea Party Time** by Eileen Lucas
It's tea party time, its tea party time.
Let everyone know it's tea party time.
We can't wait to get in our seats
And let everyone know its tea party time.

 Eileen Lucas, Fort McMurray, Alberta, Canada

Tortillas

Learning Objectives The children will:
1. Recognize things that are round.
2. Learn about tortillas.
3. Develop small motor skills.

Circle or Group Time Activity
- Show the children pictures of foods that are different shapes (round foods, square containers of food, triangular foods such as pizza slices, and so on). Engage the children in a discussion about the shapes of the foods.

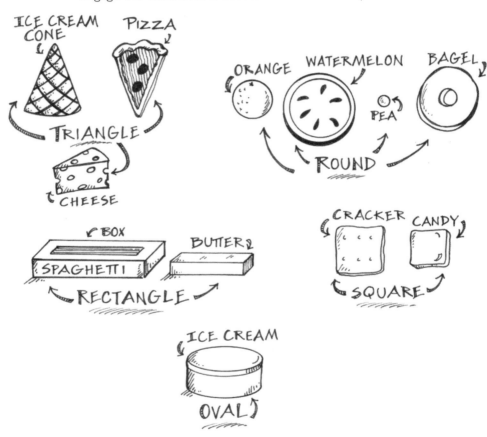

- Ask the children to name some foods that are round.
- Show the children a flattened corn tortilla and ask them if they know what it is and what shape it is. Explain to the children that tortillas are a type of bread.
- Explain to the children that they will be making tortillas today. Set out the ingredients, including masa. Have the children mix the masa according to the directions on the packaging. Give each child a chance to roll a piece of mixed masa into a ball and cover the rest with a damp cloth.

- Next, show the children how to pat the masa with their hands, or use a tortilla press to shape balls of masa into round tortillas. Explain to the children that the next step is to fry the tortilla on a griddle, which they will do later in the Cooking Center.

Learning Centers

Art
Invite the children to stamp round cookie or biscuit cutters onto paper using paint.

Dramatic Play
Provide felt tortillas and other pretend toppings for children to make pretend tacos and burritos.

Math
Set out pieces of several brown and yellow construction paper circles, representing flour and corn tortillas, each with a number on it, and challenge the children to put them in order according to number and type.

Small Motor
Provide playdough and encourage children to make round shapes with it and to roll and pound it like they did when making tortillas.

Snack and Cooking
Help children finish preparing their tortillas on a griddle. Be sure that the tortillas cook on both sides. **Safety Note:** Only adults should actually use the griddle.

Book Suggestions

Bread, Bread, Bread by Ann Morris
Tiny Tortilla by Arlene L. Williams
The Tortilla Factory by Gary Paulsen

Snack

Serve tortillas from the Snack and Cooking Center activity with grated cheese and black beans (warm canned beans in a crock pot).

Review

Ask the children to describe the process of making tortillas.

Assessment

Show the children a loaf of bread, tortillas, dry rice, and hamburger buns, and ask the children to identify which are round.

Related Song

Ten Tortillas by Cassandra Reigel Whetstone
(Tune: "Bumping Up and Down in My Little Red Wagon")
Uno, dos, tres tortillas,
Quatro, cinco, seis tortillas,
Siete, ocho, nueve tortillas,
Diez tortillas para comer.

One, two three tortillas,
Four, five, six tortillas,
Seven, eight, nine tortillas,
Ten tortillas we can eat.

 Cassandra Reigel Whetstone, Folsom, CA

Vegetables

Learning Objectives The children will:
1. Identify common vegetables, matching names with pictures.
2. Taste a variety of raw vegetables.
3. Understand the importance of having a healthy diet.
4. Observe the baby plant within a lima bean seed.

Circle or Group Time Activity
- Engage the children in a discussion about the plants that we eat, such as beans, spinach, carrots, corn, and peas. Explain that we eat different parts of plants, and that all vegetables grow from seeds.
- Show the children a sprouting lima bean, pointing out the tiny sprout emerging from the seed.
- Explain that plants need water to grow, and that water is what makes seeds pop open. Explain that plants use sunshine and soil the way we use food: as fuel to make themselves grow.
- Tell the children that they will be learning about vegetables today.

Learning Centers **Dramatic Play**
Provide straw hats, trowel, and a watering can so the children can pretend to garden.

Literacy
Provide the children with several sheets of paper that read, "My favorite vegetable is _____." Ask each child for her response and write it in the blank, then ask the children to illustrate their papers.

Small Motor
Set out a muffin tin and several packets of various vegetable seeds for the children to sort. Attach an image of each seed to one of the sections of the tin so the children can compare the seeds they hold to see what should go where.

Art

Set out playdough, paper, paint, and other art materials so the children can paint and sculpt images of their favorite vegetables.

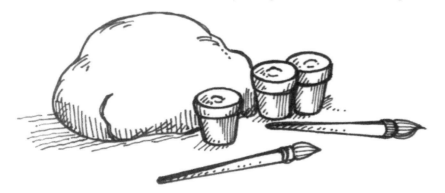

RED TOMATO

ORANGE CARROT

BROWN POTATO

Snack and Cooking

Have a taste test. Provide several various vegetables for the children to taste.

Snack
Serve carrot sticks with dip for the children.

Review
Collect the children's "My favorite vegetable" sheets and count how many responses each vegetable received, then make a graph out of the sheets by attaching them to the wall. Ask the children to say which vegetables were the most and least favorite.

Assessment
Can the children name the vegetables on the favorite vegetable chart?

 *Mary Jo Shannon, Roanoke, VA*

Very Blueberry

Learning Objectives   The children will:
1. Learn about blueberries.
2. Develop their small motor skills.
3. Practice counting to 10.
4. Learn about the parts of a plant.

Circle or Group Time Activity
■ Hold up a jar filled with blueberries, and have each child guess how many blueberries are in the jar.
■ After every child has had a chance to respond, count how many blueberries are in the jar to see whose guess was closest.
■ Tell the children they will be learning about blueberries today.

Learning Centers   **Art**
Provide white construction paper, paintbrushes, trays, and various shades of blue tempera paint that have been mixed with dry blueberry gelatin so the children can paint pictures with blueberry-scented paint.
Literacy
Set out several sheets of paper with "Blueberries make me feel _____" written on them. Ask the children to complete the statement, and then write their answers for them with a blue marker. Next, give the children the sheets and invite them to illustrate the responses.

Math
Provide several small blue marbles (if age appropriate) and 10 small paper cups numbered 1–10. Invite the children to place the corresponding number of blue marbles into each cup.

Science
Purchase a small, potted blueberry bush the children can examine. If this is not possible, show them a picture of a blueberry bush. Encourage them to discuss the different parts of the plant. Be sure to point out the roots, stems, leaves, berries, and flowers (if any).

Small Motor
Provide child-safe scissors and blue construction paper with printed circles. Invite the children to cut out the outlines of the blue circles, making construction paper blueberries.

Book Suggestions   *Blueberries for Sal* by Robert McCloskey
Blueberry Mouse by Alice Low
Blueberry Shoe by Ann Dixon
Jamberry by Bruce Degen
White Is for Blueberry by George Shannon

Snack   Provide foods made with blueberries, such as blueberry muffins, blueberry bread, blueberry pie, or fresh blueberries and cream. You can also serve blueberry gelatin snack, topped, of course, with fresh blueberries.

Review   Ask the children to use their senses to describe blueberries. How do they look, feel, smell, and taste?

Assessment   Given an assortment of berries, can the children pick out the blueberries? Ask them, "Does a blueberry look like a circle or a square?"

 *Laura D. Wynkoop, San Dimas, CA*

We All Scream for Ice Cream

Learning Objectives The children will:
1. Practice counting.
2. Learn about the ingredients that go into ice cream.
3. Improve their oral and written language skills.
4. Develop their large motor skills.

Circle or Group Time Activity

- Introduce the children to the topic of ice cream and talk with them about its main ingredients. Provide a large paper cutout of an ice-cream cone.
- Give a paper cutout of a scoop of ice cream to each child.
- Invite the children to lay their paper scoops on the floor above the cone, stacking them one on top of the other to create a giant ice-cream cone.
- Invite the children to share aloud their favorite flavor of ice cream, and then pick up and hold new scoops of ice cream.
- Teach the children the ice cream chant "I scream, you scream, we all scream for ice cream." Encourage the children to skip around the room with their paper scoops as they all chant together. Then ring the ice-cream bell.
- When the bell rings, direct the children to scurry to the floor and stack their scoops on top of the paper cone, and then count the stack of scoops.
- After the children stack all the scoops on top of the cone, remove each scoop and count backwards. Invite the children to pick up different scoops, and then play the game again.
- Ask the children to tell you their favorite flavors of ice cream again, and copy what they say onto chart paper. Consider making a graph of the information.

Learning Centers **Art**
Provide children with ice-cream cone paper cutouts to paste to sheets of art paper. Set out art supplies so the children to create a variety of differently flavored ice-cream scoops on top of the cones.

Blocks
Use masking tape to stick a paper ice-cream cone cutout to one block and a paper scoop of ice cream to several other blocks. Invite children to stack the blocks with the cone on bottom and the scoops on top. See how tall the children can build the ice-cream cone before it falls down.

Sand and Water
Invite children to scoop wet sand and stack the scoopfuls like scoops on an ice-cream cone.

Small Motor
Invite children to create ice-cream cone shapes from modeling dough and then stack a scoop on top.
Writing
Invite children to write down some of their favorite flavors of ice cream on a cone-shaped piece of paper. Let them refer to the list as they record their favorites.

Book Suggestions

From Cow to Ice Cream by Bertram T. Knight
I Like Ice Cream by Robin Pickering
Milk to Ice Cream by Inez Snyder

Snack

Provide children with an empty ice-cream cone. Invite children to place a handful of berries in the bottom of the cone. Then scoop in vanilla ice cream to top it off. Another day, have an ice cream tasting party. Bring in several of your favorite flavors and a large number of plastic or wooden spoons. Invite children to taste them all (one clean spoon per taste) and decide on their favorite.

Review

Provide four buckets of tissue ball scoops of ice cream and four ice-cream scoops with bowls. Divide the class into four teams. Invite teams to race as they take turns removing scoops of ice cream from the bucket and placing the scoops in their bowl. Players should pass the scoop around so that everyone has several opportunities to scoop ice cream into the bowl. The first team to fill their bowl and empty their bucket is the winner. Have the winning team recite things they have learned from the ice-cream activities.

Assessment

Invite the child to stack several paper scoops on top of a paper cone as he names the ingredients in ice cream, describes the different flavors of the scoops he is stacking, and then names his favorite flavor.

 Mary J. Murray. Mazomanie, WI

Wonderful Watermelon

Learning Objectives The children will:
1. Learn how watermelon grows.
2. Learn to estimate weight, length, and circumference.
3. Use their five senses.
4. Improve their large and fine motor skills.

Circle or Group Time Activity

- Before the children arrive, place a brown blanket or mural paper on the floor.
- Put at least three real watermelons on the blanket. String a "watermelon vine" (green yarn with paper leaves) between the watermelons, to represent watermelon growing in a watermelon patch. Place a bed sheet over the watermelon patch.

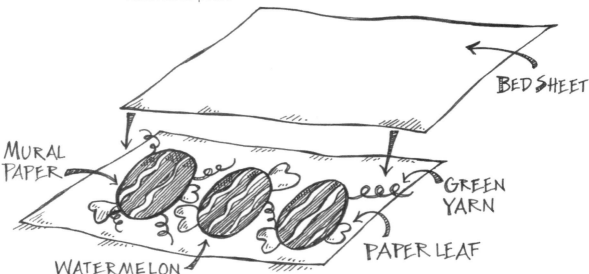

- Invite children to look at the covered shapes and guess what is beneath the sheet.
- Let the children touch the hidden shapes and make another guess. Then lift the sheet and display the watermelon patch.
- Teach the children the following poem:

Watermelon, Fruit so Fine by Mary J. Murray
Look at the watermelon growing on the vine.
I never did see a fruit so fine.
Seed in the soil, water and sun.
I never did eat a fruit so fun.

■ Invite the children to stand or sit in the watermelon patch. Then invite three children to come forward and hold onto a watermelon seed, paper sun, and watering can as the other children chant the poem repeatedly.

Learning Centers

Art
Provide colorful paper cut to resemble watermelon slices. Invite children to press their pointer fingers onto a washable ink pad and make fingerprint seeds on their slices. Older children can cut out their own slices.

Dramatic Play
Provide sun hats, garden gloves, trowels, and a hoe for the children to use to pretend they are working in a watermelon patch. Also provide watermelon-shaped cutouts that the children can pretend to harvest.

Large Motor
Invite children to have a watermelon seed-planting relay. The children place three "seeds" (black tissue balls) on top of the red "watermelon" (towel). The children hold onto the two ends of the towel and carry the seeds to a designated area, flip the towel up and over so the seeds land in the grass (green paper), and then go back for more.

Math
Set out a real watermelon, along with a bathroom scale and tape measure. Invite the children to estimate the weight, length, and circumference of the watermelon and then measure it to determine how accurate their estimates were. Set out paper and encourage the children to record their estimates and findings.

Writing
Provide several watermelon seeds and sheets of paper with the word *watermelon* written on them. Invite the children to spell out the word *watermelon* by laying the watermelon seeds along the letters.

Book Suggestions
Green by Mary Elizabeth Salzmann
One Watermelon Seed by Celia Barker Lottridge
Watermelon Day by Kathi Appelt

Snack
Cut up the watermelon from the Math Center for the children to enjoy.

Review
Invite several children to hold onto the edges of a pink or red sheet. Toss 10 black seeds (tight balls of black tissue paper) onto the sheet. Invite children to move the sheet up and down until all the seeds bounce off of the watermelon.

Assessment
Give the children handfuls of dry watermelon seeds. Display a red piece of felt. Make various true and false statements about watermelon, and ask the children to put their seeds on the red felt if they think the statements are true, and to shake their heads if they think the statements are false.

 Mary J. Murray, Mazomanie, WI

Finding Friends

Learning Objectives The children will:
1. Understand the importance of friendship.
2. Enhance their oral language skills.
3. Practice counting and telling story problems.
4. Practice writing their names and friends' names.

Circle or Group Time Activity
- Display a picture of two friends together. Invite children to talk about what makes someone a friend.
- Encourage the children to name some things that friends do together and how friends should treat each other. After the discussion play the following game.
- Have children sit in two rows facing each other.
- Display a row of common objects down the center of the game area. Invite the first two children, one from each line, to pick up an object from the center of the playing area and then join hands as each one talks about how to use the object with their friend. ("I can read this book with my friend Joe." "I can share this snack with my friend Sophie.")
- The two children then join hands and walk with their objects around the game area, then sit back down.
- Invite the next pair of children (one from each line) to pick up an item and do the same.
- Continue until all the children have walked with a friend and talked about a friend in the class. Play again as children walk and talk with a different "friend" and pick up a different object.

Learning Centers ### Art
Invite the children to glue two blank face-shaped cutouts to a piece of art paper. Have them use markers, crayons, and other collage materials to create pictures of themselves with their special friends. Set up an area in the center where they can display the artwork and take turns telling one another about their special friends.
Literacy
Set out a list of all the children's names, so they can read the names of their friends and then verbalize why each classmate makes a good friend.
Math
Prior to this activity, take several photos of the children in your classroom. When the photos are ready, set them out so the children can count how many friends are in each picture, and then lay matching number cards next to the pictures.

Blocks

Attach a photocopy of a picture of each child to a wood block, cover it with clear contact paper, and use these "friendship" blocks in the center. Each time the children incorporate the "friendship" blocks into their creations, invite them to tell how they can be good friends to the people on those blocks.

Writing

Provide each child with a few pages of paper stapled into book form and encourage all the children to sign or mark one another's books in some way, and encourage the children to describe to one another who signed their books and why they are friends.

Book Suggestions

Do You Want to Be My Friend? by Eric Carle
Finding a Friend in the Forest by Dean Bennett
Little Critter's This Is My Friend by Mercer Mayer

Snack

Invite children to spread cream cheese or peanut butter on two round crackers or rice cakes. The children then add edible toppings to create a face and hair, depicting themselves and a friend.

Review

Crumple up several sheets of different-colored paper and put them in a pile in front of the children and have them kick around one piece of paper each. After a short while, ring a bell, and ask the children to pick up their crumpled sheets of paper and find a friend with a sheet of paper that is the same color, and then sit down together.

Assessment

Invite the children to talk about a good friend of theirs in the classroom, describing activities they have done together and why they like their friends.

 *Mary J. Murray, Mazomanie, WI*

Friends Forever

Learning Objectives The children will:
1. Develop an awareness of what it means to be a friend.
2. Talk about what kinds of things friends do for and with each other.
3. Gain an appreciation for one's own friends.
4. Develop number and letter awareness.

Circle or Group Time Activity

- Engage the children in a discussion about friendship. Talk about what kinds of things friends do for and with each other. Ask them to tell you how they can be a good friend (take turns, use friendly words, talk about problems, and so on).

- Show them a piece of poster board with the following poem on it, and recite it together:

Friends by Jackie Wright
Friends care.
Friends share.
We need friends
Everywhere!

- After all the children know the poem, have them recite it in rounds. Break the children into four groups, and have each group start the poem after the previous group finishes the first line.

Learning Centers

Art
Set out several sheets of paper, markers, crayons, and so on, and invite the children to make drawings of themselves being good friends.

Listening
Place a copy and recording of the book *Little Bear's Friend* by Else Holmelund Minarik in this center for the children to listen to and explore.

Math Center
Make a simple graph with "yes" and "no" and invite the children to mark one side of the graph in response to the question "Have you ever spent the night at a friend's house?" Encourage the children to count and compare the results.

Writing
Provide markers, crayons, and sheets of paper with dotted outlines of the word *friend* on them. Invite the children to practice writing the word.

Music

Give the children several instruments and invite them to play them as they recite the following song:

Rig-A-Jig-Jig (Traditional)
As I was walking down the street,
Down the street, down the street,
A friend of mine I chanced to meet,
Hi-ho, hi-ho, hi-ho!
Rig-a-jig-jig and away we did go,
Away we did go, away we did go.
Rid-a-jig-jig and away we did go,
Hi-ho, hi-ho, hi-ho!

Book Suggestions

Alexander and the Wind-Up Mouse by Leo Lionni
Frog and Toad Are Friends by Arnold Lobel
Frog and Toad Together by Arnold Lobel
George and Martha by James Marshall
George and Martha One Fine Day by James Marshall
Little Bear's Friend by Else Holmelund Minarik
The Rainbow Fish by Marcus Pfister
That's What a Friend Is by P. K. Hallinan

Review

Ask the children to share their Art-Center illustrations and describe how they show being good friends.

Assessment

Can the children describe why it is important to share and be a thoughtful friend? Do the children act out these ideas in the centers?

 *Jackie Wright, Enid, OK*

Friendship

Learning Objectives The children will:
1. Learn the characteristics of a good friend.
2. Come to understand why their friends are special.
3. Learn how to resolve conflicts with friends.

Circle or Group Time Activity

- Engage the children in a discussion about what qualities they want in their friends, what they like to do with their friends, and why it is important to have friends in their lives.
- Read *Will I Have a Friend?* by Miriam Cohen and discuss it with the children. Brainstorm ways they can be good friends (by being nice, sharing, taking turns, be good listeners, playing fairly, and so on).
- Ask the children, "What if you have a problem with a friend? How can you solve a problem with a friend?"

Learning Centers **Art**

The children create friendship puzzle pieces. Children choose two large, connecting puzzle pieces, and then paint them with glue and cover them with glitter, attaching two wiggle eyes on each. When the children finish decorating them, set them out to dry. Encourage the children to decorate each of their pieces as similarly as possible. Once dry, help the children add the line "We Are Perfect-Fit Friends" along the tops of the pieces, and invite the children to keep one piece, then exchange the other with friends.

"We Are Perfect-Fit Friends"

WIGGLE EYES

GLITTER and PAINT

Dramatic Play

Set out puppets and encourage the children to act out problems that might arise with friends, and then practice solving the problems.

Library

Set out recordings and copies of books about friendship for the children to listen to and look through with friends.

Science

Plant seeds of friendship. Provide pairs of children with glitter, glue, markers, and small paper cups or pots that they can decorate. Once decorated, provide the pairs of children with seeds to plant in their decorated pots. Explain how taking care of a plant to make sure it blooms is like taking care of friends to make sure they are happy and healthy. Set the containers out where they will get plenty of light.

Writing

Provide the children with several sheets of paper with the statement "A good friend _____" written on them and invite the children to dictate to you responses and then illustrate the responses with markers, crayons, and so on.

Book Suggestions

Friends by Helme Heine
The Rainbow Fish by Marcus Pfister
Will I Have a Friend? by Miriam Cohen

Snack

Make a friendship salad. The day before, write the names of pieces of fruit on several cards and ask each child to select one. Ask each child to bring in two of the fruit on their cards to help make a big salad. (Be sure to have extra on hand for those children who forget to bring in their fruits.) Help the children cut up, prepare, and enjoy the salad.

Review

Talk with the children about what they want in a friend.

Assessment

Are the children sharing and working together as friends in the centers?

 *Sherry Harper, Coventry, RI*

Friendship Letters

Learning Objectives The children will:

1. Learn about how to foster and develop friendships.
2. Learn about some of the workings of the postal system where they live.
3. Create original artwork for a friend.
4. Gain literacy skills through articulating their thoughts for dictation.

Circle or Group Time Activity

- Gather the children on the floor. Display letters and stamps. Consider using trays to hold them, to keep the activity more organized.
- Ask the children what they think the letters and stamps are for. Listen carefully to their ideas, perhaps recording them with paper and pen for later reference. Explain that some of these letters are from friends and how you received them from the postal worker.
- Ask children if they would like to send or receive a letter from one of their classmates. This can be a way to warm up your class atmosphere at the beginning of the year, or extend friendships at the end of the year.
- Draw names out of a hat to determine who should send letters to whom. Observe children carefully to prevent anyone's feelings being hurt.

Learning Centers   **Art**

Provide markers, crayons, paint, and brushes, as well as various colors of heart-shaped construction paper cutouts and encourage children to "put their hearts" into making letter and pictures for their friends. Also, set out several empty boxes the children can decorate and use as mailboxes.

Blocks

The children can use the blocks to create a post office. Provide small toy people the children can put in their post offices.

Dramatic Play

Offer children mail bags, hats, and uniform-colored clothes for dressing up as postal workers. Also provide play money, stamps and envelopes for buying and selling, or writing more letters to one another. The children can deliver these to the mailboxes the children create and decorate.

Literacy

Set out several envelopes that have addresses on them so the children can see how to label envelopes, and then encourage them to replicate it using markers and crayons to draw similar designs on more blank envelopes. Ask them to verbalize who they are addressing their envelopes to. Consider posting a list of who was chosen to send letters to whom so children can refer to it. Some children may be able to recognize their own names.

Small Motor
Provide several envelopes so the children, so the children can fold letters, put them in the envelopes, and the seal the envelopes shut.

Book Suggestion   *Little Bear's Friend* by Else Holmelund Minarik

Snack   At snack time, play "Snack Postman." The children "deliver" snacks to their designated mail recipients. Alternatively, during the week you do this project, allow a few children to be Snack Postman every day until everyone has had a turn.

Review   Ask the children to name who they wrote letters to, and to think of other people they might want to stay in touch with by mail.

Assessment   To get an idea how well children understand the postal process, ask them to tell you how the letter they received got to them, or write a story together about a friendship letter.

 Elisheva Leah Nadler, Jerusalem, Israel

My Friends

Learning Objectives The children will:
1. Name their friends.
2. Play a game that helps to make new friends feel welcome.
3. Name things that friends do together.

Circle or Group Time Activity
- Teach the children the following song:

    Where Are All My Friends Today? by Shelley Hoster
    (Tune: "The Bear Went Over the Mountain")
    Where are all my friends today?
    Where are all my friends today?
    Where are all my friends today?
    Please join me in the circle!

    There is my friend _____.
    There is my friend_____.
    There is my friend_____.
    He (she)'s sitting in the circle!

- Repeat the song, naming a different child each time, until everyone has been greeted.
- After greeting all the friends in the circle, divide the children into two groups, and explain that they will be playing a game called "Friendship Hot Potato," in which they pass the beanbag around the circle while the music plays. When the music stops, whoever has the beanbag must go to the other circle. The other circle must make their new friend feel welcome.
- Play a few rounds. Afterwards, talk with the children about how it felt being welcomed into the new circle, and how the children felt welcoming their new friends. Tell the children that you are going to talk about friends today.

Learning Centers **Art**
Separate the children into pairs to paint pictures together. When the pictures are dry, help the children cut them in half so they all can take parts of their work home. **Note:** Some children may not want to change their artwork in this way. If that is the case, allow them to create their own drawings next to each other.
Blocks
The children work cooperatively in groups of two or three to build structures, each taking turns placing one block at a time until they complete building their structures.

Dramatic Play

Set out party-related props and invite the children to have a friendship party.

Library

Take a picture of each child. Make two copies. Attach each copy to different sides of a single sheet of paper, and then bind all the pages together or put them in a picture album, creating a book in the style of *Brown Bear, Brown Bear, What Do You See?* Above and below each child's first image, write text, such as, "Ryan, Ryan, who do you see? I see Kaylie looking at me." Invite the children to decorate each side of their pages. On the last page, include a picture of yourself. Leave the book in the library for the children to enjoy.

Writing

Children can use envelopes and cards to send letters to their friends. They can draw pictures, sign their names, or decorate the cards at the art area. They can also write their friends' names on their envelopes and put them in their cubbies or mailboxes.

Book Suggestions

Brown Bear, Brown Bear, What Do You See? by Bill Martin, Jr.
Do You Want to Be My Friend? by Eric Carle
My Best Friend by Pat Hutchins
Will I Have a Friend? by Miriam Cohen

Snack

Children make snacks for their friends. They can spread icing on round cookies and decorate with sprinkles. They must ask their friends what they want. They present them to each other, offering thanks for being such good friends!

Review

Bring over the *Friend, Friend, Who Do You See?* book the children made in the Library Center and share it with the children. See if they can help you read it and say all the names of their friends. The children can share ideas on chart paper of things friends do together.

Assessment

How well does the child play together with friends? Can the child identify friends by their names? Can the child identify friends in photographs? In conversations or in play, does the child talk about things friends can do together?

Shelley Hoster, Norcross, GA

Sharing Soup

Learning Objectives The children will:
1. Learn about the idea of sharing.
2. Practice using verbal communication to share.
3. Practice listening to peers and responding to their verbal communication.

Circle or Group Time Activity

- The day before, ask each child to bring one ingredient for a sharing soup.
- Set out a crock pot, and cut up several vegetables and put them in the pot. Add a small can of beans and can of tomato or vegetable juice to the pot.
- Ask the children what it means to share. Discuss different things that the children share, such as toys, food, carpools, ideas, and greetings.
- Say, "Today we are going to make a sharing soup." Ask the children to take out the soup ingredients they brought in for the sharing soup. Provide the extra ingredients to those children who did not bring something.
- Say, "I'm sharing my broth to make our sharing soup," and direct the children to respond by saying, "Thank you for the broth."
- Ask the children to take turns adding their ingredients to the pot, saying, "I'm sharing my _____ to make our sharing soup," to which the rest of the children respond "Thank you for the _____."
- After the children add their ingredients, turn the crock pot on high and cook until snack time. Add water to the pot if the soup looks too thick.

Learning Centers **Art**

Hang a large piece of butcher paper on an outside wall. Encourage the children to

BUTCHER PAPER

DUCT TAPE

PAINT

BRUSHES

share paints and brushes and work together to make a group picture. Encourage children's verbal communication by prompting them to ask, "When you're done with the blue, may I have a turn?" and "I'm done with the yellow. Does anyone want to use it?"

Dramatic Play
Give the children sheets of small stickers and ask them to offer them to their classmates, asking, "Would you like a sticker?" Remind the children only to give out stickers if the other children say yes.

Literacy
Set out several sheets of paper with the statement, "When I share, I feel_____" written on them. Help the children write their responses in the blank and then give them the pages to illustrate.

Small Motor
Provide beads and chenille stems for the children to use to make friendship bracelets they can then share with one another.

Snack and Cooking
Using a mix, the children can make a pan of cornbread. Bake according to directions on package. Cut into squares and serve at snack time.

Book Suggestions

Benny's Pennies by Pat Brisson
Mine! Mine! Mine! by Shelly Becker

Snack

Serve the sharing soup the children made during circle time along with the cornbread they prepared in the Snack and Cooking Center.

Review

Put children into groups of two or three. Ask them to take turns telling their groups about their favorite part of the day's class.

Assessment

Provide two dolls and a bowl of crumpled paper to resemble popcorn. Ask a child to pretend one friend has a bowl of popcorn and then ask him to show how the two dolls might share the popcorn. Can the child role-play the sharing of popcorn? (The child does not have to divide the popcorn evenly.)

Related Song

When We Share by Cassandra Reigel Whetstone
(Tune: "Mary Had a Little Lamb")
When we share, it makes me smile,
Makes me smile, Makes me smile.
When we share, it makes me smile
'Cause we're friends.

 *Cassandra Reigel Whetstone, Folsom, CA*

Sharing with Our Friends

Learning Objectives The children will:
1. Describe what sharing means.
2. Learn how to divide objects into equal parts.
3. Demonstrate sharing through role-playing.

Circle or Group Time Activity
- Talk about friendship and sharing with our friends.
- Read *Maebelle's Suitcase* by Tricia Tusa, a story about a bird who filled a suitcase with his favorite things. When he discovered that it was so heavy that he could not fly south for the winter, he shared all his treasures with an elderly friend.
- Pass a small suitcase or a picture of a suitcase around the circle and encourage each child to complete this statement: "I am flying south, and in my suitcase I'm going to pack_____."
- Transcribe each child's reply and read back the cumulative results. For example, "I'm flying south and in my suitcase I'm going to pack my teddy bear, a candy bar, my pet turtle, my blanket, five books, my pajamas, and my cat."
- Say, "This suitcase feels very heavy! Who can we share our treasures with?"

Learning Centers

Art
Review the story *Rainbow Fish* by Marcus Pfister with the children. Talk about how Rainbow Fish shared his scales. Ask each child to draw a fish shape on poster board and paint it with watercolors. Once the paint has dried, give the children silver sequins to glue on their fish.

Dramatic Play
Place plastic plates and plastic poker chips (representing cookies) on a table. Encourage the children to divide and share these "cookies" with dolls or stuffed animals. By asking the children to count and divide the "cookies" evenly among the stuffed animals, this center can provide a great math lesson as well. Have them dramatize the story, too.

Math
Provide a bowl of 12 small objects, such as teddy bear counters, and six paper plates. Help the children count and sort the objects into sets of two, three, four, and six. Explain that this is a great example of how to share fairly with others.

Small Motor
Place a container of Legos or other manipulatives on a table or carpet. Set out a tray for each child. Show them how to divide and share the toys equally among one another.

Snack and Cooking

Make "Stone Soup," according to the folktale, a classic example of sharing. One child plays the part of a soldier and places a stone in a soup pot (or crock pot, if time allows) of water. The other children play the part of the villagers to add various vegetables (cleaned, chopped, and measured in advance or as part of the activity) and seasonings. Cook the soup until vegetables are tender.

Book Suggestions

The Doorbell Rang by Pat Hutchins
If You Give a Mouse a Cookie by Laura Joffe Numeroff
It's Mine! by Leo Lionni
Maebelle's Suitcase by Tricia Tusa
Rainbow Fish by Marcus Pfister

Snack

Read *The Doorbell Rang* and reenact it with the children, using a plate of chocolate chip cookies. Make a doorbell sound (ding, dong!) to invite each child to come to the table for snack. Make up a calendar and ask parents to send a snack for their child to share each day.

Review

Ask the children to name things they might share with others.

Assessment

Set up the dramatic play scene as described above. Ask each child to describe or demonstrate sharing.

 Susan Arentson Sharkey, La Mesa, CA

We're Friends

Learning Objectives   The children will:
1. Talk about why we have friends.
2. Engage in activities we can do with friends.
3. Discuss where we can make friends.

Circle or Group Time Activity
- Read *The Enormous Carrot* by Vladimir Vagin to the children.
- After finishing the book, ask the children to act out the story.
- Talk with the children about how they were able to pull the carrot out of the ground.
- Engage the children in a discussion about the ways that they have helped their friends, and the ways their friends have helped them.

Learning Centers   **Art**
Provide each child with a piece of paper with "To: _____" typed in the upper left corner and "From: _____" typed on the bottom of the paper, and set out collage materials and glue the children can use to create a picture for a friend.

Blocks
Provide a balance beam in the block center so each child can help one another balance as they cross it.

Literacy
Provide a list of classmates' names and ask the children to find their friends' name on the list, and then to try copying them or recreating them with plastic letters.

Math
Set out several board games the children can play together in pairs.

Small Motor
Ask one child to make a pattern using unifix cubes, and then have a friend copy that pattern. Also, set out playdough so one child can make a sculpture and then another child can copy it.

PLAYDOUGH

Book Suggestions

The Enormous Carrot by Vladimir Vagin
Friends by Helme Heine
Friends at School by Rochelle Bunnett
Just My Friend and Me by Mercer Mayer
We Are Best Friends by Aliki
We Can Share at School by Rozanne Lanczak Williams
Will I Have a Friend? By Miriam Cohen

Snack

Make a friendship fruit salad by pairing up two children to cut the same fruit for the salad together.

Review

Talk with the children about what activities they like to do with their friends, how friends help each other, how to make friends, and how to be a good friend.

Assessment

Observe how the children create and maintain friendships throughout the day.

Kaethe Lewandowski, Centreville, VA

Apple Seeds

Learning Objectives The children will:
1. Sequence pictures of an apple tree growing from a seed.
2. Develop their small and large motor skills.

Circle or Group Time Activity

- Beforehand, make apple sequence pictures. Draw someone planting a seed, a root growing below ground, a plant pushing up through the ground, a small seedling, a larger seedling, a young tree, a mature tree, and a tree with apples).
- Show the children a picture of Johnny Appleseed and explain that a long time ago, he traveled around distributing apple seeds to farmers. Show the children apple seeds and pass them around so they can examine them.
- Cut open an apple and point out the seeds inside.
- Display apple sequence pictures, one at a time. (**Note:** Use a smaller number of pictures for a younger group of children.) Explain that things happen in a certain order and cannot happen out of order.
- Show examples of three-part sequence pictures. Ask children to put them in correct order. Next, rearrange the pictures in an illogical way. Ask the children to explain why the sequence is illogical.
- Tell the children that they will be practicing putting things in the correct order.

Learning Centers **Art**
Before the activity, make edible paint by mixing food coloring with corn syrup, sweetened condensed milk, or vanilla pudding. Make a variety of colors. Provide 12" x 18" construction paper in white, gray, and dark blue. Show the children how to dip apple halves lightly into the "paint," and then press them onto their papers to print an apple shape. Explain to the children about holding the apple still when they are printing, instead of sliding it across the paper. The apple is safe to eat when done (rinse them off first, if desired).

Blocks
Provide small red and green beads in containers for the children to transport from "apple farm" to "market" (farm and market made from blocks).

Library
Set out a recording of *Apples* by Gail Gibbons for the children to listen to as they look through a copy of the book.

Literacy

Display the apple growth sequence cards. Ask the children to guess the answer to the following riddles:

- *I'm the first thing that starts to grow, even though it does not show. What am I?* (root)
- *I like to shine; I'm very bright. But I do not work at night! What am I?* (sun)
- *I push myself up through the soil with a lot of work and toil. What am I?* (stem)
- *I'm very small and not so tall; the farmer plants me in the soil. What am I?* (seed)
- *I have some leaves, though I am small. I'm not through growing, not at all! What am I?* (seedling or young tree)
- *I fall down from the sky. I give a drink from way up high. What am I?* (rain)
- *I'm very tall with leaves of green. I grow the best apples you've ever seen. What am I?* (mature tree)

Math

Ahead of time, prepare 11 apple cutouts from sturdy tagboard. Leave the first one empty, drawing one seed on the next cutout, two seeds on the next, and so on. Explain to the children that for this game, they are to count the seeds and put them in order from 0–10, starting at the left end of the math table and working from left to right.

Book Suggestions

Apples by Gail Gibbons
Apples and Pumpkins by Anne Rockwell
The Seasons of Arnold's Apple Tree by Gail Gibbons

Snack

Make homemade applesauce with the children.

Review

Display the apple sequence pictures one at a time, asking the children to explain the first picture and guess which picture comes next. Review the entire sequence, putting one picture out of order at a time. Ask the children to correct the sequence, telling the rest of the children why it could not happen out of order.

Assessment

Give the children a three-part sequence of pictures (such as a snowman being built). Ask them to put them in correct order. Repeat with another three-part set, and then ask the children to put the apple pictures in the correct sequence.

 *Susan Oldham Hill, Lakeland, FL*

Bean Plants

Learning Objectives The children will:
1. Learn about the bean plant.
2. Plant a bean.
3. Perform action rhymes.

Circle or Group Time Activity

- Show the children a large poster of a bean plant including its parts: root, stem, leaf, and flower. Talk about the parts.
- Teach the children the following action rhyme:

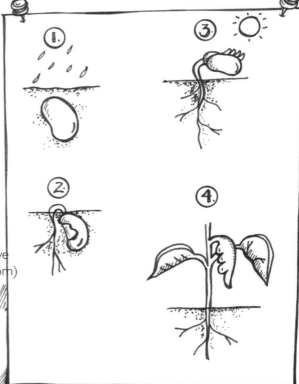

Twinkle, Twinkle Little Bean
   by Lily Erlic
(Tune: "Twinkle, Twinkle
   Little Star")
Twinkle, twinkle little bean,
   (open and close hands)
Oh, where, where can you
   be seen? (place hand above
   eyes and look around room)
Are you hiding in the ground?
   (crouch down)
I am looking all around,
   (point around room)
Twinkle, twinkle little bean,
   (open and close hands)
Oh, where, where can you
   be seen? (place hand above
   eyes and look around room)
There you are!

Learning Centers   **Art**
Display a variety of dried beans in a large basket. Ask the children to make a collage with the beans on paper with glue.
Blocks
Place bean stickers or bean pictures on blocks.

Dramatic Play
Provide the children with dried beans, pots, pans, and a wooden spoon for the housekeeping area for pretend play. Ask them to make "bean soup."

Literacy
Give each child a reproducible of a bean plant. Ask them to color the drawing and then title the page "Bean Plant." Ask the children to print the word "bean" on the paper too. Ask older children to label the parts of the bean if possible.

Small Motor
Provide a variety of dried beans and place them in a basket. Tell the children to sort the beans by color or size in other baskets. Give each child a bean seed, soil, and water. Ask them to plant their own bean in a cup.

Book Suggestions

Lucas and His Loco Beans: A Tale of the Mexican Jumping Bean by Ramona Moreno Winner

Read to Me Rhymes: Seasons by Totline

Snack

Use canned white beans or black beans to make a bean dip or use a prepared bean dip. Serve with tortilla chips or crackers.

Review

Sort beans with the children as a group. Show the bean plant picture.

Assessment

During sorting, ask questions like "Why do these beans belong together?" Ask about each part of the plant. "Where is the root?" "Where is the stem?" and "Where are the leaves?"

Related Song

I'm a Little Bean by Lily Erlic
(Tune: "I'm a Little Teapot")
I'm a little bean,
So round and plump,
I like to hop,
I like to jump.
I'm a little bean,
Under the ground,
When I'm watered
I grow without a sound.

 *Lily Erlic, Victoria, British Columbia, Canada*

Growing Nutritious Gardens

Learning Objectives
The children will:
1. Grow a fruit or vegetable from a seed.
2. Learn what plants need to grow.
3. Care for something over time and see the results.
4. Develop their environmental awareness.

Circle or Group Time Activity
■ Teach the children the following fingerplay:

Pop Goes the Flower (author unknown)
(Tune: "Pop Goes the Weasel")
The seed goes down inside the ground, (sing slowly)
Waiting for some water. (children bend as if tipping watering cans)
The sun shines brightly on the seed, (children stretch arms above head)
Pop goes the flower! (children jump up)

Learning Centers

Construction
Provide dry straw, hat, broomstick for the arms, old boots, and old children's clothes, so the children can make a classroom scarecrow. Let them use doll clothes and straw to make smaller scarecrows.

Library
Place a recording and copy of *The Carrot Seed* by Ruth Krauss in this center for the children to listen to as they look through the book.

Math
Provide several dried seeds from green peppers, apples, oranges, and other fruits, and invite the children to count how many of each type of see there are.

Sand and Water
Put gardening tools, plastic containers, a watering can, and soil in the sand and water table for the children to play with and explore.

Science
Provide simple, quickly germinating seeds, such as alfalfa, pea, and radish seeds, along with several cups and small containers of planting soil, so the children can plant their own seeds and watch them grow over time. Help the children label their cups, and then fill them with soil and a couple of seeds. Place the cups in a bright and sunny spot.

Snack and Cooking
Set out various fresh produce so the children can make their own vegetable or fruit salads. Talk with the children about the foods, what they could do with the seeds from the fruits and vegetables, whether they grow in the ground or on trees, what they would need to be able to grow these foods themselves.

Book Suggestions   *And the Good Brown Earth* by Kathy Henderson
The Carrot Seed by Ruth Krauss
The Surprise Garden by Zoe Hall

Snack   Serve the fruit and vegetable salads the children made in the Snack and Cooking Center.

Review   Repeat the fingerplay from the Circle or Group Time Activity with the children. Discuss with the children the different things a flower needs to grow.

Assessment   Show pictures of gardening tools and carpentry tools and ask the children to choose the photos of gardening tools, and, if they are able to, ask them to describe how to use the tools.

Eileen Lucas, Fort McMurray, Alberta, Canada

How Does Your Garden Grow?

Learning Objectives   The children will:
1. Gain an appreciation for all plant life.
2. Recognize the colors of plants.
3. Develop their literacy skills.
4. Develop their fine and gross motor skills.

Circle or Group Time Activity
- Teach the children the following song. At the mention of the various foods, put the felt cutouts of them on the flannel board.

   Step into My Garden (author unknown)
   When I step into my garden
   In the early morning,
   What do you think I see?
   I see a patch of red tomatoes
   As happy as can be.

- Repeat the verse adding a different food each time: yellow squash, blueberries, green string beans, orange carrots, purple cabbages, and brown potatoes.

Learning Centers   **Art**
Pour tempera paint into pie tins and dilute with water. Thinned paint leaves more accurate prints than thick paint. Children dip the bottoms of strawberry baskets in the paint and use the baskets to make prints on paper. Encourage them to overlap colors or leave them separate.

Dramatic Play
Create a "garden" in the Dramatic Play area with gardening gloves, hats, overalls, hand shovels, rakes, baskets, empty seed packages and catalogs, and watering cans.

Library
Place a recording and copy of *Jack and the Beanstalk* in the center for the children to listen to and look through. Consider adding a bag of "magic" beans that the children can explore and count.

Math
Provide the children with several magazine photos or construction paper cutouts of flowers that they can arrange according to size, color, and so on.

Sand and Water
Put plastic garden tools in the sand table for the children to play with and explore.

Small Motor
Gather seeds from several kinds of foods, such as watermelon seeds, lima beans, yellow corn seeds, pumpkin seeds, and so on, and invite the children to separate them into the divided portions of an egg crate.

Book Suggestions   *How a Seed Grows* by Helene J. Jordan
                         Miss Rumphius by Barbara Cooney
                         Planting a Rainbow by Lois Ehlert
                         This Year's Garden by Cynthia Rylant
                         Tops and Bottoms by Janet Stevens

Snack   Serve ready-to-eat sunflower seeds
              watermelon slices. Encourage the
              children to count the number of
              seeds in their slices of watermelon,
              and see who has the most seeds
              and who has the fewest.

Review   Show the children photographs of
               various fruits and vegetables growing
               engage them in a discussion about the
               parts of the plants that people do and
               do not eat.

Assessment   Can the child describe how fruits an
                   vegetables grow? Can the child distir
                   between various fruits and vegetable

Related Fingerplay   **Dig a Little Hole** (Traditional)
                           Dig a little hole. (move arms as thoug
                           Plant a little seed. (drop an imaginary
                           Pour a little water. (pretend to pour)
                           Pull a little weed. (pull weeds)

                           Chase a little bug. (make chasing motion with hands)
                           Hi-ho, there he goes! (shade eyes)
                           Give a little sunshine, (cup hands, lift to the sun)
                           Grow a little rose. (smell flower a with eyes closed, smiling)

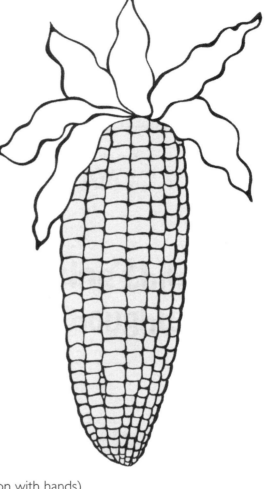

 *Jackie Wright, Enid, OK*

Our Garden Grows

Learning Objectives

The children will:
1. Learn what grows in gardens.
2. Taste fresh food from a garden.
3. Develop small motor skills.
4. Learn how to plant seeds.

Circle or Group Time Activity

- Talk with the children about gardens. Ask the children to name some fruits and vegetables, and describe the different ways that things in gardens can grow.
- Explain to the children that they will be bringing potted plants home with them at the end of the day. Discuss how to water and care for the potted seeds.
- Show the children a plastic plant pot like the ones they will take home that day, and talk with them about the pot. Have they seen a pot before? Do they know what people use pots for?

Learning Centers

Art

Provide paper, pencils, markers, and crayons, and encourage the children to draw flowers and vegetables.

Dramatic Play

Set out several plastic fruits and vegetables, as well as various gardening tools, and invite the children to pretend they are working in gardens. They can also set out the fruits and vegetables and pretend they are running a fruit stand.

Literacy

Set out several sheets of paper with "When I see a flower I feel _____" written on them. Ask the children to complete the statement. Help them write down their responses in the blanks, then hand out markers and crayons and invite the children to illustrate their papers with flowers.

Sand and Water
Encourage the children to use their fingers or small stick to draw pictures of vegetables or flowers in lightly dampened sand.

Small Motor
Set out a container of potting soil, along with several small plastic pots for the children to fill with the soil. Also set out several seeds for the children to plant in the pots. Help the children write their names on stickers or tape and attach it to their pots so they can identify their pots at the end of the day, when they take them home.

Book Suggestions

I Plant a Garden with My Mom by Paula Papazoglu
Planting a Rainbow by Lois Ehlert
This Year's Garden by Cynthia Rylant

Snack

Serve fresh vegetables, such as carrots and celery.

Review

Ask the children to tell you what they would like to grow in their own gardens.

Assessment

Show the children pictures of flowers and vegetables and other objects and ask them to say where each object would grow or belong.

 Shirley Anne Ramaley, Sun City, AZ

Plant Me a Garden

Learning Objectives The children will:
1. Plant a small garden.
2. Practice responsibility by taking care of their garden over an extended period.
3. Experience a variety of tactile stimuli, such as moist earth, hard seeds, and water.
4. Learn to distinguish seeds from other items.

Circle or Group Time Activity
■ Teach the children the following fingerplay:

I Am a Tree (author unknown)
I am a tree, (stand and reach hands high)
Whee, whee, whee.
I reach up in the sky, so very high!
Now I am a seed, (crouch down to the floor)
Curled like a little bead!
(Repeat)

Learning Centers **Art**
Give the children unwrapped crayons, leaves, and paper for them to make leaf rubbings. For smaller children, use paper slightly larger than the leaves so they won't have to guess where to rub with their crayon. Compare the designs made by various types of leaves. Explain that the lines we see on the rubbings are veins, which bring food to all the parts of the leaf.

Math
Provide egg cartons, ice cube trays, or cupcake tins in which the children can sort various types of seeds.

Science
Provide plastic cups and soil. Have the children fill their cups halfway with soil, then add several seeds. Encourage them to water the seeds, put them in sunlight, and watch them grow.

Small Motor
Collect long wild grass and place several piles of the grass next to pieces of cardboard with slits cut into them. Show the children how to weave the grass into patterns on the cardboard.

Writing
Provide gardening catalogs and magazines for the children to explore. Give them several plastic letters and encourage them to copy the spelling of various words from the catalogs.

Book Suggestions

The Carrot Seed by Ruth Krauss
Seeds by Wind and Water by Helene J. Jordan
The Tiny Seed by Eric Carle

Snack

Let children help prepare a food that grew from one of the kinds of seeds they planted in the Science Center, such as chickpeas, wheat berries, or beans.

Review

Ask the children what they must do to help their plants grow.

Assessment

Show children a few seeds and some items with similar shapes, such as beads or buttons. Can the child identify which are seeds?

 *Elisheva Leah Nadler, Jerusalem, Israel*

Very Veggie Garden

Learning Objectives The children will:
1. Identify a variety of vegetables.
2. Learn how vegetables grow.
3. Estimate and test what vegetables sink and float.
4. Practice their counting skills.
5. Improve their oral language and pre-reading skills.
6. Use their five senses to explore vegetables.

Circle or Group Time Activity
- Put on gardening clothing (straw hat, apron or overalls, clogs) and use garden tools and seeds as you pretend to plant a garden on brown soil (brown blanket).
- As you work, talk about what plants need to grow, including sun, water, air, and soil.
- Invite the children to close their eyes and chant the following rhyme three times, starting softly and then getting louder each time.

Sun and Rain by Mary J. Murray
Sun and rain, sun and rain,
Seeds in a row.
Sun and rain, sun and rain,
Vegetables grow!

- While the children's eyes are closed, place various vegetables on the blanket so that when children open their eyes, they will see the wonderful harvest of vegetables.
- Invite the children to "pick" the vegetables, pass them around the circle, and use their five senses to explore each vegetable.

Learning Centers **Art**
Put a bowl of vegetables on a table in the Art Center. Invite children to use watercolor paints at the easel to create still-life paintings of the bowl of fresh vegetables.

Dramatic Play
Put the materials from the Circle or Group Time Activity in the center. Invite children to explore the materials as they practice planting and growing vegetables.

Math
Invite children to plant mini gardens and practice their counting skills at the same time. Have them pour out each packet of "seeds" (buttons) onto a piece of brown felt and then count each set of seeds as they plant them in rows in the "soil" (brown felt).

Sand and Water

Display an assortment of vegetables and seeds at the Water Table. Invite children to estimate whether the vegetables and seeds will sink or float and then try floating them.

Writing

Provide dry-erase boards and markers, images of fresh vegetables, and matching picture-word cards. Invite children to practice matching each word card to the correct vegetable and practice writing the words on the dry-erase board.

Book Suggestions

Eating the Alphabet by Lois Ehlert
Food for Thought by Saxton Freymann and Joost Elffers
Growing Vegetable Soup by Lois Ehlert
The Surprise Garden by Zoe Hall

Snack

Mix up a batch of vegetable antipasto. Cut up a selection of vegetables including green, red, and yellow pepper; cucumber; celery; cherry tomatoes; and more. Invite children to sprinkle a little Italian dressing on the mix and enjoy.

Review

Cover an assortment of vegetables with pieces of brown paper or fabric. Invite the children to uncover the vegetables one at a time, identify them by name, and then say what they know about the vegetables.

Assessment

Display an assortment of vegetables on a tray along with other objects. Invite the child to identify which items are vegetables and which are not.

Related Song

The Vegetables Will Grow by Mary J. Murray
(Tune: "The Farmer in the Dell")
The vegetables will grow. The vegetables will grow.
Air, soil, sun, and rain, the vegetables will grow.

The carrots will grow. The carrots will grow.
Air, soil, sun, and rain, the carrots will grow.

The _____ will grow. The _____ will grow.
Air, soil, sun, and rain, the _____ will grow.

(In the final stanza, add the name of a different vegetable.)

 *Mary J. Murray, Mazomanie, WI*

Brush Your Teeth

Learning Objectives The children will:
1. Develop an interest in basic dental care.
2. Learn about teeth.
3. Develop word-recognition and literacy skills.

Circle or Group Time Activity

- On poster board, copy the following statements:

  Keep Your Teeth Healthy
  Brush your teeth after eating.
  Floss your teeth every day.
  Go to a dentist regularly.
  Eat healthful food.

- Find images that illustrate various words in the statements, such as a toothbrush for the word "brush," an image of teeth, a container of floss, a dentist, healthy food, and so on.
- Show the children the poster board and engage them in a discussion about dental care. Do the children brush their teeth every day? Do they floss? What foods do they think are good for helping strong teeth grow?
- Read through the statements on the poster board, and then show the children the images that match the various words. Give a child one of the images, and ask the other children to help him pick the word on the board that describes the image, and then cover that word with it.
- After the child places the image, repeat the statements, making a motion that mimics the image the child put up on the board.
- Repeat with a different child until all the images are on the board.

Learning Centers   **Literacy**
Draw or cut out a picture of a tooth, and write the word "tooth" below it. Do the same thing with several teeth, and write the word "teeth" below the picture. Make copies of both images and words, and provide several magnetic letters. Invite the children to copy the spelling of the two words and talk about the differences between them.

Math
Make a graph on chart paper with the question "Have you ever lost a tooth?" at the top. Form two columns. Let each child respond under the "Yes" or "No" column. Record their answers. Compare the number in each column and compare the results.

Art

Cut construction paper into the shape of an open mouth (with lips but no teeth). Have the children draw teeth in the mouth, and then use a toothbrush to paint white paint on the teeth.

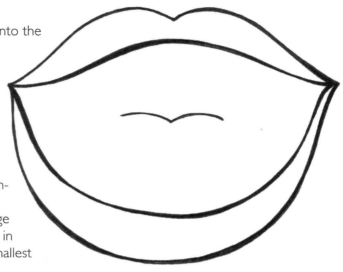

More Math

Provide four construction-paper tooth cutouts of various sizes and challenge the children to put them in graduated order from smallest to largest.

Writing

Set out sheets of paper with dots making the outline of the word *tooth* on them for the children to use markers and crayons trace and fill in.

Book Suggestions

Little Rabbit's Loose Tooth by Lucy Bates
The Selfish Crocodile Counting Book by Faustin Charles
Tooth Fairy by Audrey Wood
The Tooth Fairy by Kirsten Hall

Snack

Serve apple slices and yogurt.

Review

Review the "Keep Your Teeth Healthy" poster with the children.

Assessment

Can the child distinguish between foods that are good and bad for the health of his teeth?

 *Jackie Wright, Enid, OK*

Brushing and Flossing

Learning Objectives   The children will:
1. Practice brushing their teeth.
2. Practice flossing their teeth.
3. Count to 10.

Circle or Group Time Activity

- Cut the bottoms off three 2-liter bottles. Paint them with white tempera paint and let dry completely.
- When dry, fasten them together side by side using clear packaging tape.
- Pass hand mirrors around the circle. Ask the children to look into their mouths. Ask them to talk about what they see.
- Show the children the teeth model. Engage the children in a discussion about why we take care of our teeth. Explain that we need healthy teeth to bite and chew and to speak clearly.
- Ask the children how they take care of our teeth (brush, floss).
- Ask the children what happens if they do not take care of their teeth (cavities, toothache, sore gums).
- Take out a toothbrush and the teeth model and show the children how to brush the teeth gently. **Note:** Do not brush too hard or the paint may scrape off!
- Use yarn to show the children how to floss between the teeth.

Learning Centers   **Art**
Provide paint, paper, and toothbrushes with which the children can paint.
Library
Set a recording and copy of *Throw Your Tooth on the Roof: Tooth Traditions from Around the World* by Selby Beeler in the center for the children to listen to and explore.
Math
Set out several red construction paper semicircles, glue, and small buttons. The

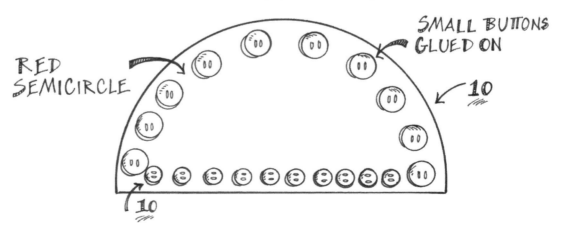

children glue a row of 10 buttons on the top and 10 buttons on the bottom of the semicircle to make teeth.

Science
Put several hardboiled eggs into plastic containers filled with lukewarm water and teabags. Set out toothpaste and brushes and invite the children to brush the eggs clean.

Small Motor
Set out yarn and egg-carton bottoms on which the children can practice flossing.

Book Suggestions

Clarabella's Teeth by An Vrombaut
Grandpa's Teeth by Rod Clement
How Many Teeth? by Paul Showers
Throw Your Tooth on the Roof: Tooth Traditions from Around the World by Selby Beeler

Snack

Serve strong teeth-building foods, such as apples, string cheese, and milk.

Review

Sing the following song with the children, asking that they model the appropriate actions as the song describes them:

This Is the Way We Brush Our Teeth by Cassandra Reigel Whetstone
(Tune: "Here We Go 'Round the Mulberry Bush")
This the way we brush our teeth, brush our teeth, brush our teeth.
This is the way we brush our teeth in the morning and evening.
This is the way we floss our teeth, floss our teeth, floss our teeth.
This is the way we floss our teeth, in the morning and evening.
This is the way we show our teeth, show our teeth, show our teeth.
This is the way we show our teeth, in the morning and evening.

Assessment

Set out the teeth model from the group or circle time activity and ask children to model how to brush and how to floss teeth.

 *Cassandra Reigel Whetstone, Folsom, CA*

Caring for My Teeth

Learning Objectives The children will:
1. Learn the importance of taking care of their teeth.
2. Understand how to take care of their teeth.
3. Recognize that the dentist is their friend.

Circle or Group Time Activity

■ Ask the children about their early morning routines. What do they do in the morning after they get out of bed? Answers might include dressing, washing faces, eating breakfast, making beds, and brushing teeth.

■ Show the children a toothbrush, toothpaste, and dental floss. Show each to the children and ask, "Who has one of these?" Listen as the children describe the sizes and colors of their own toothbrushes, toothpaste tubes, and containers of dental floss.

■ Teach the children the following rhyme:

My Toothbrush by Sandra Bynum
I have a little toothbrush.
I hold it very tight.
I brush my teeth each morning,
And then again at night.

■ Encourage the children to mimic brushing their teeth while repeating the rhyme.

Learning Centers **Art**
Set out several sheets of paper, markers, crayons, and so on. Invite the children to draw smiling faces with teeth showing between the lips.

Dramatic Play
Provide a chair and several stuffed animals and invite the children to pretend they are dentists giving the stuffed animals dental exams.

Library
Set out a copy and recording of *Going to the Dentist* by Anne Civardi for the children to listen to and read through.

Math
Prepare several photocopies of sets of teeth, some with all teeth showing, and some with a few teeth missing here and there. The children compare them and say how many are missing from the one with fewer teeth. Also provide markers and crayons so the children can color in the teeth if they want to.

Snack and Cooking

The children help to prepare a healthy snack made of dairy foods. Explain that dairy contains calcium that helps build strong teeth. Use dairy foods such as yogurt (add crunchy cereal for added texture), cheese cubes, cottage cheese and fruit, and cream and berries. Remind the children that sweet, sticky foods, such as gumdrops and caramel candy, stick to the teeth and can cause cavities or tooth decay.

Book Suggestions

Brush Your Teeth Please Pop-Up by Reader's Digest
Fresh & Fun: Teeth by Jacqueline Clarke
How Many Teeth? by Paul Showers
Show Me Your Smile! A Visit to the Dentist by Christine Ricci

Snack

Serve the dairy-based snacks prepared by the children in the Snack and Cooking Center.

Review

Ask the children to share what they know or learned about the importance of having healthy teeth, and why they go to the dentist.

Assessment

Play "Who Knows This?" Give everyone opportunities to participate so each can answer at least one question. Ask these and similar open-ended questions:

Why do we brush our teeth?
How often should we brush our teeth?
Why should we floss our teeth?
What kinds of foods help keep our teeth strong?
What kinds of foods can cause cavities (or decay)?
Why should we go to the dentist?
What happens to our baby teeth? Why?

 *Sandra Bynum, Blackfoot, ID*

Elbows and Hands

Learning Objectives The children will:
1. Learn some of the occasions when they need to wash their hands.
2. Learn the appropriate way to handle a cough or sneeze.
3. Start to distinguish their left from their right.

Circle or Group Time Activity
- Teach the children the following chant and movements:

Wash Your Hands by Christina Chilcote
You play outside in dirt or sand. (point outside)
Wash, wash, wash your hands. (pretend to scrub hands vigorously)
The teacher says it's snack time and (point to watch on wrist)
Wash, wash, wash your hands. (pretend to scrub hands vigorously)
You blow your runny nose and (point to nose)
Wash, wash, wash your hands. (pretend to scrub hands vigorously)
You pet a friendly animal and (lean down and pet pretend animal)
Wash, wash, wash your hands. (pretend to scrub hands vigorously)

- Once the children know the chant, repeat it with them two more times.
- Engage the children in a discussion about germs. Talk about why the children should wash their hands after certain activities.

Learning Centers

Large Motor
Set out several soft sponge balls and a crate or basket. Encourage the children to use their hands (first right, then left) to toss the balls into the basket from 2'–4' away, and to try using their elbows to carry the balls back from the basket to the tossing point.

Library
Place a recording and copy of *Ah-Choo!* by Margery Cuyler, or another similar "sneeze-themed" picture book in this center for the children to explore.

Math
Mark the children's left hands with green dots and right hands with red dots. Provide green and red items the children can use as counters. The children pick up a certain number of green or red counters with the appropriately marked hands, counting them aloud as they go.

Music
Play a recording of "The Hokey Pokey" and do the dance with the children. Make sure to emphasize "left" and "right."

Sand and Water
Add liquid detergent or bubble bath to the water in the water table for the children to enjoy as they wash their hands.

Small Motor

Place an assortment of red and green counters on a table. Put a green dot sticker on each child's left hand. The children use their green-dotted left hands to put the green counters in the green basket, and then use their non-dotted right hands to put the red counters in the red basket.

Book Suggestions

The Flea's Sneeze by Lynn Downey
Hands Can by Cheryl Willis Hudson
My Hands by Aliki
Stop That Nose! by Martha Peaslee Levine
Washing My Hands by Elizabeth Vogel

Snack

Make "hand" sandwiches by using a hand-shaped cookie cutter to cut the shapes out of sandwiches. Encourage the children to add halved grapes as fingernails, or segments of mandarin oranges as bracelets.

Review

Play "Simon Says" with the children, asking them to do things like sneeze in their elbows or raise their left hands.

Assessment

Ask the children what they should do after they finish playing in the dirt, petting an animal, or blowing their noses.

Related Song

This Is the Way We Wash Our Hands by Christina Chilcote
(Tune: "Here We Go 'Round the Mulberry Bush")
This is the way we wash our hands, (mimic washing hands)
Wash our hands, wash our hands,
This is the way we wash our hands,
Before we eat a meal. (pretend to put food in mouth)

Additional verses:
After we play outside.
After we blow our nose.

 *Christina Chilcote, New Freedom, PA*

Exercise by Dancing!

Learning Objectives The children will:
1. Learn how daily exercise helps to keep our bodies healthy.
2. Develop large motor skills.
3. Discover the many forms of dance.

Circle or Group Time Activity
- Talk about exercise and its health benefits. Create a word web about dance through brainstorming with the children. Find out what they know about types of dance, classes, and so on.
- Read *Dance Tanya* by Patricia Lee Gauch.

Learning Centers **Dramatic Play**
Place unbreakable mirrors, costumes, dance shoes, music, and perhaps a dance bar in the Dramatic Play Center for the children to use to pretend they are dancing in a dance studio.

Library
Place informational dance books to help teach content areas about different forms of dance and the history of dance. Also provide dance magazines.

Listening
Provide headphones with different types of music to hear and learn about, such as jazz, classical, and so on. This can include ritual or ceremonial dance music.

Math
Encourage children to seriate a small number of objects such as dance shoes from smallest to largest. Their height and feet sizes can be measured and then placed in a series from largest to smallest.

Music
Provide musical instruments and rhythm sticks for students to experiment with rhythm and sound.

Book Suggestions
Angelina on Stage by Helen Craig
Barn Dance! by Bill Martin
Clap Your Hands by Lorinda Bryan Cauley
Moondance by Frank Asch
Song and Dance Man by Karen Ackerman

Snack
Children can help prepare healthy snacks that give our body energy to exercise, such as fruits and vegetables.

Review
Ask children to retell stories about dancing.

Assessment
Host a recital at the end of a dance unit so children can showcase what they have learned. Children could make posters and invite families to a dance celebration.

 *Sherry Harper, Coventry, RI*

Fun to Be Fit

Learning Objectives The children will:
1. Begin to understand the basic health need for physical fitness.
2. Develop phonemic awareness.
3. Demonstrate coordination skills and strength.
4. Develop basic math skills.

Circle or Group Time Activity

■ Present a puppet to the children. Explain that the puppet's name is Jolly Jogger. Accentuate the J sounds in the puppet's name, and ask the children if they can say the letter the jogger's name starts with.

■ With the puppet, invite the children to recite the song below, emphasizing each instance of the letter J.

Jolly Jogger by Jackie Wright
(Tune: "London Bridge")
Jolly Jogger is a jogger,
Is a jogger, is a jogger.
Jolly Jogger is a jogger,
She likes jogging.

■ Invite the children to make up additional verses that use alliteration. They can be about Jolly Jogger or any other character with n alliterative name.

Learning Centers **Dramatic Play**
Put jump ropes, an exercise mat, and one-pound weights in the Dramatic Play Center, along with a book showing yoga stretches and postures for the children to use and explore.

Library
After reading and acting out *Calico Cat's Exercise Book* by Donald Charles, put it in the library area along with an exercise mat so that the children can refer to it again. Place a full-length unbreakable mirror nearby.

Small Motor
Set out sheets of colored construction paper with a person's outline on them. The children can make their own "Jolly Jogger" alphabet puppets by drawing features on the outlines, cutting them out using child-safe scissors, and attaching them to straws using tape.

Math
Make a simple graph showing the children's favorite playground activities, such as riding bikes, jumping rope, and swinging on a swing. Set out images that represent each activity, and ask the children to choose their personal favorite activities, take a

corresponding image, and attach it to the graph. After the children all add their pictures, they can compare the popularity of the various activities.

Music
10 children at a time can sing and act out the following song:

Ten Little Joggers by Jackie Wright
(Tune: "Bumping Up and Down in My Little Red Wagon")
One little, two little, three little joggers,
Four little, five little, six little joggers,
Seven little, eight little, nine little joggers,
Ten little joggers fit and fine.

Book Suggestions   *I'm Walking, I'm Running, I'm Jumping, I'm Hopping* by Richard Harris
A Piece of Cake by Jill Murphy
What Shall We Do When We All Go Out? by Shari Halpern

Snack   Serve gelatin with fruit juice.

Review   Play a game of playground riddles with the children, giving them hints about a particular playground activity and challenging them to guess which it is. For example, "Over my head and under my feet, the rope twirls around, and I jump to the beat. What am I playing?" (jump rope). Continue making up riddles for hula-hoop, seesaw, basketball, baseball, soccer, hopscotch, tag, and so on.

Assessment   Do the children understand that there is a connection between exercise and body health?

 *Jackie Wright, Enid, OK*

Germs Busters!

Learning Objectives The children will:
1. Learn appropriate hand washing techniques.
2. Learn how to use a tissue and/or cough in their sleeve.
3. Develop healthy skills.

Circle or Group Time Activity
- Pretend to cough or sneeze in your hands, then squirt a small amount of shaving cream (germs) in your hands.
- Show the children the "germs" that come from your mouth and nose when coughing or sneezing. Then touch other objects, such as a book, a block, a chair, or doorknob, to show how the germs spread.
- Next, pretend to cough or sneeze in a tissue, squirt a small amount of shaving cream into it, and demonstrate how you fold it over the "germs" and throw it away.

Learning Centers **Art**
Substitute shaving cream for fingerpaint. Also, provide several tissues and pairs of child-safe scissors and help the children make tissue snowflakes. If the children are not yet ready to use scissors, provide crayons for them to draw noses on the tissues.

Blocks
Put child-sized life jackets in the area, and encourage the children to build a boat out of blocks. (If you have a wooden rocking boat, put the life jackets in it.)

Dramatic Play
Set up a hospital or doctor's office in the area. Invite the children to pretend to take care of sick patients (dolls, stuffed animals, or children volunteers).

Literacy
Make a "book of germs." Give each child a sheet of paper with the name of a germ on it and invite the children to draw what they think the germ looks like. Collect the images, bind them together with a cover that reads "The Germ Book," and place it in the center for the children to enjoy.

Sand and Water
Provide buckets, dish towels, and plastic dishes for the children to wash. Talk about the importance of using clean dishes and not using other people's cups or plates.

Small Motor
Provide small wrapped bars of hotel soap for the children to categorize, such as same/different, large/small, smells good/bad, and so on. Use this as an opportunity to stress the importance of hand washing.

Book Suggestions

Germs! Germs! Germs! by Bobbi Katz
Germs Make Me Sick by Melvin Berger
Wash Your Hands by Tony Ross

Snack

Serve apple slices. Recite the old saying, "An apple a day keeps the doctor way," and explain to the children that a healthy diet can keep their bodies healthy, so it is able to fight germs and not get sick.

Review

Engage the children in a discussion about ways to stop germs from spreading.

Assessment

In the bathroom, do the children demonstrate an understanding of how to wash their hands, getting them wet, adding soap, scrubbing, and then rinsing with water again? Do the children use tissues when they sneeze?

 *Lauri Robinson, Big Lake, MN*

Healthy Habits

Learning Objectives The children will:
1. Learn ways to stay healthy.
2. Distinguish between healthy and unhealthy food.

Circle or Group Time Activity
- Talk to children about how exercise helps to keep them healthy.
- Have the children stand in a circle. Make different movements and ask the children to copy the movements as well, for instance, put hands on hips or touch your toes.
- After the children follow you through several different motions, ask a child to perform an exercise movement and ask the other children to copy that movement.
- Repeat, choosing a different child at the end each time.
- After each child has a chance to lead the exercise movement, brainstorm with the children about different ways they can stay healthy (good eating habits, exercise, going to the dentist, washing hands, and so on). Specifically discuss healthy food and maintaining a good diet.

Learning Centers ### Art
Have the children cut out pictures of all kinds of food, healthy and unhealthy, from magazines. Invite them to glue the healthy food pictures to paper plates to make a healthy meal collage.

Dramatic Play
Set out toothbrushes, empty toothpaste boxes, and any donations that you can get from a local dentist (dentist bibs, small round mirrors, scrubs, rubber gloves, and so on) so the children can pretend to be dentists. Provide large stuffed animals or dolls, small chairs, a phone, small pads of paper, crayons, and magazines for the waiting area. A doll highchair can be a good dentist chair.

Literacy
Give each child a brown paper bag. Ask the children to draw a picture of a favorite healthy food on it. Help the children write the name of the food underneath their drawing. Staple all of the bags together to make a paper-bag book. Add a title page that reads, "I like to eat, eat, eat…."

Math

Provide a variety of plastic toy foods that represent all the food groups. Also set out a milk jug (cleaned well and the top cut off), a white paper bag, a clean Styrofoam tray, a bowl, and baskets that the children can use as containers into which they sort the food. Explain how each container represents a different food group, and ask the children to sort the foods into the appropriate containers.

Science

Provide stethoscopes, illustrations of X-rays, and books or pictures about the body. Encourage the children to take turns using the stethoscope to listen to their heartbeats. After the children listen to their heartbeats, they engage in active play for a short while, and then listen to their heartbeats again. Encourage the children to discuss the differences and talk about why their heart rates increased.

Book Suggestions

From Head to Toe by Eric Carle
Good for Me and You by Mercer Mayer
I Know Why I Brush My Teeth by Kate Rowan
Mr. Sugar Came to Town by Harriet Rohmer

Snack

Set out an assortment healthy foods and ask the children to try each one. Write the names of each food along the top of a sheet of poster board and help the children write their names or somehow mark the column for each food they try.

Review

Show the children images of various foods and ask them to identify those that are healthy.

Assessment

Do the children exhibit an interest in getting exercise and having a healthy diet?

 *Gail Morris, Kemah, TX*

Safety

Learning Objectives   The children will:
1. Learn about fire safety.
2. Learn about personal safety.
3. Role-play using skills they have learned.

Circle or Group Time Activity

■ Teach the children the following song:

911 (author unknown)
(Tune: "B-I-N-G-O")
*There is a number
You can call,
When you need someone to help you.
Just call 911.
Just call 911.
Just call 911,
And someone will come help you!*

■ Ask the children what they already know about personal safety and record their answers on a piece of chart paper.
■ If a child mentions the phrase, "stop, drop, and roll," use it as an opportunity to illustrate the phrase. Demonstrate how to stop, drop, and roll the flames out of clothing.
■ Pick one child to start this activity by placing the colored felt "flames" on her and having the child stop, drop, and roll the flames off.
■ Explain to the children that if their house catches on fire, or if they smell smoke, it is important that they get down on the floor and crawl underneath the smoke. To demonstrate this, place two chairs about four feet apart. Drape a blanket over the tops of the chairs, explaining to the children that the blanket represents the "smoke."
■ The children take turns crawling under the smoke.

Learning Centers   **Art**
Have the children draw pictures of "strangers" and record their dictations on their drawings. Bind the pages together to make a book called, "Stranger Danger."
On another day, have the children make a book, "Fire Safety." Place both books in the Library Center for the children to read.
Dramatic Play
Provide the children with fire department and police department costumes. Also, drape a blanket over two chairs and encourage the children to practice crawling under the "smoke."

Blocks
The children make buildings and use small toy figures to act out safety concerns.

Library
Set out a recording and copy of *The Berenstain Bears Learn About Strangers* by Stan and Jan Berenstain for the children to listen to and look through.

Writing
Cut out stop signs from construction paper and write "stop, drop, and roll" on them. Provide paper, markers, and plastic letters that spell out all the words. Invite the children to arrange the plastic letters to match the signs, and then trace around them, making copies of the signs.

Book Suggestions

The Berenstain Bears Learn About Strangers by Stan and Jan Berenstain
Fire Safety by Peggy Pancella
I Can Be Safe: A First Look at Safety by Pat Thomas
Please Play Safe! Penguin's Guide to Playground Safety by Margery Cuyler

Snack

Serve toast cut into the shapes of flames.

Review

Ask the children to take turns telling you the "most important thing" they have learned about safety.

Assessment

Do the children know the "stop, drop, and roll" phrase, and how to act it out?

 *Jodi Sykes, Lake Worth, FL*

Staying Healthy and Safe

Learning Objectives   The children will:
1. Learn what can make us sick or unsafe.
2. Learn about the equipment doctors and nurses use.
3. Learn how to stay healthy and safe.

Circle or Group Time Activity

■ Take the children on a walk through the neighborhood to see if they can be good detectives by spotting things they think may be unsafe or not healthy. Examples include riding bikes without helmets, not wearing seatbelts, picking up things on the ground that could be harmful, eating food off the ground, not looking both ways before crossing the street, and so on.

■ Bring the children back into the classroom and engage them in a discussion about what they saw.

■ Record the children's answers on poster board for further reference.

Learning Centers   **Art**

Make paper binoculars to take on a neighborhood walk. Children use child-safe scissors to cut paper towel rolls in half and tape or glue their lengths beside one another, and then add string to put around their necks.

Small Motor

Attach several bandages of various sizes to the inside flaps of a file folder, and laminate it. Set out several additional individual bandages for the children to match to those on the folder.

FILE FOLDER

BANDAGES

LAMINATED

VARIOUS SIZES
to MATCH

Blocks

Put out toy ambulances, helicopters, and figures that relate to hospitals and encourage the children to make a hospital out of blocks.

Dramatic Play

Put an inflatable mattress or blanket, toy stethoscopes, a doctor's bag, bandages, prescription pads, and so on in this area for the children to pretend they are doctors or patients.

Writing

Provide pretend prescription pads and pretend casts (made from white fabric or foam) that the children can write on, as though making prescriptions or signing friends' casts.

Book Suggestions

Curious George Goes to the Hospital by H. A. Rey and Margret Rey
How Do Dinosaurs Get Well Soon? by Jane Yolen

Snack

Serve chicken soup while the children pretend they are all sick. After they finish eating the soup, the children are healthy again.

Review

Children describe to the group times when they felt unwell.

Assessment

Set out two boxes, one marked "Healthy/Safe," the other marked "Unhealthy/Unsafe." Ask the children to look at some pictures and tell whether they belong in the healthy/safe or unhealthy/unsafe box. (Boxes are available with slits in them.) When they decide which box the picture belongs in they put the picture in the slot.

Related Song

Miss Molly Had a Dolly (traditional)
Miss Molloy had a dolly who was sick, sick, sick.
So she called the doctor to come quick, quick, quick.
The doctor came with his bag and his hat.
And he rapped on the door with a rat-a-tat-tat.
He looked at the dolly and he shook his head.
And he said, "Miss Molly put her straight to bed."
He wrote on a paper for the pill, pill, pill.
I'll be back in the morning with my bill, bill, bill.

 *Eileen Lucas, Fort McMurray, Alberta, Canada*

Taking Care of Me

Learning Objectives The children will:
1. Learn basic ways to care for their bodies.
2. Develop their small motor skills.
3. Practice beginning reading skills.
4. Measure ingredients.
5. Practice number recognition and counting skills.

Circle or Group Time Activity

- Display an assortment of objects related to healthy living, such as a toothbrush, toothpaste, washcloth, soap, pillow, bike helmet, tissues, a water bottle, a vitamin bottle, and containers and wrappers from healthy foods. Place them in a line down the center of the circle area.
- Teach the children the following song:

  I Want to Be Healthy by Mary J. Murray
  (Tune: "Did You Ever See a Lassie?")
  Oh, I want to be healthy, be healthy,
  *   be healthy.*
  Oh, I want to be healthy, so here's what
  *   I'll do.*
  I'll eat right and sleep well.
  I'll get lots of exercise.
  Oh, I want to be healthy, so here's what I'll do.

- When the song ends, each child picks up one of the items from the line in the circle area and the children each take a turn discussing how their objects contribute to health and safety.
- Repeat the song several times.

Learning Centers

Art
Invite children to draw or paint self-portraits in which they are participating in healthy activities.

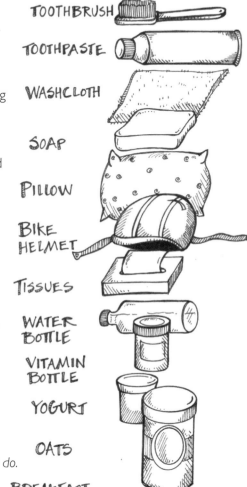

TOOTHBRUSH

TOOTHPASTE

WASHCLOTH

SOAP

PILLOW

BIKE HELMET

TISSUES

WATER BOTTLE

VITAMIN BOTTLE

YOGURT

OATS

BREAKFAST BAR WRAPPER

Dramatic Play

Provide food containers and boxes, along with baskets, a toy cash register, and so on, so the children can set up a health food store where they buy and sell healthy food items.

Literacy

Set out markers, crayons, and several sentence strips with statements on them, such as, "I will brush my teeth," "I will get enough sleep," "I will wear my helmet," "I will eat healthy food," and so on, and invite the children to illustrate the healthy behaviors each strip describes.

Math

Set out several sample food packages that have their nutritional information listed for the children to explore. The children then separate the containers and packages based on whether they are for healthy or unhealthy foods.

Snack and Cooking

The children select one of the following healthy choices, and then put the ingredients together for a healthy snack for later.

- ¼ cup yogurt
- 1 tablespoon fruit bits
- celery spread with peanut butter
- whole grain cracker topped with cheese and olive slice

Book Suggestions

Eating the Alphabet by Lois Ehlert
Staying Healthy, Dental Care by Alice B. McGinty

Snack

Set out the snacks the children prepared for themselves earlier. Add food items so all food groups are represented.

Review

Invite children to bring one item from the learning centers to the circle area and line up in a single-file line. Set out a small stepstool and invite the children to take turns standing on the stool to explain why the objects they picked are healthy.

Assessment

Display a healthy habits poster and ask the children to use the poster to tell you what they have learned about being healthy.

 *Mary J. Murray, Mazomanie, WI*

What's Inside the Body?

Learning Objectives The children will:

1. Learn why our bones are important.
2. Discover ways to keep our bones healthy.
3. Learn about the heart, brain, and lungs.
4. Find out ways to keep the heart, lungs, and brain healthy.

Circle or Group Time Activity

- Discuss what is underneath our skin, including our bones, organs, muscles, joints, and so on. Talk about how everything works together to make our bodies function.
- Talk about the skeletal system. Show the children a model or picture of the skeletal system and talk about how the bones protect our brain, heart, lungs, and spinal cord. Explain that bones come in all sizes.
- Tell the children that healthy foods and exercise help keep us strong and healthy.
- Ask the children to use their hands to find their heartbeats on their chests.
- After the children find their heartbeats, ask them to run in place for a minute, then feel their heartbeats again. Ask them to describe the difference.
- Explain to the children that the body needs air to survive, and that their lungs take in the air.
- Show the children a balloon. Blow it up, and then let its air out so that they can see how the lungs work.

Learning Centers **Art**

Give the children white paint and cotton swabs and encourage them to paint X-ray designs on black construction paper.

BLACK CONSTRUCTION PAPER

WHITE PAINT

COTTON SWAB

Blocks

Cut out heads from magazines and glue them onto paper plates. Older children may help with this step. Encourage the children to use blocks to create skeletal systems for the paper plate heads.

Math

Cut out bones in a variety of sizes from construction paper. Challenge the children to find matching bones and put them in order from largest to smallest.

Science

On large sheets of butcher paper, trace the children's bodies, and then have them use markers and crayons to draw their body parts.

Writing

On sentence strips, copy the words *bone* and *femur* and encourage the children to copy the letters or match plastic copies of the letters to the letters in the words. (**Note:** Tell the children that the femur is their thigh bone.)

Book Suggestions

Dem Bones by Bob Barner
The Magic School Bus Inside Ralphie by Joanna Cole
Me and My Amazing Body by Joan Sweeney

Snack

Serve toast and cheese cut into the shapes of bones as well as milk and other bone-fortifying foods.

Review

Ask the children to identify the body parts that they painted and drew onto the butcher paper outlines of their bodies.

Assessment

Do the children seem to recognize that they have bones and organs in their bodies that help them move and function?

 *Holly Dzierzanowski, Brenham, TX*

An Ant's World

Learning Objectives   The children will:
1. Learn how ants use teamwork.
2. Learn about ant colonies.
3. Reinforce math skills (geometric shapes, counting).

Circle or Group Time Activity
- Make several tape arrows on the floor, with each leading to a carpet square.
- Set a tall chair or stool at the center of all the arrows and carpet squares. Put up a large image of an anthill behind the chair.
- Sit on the tall chair or stand on the stool, and say that you are the queen ant. (Consider wearing a crown.)
- The children crawl, following the tape arrows on the floor, until they all come to carpet squares.
- Tell the children that today they will learn about ants, and engage them in a conversation about ants. Ask them where ants live (in anthills), why they are called hills, and what they look like (piles of sand or dirt), and whether the ants live alone or in groups (introduce the word "colony" here). Also ask them which ant is in charge of a colony.
- Read Chris Van Allsburg's *Two Bad Ants* to the children, and discuss it with the children.
- Ask the children what good and poor choices the ants made. Using chart paper, make a list of the good and poor choices they discuss. Draw a checkmark over the positive behaviors and a red circle with a slash through it for the negative ones.

Learning Centers   **Art**
Give each child a page from a coloring book with an ant outline and crayons. Post the pictures on the wall so that the ants are marching in a line toward an anthill, a picnic basket, a cookie, the ant queen, or some other image.

Math
Draw or find pictures of 10 ants. On five ants, draw them carrying sugar cubes. On three, draw them carrying pieces of cake, and on two, draw them carrying seeds. Ask the children to count how many ants are carrying each type of food, and which kinds of food the largest and smallest numbers of ants are carrying.

Music
Play a recording of "The Ants Go Marching," or another similar ant-related song, and encourage the children to act out the gestures the song's lyrics describe.

Sand and Water

Provide a large box with sand in it or fill the table with sand. Encourage the children to make anthills and walking paths around the anthills.

Small Motor

Make several photocopies of simple mazes with images of anthills at their centers and challenge the children to move their fingers through the maze to the anthill at the center.

Book Suggestions

512 Ants on Sullivan Street by Carol A. Losi
Are You an Ant? by Judy Allen
I Saw an Ant in a Parking Lot by Joshua Prince
One Hundred Hungry Ants by Elinor J. Pinczes
Two Bad Ants by Chris Van Allsburg

Snack

Break long pretzel logs in half. Spread peanut butter (check for allergies) or cream cheese on one side, and let the children add "ants" (raisins) on the logs.

Review

Gather the children in a circle. Explain that ants get their work done because they work as a unit. Hold up a ball and say the ball needs to come back around to you, and that all the ants must do their part for this to happen. Pass the ball to your right, and watch as the children pass the ball around the circle and back to you.

Assessment

Can children identify the ant if shown images of an ant, a ladybug, and a snail?

Related Fingerplay

Five Little Ants by Theresa Callahan
Five little ants were walking to their home. (walk in place)
One saw a flower and wanted to roam. (walk in a tight circle)
One fell down and hurt his knee. (rub knee)
One decided to stop for tea. (pretend to sip from a mug)
One saw a bird and stooped to hide. (stoop down)
One dropped his food, and sat and cried. (rub eyes and make appropriate sound)
Five little ants in the sun's bright glare, (shade eyes from sun)
They saw their anthill, and they were there. (point to anthill and cheer)

 *Theresa Callahan, Easton, MD*

Beehives and Honey

Learning Objectives The children will:
1. Learn about honeybees.
2. Recognize the colors black and yellow.
3. Engage in dramatic play with their peers.

Circle or Group Time Activity

- Show the children pictures of bees. Ask the children if they have seen bees before. Talk about how bees live in groups called colonies, and that they collect pollen and nectar to take back to their hives.
- Divide the children into two groups. Tell one group they are the flowers. Give each child in this group a pinch of "pollen" (a piece of yellow paper) to hold. Ask the "flowers" to sit on the ground and hold the papers over their heads.
- Tell the other group that they are the bees. Ask them to buzz around the flowers to collect the pollen. When the "bees" collect most of the pollen, they fly back to their hive (where you stand) and give the pollen to their colony.
- Have the children switch roles and repeat the activity.

Learning Centers ### Art
Provide yellow construction paper, yellow paint, sponges, and stripe stencils. Encourage children to put the stencil onto the paper and to sponge paint black stripes on the paper.

Snack and Cooking
Provide brown paper hive cutouts and bowls of honeycomb-shaped cereal. Encourage the children to arrange the cereal on the hive cutouts to make beehives. When they are finished, they can eat their creations.

BROWN PAPER HIVE CUTOUT

START LAYERING CEREAL

HONEYCOMB-SHAPED CEREAL

Dramatic Play
Put a row of large cardboard boxes on their sides. Tape them together with duct tape. Encourage children to use the boxes as a beehive for their dramatic play.
Science
Put honeycomb on a paper plate and let children explore it with magnifying glasses.
Small Motor
Have children make fingerprint bees. Provide paper, a yellow ink pad, and black colored pencils. Encourage children to make thumbprints on the paper. Have them use the pencil to draw black stripes and antennae on their bees.

Book Suggestions   *Are You a Bee?* by Judy Allen
The Honey Makers by Gail Gibbons
In Enzo's Splendid Garden by Patricia Polacco

Snack   Pretend a straw is a bee's proboscis and suck nectar from flowers (cups). Serve bread with honey.

Review   Have the children sit in the circle. Say, "I'm a dizzy, buzzy bee and I've gotten lost. I'm out here in a field of flowers but I don't remember why. What am I supposed to do?" (Collect pollen and nectar.) Pretend to collect pollen and sip nectar. Say, "Okay, I have pollen and I have nectar, now where do I go?" (Home, to the beehive.) Thank the children for their help and then buzz away.

Assessment   If shown a picture of a bee, can the child state two facts about bees? (It may be necessary to prompt with "What does the bee collect from the flowers?" "Where is it going to take the pollen?")

Related Fingerplay   **Here Is the Beehive** (Traditional)
Here is the beehive (hold up fist)
But where are the bees?
Hidden away, where nobody sees.
Watch and we'll see them come out of the hive.
One, two, three, four, five! (raise fingers one at a time)

 *Cassandra Reigel Whetstone, Folsom, CA*

Bees Are Busy!

Learning Objectives The children will:
1. Learn where bees live.
2. Learn about the sound bees make.
3. Talk about how honey looks and feels.

Circle or Group Time Activity
- Ask children what sounds bees make. Encourage them to practice buzzing like bees.
- Show the children a photo of a beehive or, if you know a beekeeper, an unused beehive.
- Teach the children the following action rhyme, making all the "B" words buzz:

Busy Bees by Christina Chilcote
Busy bees, buzzing around (with one finger, circle around your head)
Flying high and low (point up, then down)
From the flower to the hive (point left to flower, then right to hive)
See how quick they go! (quickly zigzag finger through the air)
(Repeat twice)

- Tell the children that they will be learning about bees today.

Learning Centers

Art
Give each child a sheet of pastel construction paper. Let each child choose three to five flowers pre-cut from wallpaper sample books and arrange them on the paper. Have the children glue the flowers to paper, and attach several bee stickers around their flowers. Help the children write their names on their flower sheets.

Dramatic Play
Provide yellow and black striped tee shirts and headbands with springy "antennae" so the children can pretend to be busy bees, going between silk or paper flowers and a "beehive."

Math
Set out sheets of paper, each with the same image of several bees flying around a few beehives. Below the image of the beehive, put the following statements and set out red and blue crayons for the children to use complete the statements:
There are _____ bees in the picture.
There are _____ beehives in the picture.
Circle the beehives in red.
Circle the bees in blue.

Music

Provide inexpensive kazoos for the children, printing each child's name on a different kazoo, and encourage them to play various songs, such as "Happy Birthday." The kazoos will make them sound like humming bees.

Small Motor

Attach four quarters of a picture of a bee onto four separate blocks. Challenge the children to put the blocks together to make the bee.

Book Suggestions

The Bee's Sneeze by Ellis Nader
Buzz, Buzz, Busy Bees by Dawn Bentley
Buzzing Bees by Wendy McLean
Happy Bees by Arthur Yorinks

Snack

Arrange apple slices or mandarin orange slices on a plate to look like the petals of a flower. Put a cherry half or a green grape in the center of the "petals." Add several mini-pretzel twists for bees.

Review

On a piece of tagboard, write the statement "Bees like _____." five times in a row, and encourage the children to complete the statements.

Assessment

Show a picture of a house and a beehive. Ask the children to point to the bees' home. Show a sandwich and a honeycomb. Ask the children to point to the bees' food. Ask the children what sound a bee makes.

Christina Chilcote, New Freedom, PA

Bees Buzz

Learning Objectives The children will:
1. Learn the importance of bees in our environment.
2. Learn about bees' habits.

Circle or Group Time Activity
- Play *Bumblebee (Buzz Buzz)* by Laurie Berkner.
- Invite the children to move to the music.
- Next, have the children sit and imagine being bees. Ask them to describe the experience.
- Lead this discussion to the importance of bees and their habitat.

Learning Centers ### Art
Provide yellow and black chenille stems and invite the children to bend them and wrap them around their fingers, shaping them to look like bees. Provide wiggle eyes for the children to add.

Blocks
Add fabric or felt bee-shaped cutouts and suggest that the children build beehives for them.

Dramatic Play
Make bee costumes and plastic flowers available for the children to pretend they are bees.

Small Motor
Draw bees on the ends of the fingers of several pairs of white gloves. Set out a chart with the words to a fingerplay like "Five Busy Bees" copied on it. Ask the children to recite the rhyme while wearing the gloves.

Literacy
Give the children markers, rubber stamps of bees, and several sheets of paper with "Be_" written on them. Invite the children to stamp pictures of bees on the sheets and to write the second "e" in the blank space on each page.

Book Suggestions

The 1, 2, 3 Bees by
    Wheldon Nicole
Are You a Bee? by
    Judy Allen
Buzz-Buzz, Busy Bees
    by Dawn Bentley
Buzz Said the Bee
    by Wendy Cheyette Lewison

Snack

Give the children honey on crackers to enjoy. Talk with them about where honey comes from. (**Note:** Check for allergies before serving honey.)

Review

Discuss the importance of bees to our world.

Assessment

Ask questions about the bees' habitat, types of bees and the significance of bees in our world.

 *Jean Potter, Greensburg, PA*

Bugs, Bugs, Bugs

Learning Objectives The children will:
1. Familiarize themselves with bugs.
2. Develop their critical thinking skills.

Circle or Group Time Activity
- Before the children come into the room, hide 10 plastic insects or pictures of insects in areas they are most likely to visit before Circle or Group Time.
- As the children enter and find the plastic insects or the pictures of insects, ask them to place the bugs in a large plastic "Bug Jar."
- After they find all the insects, gather the children together. Show them the bug jar and remove the bugs. Engage the children in a discussion about the insects. Help them identify each different species, and so on.
- Tell the children that some creepy crawly things are insects and some are not.
- Display large photographs of eight different types of insects.
- Ask the children to look for ways the bugs are similar. To help the children think this through, ask them questions, such as "How many wings do they have?" and "Are they all the same color?"
- Continue asking questions about size, shape, antennae, number of legs, and number of body parts until the children come up with these requirements:
  - six legs
  - two wings
  - antennae
  - three body parts
- Show the children a picture of a spider. Go through the checklist of insect characteristics with the children so they can see whether the spider falls into the insect category. Help the children see that because a spider has eight legs, the spider is not an insect.
- Teach the children the following song to help them remember the characteristics for insects.

Insect Body Parts by Susan Oldham Hill
(Tune: "The Ants Go Marching")
I'm counting all the body parts, one, two, three.
I'm counting all the wings in view, one and two.
I see antennae to feel their way,
And six little feet walk every day.
I'm counting insects,
Counting each one I see.

Learning Centers

Art
Set out glue; large sheets of uncut construction paper; construction paper cutouts of ovals, black legs, and antennae; and tissue paper wings of various sizes. On the uncut sheets of paper, the children glue three ovals in a row, making an insect's body, and then add two antennae, two wings, and six legs. Next, the children illustrate their insects. Encourage the children to draw around their insects, giving the insects landscapes in which to live.

Library
Place a variety of informational insect books in the Library Center for the children to explore and read.

Math
Set out laminated construction-paper cutouts of insect bodies that have varying numbers of legs, from zero to six, as well as the corresponding numbers written on them. Ask the children to put the insects in order. Also, consider cutting out six insect outlines, each with one different leg, and setting it out so the children can lay them on top of one another, counting as they go. In the end, the stack will make one insect with all six legs.

Small Motor
Cut out six 8" insect bodies from cardboard and laminate. Invite the children to add playdough antennae, wings, and legs.

Writing
Using the children's insect creations from the Art Center, ask the children what their insects' names are, as well as what the insects are doing. Copy this information onto separate sheets of construction paper, leaving blanks where the children can fill in words or illustrations that complete the statements.

Book Suggestions

Bugs by Nancy Winslow Parker and Joan Richards Wright
The Icky Bug Alphabet Book by Jerry Pallotta
I Like Bugs by Margaret Wise Brown
Insects in the Garden by D. M. Souza

Snack

Slice several miniature muffins into thirds. Ask the children to place the three slices in a row, making the three body parts of the insect. Next, give them raisins for eyes and spots. Show them how to use licorice for antennae, legs, and the outlines of wings.

Review

Recite the following song with the children:

Are You an Insect? by Susan Oldham Hill   (Tune: "Do You Know the Muffin Man?")
Oh, do you have six legs to walk   *If you have six legs to walk*
Up and down a tall beanstalk?   *And wings to fly up on a rock;*
Oh, do you have two wings to fly   *If your body has three parts,*
And three parts to your body?   *Then you are an insect!*

Assessment

Given a laminated outline of an insect body, can the child attach the correct number of playdough legs to it?

 Susan Oldham Hill, Lakeland, FL

Butterflies

Learning Objectives   The children will:
1. Learn about the life cycle stages of a butterfly.
2. Develop their memory skills.
3. Develop their small and large motor skills.

Circle or Group Time Activity
- Begin by explaining that the class will be learning about butterflies today.
- Show the children photos of each stage of a butterfly's life cycle: egg, caterpillar, chrysalis (pupa), and adult butterfly.
- Give each child a life cycle picture. Say the name of one of the stages of the life cycle, and have the children holding images of that stage hold the pictures up high and repeat the stage's name.

Learning Centers   ### Art
Paint the children's middle fingers with one color of tempera paint, and have them press their fingers onto the center of sheets of construction paper. Wash the children's hands, set out containers of various colors of paint for them to press their entire hands into, and then press their hands on either side of the prints of their pointer fingers. Wash the children's hands again. When the paint dries, provide markers and crayons and encourage the children to illustrate their finger butterflies, adding faces and antennae.

Large Motor
Play music and encourage the children to flap their arms and dance around the room as if they were butterflies.

Library
Put books about butterflies in this center for children to explore.

Math
Make five matching pairs of construction paper butterflies with which the children can play memory games.

THE BUTTERFLY LIFE CYCLE

egg

caterpillar (larva)

chrysalis (pupa)

butterfly

Writing
Provide several block letters that spell *butterfly* and encourage the children to trace them. Give them several sheets of paper with the letters already traced in proper order so they can arrange the block letters on top of them, spelling *butterfly.*

Book Suggestions
Are You a Butterfly? by Judy Allen
Butterfly House by Eve Bunting
My, Oh My, a Butterfly: All About Butterflies by Tish Rabe
The Very Hungry Caterpillar by Eric Carle

Snack
Make Caterpillar Biscuit Snacks with the children.
Ingredients:
- refrigerator biscuits
- sesame seeds
- poppy seeds
- shredded cheddar cheese
- pretzel sticks
- raisins
- butter or margarine (melted)

Prepare small bowls of sesame seeds, poppy seeds, and grated cheese. Use two biscuits to form four small dough balls. Dip the dough balls into the melted butter and then roll them into seeds or cheese. Press the balls together on a cookie sheet to form a caterpillar shape. Bake the biscuits according to package directions. When the caterpillar biscuits are done, poke two pretzel sticks into the head of the biscuit caterpillar for antennae, and use raisins for eyes.

Review
Recite the following song with the children:

Butterfly Bustle by Kimberly M. Hutmacher
Dancing on a bush,
Darting out of trees,
Swooping over grass,
Sailing in the breeze.
Roaming through yards,
Rushing to sky,
Whisking past nets,
Waving goodbye!

Assessment
Show the children the life-cycle pictures again and ask them to name each cycle.

 *Kimberly Hutmacher, Illiopolis, IL*

Butterflies Are Beautiful

Learning Objectives The children will:
1. Learn about caterpillars and butterflies.
2. Develop their small and large motor skills.
3. Use their observations skills.

Circle or Group Time Activity

- Create a "Curly Caterpillar" puppet by cutting out a construction paper C shape. Draw a caterpillar's face and characteristics on it, and then attach it to a straw or stick.
- Show the children the Curly Caterpillar puppet.
- Ask the children what letter is at the start of Curly Caterpillar's name.
- After the children identify the correct letter, ask the children if they can think of other words that start with C. Ask the children to think of things that start with C that Curly Caterpillar might do. Make a list of their responses.
- Recite the following song with the children. Once they finish singing the lines below, encourage them to make up verses using the suggestions they made in the previous step.

Curly the Caterpillar by Jackie Wright
(Tune: "Skip to My Lou")
What can we do with Curly?
What can we do with Curly?
What can we do with Curly,
Curly the Caterpillar?

Learning Centers

Art
Set out a container of tempera paint and several large sheets of construction paper. The children dip their feet into the paint and then carefully step on the construction paper, with each foot a short distance from the other, so they resemble butterfly wings. After the paint dries, the children use markers, crayons, and glitter to decorate their own butterflies.

Dramatic Play
Add a butterfly costume or large, colorful, flowing articles of clothing to the dress-up clothes so the children can pretend to be butterflies.

Math

Make a simple graph with "yes" and "no" columns that show how the children respond the question "Would you like to be a butterfly?" The children can count and compare the results.

Sand and Water

Hide halves of matching pairs of painted construction paper butterflies in the sand for the children to find. As the children find the butterflies, have them match the butterflies to their twins in a file folder.

Small Motor

Set out markers, child-safe scissors, tape, straws, and several pieces of construction paper with Curly Caterpillar outlines on them. The children use the child-safe scissors to cut out the outlines of the puppets, decorate the puppets using markers, and then use glue to attach the puppets to straws.

Book Suggestions

Monarch Butterfly by Gail Gibbons
A Monarch Butterfly's Life by John Himmelman
The Very Hungry Caterpillar by Eric Carle

Snack

Serve the different foods that the caterpillar eats in *The Very Hungry Caterpillar.*

Review

Reread *The Very Hungry Caterpillar* by Eric Carle, asking the children to name the objects that the story mentions.

Assessment

Can the children identify a butterfly when you show them pictures of various insects? Do the children recognize that caterpillars become butterflies?

Related Song

Five Little Butterflies (Traditional)

Five little butterflies
Resting at the door,
One flew away and then there were four.
Butterfly, butterfly, happy and gay,
Butterfly, butterfly, fly away.

Four little butterflies
Sitting in a tree,
One flew away
And then there were three.
Butterfly, butterfly, happy and gay,
Butterfly, butterfly, fly away.

Three little butterflies
Looking at you,
One flew away
And then there were two.

Butterfly, butterfly, happy and gay,
Butterfly, butterfly, fly away.

Two little butterflies
Sitting in the sun,
One flew away
And then there was one.
Butterfly, butterfly, happy and gay,
Butterfly, butterfly, fly away.

One little butterfly
Left all alone,
He flew away
And then there was none.
Butterfly, butterfly, happy and gay,
Butterfly, butterfly, fly away.

 *Jackie Wright, Enid, OK*

Butterfly Life Cycle

Learning Objectives The children will:
1. Learn about butterflies and moths.
2. Explore the life cycle of a butterfly through a fingerplay.
3. Explore symmetry in design.
4. Develop small motor skills.

Circle or Group Time Activity

■ Teach the children the following fingerplay:

The Butterfly by Sandra Bynum
I am a tiny little egg, stuck to a leaf on a tree. (touch outstretched fingers to fingers of other hand, making an egg shape)
Now I'm a little caterpillar, as wiggly as I can be! (raise and wiggle index finger)
I eat all day and I eat all night, then I climb to a branch on high. (mimic eating, slide wiggly finger up other arm to tips of fingers)
I make a cocoon and before too long, I'm a beautiful butterfly! (form a fist, open hand, intertwine thumbs, and flap both hands)

■ Practice just the rhyme a few times with the children, and then demonstrate the fingerplay actions as the children follow along.
■ Once the children know the rhyme and the fingerplay, show the children a live butterfly and ask them to describe what they see. Tell the children that today they will be learning about butterflies.

Learning Centers

Art
Invite the children to color coffee filters with markers. When they finish drawing, help them spray the coffee filters with water to blend the colors, and let the filters dry. When dry, show them how to pinch the filters together in the middle, and twist pipe cleaners around the center. Twist the two ends of the pipe cleaner to one side, so that they resemble a butterfly's antennae.

Library
Place a copy of a pictorial butterfly book, such as *Eyewitness: Butterfly & Moth* by Paul Whalley or *Are You a Butterfly?* by Judy Allen in the center for the children to explore.

Science
Provide specimen jars that contain live butterflies, moths, and caterpillars for the children to observe. Encourage the children to describe the creatures, and then make drawings of each. Release them when you are finished.

Small Motor
Give the children paper, child-safe scissors, and several cardboard cutouts of halved butterfly shapes and show them how to fold a sheet of paper in half, lay the butterfly template on the paper so its edge is along the paper's crease, copy its

outline, and then cut out the outline to make a whole butterfly. Set out markers and crayons so the children can illustrate their butterflies as they like, and then attach the butterflies to the walls.

Dramatic Play

Invite the children to act out the fingerplay "The Butterfly" from Circle or Group Time using their entire bodies.

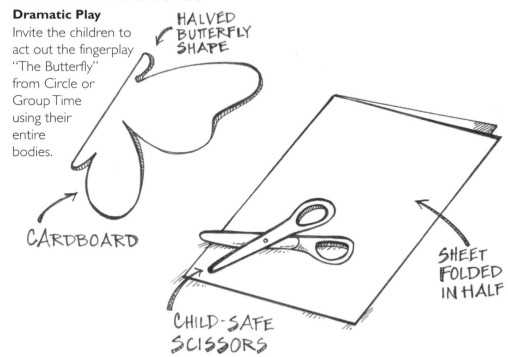

HALVED BUTTERFLY SHAPE

CARDBOARD

CHILD-SAFE SCISSORS

SHEET FOLDED IN HALF

Book Suggestions

Are You a Butterfly? by Judy Allen
Butterflies in the Garden by Carol Lerner
Clara Caterpillar by Pamela Duncan Edwards
The Crunching Munching Caterpillar by Sheridan Cain
From Egg to Butterfly by Shannon Zemlicka and Shannon Knudsen
Where Butterflies Grow by Joanne Ryder

Snack

Serve juice, such as apricot nectar or any other sweet fruit juice, with straws so children can drink nectar just like butterflies. Also, consider serving juicy fruits such as orange segments or cut up peaches or pineapples.

Review

As a group, ask the children to share their butterfly art projects with one another. Draw their attention to all of the mounted butterflies on the window or wall and encourage them to talk about the different designs and colors.

Assessment

Ask the children to finish the following statements:

A caterpillar comes from a tiny _____. (egg)
Moths are most active at _____. (night)
A butterfly's favorite food is _____. (flower nectar)
After a long rest, butterfly emerges from a _____. (cocoon)

 *Sandra Bynum, Blackfoot, ID*

Butterfly Wings

Learning Objectives   The children will:
1. Act out the life cycle of a butterfly.
2. Describe the order of development.
3. Observe a caterpillar as it hatches into a butterfly.
4. Listen to stories about butterflies and caterpillars.

Circle or Group Time Activity
- Read *Butterfly* by Susan Canizares to the children.
- As you read the story, ask the children to act out all of the various actions the story describes, such as the caterpillar crawling, the caterpillar spinning a chrysalis, and the beautiful wings of a butterfly.
- After finishing the story, talk with the children about the story. Ask them to name the different parts of the butterfly's life cycle.

Learning Centers   ### Blocks
Provide paints, brushes, and several blocks that the children can paint. Make sure they paint a face on one of the blocks, as well as black dots on the sides of the other blocks to make feet. Once the blocks are dry, encourage the children to use the blocks to create a colorful caterpillar.

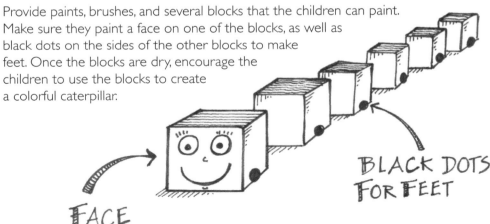

FACE

BLACK DOTS FOR FEET

Dramatic Play
Set out wings that the children can attach to their backs so they can pretend to fly around as butterflies.

Library
Place a flannel-board version of Eric Carle's *The Very Hungry Caterpillar* in the Library Center for the children to look at and explore.

Math
Cut several sheets of paper into butterfly shapes. Have the children choose a butterfly-shaped paper, fold it in half, and then open it again. Invite them to drop one or two colors of paint on one side of the fold, fold the paper over, and press the halves together to create a unique mirror image design. Talk about pairs and symmetry with the children.

Science
Order caterpillars that form chrysalis and then emerge as butterflies. When the caterpillars arrive, place them in a fish tank for the children to observe.

Small Motor
Cut several images of butterflies into simple puzzles and challenge the children to put them together. Use commercially available butterfly puzzles, if available.

Writing
Write the statement "It feels _____ to be a butterfly" on pieces of paper. Give one to each child. Ask the children to complete the statement as you copy their statements into the blank. Have the children illustrate their answers on the page.

Book Suggestions

Butterfly by Susan Canizares
The Butterfly Alphabet by Kjell B. Sandved
The Caterpillow Fight by Sam McBratney
The Crunching Munching Caterpillar by Sheridan Cain
The Very Hungry Caterpillar by Eric Carle

Snack

Make a butterfly snack with celery, cream cheese, two oval shaped crackers, and two stick pretzels. Spread the cream cheese in the celery, add the crackers to the cream cheese, making wings, and then add the pretzels as antennae.

Review

Re-read *Butterfly* with the children. Discuss the life cycle of the butterfly.

Assessment

Can the child explain the steps involved in a caterpillar's transformation into a butterfly?

 *Sandy Scott, Meridian, ID*

Caterpillars to Butterflies

Learning Objectives The children will:
1. Move like a caterpillar and butterfly.
2. Learn about the habitat and feeding habits of the caterpillar.
3. Compare butterflies and caterpillars.

Circle or Group Time Activity
- Gather the children together on the floor, and engage them in a discussion about caterpillars.
- After talking about the life cycles of caterpillars and butterflies, ask the children to get down in a row on their hands and knees.
- Tell them to crawl toward you when you say "crawl like a caterpillar," and then to freeze when you say "freeze."
- Let the first child to reach you take your place, and repeat the activity.

Learning Centers ### Art
Cut large butterfly and caterpillar shapes from sponges and set them out beside construction paper and containers of paint and encourage the children to paint with them.

Construction
Set out empty plastic wrap and aluminum foil boxes, containers of glue, and cotton balls, and show the children how to glue cotton balls to the boxes until they are covered and resemble cocoons. Set out foam, felt, and pipe cleaners with which the children can make caterpillars to put inside their cocoons.

Library
Place a copy of the story *From Caterpillar to Butterfly* by Deborah Heiligman in the center for the children to listen to and explore.

Math
Set out two large 12" laminated construction paper caterpillar cutouts with inch measurements marked along their sides, as well as several other caterpillar cutouts of various sizes for the children to measure and arrange according to size.

Small Motor
Cut several images of caterpillars and butterflies into puzzles and invite the children to put them together.

Book Suggestions   *Butterfly House* by Eve Bunting
From Caterpillar to Butterfly by Deborah Heiligman

Snack   On a tray, set out several muffins in the shape of a caterpillar, and add pretzel sticks as legs.

Review   Recite the following song with the children, inviting them to act out the movements the song describes:

Fuzzy, Wuzzy Caterpillar (Traditional)
Fuzzy, wuzzy caterpillar,
Into the corner she crept, (creep on ground)
Spun herself a blanket
And then went fast asleep. (curl up)
Fuzzy, wuzzy caterpillar
Wakes up by and by, (get up and dance around)
Finds herself with beautiful wings (flap hands like wings)
Changed to a butterfly.

Assessment   Set out images of the different stages of a butterfly's life cycle and ask the child to put them in the correct order.

Related Song   **Ten Little Butterflies** by Eileen Lucas
(Tune: "Bumping Up and Down in My Little Red Wagon")
One little, two little, three little caterpillars.
Four little, five little, six little caterpillars.
Seven little, eight little, nine little caterpillars.
Wait! Ten little butterflies.

 Eileen Lucas, Fort McMurray, Alberta, Canada

Crazy for Bugs

Learning Objectives   The children will:
1. Identify four types of insects (ladybug, butterfly, bee, ant).
2. Discover the butterfly life cycle.
3. Learn about the natural world.

Circle or Group Time Activity
■ Teach the children the following song:

The Bees in the Garden by Renee Kirchner
(Tune: "Wheels on The Bus")
The bees in the garden go buzz, buzz, buzz.
Buzz, buzz, buzz, buzz, buzz, buzz
The bees in the garden go buzz, buzz, buzz.
All around the garden.

The butterflies in the garden go flutter,
*   flutter, flutter.*
Flutter, flutter, flutter, flutter, flutter, flutter.
The butterflies in the garden go flutter,
*   flutter, flutter.*
All around the garden.

The ladybugs on the grass go chew, chew, chew
Chew, chew, chew, chew, chew, chew.
The ladybugs on the grass go chew, chew, chew
All around the garden.

The ant in the garden goes march,
*   march, march.*
March, march, march, march, march, march.
The ant in the garden goes march,
*   march, march.*
All around the garden.

■ Tell children that today they will learn about insects, especially ants, bees, ladybugs, and butterflies.
■ Engage the children in a discussion about insects. Be sure to explain that insects have three body parts and six legs.

Learning Centers   **Literacy**
Give each child four pieces of paper, each with the name of a different kind of insect written on them (ant, bee, butterfly, or ladybug). Also set out several sheets with "Bug Book by _____" written on them. Ask the children to draw pictures of each of the insects, and then collect the images into a four-page "Bug Book," and help the children write their names on the cover pages as well. Bind the pages with staples and place the books in the Library Center.

Math
Away from the children, paint rocks with red spray paint. Put one, two, three, four, or five magic marker dots on each rock and encourage the children to sort the "ladybugs" by number of dots.

Science
Place a variety of insects into an aquarium for the children to observe and discuss. Put *Don't Squash That Bug! The Curious Kid's Guide to Insects* by Natalie Rompella next to the tank so the children can try to identify the different insects.

Art

Cut tissue paper into 6" squares. Ask each child to choose two different colors of tissue paper. Show the children how to gather the paper in the middle and clamp a clothespin over it, and then spread out the paper, so it resembles wings. Have them glue 4" lengths of chenille stems to the butterflies to make antennae. They can use markers to add faces.

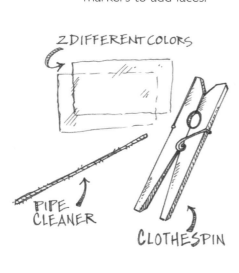

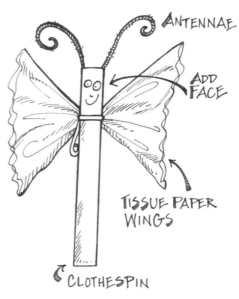

Writing

Set out several block letters that spell the names of various insects, as well as several sheets of paper with the insects' names written on them, and encourage the children to match the block letters to the letters on the pages. When the children finish, have them draw the letters on paper.

Book Suggestions

Bugs Are Insects by Anne F. Rockwell
Butterfly House by Eve Bunting
Don't Squash That Bug! The Curious Kid's Guide to Insects by Natalie Rompella
Roberto: The Insect Architect by Nina Laden
The Very Hungry Caterpillar by Eric Carle

Snack

Cut apples in half and take out the core and seeds. Set out peanut butter for the children to spread on the apple skin, and then press raisins into the peanut butter, making edible ladybugs. Put grapes on toothpicks and stick them in one end of the apple halves, making the ladybugs' heads.

Review

Go outside to a playground or a garden and have children look for and identify insects.

Assessment

Show the children pictures of a bee, a ladybug, a butterfly, and an ant. See if they can name each insect. Ask the children what type of insect the butterfly is before it turns into a butterfly.

 Renee Kirchner, Carrollton, TX

Five Little Ladybugs

Learning Objectives The children will:
1. Learn about ladybugs.
2. Refine their small motor skills.
3. Write the letters L, A, D, Y, B, U, and G.

Circle or Group Time Activity
- Teach the children the following fingerplay:

    Five Little Ladybugs (author unknown)
    Five little ladybugs climbing up the door. (hold up five fingers on one hand)
    One flew away and then there were four. (hold up four fingers)
    Four little ladybugs sitting on the tree.
    One flew away and then there were three. (hold up three fingers)
    Three little ladybugs landed on my shoe!
    One flew away and then there were two. (hold up two fingers)
    Two little ladybugs out for some fun.
    One flew away and then there was one. (hold up one finger)
    One little ladybug sitting in the sun.
    She flew away and then there were none! (close hand)

- Repeat the fingerplay and tell the children they will be learning about ladybugs today.

Learning Centers

Art
Provide, crayons, markers, and white construction paper. Encourage the children to use red and black for their drawings. Provide a picture of a ladybug to copy.

Construction
Provide scissors; black, red and white construction paper; and glue. Have the children cut out red circles. Have them cut out smaller black circles. Encourage them to glue to small black circles on the larger red ones, for their own ladybugs. Glue the ladybugs onto white construction paper.

Dramatic Play
Provide red and black shirts, pants, and shoes in the dress-up area for the children to use in their pretend play.

Literacy
Have each child finish the following sentence: "If I were a ladybug I would _____." Write their answers on a piece of paper. Encourage them to illustrate their answers.

Science
Provide pictures of ladybugs and other bugs. Ask the children to identify the ladybugs. Discuss ladybugs and where they live.
Writing
Provide writing paper and pencils for the children to practice writing the letters L, A, D, Y, B, U, and G.

Book Suggestions

Are You a Ladybug? by Judy Allen
Hungry Ladybugs by Judith Jango-Cohen
Ladybugs: Red, Fiery, and Bright by Mia Posada
Lara Ladybug by Christine Florie

Snack

Core red apples and slice them in half, and give one half to each child. Have the children place the apple half on a plate with the red skin side facing up. They dab raisins into peanut butter or cream cheese and then stick the raisins onto the apples to make spots and faces.

Review

Ask the children to look around the room and find red and black objects. Ask them what they like about ladybugs. What did they learn about ladybugs today?

Assessment

Show the children pictures of ladybugs and other bugs. Can they pick out which are ladybugs?

Related Poem

We Love Ladybugs by Shirley Anne Ramaley
We love ladybugs, did you know?
They eat lots of bugs, so plants will grow!

 Shirley Anne Ramaley, Sun City, AZ

Ladybugs

Learning Objectives The children will:
1. Learn about the life cycles and habits of ladybugs.
2. Develop their small and large motor skills.

Circle or Group Time Activity
- Read *The Very Lazy Ladybug* by Isobel Finn to the children.
- After reading the book, engage the children in a discussion about ladybugs.
- Show the children some images of ladybugs, and ask them to describe the specific characteristics of the insect.

Learning Centers **Art**

Give each child two paper plates. Have the children paint the bottoms of their two plates red. When dry, help them cut one of the plates in half. Provide small black construction paper circles for the children to glue to the two halves of their plate. Have them glue another black circle to the top of the uncut plate to make the head. Help them fasten the two cut halves just behind the head using brads to resemble wings. Encourage the children to draw faces using white crayon or pencil on their ladybugs.

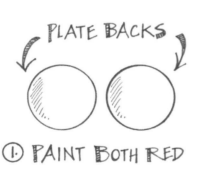

Dramatic Play

Set out several sheets of red poster board, glue, and black circular cutouts the children can attach to the poster board, making ladybug shells for themselves to wear on their backs. Help them punch holes along the edges of their shells and attach yarn to them to hold the shells on their backs.

Library

Provide a recording and copy of *Are You a Ladybug?* by Judy Allen in the center for the children to listen to and look through.

Math

Cut out 10 red construction paper ladybug shapes. Put the shapes in pairs, and draw an equal number of between one and five dots on the pairs. Mix them up, and challenge the children to find the matching ladybug cutouts by counting the numbers of dots on each.

Music

Write the following poem on a piece of poster board for the children to recite:

I'm a Little Ladybug by Cookie Zingarelli
(Tune: "I'm a Little Teapot")
I'm a little ladybug fat and round,
Here on my back my spots to be found,
I set all day on a nice big leaf,
Eating aphids nice and sweet.

Book Suggestions

Are You a Ladybug? by Judy Allen
Creepy Beetles! by Fay Robinson
Ladybug at Orchard Avenue by Kathleen Weidner Zoehfeld
Ladybug on the Move by Richard Fowler
Ladybugs: Red, Fiery, and Bright by Mia Posada
The Very Lazy Ladybug by Isobel Finn

Snack

Make a ladybug snack by providing sugar cookies, red frosting, four grapes, and two pieces of circular cereal. The children cover the cookies in frosting, put grape halves in the frosting to simulate dots, and then add the cereal "eyes."

Review

Talk about ladybugs with the children, asking different children to name facts about them.

Assessment

Show the children pictures of several different kinds of insects, and ask them to identify the ladybug. Ask them to explain how they could differentiate between the ladybug and the other insects.

 Cookie Zingarelli, Columbus, OH

Magnificent Ladybugs

Learning Objectives The children will:
1. Learn to identify ladybugs.
2. Practice counting and comparing skills.
3. Enhance their large and small motor skills.
4. Improve their oral language skills.

Circle or Group Time Activity
- Randomly set several large construction paper cutouts of green leaves and flowers on the floor, leaving several feet between them.
- Talk with the children about ladybugs. Share the following facts with the children as you show them several ladybugs or ladybug pictures.
  - A ladybug is a small round flying beetle.
  - Ladybugs have red or orange outer wings.
  - Ladybugs have black spots.
  - Ladybugs eat aphids and other insects.
  - Ladybugs hibernate in groups in the winter.
- Hand each child a paper or felt ladybug. Invite the children to "fly" their ladybug around and land on the various leaves and flowers.
- As the children bustle about, occasionally say, "Winter time—hibernate!" The children huddle together in the middle of the room.
- After a few moments, call "springtime," and release the children to go back to having their ladybugs fly around the room.
- Repeat the activity several times.
- Read *Are You a Ladybug?* by Judy Allen to the children.

Learning Centers

Art
Provide construction paper cutouts of ladybugs and invite the children to paint and decorate the cutouts. Help the children sign their names to their ladybugs.

Library
Place a recording and copy of *Ladybugs and Beetles* by Sally Morgan in the library for the children to listen to and look through.

Literacy
Write the letters of the alphabet on a large sheet of poster board. Provide the children with a ladybug-shaped beanbag. The children toss the beanbag onto the letters on the poster board and name the letter that the ladybug lands closest to.

Math
Write the numbers 1–10 on construction paper cutouts of ladybugs and challenge the children to put them in order. Also make construction paper cutouts of ladybugs with between 1 and 10 dots on their backs and challenge the children to match the corresponding ladybugs together.

Small Motor

Invite the children to cut out "ladybug" circles from red construction paper and use a black marker to add black dots on their ladybugs' backs. Help them attach several ladybugs to a strand of green yarn and display them in the classroom. Consider challenging the children to put the ladybugs in order according to the number of dots they have on their backs.

Book Suggestions

Are You a Ladybug? by Judy Allen
Ladybugs and Beetles by Sally Morgan
More Bugs? Less Bugs? by Don L. Curry and Johanna Kaufman

Snack

The children spread strawberry jam on a round cracker and top it off with raisins. Children will enjoy this spotted ladybug snack.

Review

Recite the following song with the children:

I'm a Little Ladybug by Mary J. Murray
(Tune: "I'm a Little Teapot")
I'm a little ladybug round and red.
I have six legs and a tiny head.
I have many spots upon my wings.
I fly and land on lots of things.

Assessment

Ask the children to describe ladybugs. Make a drawing based on their descriptions. When finished, compare the illustration to an actual image of a ladybug, and ask the children to describe the similarities and differences.

 *Mary J. Murray, Mazomanie, WI*

Spinning a Web

Learning Objectives The children will:
1. Learn that spiders have eight legs.
2. Practice their counting skills.
3. Improve their large and small motor skills.

Circle or Group Time Activity
- Gather the children in a circle. Show the children a spider-web design made of string on black paper, and ask them to guess what today's lesson is about.
- After the children determine that they will be learning about spiders, engage them in a discussion about spiders. Explain to the children that a spider is an insect, called an arachnid, and that most spiders spin webs and all have eight legs.
- Invite one child to hold onto the end of a string from a ball of yarn, and to roll the ball to a friend across the circle.
- That child picks up the yarn, holds onto a portion of it, and rolls it to someone else in the circle.
- Continue in this manner as the class spins a spider web. Then drop a spider-shaped beanbag into the web, along with a few plastic toy insects on the web as well for the spider to eat.

Learning Centers

Art
Provide several individual cutout cups from egg crates. The children attach two circular stickers to the cup, and then insert four chenille stems through one side, and another four through the opposite side. Help the children poke a small hole through the top of the crate, and insert a length of yarn the children can use to raise and lower the spider.

Large Motor
Make a large spider web by wrapping yarn between the legs of various chairs and tables, leaving space for the children to step through. The children then go through the yarn as though it were a spidery obstacle course.

Math
Set out construction paper cutouts of various spiders, each with a different number of legs and the corresponding digit written on the spider's back. Invite the children to put them in the correct order.

Science
Set out a fish tank with a real spider in it. Provide a magnifying glass and a book about spiders beside the tank so the children can observe and learn about the class pet.

Small Motor
Invite the children to wind lengths of colorful yarn through slits cut into paper plates, making a web design.

Book Suggestions   *Aaaarrgghh! Spider* by Lydia Monks
Diary of a Spider by Doreen Cronin
Little Miss Spider by David Kirk

Snack   Set out eight lengths of licorice per child, and show the children how to attach the licorice to marshmallows to make edible spiders.

Review   Display a collection of plastic spider rings on a paper spider web. Invite children to slide the web around the circle and select a ring to keep as they share something they've learned about spiders.

Assessment   Display an assortment of plastic insects and spiders. Have the children select the spiders from the tray and display them on their hands and climbing up their arms. Ask the children how they were able to identify the spiders from among the other insects.

Related Song   Recite "Little Miss Muffet" or "The Itsy Bitsy Spider" with the children.

Mary J. Murray, Mazomanie, WI

What Is an Insect?

Learning Objectives The children will:
1. Learn that insects have six legs.
2. Discover why insects are important.
3. Learn that insects come from eggs.
4. Discover where insects can be found.

Circle or Group Time Activity
- Show the children several pictures of different insects and talk with them about what the insects all have in common and how they are different.
- Talk about the life cycle of insects and introduce new vocabulary words, such as "egg," "larvae," and "insects."
- Discuss why insects are necessary in the world. Talk about how they help pollinate flowers, make honey, and provide a food source for larger animals.
- Look at real insects or plastic insects and point out the parts of the insects bodies: antenna, six legs, thorax, and abdomen.

Learning Centers
Art
Draw outlines of various insects on sheets of construction paper. Invite the children to paint the insects, and then label the various parts of their bodies.
Blocks
Put plastic insects in the Blocks Center and encourage the children to make block homes for the insects.
Dramatic Play
Put out picnic props and plastic ants and invite the children to have a pretend picnic.
Math
Put plastic spiders and insects on a tray. The children count the legs on the different plastic creatures and then sort them into two categories: spiders and insects.
Science
Put real insects in jars for the children to observe. Ladybugs and other insects are available for purchase at plant nurseries.
Small Motor
Collect 24 juice lids and place 12 pairs of insect stickers on the tops of the lids. Set them out face-down and challenge the children to a game of memory.

Book Suggestions
Ladybug on the Move by Richard Fowler
Ladybugs: Red, Fiery, and Bright by Mia Posada
The Magic School Bus Gets Ants in Their Pants by Joanna Cole
The Very Quiet Cricket by Eric Carle

Snack
Serve fruit and honey.

Review
Ask the children to tell you what they know about insects. Copy this information onto construction paper, and then provide the children with markers and crayons so they can illustrate the pages.

Assessment
Can the children tell the difference between insects and spiders based on the number of legs on each creature?

Related Fingerplay
The Beehive (Traditional)
Here is the beehive, (close fist)
But where are the bees?
They are hiding inside so nobody sees.
Now they come creeping out of the hive,
Let's count them, 1, 2, 3, 4, 5. (unfold one finger at a time)
Bzzzzzzzzzzzzzz, (move fingers around)
Back in the hive! (zoom hand into other fist)

 *Holly Dzierzanowski, Brenham, TX*

Worms

Learning Objectives The children will:
1. Observe how worms live.
2. Discover what worms eat.
3. Develop their literacy skills.

Circle or Group time Activity
- Read *Diary of a Worm* by Doreen Cronin to the children. After finishing the book, engage the children in a discussion about worms.
- Ask the children where they see worms, and to describe them to one another.
- Teach the children the following song, and invite them to make the movements the song describes:

Worm, Worm by Cookie Zingarelli
(Tune: "Teddy Bear, Teddy Bear, Turn Around")
Worm, Worm, wiggle around. (wiggle around)
Dig a hole in the ground. (pretend to dig)
Worm, Worm, wiggle around. (wiggle around)
Worm, Worm, that will do. (turn around)

- Share these worm facts with the children:
  - Baby worms hatch from a cocoon that is smaller than a piece of rice.
  - Most earthworms are no more than 1' long. In Australia and Southern Africa, some giant earthworms can reach over 6' when stretched out.
  - Earthworms have no teeth so they coat their food with saliva to aid digestion.
  - The bodies of worms have small, invisible bristles that they use to grip the walls of their tunnels as they move through the soil.
  - As the worms travel through the soil, digging, eating and digesting, they improve the quality of the soil. Their waste material, called castings, contain nutrients that are valuable for plants.
  - Earthworms have a very important job because they recycle leaves that can then be reused by other organisms.
  - In the winter, worms curl up in underground shelters known as burrows.
  - There are over 1,800 different species of earthworms all over the world.
  - The largest earthworm ever found was in South Africa and measured 22' from nose to tail tip.

Learning Centers

Art
Provide several fake worms (available wherever fishing supplies are sold), paper, and tempera paint, and invite the children to paint using the worms. They can make slithery shapes, coil the worms, or use them in any way they can think of.

Large Motor
Make a line on the ground and challenge the children to have worm races by slithering along on the ground, moving the way they think worms would move.

Literacy
Set out sheets of paper with the word *Worm* written on it, along with several plastic worms. Invite the children to shape the worms into the forms of the letters.

Math
Using red construction board, cut out 1–10 red apple shapes. Put a number on each apple, and punch the same number of holes in it. Cut out several brown construction paper worm shapes (laminate if possible) and invite the children to put the correct number of worms through the holes in each of the numbered apple shapes.

Science
Set out a large glass jar with dirt, coffee grounds, and several real worms in it. Encourage the children to observe the worms. Set a magnifying glass out by the jar so the children can observe the worms more closely. Consider adding food scraps to the jar so the children can observe what happens to the scraps over time.

Book Suggestions

Diary of a Worm by Doreen Cronin
Inch by Inch by Leo Leonni
Wonderful Worms by Linda Glaser

Snack

Make worm pretzels with the children. Set out bread dough and let the children roll the dough into long "worm" shapes. Blend together an egg yolk and 2 tablespoons of water and have the children brush some of the mixture on their worm pretzels. Sprinkle some coarse salt or sesame seeds onto the worms. Lay their worms on a cookie sheet lined with a baking sheet and bake at 450 degrees for 12 minutes. Have fun!

Review

Ask the children to recite the song they learning in Circle or Group Time.

Assessment

Can the child name some facts about worms?

 *Cookie Zingarelli, Columbus, OH*

Worms and Measurement

Learning Objectives   The children will:
1. Learn about worms and how they live.
2. Use worms as a form of measurement.
3. Practice measuring things around the room.
4. Discuss the characteristics of a worm.

Circle or Group Time Activity

- Before doing this activity, cut construction paper into 1" segments and write *one inch* on them.
- Engage the children in a discussion about measurement. Ask the children if they have heard the word *inch* before.
- Talk to the children about inchworms.
- Show the children the paper inchworms and have them use the inchworms to measure various things in the classroom. When they are done, have them come back and report on the lengths of the objects they measured.
- On poster board or chart paper, write down all of the objects the children measured, as well as their sizes.

Learning Centers

Art
Precut leaf shapes from green construction paper. Provide leaf shapes and pompoms. Invite the children to glue the pompoms to the leaf shapes to make inchworms and to use scissors to make small jagged cuts along the edge of the paper to look like the worm has been munching on its edge.

Blocks
Add rubber worms to the Blocks Center and encourage the children to make tunnels for the worms to move through.

Sand and Water
Add dirt and worms to the sensory table. Be sure to continue to add water so that the worms do not dry out.

Science
If possible, set up a worm habitat so the children can see the tunnels that the worms create in the dirt (you may be able to create your own with resources found on the Internet).

Small Motor
Play a worm match with craft sticks. Draw matching pairs of worm faces on the ends of several craft sticks, separate the pairs, and stick one from each pair of faces down in two separate containers of sand. The children take turns picking up one

stick from each container and checking to see if the faces match. If they do, the child who picked them continues by picking two more. If they do not match, another child picks two sticks. Continue until the children match all the pairs.

Snack and Cooking

Make "dirt cups" by giving the children crushed Oreo cookies, chocolate pudding, and gummy worms to mix into cups. Use clear cups so that the children can see the "dirt."

Book Suggestions

Inch by Inch by Leo Lionni
Inch Worm and a Half by Elinor J. Pinczes
The Very Hungry Caterpillar by Eric Carle

Snack

The children enjoy the "dirt cups" they made in the Snack and Cooking Center.

Review

Ask the children to measure a specific item using construction paper cutouts of inchworms.

Assessment

Can the child explain where worms live and how they move?

Sandy L. Scott, Meridian, ID

Beginning Letter Sounds

Learning Objectives   The children will:

1. Say beginning letter sounds.
2. Name the letter corresponding to beginning sounds.

Circle or Group Time Activity

- Place a variety of objects that all start with the same letter in a large box, one for each child (for example, cup, carrot, pompom caterpillar, car).

- Invite each child to take one item from the box and identify it. Explain that all of the items have the same beginning sound, then say the beginning sound slowly.
- As items are revealed, encourage all the children to repeat the names of items to hear the beginning sound. Teach children the corresponding letter name.
- Tape each child naming an item (save this for the Listening Center activity).

Learning Centers   **Art**

Provide magazines, construction paper, scissors, and glue. Ask children to find pictures of things that start with the same letter, cut them out, and make a collage.

Listening

Play the tape recording of the children naming the items taken from the box during Circle or Group Time.

Literacy

Give each child paper and crayons. Ask them to choose items that start with each letter of the alphabet and write one on each sheet of paper. Encourage them to illustrate their pages. Bind all of the pages together with yarn or staples to make individualized alphabet books for each child.

Science

Provide plush animals for children to name and play with. Have them identify the beginning letters of each animal.

Outdoors
Make a mural with the children. Hang a large piece of bulletin board outdoors and invite the children to paint or color on it. Before starting, choose a letter and brainstorm words that begin with that letter. Write the words on a list and keep it handy for the children to refer to when painting.

Book Suggestions *A My Name Is Alice* by Jane E. Bayer
You're Adorable by Buddy Kaye, Fred Wise, and Sidney Lippman

Snack Provide snacks that begin with the letter the children are learning about.

Review Repeat the Group or Circle Time activity with new items, but this time the teacher removes each item and the children call out names together. Intentionally place a few items in the box that do not begin with the correct letter, and demonstrate how the beginning sound is different.

Assessment Show a child an assortment of objects and ask him to name them and identify which have the same beginning letter as was studied in class.

Related Song Sing the alphabet song or "A You're Adorable" with the children.

 *Karyn F. Everham, Fort Myers, FL*

Days of the Week

Learning Objectives The children will:
1. Recite the days of the week in order.
2. Improve their oral language skills.
3. Enhance their large and fine motor skills.
4. Learn about the calendar and measuring time.

Circle or Group Time Activity

- Before doing this activity, make "day-of-the-week" word-picture cards, using the suggestions below. Write the words and draw or find a picture to illustrate. These pictures will help children to read the words as they associate another word with a similar sound.
    - Sunday (image of the sun)
    - Monday (image of a monkey)
    - Tuesday (image of the number 2)
    - Wednesday (image of a clock)
    - Thursday (image of a cup of water)
    - Friday (image of a frying pan)
    - Saturday (image of a chair)

- Hang the cards on the walls around the room, in order, in a clockwise direction.
- Introduce the children to the topic of the days of the week by pointing out the days of the week on the class calendar.
- Next, walk around the room in a clockwise direction, reciting the names of the days aloud and drawing the children's attention to the cards. Ask them if they see a correlation between the images and the names of the days.
- Invite children to line up beneath the Sunday word card, and then walk to each card and recite the names of each day.

■ After the children move through the days of the week a few times, bring them back into a circle and recite the days of the week. Then sing the following song:

Seven Days in a Week (Traditional)
(Tune: "The Bear Went Over the Mountain")
There are seven days in a week,
Seven days in a week,
Seven days in a week and I can say them all.
Sunday, Monday, Tuesday, Wednesday, Thursday,
Friday, Saturday, and Sunday.
I can say them all.

Learning Centers

Art
Invite the children to paint or use markers to decorate each square on a calendar page as they recite the days of the week. Encourage the children to decorate each square in a unique way.

Dramatic Play
Provide puppets for children to manipulate as they talk about the various days of the week. For example, a bear puppet might say, "I am going to hunt for fish in the creek on Monday. On Tuesday, I will hibernate in my cave."

Large Motor
Ask children to hop like frogs from one "days-of-the-week" card to another, croaking out the names of the days they pass.

Literacy
Put out four sets of cards with the names of the days of the week written on each for the children to match or put them in order.

Math
Set out "days-of-the-week" word strips in chronological order. Ask the children to place a paper square beneath each word and recite the day aloud. Have children lay out four rows of squares beneath the strips, creating a four-week calendar.

Small Motor
Set out calendars and child-safe scissors, inviting the children to cut the words off a calendar and then paste them in order on another sheet of paper.

Book Suggestions
A Busy Guy by Charnan Simon
Day by Day a Week Goes Round by Carol Diggory Shields

Snack
Enjoy any snack and recite simple statements signaling children to eat the snack. "On Sunday I ate two carrots. On Monday I ate one grape," and so on.

Review
Make a row of seven Xs on the floor with masking tape. Invite the children to jump from X to X, reciting the days of the week in order as they go.

Assessment
Display a row of seven colored blocks. Invite the children to say the seven days of the week in order as they touch the seven squares.

 *Mary J. Murray, Mazomanie, WI*

Giants

Learning Objectives The children will:
1. Learn about real giants.
2. Learn empathy for those who are different.
3. Make size comparisons.
4. Express themselves dramatically.
5. Practice social skills, such as listening and talking in a group.
6. Understand and apply the term "giant" to things other than mythical people.

Circle or Group Time Activity
■ Have the children bring in their favorite books featuring giants. Make sure you have a supply of books about giants for those who have none of their own.
■ Let children either show the group their favorite illustration or tell the others what they think is the best thing about the book.
■ Talk about how giants are different. Ask the children if they think giants are real. Explain that some people might be very tall, but they are not "giants."

Learning Centers

Blocks
Ask the smallest child (make sure the child volunteers for this) to stand beside the tallest adult in the class. Have the children build towers of blocks to show comparisons between a small child, an adult, and a giant (for example, three blocks for a child, six blocks for a man, nine for a giant).

Dramatic Play
After reading the story of "Jack and the Beanstalk," say the giant's chant: "Fee, fie, foe, fum, I smell the blood of an Englishman! Be he alive, or be he dead, I'll grind his bones to make my bread." Make this as dramatic as possible, then get the children to practice it. Then get everyone to demonstrate how scarily they can chant it. Let them do this individually or in groups, according to their level of self-confidence.
Note: This may be too scary for some children, especially younger children. If so, just say, "Fee, fie, foe, fum!"

Literacy
Read stories about giants, including Goliath and Paul Bunyan. Draw a giant on a large piece of paper and ask the children to brainstorm words to describe the giant. Write their words around the giant, with their help if they are able. Read each word and ask the children if it could describe someone who isn't a giant. Ask them what this tells us about giants. Explain that we apply the term "giant" to many things other than large mythical people or creatures, such as "giants" of history, sport, music, and so on.

Math

Hang a height chart on the wall. Mark the heights of all the children and adults in the class. Then mark the heights of the tallest man ever (8' 1"), and the tallest man (7' 9") and tallest woman (7') alive today. Ask them questions such as, "Who is the tallest child?" "Who is the tallest adult present?" If there are any twins or siblings, compare their heights. Help them work out how many times a child could fit into the body of the tallest person today.

Snack and Cooking

Cutting food in a different way than usual can give the children experience of "giant" servings. For example, instead of serving bananas as a pile of small slices, cut each banana into four length-wise pieces. Cut a baguette lengthwise into long, narrow pieces. Invite the children to spread their slice with soft cheese, peanut butter, or a simple ranch dip.

Book Suggestions

The Giant of Seville: A "Tall" Tale Based on a True Story by Dan Andreasen
Giants Have Feeling Too/Jack and the Beanstalk by Alvin Grawowsky
Jack and the Beanstalk by Anne Adeney
My Daddy Is a Giant by Carl Norac
When Giants Come to Play by Andrea Beaty

Snack

Serve the giant nibbles the children prepared in the Snack and Cooking Center.

Review

Ask the children who is bigger: their tallest family members, or a giant.

Assessment

In pictures, can the children differentiate between giants and people of normal size?

 Anne Adeney, Plymouth, United Kingdom

Introducing Laura Ingalls Wilder

Learning Objectives The children will:
1. Learn about the author Laura Ingalls Wilder.
2. Discover the similarities and differences between pioneer life and life today.
3. Become aware of the concepts *then* and *now*.
4. Make and taste a "pioneer" food.

Circle or Group Time Activity

- Teach children the following traditional rhyme:

  Wait for the wagon, wait for the wagon,
  Wait for the wagon and we'll all take a ride.

- Once the children know this chorus, invite them to move around the room pretending to "drive" a wagon while holding imaginary reins.
- Choose one child to be the driver. The driver starts by moving through the room alone, then stops by each child so everyone can get on the "wagon" (following the driver).
- After a short while, announce that the wagon needs to "change drivers," and have the driver get off the wagon, so that the child behind the driver becomes the new driver. Repeat this until everyone has had a turn to drive.
- After all the children have had a chance to drive, show the children a picture of Laura Ingalls Wilder, and talk with them about who she was and the books she wrote. Explain that she spent part of her childhood in wagons, traveling west.
- Read one of her books to the children. Many of her stories are short storybooks with illustrations.

Learning Centers

Art
Provide paper and coloring tools. Let children draw a picture illustrating a scene from one of the suggested books, or let them draw "little houses" of their own.

Blocks
Put plastic farm animals in the center so the children can create a little house or farm for them to live on.

Dramatic Play
Provide old clothes or period costumes and invite the children to dress up and pretend they are living long ago. Ask each child to look around the room and find one item Laura might have used (pencils, books, a dress, and so on). Ask them to look around the room and find one item Laura would never have used (computers, electric lights, backpacks, and so on).

Music
"Skip to My Lou" is a traditional song that was popular in Laura Ingalls Wilder's era. Find a copy of the lyrics and sing the song with the children.

Small Motor

Provide children with a square of white cardboard (4" x 6") and pass out strips of construction paper, glue sticks, and child-safe scissors. Show children a picture of a quilt. Let them cut the colored paper into interesting shapes and glue them on the cardboard to make their own "quilt."

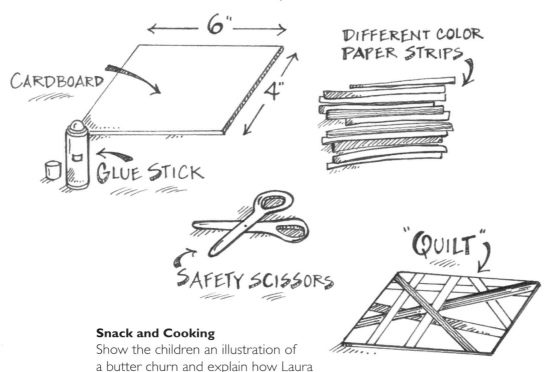

Snack and Cooking

Show the children an illustration of a butter churn and explain how Laura Ingall Wilder's family had to make most of their own food and clothing. Give each child a baby-food jar with 1–2 teaspoons of heavy cream inside. Children shake the jars until butter forms. **Note:** Chilled cream works faster.

Book Suggestions

County Fair by Laura Ingalls Wilder
Dance at Grandpa's by Laura Ingalls Wilder
A Little House Birthday by Laura Ingalls Wilder
Sugar Snow by Laura Ingalls Wilder
Summertime in the Big Woods by Laura Ingalls Wilder

Snack

Serve the butter the children made on crackers. Other authentic pioneer food could include apple slices, licorice, hoarhound candy, beef jerky, or popcorn.

Review

Ask the children to remember one thing they learned about Laura Ingalls Wilder or pioneer life. Let each child give an answer.

Assessment

Make two columns on the blackboard or paper, one titled "Now" and and one titled "Then." Ask children to list items we use now and items Laura used then.

 *Donna Alice Patton, Hillsboro, OH*

The Letter B

Learning Objectives The children will:
1. Identify the sound of the letter B.
2. Practice writing the letter B.
3. Develop small motor skills.

Circle or Group Time Activity
- Engage the children in a discussion about the letter B.
- Ask the children to name some words that begin with the letter B.
- Show the children several flashcards of various objects, and ask them to say the names of the objects, and then say whether the names of the objects begin with the letter B.

Learning Centers
Art
Provide paper and crayons. Ask the children to draw a brown bear holding a blue balloon.
Blocks
Using blocks, the children make the shape of the letter B.

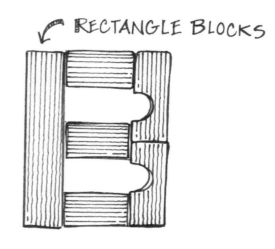

← RECTANGLE BLOCKS

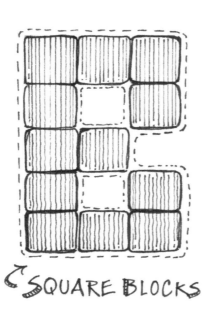

↖ SQUARE BLOCKS

Dramatic Play

Play the "Big Boat B" game. Tell the children to pretend they are a big boat. Tell them to softly and continuously repeat the /b/ sound. Tell them to chug using the /b/ sound and look around the classroom for things that start with B. List them on the board (book, block, blue, boat, boy, brown).

Small Motor

Blow up a blue balloon. The children sit in a circle, toss the balloon in the air, and gently tap the balloon to keep it in the air. Ask each child to say a word that starts with B when they tap the ball.

Snack and Cooking

Pour heavy cream into a jar with a lid. Screw the lid on tightly. Give the children turns to shake the jar back and forth until the heavy cream turns to butter.

Writing

Set out several sheets of paper with both uppercase and lowercase versions of the letter B on them for the children to trace over with their fingers. Set out blue markers and paint and encourage the children to make their own blue Bs. After they copy the letter B, encourage the children to make a drawing of something that starts with the letter B.

Book Suggestions

ABC by Dr. Seuss
Andy Learns the Letter Bb by J.P. Curington
Bernard, Me, and the Letter B by Cynthia Fitterer Klingel and Robert B. Noyed

Snack

Serve slices of bread with the butter the children made in the Snack and Cooking Center.

Review

Given an assortment of objects, ask the children to identify things that begin the letter B.

Assessment

Given a worksheet with pictures of a balloon, ball, cat, bread, carrot, and boat, can the child distinguish the things with names that begin with the letter B from those with names that do not begin with the letter B?

 *Lynn Smaagaard, Minneapolis, MN*

Letters of the Alphabet

Learning Objectives   The children will:
1. Gain familiarity with one of the letters of the alphabet.
2. Visually discriminate and name one of the letters of the alphabet.

Circle or Group Time Activity
- Give one wooden or clay letter to each child and tell them the name of the letter.
- Ask them to hold it in their palm and feel the shape, run their finger over the top with eyes open and again with eyes closed, sandwich the letter between their palms, put it in their lap, and by memory trace the shape of letter in their palm with their finger.
- Then ask questions, such as "What does it feel like?" "What does the shape remind you of?"

Learning Centers   ### Art
Provide paint for children to paint wood or clay letters. As an art and small motor activity for older children, provide modeling clay for them to make their own letters. Let them dry overnight and then have the children paint them.

Blocks
Draw a letter on poster board and tape it onto the floor. Encourage the children to place blocks over the letter, imitating its shape.

Math
Show children how to make a stamp with a wooden letter by brushing poster paint on one side then pressing it onto a piece of paper. After they have made as many stamps as desired, count them, and write, "_____ (child's name) has _____(number of stamps) Cs."

Sand and Water
Hide several letters in the sand. Let children dig for buried letter treasure.

Small Motor
Using a wooden letter, show the children how to trace it on a piece of paper.

Book Suggestions   *The Alphabet Book* by P.D. Eastman
Chicka Chicka ABC by Bill Martin, Jr. and John Archambault
Dr. Seuss's ABC: An Amazing Alphabet Book by Dr. Seuss
Miss Spider's ABC by David Kirk

Snack   Serve alphabet soup and ask children to name the letters they see.

Review   Set out several sheets of construction paper with letters written on them, so they are in the pattern of a hopscotch board. Invite the children to take turns calling out letters, and having other children hop to and stop on the correct letter.

Assessment   Given an assortment of letters, can the child find the letter you studied?

Karyn F. Everham, Fort Myers, FL

The Lion and the Mouse

Learning Objectives   The children will:
1. Participate in storytelling.
2. Gain awareness of helpful and kind behavior.

Circle or Group Time Activity
- Prior to the activity, learn the very short story "The Lion and the Mouse," found in *The McElderry Book of Aesop's Fables* by Michael Morpurgo, well enough to tell without the book. Use plush animals and a hairnet as props.
- Talk about fables with the children. Explain that they are stories with animals that teach a lesson.
- Invite children to participate in storytelling: When the mouse begs the lion, "Please, please, don't eat me," ask the children to say, "Please, please, don't eat the mouse!" When the mouse gnaws at the net ropes to free the lion, ask the children to say, "Gnaw, little mouse! You can do it!"

Learning Centers   **Art**
Dilute brown and gold poster paint with water. Cut off the fingers of old child-size gloves to use as finger puppets. Have children make lion hand puppets by painting a mitten with gold paint and decorating a face. Children can make mouse finger puppets by painting a glove finger with brown paint and adding mouse features. Use the puppets to retell the story.

Dramatic Play

Encourage children to act out the story with their puppets from the Art Center activity.

Listening

Encourage children to listen to animal sounds tape. Challenge them to pick out the lions' roars.

Literacy

Ask children to complete the sentence: "I help_____." At the end of the day, post all of the sentences by the front door of class for family members to read.

Science

Set up a cage with a live mouse for the children to observe. (Contact a local pet store; feeder mice are often available at a very low cost.)

Book Suggestions

Frederick by Leo Lionni
The McElderry Book of Aesop's Fables by Michael Morpurgo
Roar! by Pamela Duncan Edwards

Snack

Make Marshmallow Mice with the children. Push two raisin "eyes" into one end of a large marshmallow, and add a licorice "tail" in the back.

Review

Share with the children all of the responses provided in the Literacy Center activity.

Assessment

Tell the story of the lion and the mouse again with the children's help. Ask the children what they think might happen next if the story continued after the mouse helped the lion.

 *Karyn F. Everham, Fort Myers, FL*

Pease Porridge Hot

Learning Objectives The children will:
1. Learn and repeat a nursery rhyme.
2. Engage in cooperative movement with another child.
3. Taste and describe oatmeal porridge.

Circle or Group Time Activity
■ With the children, recite the following classic nursery rhyme:

Pease Porridge Hot (Traditional)
Pease porridge hot,
Pease porridge cold,
Pease porridge in the pot
Nine days old.

Some like it hot,
Some like it cold,
Some like it in the pot,
Nine days old.

■ Ask children, "What is porridge?" "Who has tasted porridge?" Explain that there are different types of porridge eaten all over the world. It can be made from oats, rice, cornmeal, and many other foods. "Pease" porridge is made from dried peas.
■ Have the children recite the rhyme two times.
■ Pair the children. Demonstrate a simple hand clap pattern to do while reciting the rhyme. The children start with a clap and then clap their partner's hands. Repeat (clap on "pease," clap partner's hands on "hot," and so on).

Learning Centers

Art
Provide small paper plates, buttons, sequins, dried rice or other small grains, glue, and paint. Encourage children to create a plate of "porridge."

Dramatic Play
Provide bowls, spoons, and aprons for children to use for pretend play.

Literacy
Ask children to draw a picture of porridge. Ask them, "How do you make your porridge?" Write down their "recipes." Bind together in a class "Porridge Cookbook."

Math
Provide pictures of things that are hot and things that are cold. Encourage children to sort the items into "hot" and "cold" groups.

Sand and Water
Add spoons and bowls to the sand table. Recite the rhyme with children while they play in the sand.

Book Suggestions
Goldilocks and the Three Bears by Jan Brett
The Magic Porridge Pot by Paul Galdone
Mary Engelbreit's Mother Goose by Mary Engelbreit

Snack
Make crock-pot oatmeal. To make 16 small servings, combine two cups of rolled oats, a teaspoon of salt, and four cups of water in a crock-pot. Cook on low for 8–10 hours. Let the children choose their toppings. Good choices include milk, berries, sunflower seeds, brown sugar, banana slices, chopped apples, or other fruit. Ask children to describe what the different toppings taste like. At the end of snack, take a poll (using raised hands) to learn which toppings were the children's favorites.

Review
Have the whole group recite the rhyme in different voices, such as quiet voices, baby voices, loud voices, or in animal talk using words like "meow" or "moo."

Assessment
If given the first part of the lines in the nursery rhyme, can child state the rhyming pairs?
Pease porridge _____,
Pease porridge _____,
Pease porridge in the _____
Nine days _____.

Related Song
Substitute other foods for "porridge" in the "Pease Porridge" rhyme:
Pizza hot,
Pizza cold,
Pizza in the pot,
Nine days old.

Macaroni hot,
Macaroni cold,
Macaroni in the pot,
Nine days old.

 Cassandra Reigel Whetstone, Folsom, CA

Rhyme Time

Learning Objectives The children will:
1. Learn how to rhyme.
2. Rhyme words that end in "ack."
3. Learn about initial sounds.
4. Understand word families.

Circle or Group Time Activity

- Make a list of "ack"-family words on sentence strips and hang them on a wall or board.
- Read *I Saw an Ant on the Railroad Track* by Joshua Prince to the children. Ask them to put their thumbs up or down when they hear an "ack" word.
- After reading the book write a few sentences from the story on sentence strips. At the end of these sentences, leave off the rhyming "ack" words and challenge the children to use the word cards on the wall to fill in the missing word. Read the sentences with the children to make sure that they make sense.
- Tell the children that they will be learning about rhyming today.

Learning Centers

Art
Provide paper, magazines, scissors, and glue. Encourage the children to use the materials to find pictures that rhyme. For example, children can find and attach pictures of a cat, a hat, a mat, and a rat.

Dramatic Play
Pick a nursery rhyme and provide props to go with it so that children can recite and act it out.

Library
Place recordings and copies of rhyming books for children to listen to in this center. This will help children hear and recognize different rhymes.

Math
Pick a rhyme with counting in it for the children to act out. Provide number cards the children can use to see the numbers in the rhyme as they say them.

Small Motor
Give the children nursery rhyme puzzles to put together.

Writing
Ask each child to come up with a one-sentence rhyme or two words that rhyme, and copy the words or sentence onto a sheet of paper for the children. Encourage the children to illustrate their pages. Bind all the papers together and place the "Book of Rhymes" in the library for the children to read.

Book Suggestions   *The Flea's Sneeze* by Lynn Downey
A Frog in the Bog by Karma Wilson
I Saw an Ant on the Railroad Track by Joshua Prince
Jake Baked the Cake by B.G. Hennessy
Miss Mary Mack by Mary Ann Hoberman
Skip to My Lou by Nadine Bernard Westcott

Snack   Make Ants on a Track with the children. Provide two short pretzel logs, cream cheese, raisins, and five pretzel sticks. Show children how to put pretzel logs parallel. Using a plastic knife, demonstrate how to spread cream cheese on top of pretzel logs, place pretzel sticks across logs, and add raisins.

Review   Provide a picture of a tree and images of 10 other objects (such as a bee, bug, knee, flea, car, three, key, cat, fish, and boy). Remind the children that they will be looking for things that rhyme with tree. Name the thing in each picture and have the children say whether or not they rhyme.

Assessment   Give the children two different pictures (one of a bug and another of a car, for example). Provide the child with pictures of objects whose names rhyme with either word. For example, *rug, hug, jug, tug, slug, chug, bar, tar, jar, far,* and *star.* Can the child sort the images into two rhyming piles?

Related Song   Sing the classic children's rhyme "Jack and Jill" with the children.

Quazonia Quarles, Newark, DE

Air and Wind

Learning Objectives The children will:
1. Learn that air is everywhere.
2. Learn that wind is moving air.
3. Introduce the idea of heavy and light.
4. Learn that air is invisible.

Circle or Group Time Activity

- Ask the children what they know about the air and wind. Ask them if they can see the air.
- Show the children a hair dryer and several different types of balls (ping pong balls, golf balls, tennis balls, and so on). Talk about what the hair dryer blows out.
- Demonstrate the different speeds of the hair dryer then let older children try moving the balls around with the hair dryer. For younger children, do this for them and allow them to observe. (Note: Supervise closely.)
- Talk about why some of the balls move faster than other balls. Introduce the words *light* and *heavy*.
- Give each child a straw to use to blow Styrofoam balls across the circle to friends. Encourage them to try this with cotton balls, feathers, and other objects.
- Talk about how our bodies have air inside and how we breathe air in using our lungs.
- Illustrate how our lungs work using a balloon. Blow up balloon to show how lungs breathe in air (inflate) and then let the air out of the balloon to show how our lungs release air (deflate).
- Talk about how all people need clean air to breathe. (This is a perfect time to introduce the children to the topic of air pollution.)

Learning Centers ### Art

Set out several straws, construction paper, and two containers of red and blue paint. Encourage the children to put dabs of each color of paint on their papers, and then to use the straws to blow them together until they make purple. Thin the paint with water so it is easier to blow. Also consider dipping cotton balls in paint for the children to blow over paper, and compare the different patterns the cotton balls leave.

Blocks

Put various balls in the Blocks Center and encourage the children to make mazes through which the balls can travel. Challenge the children to push the balls through the mazes by blowing on them or waving at them with blocks or sheets of paper.

Library
Set out a recording and copy of *The Wind Blew* by Pat Hutchins for the children to listen to and explore.

Sand and Water
Fill a tub with water. Place Styrofoam balls inside the tub for the children to blow around the water. Consider adding soap to the tub so the children can blow the balls around in the bubbly water.

Science
Find some fallen sticks outside that still have a few leaves attached to them. Bring the sticks inside, place them beside a fan, and invite the children to take turns blowing the leaves off the sticks with the fan, like the wind blows leaves off tree branches.

Writing
Ask the children to dictate a story to you about a windy day. Afterward, give them the sheets of paper and encourage them to illustrate their stories.

Book Suggestions
Gilberto and the Wind by Marie Hall Ets
The Sun, the Wind, and the Rain by Lisa Westberg Peters
The Wind Blew by Pat Hutchins

Snack
Serve rice cakes and pears to the children. As they take bites from each, ask them to think about how easy or difficult it would be to blow the two foods.

Review
On a large sheet of chart paper, make two columns. Write "heavy" on one column and "light" on the other column. Set out a variety of objects, from feathers to books, and ask the children to blow on them with a straw, and then blow on them with a fan. Ask the children say which items were "light," and which items were "heavy."

Assessment
Does the child illustrate an understanding that the air is invisible, and that it surrounds us?

 *Holly Dzierzanowski, Brenham, TX*

Caves

Learning Objectives The children will:
1. Understand "out" and "in."
2. Learn about caves.
3. Develop their small motor skills.

Circle or Group Time Activity

- Show several pictures of caves, and engage the children in a discussion about caves. Explain that caves have "chambers" or rooms and they are found in the sides of hills, mountains, and cliffs, and sometimes even in the ocean.
- Show the children a small box draped in a scarf of small blanket, and explain to them that this is the class "cave." Show the children a stuffed bear, and ask the children what a bear might do inside a cave (sleep), and what it might do outside the cave (hunt or gather food).
- Walk the bear "in" the cave and put bear to sleep. Ask, "Where is the bear?"
- Wake the bear up and walk it "out" of the cave to hunt for food and water. Ask, "Where is the bear now?"
- Invite the children to help move the bear in and out of the cave.

Learning Centers ### Art
Tape brown paper cut from paper bags to the underside of a table. Provide crayons and invite the children to crawl into the "cave" and make "cave paintings."
Blocks
Provide blocks, scarves or baby blankets, and small toy animals or dolls and encourage the children to build small caves for the animals or dolls.
Dramatic Play
Create "caves" from small tents, large cardboard boxes, or chairs and sheets. Put a few toy animals in the caves. When children are playing, ask them "Who is in the cave?" and "Who is out of the cave?"
Small Motor
Encourage children to use playdough or modeling clay to create caves.
Snack and Cooking
Provide graham crackers and cream cheese frosting to use as glue. Help children put two halves of graham crackers together to form a triangle. Use just enough frosting to glue the crackers together. Put in small bowls or plates and if possible chill the cracker caves until snack time.

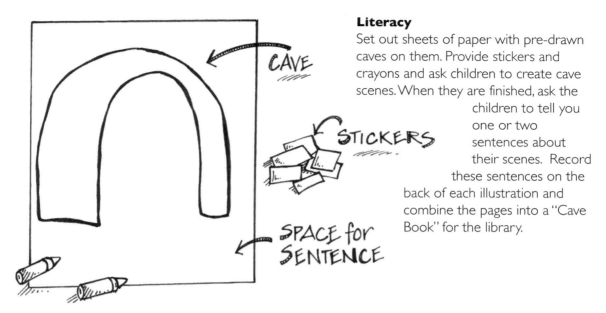

Literacy
Set out sheets of paper with pre-drawn caves on them. Provide stickers and crayons and ask children to create cave scenes. When they are finished, ask the children to tell you one or two sentences about their scenes. Record these sentences on the back of each illustration and combine the pages into a "Cave Book" for the library.

Book Suggestions *Bear Snores On* by Karma Wilson
Good Night, Good Knight by Shelley Moore Thomas
We're Going on a Bear Hunt by Michael Rosen

Snack Serve cracker caves with a handful of berries on each plate. As children are eating, ask them how many berries are in their caves and how many are out of their caves.

Review Using the props from circle time, put the bear inside the cave and ask "Where is the bear?" (in the cave) and "What is he doing?" (sleeping). Take the bear out of the cave and ask, "Where is the bear now?" (out of the cave). Say, "That's right, and he's come out to say goodbye to you!"

Assessment When asked, can the child put an object in a box and out of a box? Can the child correctly state whether the object is in or out of the box?

Related Song **Bear Is Sleeping** by Cassandra Reigel Whetstone
(Tune: "Mary Had a Little Lamb")

Bear is sleeping in a cave,   *Bear is out and hunting food,*
In a cave, in a cave.   *Hunting food, hunting food.*
Bear is sleeping in a cave   *Bear is out and hunting food*
Until the winter's through.   *Until his tummy's full.*

 Cassandra Reigel Whetstone, Folsom, CA

Flower Power

● ●

Learning Objectives The children will:
1. Recognize different flowers.
2. Learn the names of some flowers.
3. Learn that flowers need soil, sun, water and air.
4. Create patterns with flowers.

Circle or Group Time Activity
- Place several artificial flowers in a circle on the floor, with a vase at their center.
- Invite the children to stand around the flowers and march as they sing the following song:

Did You Ever See Flowers? by Mary J. Murray
(Tune: "Did You Ever See a Lassie?")
Did you ever see flowers, see flowers, see flowers?
Did you ever see flowers as pretty as these?
There's blue ones and red ones and pink ones and white ones.
Did you ever see flowers as pretty as these?

- At the end of the song, ask the children to stop marching, stand by a flower, and pick it up. Then say, "Let's make a _____ bouquet" (fill in the blank with a color word).
- The children with the flowers of the color you name take their stems to the center of the circle and place their flowers in the vase.
- Invite the children to sing the following verse as they admire the colorful bouquet:

This Bouquet Is Beautiful by Mary J. Murray
(Tune: "Here We Go 'Round the Mulberry Bush")
This bouquet is beautiful, beautiful, beautiful.
This bouquet is beautiful. Let's make one more.

- Invite children to come to the vase and pick up their flowers.
- Set all the flowers back in the circle. Share a fact about flowers that starts with the sentence "Did you know…?" (Options include "flowers grow in soil," " flowers need sun and water," "marigolds are flowers," "roses are flowers," "flowers have stems," and so on.)
- Repeat the activity, creating several beautiful vases of flowers as you share other facts about flowers. Use a different color or mix of colors for each new bouquet.

Nature and the Environment

Learning Centers

Blocks
Give the children blue art paper and a collection of pattern blocks. Invite them to use the blocks to create an assortment of flowers, putting a different flower on each sheet of blue paper.

Dramatic Play
Display an apron, artificial flowers, empty vases, cash register, and blank note cards, which the children can use to make a shop and pretend to make and purchase flower bouquets for various family members and friends.

Library
Put a copy of *Planting a Rainbow* by Lois Ehlert in the center for the children to look through. Encourage them to name the various flowers they see in the book.

Math
Set out an assortment of stems of artificial flowers, along with several blocks of floral arrangement foam. Invite the children to create patterns by standing a variety of flowers in the foam bricks in a row, and then repeating the pattern.

Science
Display two or more real flowers. Invite the children to study the likenesses and differences between the two flowers and to observe the various parts of the plant.

Book Suggestions

The Flower Alphabet Book by Jerry Pallotta
Flower Garden by Eve Bunting
Planting a Rainbow by Lois Ehlert

Snack

Draw a flower stem with leaves near the bottom of each child's paper plate. Provide the children with cups of assorted fruit pieces and encourage them to use the fruit pieces to create a flower at the top of their stems and then eat them for snack.

Review

Display several flower pictures on a bulletin board. Hand the stem of an artificial flower to one child, and ask the child to come forward, point to a favorite flower with the stem, and then say something about flowers. Give each child a chance to say something about flowers.

Assessment

Display an assortment of flower pictures along with pictures of trees, mushrooms, moss, grass, and other living plants. Invite each child to point to each picture and tell if it shows a flower or some other kind of living plant.

Related Poem

The Amazing Flower by Mary J. Murray
There are things about flowers that I already know.
They need sun, soil, air, and water to grow.
But how a flower forms from a tiny little seed.
Now that is amazing, yes indeed.

 *Mary J. Murray, Mazomanie, WI*

Grasslands

Learning Objectives The children will:
1. Learn about grasslands.
2. Grow grass.
3. Recite various rhymes.

Circle or Group Time Activity
- Show the children pictures of grasslands. Engage the children in a discussion about the different types of grass. Point to each item and talk about the animals that live in the grasslands.
- Ask, "Do you think it is hot or cold there?" Show the children a piece of sod. Ask, "What is this?"
- Pass the sod around so the children may feel the grass. Ask, "How does it feel? What other plants grow in grass? What insects live in the grass?"
- Recite the following action rhyme with the children:

Two Ladybugs in the Grass by Lily Erlic
Two ladybugs in the grass, (hold up two fingers and stretch)
Climbing and jumping all day, (pretend to climb and jump)
"Look over there!" said one ladybug, (point)
The spider is on its way!" (make a circle with arms)
"Oh my, Oh me, Oh dear,
We'll be caught, I fear!" (shiver)
The spider said,
"You're not in my way,
I'm just looking for a fly,
Who passed by here today."
So the spider,
Searching for fly, (pretend to search)
Winked an eye, (wink eye)
And caught the ladybugs
In his trap! (clap once loudly)
They squirmed
Like worms!
Two ladybugs in a web, (pretend to squirm whole body)
Waiting in the sun, (make circle with arms)
The spider winked an eye, (wink eye)
He said, "I was only having fun!" (laugh)
So the spider unraveled them. (pretend to unravel)
The two ladybugs flew away. (pretend to fly)
They went back to the grass, (stretch tall like grass)
Where they climbed and jumped all day! (pretend to climb and jump)

Learning Centers

Dramatic Play
Place a sign in the center that reads "Grassland," above large pieces of artificial grass and stuffed grassland animals, so the children can pretend they live among the animals in the grassland.

Literacy
Provide sheets of paper with photocopied images of grassland and the phrase "My Grassland" written on them. Encourage the children to draw creatures on the grassland images, and to color in the letters at the top of the page. Have them dictate a sentence or two about their work. Write it underneath.

Math
Give the children a basket of green straws of various lengths to count. Ask them to count the straws in pairs, and to order them according to height.

Science
Help the children grow grass. Set out containers of topsoil and small shovels. Ask the children to sprinkle grass seeds on top of the soil, pat the soil, and water the seeds. The children place their containers on the windowsill and water them everyday. When the grass is grown, give them a plastic grassland animal to place in their grass.

Small Motor
Mix a variety of pairs of plastic grassland animals and encourage the children to find the pairs of animals and place them in another basket.

Book Suggestions

Animal Babies in Grasslands by Houghton Mifflin Editorial
Grasslands by Lily Erlic
Over in the Grasslands by Anna Wilson and Alison Bartlett

Snack

Serve animal cookies for the children to enjoy.

Review

Read *Over in the Grasslands* by Anna Wilson and Alison Bartlett to the children. Show the children grassland pictures. Talk about grasslands.

Assessment

Show the children pictures of different biomes. Can the child pick out the grassland biome? Ask, "Can you tell me about your favorite animals in the grassland?"

 Lily Erlic, Victoria, British Columbia, Canada

Leaf Exploration

Learning Objectives The children will:
1. Gain sensory experience with the natural environment.
2. Become aware of leaf variety.

Circle or Group Time Activity
- Prior to doing this activity, put single leaves into several paper lunch bags. For your reference, label the outside of each bag with the name of the type of tree from which the leaf came.
- Give each child a bag, asking that the children not look inside the bags.
- Ask each child to place a hand inside her bag, touch the object inside it, and describe what she feels.
- Provide words such as *rough, smooth, cold, warm, pointy, round,* and *flat* to guide the children's descriptions.
- Next, ask them to pass their bags to their neighbors. Again, have them use their fingers to explore the leaves. Ask them to describe and compare the new leaf with the first leaf.
- Finish by opening bags and talking about how the leaves look and feel.

Learning Centers ### Construction
Prior to the activity, draw an outline of a tree on butcher paper. Make it slightly taller than the children, but not so tall that they can't reach the top. Invite the children to glue or tape real leaves or cutout leaf rubbings from the Art Center activity to the tree. Hang the tree on a wall inside or outside the classroom.

TREE OUTLINE ON BUTCHER PAPER

LEAF

Art

The children make leaf rubbings by placing leaves between two sheets of white paper and rubbing unwrapped crayons over the top sheets.

Library

Set out a recording and copy of *Leaves* by David Ezra Stein for the children to listen to and look through.

Math

Tape a large sheet of butcher paper or chart paper on the wall in a dark part of the classroom. Provide flashlights and encourage children to create shadow puppets using their hands.

Science

Trace the outlines of a variety of leaves onto paper. Put individual leaves in plastic zippered bags and encourage the children to match the leaves in the bags to their paper outlines.

Book Suggestions

Leaves by David Ezra Stein
Leaves! Leaves! Leaves! by Nancy Elizabeth Wallace
Ruby's Falling Leaves by Rosemary Wells

Snack

Invite a child's family member or a local cake baker to demonstrate how to use icing to decorate a cake with leaf shapes.

Review

Talk with the children about the tree in the Construction Center. Encourage the children to point out the leaves and talk about how they differ.

Assessment

Set out several mixed pairs of leaves and ask the children to match similar leaves together.

 *Karyn F. Everham, Fort Myers, FL*

Leaves on the Loose

Learning Objectives   The children will:
1. Collect, examine, and compare leaves
2. Look at leaf characteristics (colors, shapes, and sizes).
3. Learn about leaves that we eat and use in drinks.
4. Determine if leaves float or sink.
5. Notice that some leaves change colors in the fall.

Circle or Group Time Activity
- Read *Why Do Leaves Change Color?* by Betsy Maestro to the children.
- Place a container of leaves in the middle of the circle and ask each child to choose one.
- Encourage children to have fun throwing and blowing their leaves like the wind, and catching them.

Learning Centers   ### Art
Make coffee filter leaf art. Use fresh-picked leaves and flowers (a variety of leaves and flowers gives the artwork more color). Place the leaves onto a hard surface and put a coffee filter on top. Children rub large craft sticks over the coffee filters and they will start to see color from the leaves appear on the coffee filter. Hang their beautiful artwork around the room.

Dramatic Play
Make a "forest" in one area of the room. Ask children to make paper leaves, and hang them from the ceiling. Drape green and brown blankets over items so they look like rocks and grass. Place leaves on the floor. Add some child-size rakes, and stuffed animals or puppets, such as birds, squirrels, raccoons, and bears.

Sand and Water
Fill the sand and water table or tubs with water. Place leaves in the water. Children can experiment with the leaves. Do the leaves float or sink in the water?

Science
Give each child a small bag and go for a walk to collect leaves from different trees. Name the trees along the way. When the children get back to the classroom, compare the shapes, sizes, and colors of the various leaves. Talk about how some leaves change colors from green to red, yellow, and orange and fall off trees before winter comes. If you want to save the leaves, layer the leaves between sheets of newspaper, place something heavy on top, and let them dry. This takes about a week.

Snack and Cooking
Brew sun tea with the children. Fill a large clear glass jar with water. Place decaffeinated tea bags or loose tea in the water. Put the jar in a sunny spot. Leave it

for several hours. When the water changes color and looks like it's been brewed, take out the tea bags. If you used loose tea, pour it through a strainer. Serve the tea at a tea party with honey, sugar, and biscuits. Tell the children that tea leaves come from a tea bush.

Book Suggestions
I Eat Leaves by JoAnn Vandine
Leaves! Leaves! Leaves! by Nancy Elizabeth Wallace
Why Do Leaves Change Color? by Betsy Maestro

Snack
Make a salad with the children using a variety of leaf vegetables, such as spinach, kale, cabbage, and lettuces. Have the children wash the leaves and tear them into smaller pieces. They can taste the leaves and then choose the ones they would like to eat in a salad. Have some tasty dressings available too.

Review
Talk about the leaves we see around us. Discuss how some leaves change color in the fall and drift to the ground. Discuss growing plants in order to eat the leaves and drink the tea.

Assessment
Present different kinds of leaves. Ask the children to tell you what they know about the leaves.

 *Monica Hay Cook, Tucson, AZ*

Making Shadows

Learning Objectives The children will:
1. See that a shadow is an area of darkness created by blocking light.
2. Learn where to look for shadows and know how to make shadows.
3. Know when the light moves, the shadow changes too.

Circle or Group Time Activity
- Read the story *Moonbear's Shadow* by Frank Asch to the children.
- After finishing the book, play a shadow game with the children. Choose one child to be the leader. The other children line up behind the leader.
- The leader runs, jumps, skips, twirls, and moves. The other children follow behind the leader, just like a shadow would.
- After about a minute, choose another child in line to become the leader and the others become shadows.

Learning Centers ### Art
Place sheets of butcher paper on the floor and put the children into pairs. One child stands near the piece of butcher paper in a position that creates his shadow on the paper and his partner traces the shadow. Have the children trade places. When finished tracing, let them color the shadows a dark color. Hang their shadow art around the room.

Blocks
Add extra lighting to the block area. As the children build with blocks, ask them to pay attention to the shadows they've created. The children can measure the shadows using blocks. How many blocks tall and wide are the structures? How many blocks tall and wide are the shadows?

Large Motor
Play shadow tag outside. The children run around and try not to get caught. If the person that is "It" steps on someone's shadow, that person becomes "It."

Sand and Water
Fill the sand and water table with water. Put it outside in the sunlight. Provide a variety of items for the children to use to make shadows in the water table.

Science
On a sunny morning, go outside with the children and look for items and their shadows. With chalk, the children draw the outlines of the shadows. Later in the

day, go outside again. Have the children trace the shadows of the same objects again. Did it change?

Book Suggestions

Gregory's Shadow by Don Freeman
Moonbear's Shadow by Frank Asch
My Shadow by Robert Louis Stevenson

Snack

On a sunny day, eat a picnic snack outside. While eating, the children can watch for and make shadows.

Review

Ask the children to look around the room and find shadows.

Assessment

When asked, the children can explain that shadows occur when light hits an object. The children can find shadows, make shadows, and see that shadows change when the light source that produces them moves.

 *Monica Hay Cook, Tucson, AZ*

Me and My Shadow

Learning Objectives The children will:
1. Identify what a shadow is and how it is made.
2. Develop their small and large motor skills.
3. Develop their language skills.

Circle or Group Time Activity
- Introduce the children to the concept of shadows.
- Read the children a book about shadows (see the list below).
- Hang a small sheet and shine a light behind it.
- Tape common items to the back of the sheet and recite the following rhyme, encouraging them to name the objects they see in the shadows (such as a comb, scissors, shapes, toothbrush, leaf, and so on):

Shadow, shadow, what do I see?
I see a _____, that's what I see.

Learning Centers **Art**

Show children how to trace each other's silhouettes. Tape white paper to the wall and shine the light toward the paper. Have a child sit sideways between the light and the paper, creating a silhouette on the paper. Trace around the silhouette on the paper. Cut shapes out of sponges and have the children dip them in black paint and make "shadow" prints on white paper.

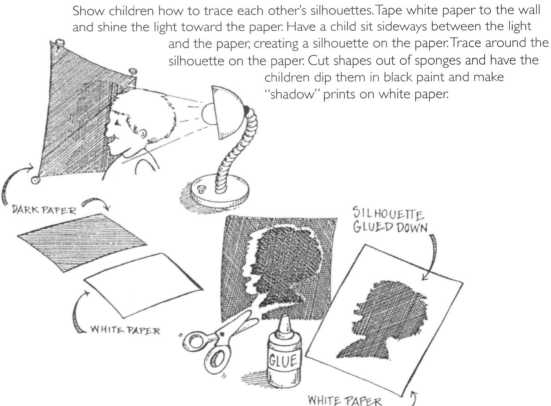

DARK PAPER

WHITE PAPER

GLUE

WHITE PAPER

SILHOUETTE GLUED DOWN

Large Motor

Hang up a large sheet and shine a light behind it. Have children take turns dancing behind the sheet (standing between the sheet and the light). Play music while they dance.

Math

Cut out pictures of animals and trace their shapes onto black paper. Have children match the animals to their "shadows."

Science

Set up a table with small flashlights and various-sized objects so the children can experiment with creating shadows.

Small Motor

The children cut out shapes from paper and tape them to dark blue construction paper. Hang the pictures on a sunny window facing out. After a few days, remove the shapes and see the "shadows" formed by the sun fading the paper around the shapes.

Book Suggestions

Gregory's Shadow by Don Freeman
Gretchen Groundhog, It's Your Day! by Abby Levine
Moonbear's Shadow by Frank Asch

Snack

Serve slices of toast. Provide cookie cutters with which the children can cut out various shapes of toast. Explain how the bread from which they cut the shapes holds the negative, or shadow of the shape.

Review

Go for a walk outside and look for shadows from street signs, light posts, fences, trees, and so on. Have children try to trace shadows on the sidewalk with chalk.

Assessment

Challenge the children to match various items to cutout "shadows."

Sandra Ryan, Buffalo, NY

Ocean Days

Learning Objectives The children will:

1. Learn about the ocean.
2. Reproduce, extend, and create patterns.
3. Use their five senses to explore at the Science Center.
4. Improve their oral language skills.

Circle or Group Time Activity

■ Display a globe or large world map. Draw the children's attention to the large bodies of water. Ask the children if they know what they are called. If the children do not know, explain that the bodies of water are called "oceans."

■ Set out a sand bucket filled with beanbag ocean animals and land animals, and show each animal to the children, asking the children to clap if the animal belongs in the ocean, and to sit quietly if the animal lives on the land.

■ After going through all the animals, place a blue blanket in the center of the circle. Put an animal behind each child's back as they sit in a circle formation. Ask the children not to look at their animals until you call their names.

■ Teach the children the following ocean chant, inviting them to bring their animals, one by one, and say the animals' names in the appropriate places:

Big Blue Ocean by Mary J. Murray
Big blue ocean, filled with life
There's so much to learn.
Show us what you have, _____ (child's name)
Now it's your turn.
I have a _____. (children take turns saying the names of their animals)

■ After the children show and name all the animals, put a pair of sunglasses in the center of the blanket. Ask the children to close their eyes. Remove one of the animals from the blanket. When they open their eyes, ask the first child who knows which animal is missing to put the sunglasses on and name the animal.

Learning Centers **Dramatic Play**
Provide plastic flippers and invite the children to lie on their stomachs and kick with the flippers on their feet, pretending to be scuba divers.
Large Motor
Put a pair of flippers at the center. Invite the children to walk around the room wearing the flippers.

Math
Give the children blue paper and invite them to create, extend, and reproduce patterns using seashells, fish, and ocean objects.

Sand and Water
Place assorted shells, coral, and toy fish, whales, and dolphins at the water table and invite the children to manipulate the objects in the water.

Science
Give the children a globe to explore. Also, display various pictures of whales and cards with the names of the various whales written on them. Invite the children to learn the names of each whale and then teach someone else about the different types of whales in the ocean.

Small Motor
Set out various shells, plastic fish, pieces of coral, and playdough. Encourage the children to press the objects into the dough to form interesting imprints.

Book Suggestions

Do You Know About Life in the Sea? by Philip Steele
The Ocean Alphabet Book by Jerry Pallotta

Snack

Serve oyster crackers (shells) and fish-shaped crackers on blue paper plates.

Review

Give one child a beanbag ocean animal. Have the children recite the following rhyme:

I Like the Ocean by Mary J. Murray
I like the ocean; it's big and blue.
I like the ocean, how about you.

Each time the children chant the word "you," the child holding the beanbag tosses it to a different child. The child who catches the beanbag responds by naming a sea creature.

Assessment

Display an assortment of ocean objects and objects that do not relate to the ocean. Ask a child to pick up the objects that "don't belong" and put them in a sand pail.

 *Mary J. Murray, Mazomanie, WI*

Sensational Sun

Learning Objectives   The children will:
1. Learn that the sun is a burning hot ball of gases and flame.
2. Understand that the sun warms the earth.
3. Learn that the sun helps keep people, animals, and plants alive and growing.
4. Enhance large and small motor skills.
5. Improve their oral language skills.

Circle or Group Time Activity
- Teach the children the following fingerplay:

  Our Sun by Mary J. Murray
  The sun shines and warms the earth. (stand with arms in circle above head)
  It also gives us light. (place hand over eyebrow to block sun)
  It causes plants and trees to grow. (arms grow upward like a plant)
  And shines on the moon at night. (head on hands—sleeping motion)

- Hold up a yellow balloon high above a globe on a table.
- Show the children how day and night arrive. Explain that the sun stays in one place as the earth rotates. Remind that the sun does not go away and come back; the earth simply spins around on its axis.
- Invite the children to stand in a large circle on the floor. Place "raindrops" (blue tissue paper balls) around the outside of the Group or Circle Time area.
- With your hands, tap the yellow balloon high into the air and invite two children to keep tapping the "sun" so that it stays up in the sky. Make sure to let all the children get a turn tapping the balloon.
- Each time a child taps the balloon, the children chant "sunny day" in unison.
- Every 30 seconds, announce a "rainy day" and hold onto the sun. Invite the children to pick up blue raindrops, toss them up into the air, and let them land on the ground.

Learning Centers   **Art**
Invite the children to paint a big yellow sun on art paper. Provide gold glitter for the children to sprinkle on the wet paint to signify that the sun is shining.
Blocks
Set out a flashlight and a large yellow piece of mural paper. Invite the children to arrange the blocks on the yellow paper to form a giant sun and its rays. The children can then point the beam of the flashlight at the sun to make it shine.

Large Motor

Separate the children into pairs. Give each child a felt or foam sun. One child in each pair holds the yellow felt sun while the other child recites the following sentence, naming various body parts: "The sun shines on my _____." The children holding the suns set them on the body parts that their partners mention. Children take turns speaking and manipulating the sun.

Sensory

Fill a shallow tub with a small bowl of yellow food coloring mixed in shaving cream, and invite the children to use their fingers write the word "sun" and draw the sun in the mixture.

Small Motor

Set out yellow modeling dough. Invite the children to create suns by rolling or cutting the dough into circles. Encourage the children to add sunrays by rolling snakes of yellow dough and attaching them to their circular suns.

Book Suggestions

Hello Sun! by Hans Wilhelm
The Sun Is My Favorite Star by Frank Asch
Sunshine by Gail Saunders-Smith

Snack

Give each child a pineapple ring or a circular slice of banana in its peel, and several thin strips of yellow pepper. Invite the children to create suns on their plates, using the bananas or pineapples as the suns, and the pepper strips as sunrays. Invite the children to eat their suns, piece by piece.

Review

Invite the children to pass the balloon around the circle, over their heads. Each child who passes the sun finishes one of the following sentences: "The sun warms _____." "The sun shines on _____." "The sun helps us by _____."

Assessment

Display a picture of the sun, the moon, and another planet. Invite each child to point out which is a picture of the sun and share some facts about the sun.

 *Mary J. Murray, Mazomanie, WI*

Sticks and Stones

Learning Objectives The children will:
1. Describe sticks and stones.
2. Develop their oral language skills.
3. Improve their large and small motor skills.
4. Practice letter recognition.

Circle or Group Time Activity

- Spread a collection of sticks and stones (five or more per child) randomly about the Circle or Group Time area, and set out two large buckets, one labeled "sticks," the other labeled "stones."
- Assign each child to pick up either sticks or stones and put them in the correct buckets, one piece at a time.
- After the children gather all the stick sand stones in the area, ask the children the following questions to encourage a class discussion.
  - How are sticks and stones alike and different?
  - Where might you find sticks and stones?
  - What safety rules should you follow when playing with sticks and stones?
  - Where do sticks and stones come from?
- Spill out the sticks and stones again. Repeat the activity to see which group can finish first, the ones picking up sticks or the ones picking up stones.

Learning Centers

Literacy

Set out sticks, stones, and various cards with alphabet letters on them, encouraging the children to use the sticks and stones to copy the individual letters. More advanced children can try spelling out their own names.

CARD WITH LETTER "A"

STONES

CARD WITH LETTER "G"

STICKS

Construction
Invite the children to arrange sticks and stones in a container of wet sand as they create various structures, teepees, designs, and so on.

Math
Create a trail in the classroom using paper or fabric. Display an assortment of sticks and stones along the edge of the trail. Invite children to walk the trail and count how many sticks they see. Then walk it again and count how many stones they see.

Music
Invite children to hit pairs of rhythm sticks and pairs of natural sticks together as they listen to recordings of their favorite songs.

Science
Set out a container of water and various sticks and stones, inviting the children to see if the objects sink or float.

Book Suggestions

Materials from Nature by Victoria Seix
More than One by Miriam Schlein

Snack

Combine an assortment of pretzel sticks and various nuts in a bowl and then serve up a cup of "sticks and stones" to each child for snack.

Review

Hand each child a stick and a stone. Create a pattern in the center of the Circle or Group Time area and invite each child to add one or two pieces to extend the pattern.

Assessment

Display an assortment of sticks, stones, seeds, pine cones, and other items from nature. Invite the child to select the sticks and the stones from among the other items and describe each one aloud.

Mary J. Murray, Mazomanie, WI

Nature and the Environment

Touch the Earth

Learning Objectives The children will:
1. Gain familiarity with different types of soil.
2. Explore the properties of soil.

Circle or Group Time Activity
- Put out three plastic bins, each containing a different type of soil (garden soil, sand, and clay soil).
- Ask the children to scoop out a sample of each into three cups.
- Invite the children to use their senses to explore the soils by squeezing, sniffing, shaping, pouring, mixing, and so on.
- Ask the children questions as they explore, such as "What do the soils feel like?" "What do they look like?" "Are they hot or cold?"

Learning Centers

Art
The children "paint" glue on paper with a paintbrush, and then sprinkle salt over the wet glue. After the glue dries, invite children to watercolor a garden scene over the salt and glue. The rough texture will look like dirt.

Library
Provide a copy and recording of *We Love the Dirt* by Tony Johnston for the children to listen to and look through.

Sand and Water
Divide the sand table into three sections, each containing a type of soil (sand, gardening soil, clay soil); also provide magnifying lenses, spoons, and shovels and encourage the children to handle and examine the soils.

Science
Encourage the children to mix spoonfuls of each type of soil with water and watch what happens. As an alternative, give each child three small paper cups with the three different types of soil. Have them plant bean seeds in each cup. Water each pot, then set them out for observation.

Small Motor
Provide modeling clay for children to handle and experiment with. Talk about how the modeling clay feels compared to clay soil.

Book Suggestions *Dirt Is Delightful* by Jannelle Cherrington
A Mudpie for Mother by Scott Beck
We Love the Dirt by Tony Johnston

Snack   Show the children images of vegetables growing out of the ground, and then show them samples of the vegetables that still have dirt on them. Encourage the children to help clean the food, and then prepare and serve it for a healthy snack.

Review   Play a guessing game challenging the children to answer the following:
"I am a grainy and dry and found on the beach."
"I am sticky and wet and very heavy."
"I am soft and very dark and get muddy when I'm wet."

Assessment   Place sand, gardening soil, and clay soil into three separate boxes. Cut holes in the lids and cover the boxes. Put three additional soil samples in visible containers. After the child touches the hidden soil, ask the child to match it with the appropriate visible container.

Related Fingerplay   **If You're Muddy and You Know It** by Karyn Everham
(Tune: "If You're Happy and You Know It")
If you're muddy and you know it,
Go squish, squish. (make feet motions indicating sticky mud)
If you're dirty and you know it,
Go rub a-dub-dub. (make hand motions indicating washing body)
If you're sandy and you know it,
Go swish-swish. (make hand motions indicating sweeping)

 Karyn F. Everham, Fort Myers, FL

Trash to Treasure

Learning Objectives The children will:
1. Learn ways to recycle.
2. Classify recycled items.
3. Create recycled art projects.

Circle or Group Time Activity
- Put several clean recyclables (plastic cartons, cans, jars, egg cartons, bottles) in a pile on the rug in front of the children.
- Ask the children, "Where does all this go if we put it into the garbage can?"
- Show the children pictures of landfills, explaining that much of our garbage ends up there, but they are rapidly filling up. Ask for ideas to solve this problem.
- Show the children a chart with the three recycling Rs: Reduce, Reuse, Recycle.
- Demonstrate "reduce" by showing a large container of juice that can be purchased in place of several small juice boxes that take up much more room in the garbage can.
- Explain "reuse" by showing the plastic grocery bag, which can be used again to line a small trashcan at home.
- Explain "recycle" by showing the children a glass jar with a lid that has been reused to store pasta, for example.
- Tell the children that they will be recycling their items into art projects, which will be displayed in an art show for their family members (or another class to view).

Learning Centers

Art
Provide recycled items (scraps of metallic paper, corrugated paper, cardboard, fabric, wrapping paper), glue, assorted art supplies (buttons, cotton balls, fabric scraps, ribbons, and yarn), markers, and crayons so the children can build three-dimensional objects for an art show.

Blocks
Provide small containers and assorted small items, such as buttons, paper clips, and cotton balls, for the children to transport in the Blocks Center. Make cardstock signs for the "Recycle Center" and add medium containers to classify the items.

Dramatic Play
Give the children three green headbands, labeled "reduce," "reuse," and "recycle." Provide clean empty cans and plastic bottles to put in a container labeled "recycle." Encourage the children to pretend they are recycling workers.

Literacy

Ask the following riddles to help the children classify the recyclable materials:

- *I'm hard and breakable. I come in different colors, but you can usually see through me. What am I?* (glass)
- *I'm bendable and lightweight. I come in many different shapes and colors. Lots of liquids fill me up. What am I?* (plastic)
- *I'm thin and come from trees. People use me for books and wrapping. What am I?* (paper)

Math

Provide 20 recyclable items, such as cans, papers, glass bottles, plastic containers, and metal items. Give the children four bins labeled "Plastic," "Glass," "Metal," and "Paper." Also provide numeral cards labeled 0–10. Explain that the recycle truck has separate sections for different types of recyclables. Ask the children to put the recycled items into the correct containers. Ask them to count the items and put the correct numeral card by each container.

Writing

Provide cardstock and markers for the children to name their art projects. Help them copy the names of their projects followed by their names.

Book Suggestions

The Earth and I by Frank Asch
Just a Dream by Chris Van Allsburg
The Lorax by Dr. Seuss
My Car by Byron Barton
Recycle! A Handbook for Kids by Gail Gibbons

Snack

Serve cheese and crackers in recycled paper plates, cups, and napkins.

Review

Ask the children to list the three recycling Rs. Show the following items (or pictures of these items) and ask how to keep the landfills from filling up:

- Small individual bags of snacks (reduce by buying large bags and dividing it up)
- Milk jug (reuse by filling half with water and freezing it to take on a picnic)
- Sunday's comics page (recycle by using it for wrapping a gift)

Assessment

Provide items for the child to classify into the categories "glass," "metal," "plastic," and "paper."

 *Susan Oldham Hill, Lakeland, FL*

Trees

Learning Objectives The children will:
1. Become familiar with the parts of a tree.
2. Learn about how animals and people need trees.
3. Gather information using sense of touch, smell, and sight.

Circle or Group Time Activity
- Show the children pictures of trees and engage them in a discussion about trees. Discuss how animals live in trees, how we eat food from trees, and harvest trees for wood.
- Point out the parts of the trees: trunk, leaves, branches, bark, roots, and so on.
- Take the children on a walk to visit a live tree. Ask them to identify the parts of the tree. Look for animals in and around the tree.
- Encourage them to describe what the tree looks like, smells like, and feels like.
- Ask children what that spot would be like without the tree.
- Gather leaves or needles from the ground to use in the Science Center.

Learning Centers **Art**
Provide leaves, bark, paper, and crayons so the children can do crayon rubbings.
Blocks
Put toy animals into the block area and encourage children to build tree trunks with spaces for the animals to live in.
Dramatic Play
Put baskets and plastic eggs in the center for children to use as nests. Encourage them to pretend they are birds caring for their young.
Library
Set out a recording and copy of *The Great Kapok Tree* by Lynne Cherry for the children to listen to and look through.
Science
Provide magnifying glasses and invite the children to use them to observe the leaves, bark, pine needles, pinecones, and other materials they collected during the Circle or Group Time activity.
Snack and Cooking
Provide tree-grown fruit, cutting boards, plastic knives, and bowls. Help children make individual bowls of fruit salad while discussing the type of tree that bears each fruit.

Nature and the Environment

Book Suggestions   *Are Trees Alive?* by Debbie S. Miller
The Great Kapok Tree by Lynne Cherry
A Tree Is Nice by Janice May Udry

Snack   Serve the fruit salad from the Snack and Cooking Center, along with almonds or walnuts and orange juice.

Review   Gather the children around a picture of a tree and ask them to point out the trunk, branches, leaves, and any other visible parts of the tree.

Assessment   Can the child look at a picture of a tree and identify the leaves and the trunk?

Related Rhyme   **I Had a Little Nut Tree** (Traditional)
I had a little nut tree,
Nothing would it bear
But a silver nutmeg
And a golden pear.
The king of Spain's daughter
Came to visit me,
All for the sake of
My little nut tree.

 *Cassandra Reigel Whetstone, Folsom, CA*

We Can Save the Earth

Learning Objectives The children will:
1. Gain an appreciation for nature and the environment.
2. Understand the importance of caring for the environment.
3. Learn that our clean and natural environment can be lots of fun.
4. Cooperate with each other and share responsibility.

Circle or Group Time Activity
- Bring the children to an outdoor garden area.
- Provide garbage bins, rubber gloves, and other materials the children can use to clean up the garden.
- Talk about the importance of having a clean environment, and ask them to help clean up the garden.
- Once the children finish cleaning up the garden, have a class picnic of raw fruits and vegetables. Serve the food on paper plates and set out a separate set of garbage containers in which the children can recycle their plates.

Learning Centers

Art
Provide paper, markers, crayons, paints, and so on, and invite the children to draw individual seeds on their paper, and then draw or paint what they imagine would grow from their seeds.

Construction
Provide all kinds of recyclables that the children can construct with, such as boxes, containers, lids, paper, writing tools, tape, scissors, sponges, string, or any other recycled item.

Library
Place a recording and copy of *The Lorax* by Dr. Seuss in the center for the children to listen to and look through.

Sensory
Make several feely bags with various natural and manufactured objects in them. Encourage the children to feel the various objects and say whether they think they are natural or not, and whether they should be recycled or thrown away.

Writing
Put postcard-sized pieces of paper, markers, paint, and other materials in the center. Encourage the children to make postcards with images of natural objects and scenes on them. When they dry, help the children write notes to family members on their postcards.

Book Suggestions   *The Lorax* by Dr. Seuss
Recycle! A Handbook for Kids by Gail Gibbons
Where Does the Garbage Go? by Paul Showers

Snack   Provide snacks that come in different recyclable containers, such as juice boxes, water bottles, paper cups, small bags of snacks, and so on. Make sure the children sort and recycle any recyclable materials used during snack time.

Review   Bring the children outside to look for garbage and recyclable materials they can put in the appropriate places, such as trash or recycling bins. Children love to use binoculars as they search for materials.

Assessment   Can the child distinguish between recyclable and nonrecyclable materials?

Related Rhyme   **My Little Seed** by Eileen Lucas
I took a little seed and planted it so deep.
I thought it would grow while I was fast asleep.
I woke up in the morning and to my surprise.
My little seed was no where to be seen and it did not rise.
So I waited and I waited
And in a few short days,
My little seed began to pop
And I was so amazed.

Eileen Lucas, Fort McMurray, Alberta, Canada

Wonderful Trees

Learning Objectives The children will:
1. Learn about trees.
2. Appreciate what trees provide to people and other creatures.
3. Eat food that comes from trees.

Circle or Group Time Activity
- Engage the children in a discussion about trees and bushes. Ask the children what trees provide (food, shade, homes, protection, and resting places for animals such as monkeys, squirrels, bears, snakes, and sloths as well as nesting places and materials for birds). Ask, "What would our world be like without forests and trees?"
- Teach the children the following fingerplay:

  The Little Lemon by Sandra Bynum
  Up in a treetop (look up)
  I spy a little lemon. (point up)
  Up in that treetop (look up)
  That lemon spies me! (point to self)
  "Hello little lemon! (wave)
  Come down little lemon!" (motion towards self)
  And that little lemon falls down on me! (hold head)
  I pick up that lemon (pretend to reach down to pick it up)
  And I open it up. (pretend to split it open)
  Whew! That lemon's as sour as it can be! (make a sour face)

- Repeat the rhyme a few times, then ask the children to name other fruits that grow on trees. If you have images of a bonsai tree or redwoods available, share them with the children. Emphasize the comparable sizes of the bonsai tree and the giant tree to sizes of people. The children will be fascinated!
- Tell the children that today they will be learning interesting facts about trees.

Learning Centers **Art**
Draw an outline of a tree on a piece of paper and make copies of it. Give an outline of a tree to each child to illustrate. Older children will not need outlines; have them draw trees however they want.
Dramatic Play
Encourage the children to build a "tree house" by draping chairs and tables with sheets, and other materials. Give the children binoculars for spying on the world below, and other items to make their tree house homier.

Library
Provide a recording and copy of *The Gift of the Tree* by Alvin R. Tresselt for the children to listen to and look through.

Outdoors
Bring the children on a nature walk to look for different types of trees. Let the children tell you how they are different and how they are the same. Collect different types of tree leaves. If it is autumn, collect beautiful fall leaves and use them to decorate the room.

Writing
On story paper, have the children write or dictate to you one or two sentences about what they like most about trees. Give the children their sheets of paper and encourage them to illustrate their stories. Post these on the wall or compile into a book entitled "Wonderful Trees." Make it available in the classroom or school library to share with others.

Book Suggestions
Are Trees Alive? by Debbie S. Miller
The Big Tree by Bruce Hiscock
The Gift of the Tree by Alvin R. Tresselt
The Giving Tree by Shel Silverstein
Tell Me, Tree: All About Trees for Kids by Gail Gibbons
The Tremendous Tree Book by Barbara Brenner

Snack
Serve various fruits and berries that come from trees and bushes. Show the children images of the trees and bushes from which they come as the children enjoy the snack.

Review
Recite "The Little Lemon" with the children again. Afterwards, engage the children in a discussion about the importance of trees to people, birds, and animals for food, shade, protection, and homes.

Assessment
Draw a simple picture of a tree. Ask the children to name the different parts of the tree. Name different kinds of fruit that grow on trees.

 *Sandra Bynum, Blackfoot, ID*

Countdown to Counting

Learning Objectives The children will:
1. Recognize the numerals 1–10.
2. Understand various numerical values.
3. Develop their small motor skills.

Circle or Group Time Activity
- Teach the children the following rhyme, asking them to clap the numbers in time:

  The Number Song (Traditional)
  One, two, tie my shoe. (pretend to tie shoe)
  Three, four, shut the door. (swing arm as if closing a door)
  Five, six, pick up sticks. (bend down to pick up pretend sticks)
  Seven, eight, lay them straight. (hands out, palms facing and parallel, move hands up and down)
  Nine, ten, a big fat hen! (hands out in front, fingers touching, making a big circle)
  Let's get ready and count again. (march in place)
  Now we all can count to 10.

- Once the children know the rhyme, divide them into two groups. Repeat the rhyme as a call and response, with one group saying the numbers and the second group completing the rhyme.
- Substitute clapping the numbers for holding up the correct numbers of fingers.
- Tell the children they will be learning about the numerals 1–10.

Learning Centers **Art**
Write numerals on paper and invite the children to create characters using the numbers as starting points. Ask, "What can you make from the numeral 2? Someone with a pointy nose?"

Blocks
Put number blocks in a pail. Ask 10 children to stand in a line. The children count off from one to 10 and pick out the blocks that match the numbers they say.

"2"   "3"

Games

Play Musical Chairs with the children. Be sure there is enough room to play this game safely. Place two rows of chairs back to back in the center of the room, one chair per child. Place a number on each chair. Give each child a corresponding number card from 1–10. If needed, repeat this with another group or use numbers more than once. Music begins and children slowly walk around the chairs watching for their number. When the music ends, they quickly sit down on the chairs that have their numbers on them. After the children are all sitting, ask them to exchange numbers with one of the children sitting beside them. In this version of the game, no one loses a chair.

Literacy

Set out several sheets of paper that have the following sentences on them: "I love _____. I wish I had _____ of them." Ask the children to name something they love. Write the names of the things they love in the first blank, and then encourage the children to write the number of those things they wish they had in the second blank, and then to illustrate and decorate their papers.

Math

Give each child 10 pieces of paper. Provide stickers, stamps, and simple shapes for them to make number books. Have them write a different number from 1–10 on each page, and then draw, stick, stamp, or glue the matching number of items on each page. Staple or bind the pages together with a hole punch and binder rings. Help the children write their names on the covers of their number books.

Small Motor

Cut openings on each end of shoebox so children can put their hands inside. Put chunky number blocks into the box and invite the children to put their hands in, feel the numbers, and then name them.

Book Suggestions

1, 2, 3 to the Zoo by Eric Carle
10 Apples Up on Top by Dr. Seuss
Counting Kisses by Karen Katz
One Fish, Two Fish, Red Fish, Blue Fish by Dr. Seuss

Snack

Use tube frosting to draw numbers on muffins. Serve with milk.

Review

Gather the children in small groups and sit each group in a circle. Roll a ball from child to child in each circle. Ask the first child to whom you roll the ball to say "one," the next child to say "two," and so on.

Assessment

Set out a large container full of several objects such as pennies, marbles, pencils, paper clips, and so on. Ask a child to find you a certain number of one object, such as three paperclips or one penny.

 *Sally Phillips, Enfield, IL*

Counting on You!

Learning Objectives   The children will:
1. Count from 1–10.
2. Begin to recognize numerals.
3. Develop their small motor skills (specifically the pincer grasp).

Circle or Group Time Activity
- Read *Chicka, Chicka 123* by Bill Martin, Jr. to the children. Point out the numerals to the children as you go through the book.
- After the children are somewhat familiar with the numerals, give each child a felt numeral from 1–10.
- Reread the book. As you read, ask the child with the corresponding numeral to hold it up or place it on the flannel board.

Learning Centers   **Dramatic Play**
Make fishing poles by attaching pieces of string or yarn to the ends of wooden dowels. On the other end of the strings, tie round magnets that have holes in their centers. Fill a container with water, put several magnetic numerals in the water, and invite the children to go fishing for numbers. Challenge the children to identify the numbers as they catch them.

Library
Put a recording and copy of *There Were Ten in the Bed* by Mary Gruetzke in the center for the children to listen to as they look through the book. Encourage them to perform the actions the book describes.

Listening
Gather the children into a group. Clap a pattern and invite the children to clap the same pattern back. Let the children take turns making up clapping patterns that the rest of the children repeat.

Math
With a permanent marker, write a numeral from 1–10 on the outsides of several paper cups. Underneath the numerals, put the corresponding number of dots. This gives the children a clue if they do not know the numeral. Give each child a clothespin. Provide several cotton balls and challenge the children to pick them up using their clothespins, and then drop the corresponding number of balls into one of the cups. Encourage the children to check the accuracy of their counting by comparing the number of cotton balls in their cups to the number of dots on the fronts of the cups.

Sand and Water
Fill the sand and water table with sand and hide several plastic numerals. Invite the children to dig the numerals up and identify them.

Book Suggestions   *10 Fat Turkeys* by Tony Johnston
10 Sly Piranhas: A Counting Story in Reverse by William Wise
Chicka, Chicka 123 by Bill Martin, Jr.
There Were Ten in the Bed by Mary Gruetzke

Snack   Place recipe cards for a salad along a table in sequential order from left to right (five pieces of lettuce, 10 carrot slices, two drops of dressing, and so on) in front of bowls of the corresponding ingredient. Invite the children to move down the line and put the correct numbers of ingredients in their bowls, then enjoy their salads together.

Review   Ask the children, "What was your favorite number activity today?" Record their responses on a piece of chart paper and post them where family members can read them.

Assessment   Some of the children may be ready to recognize all of the numerals, other may not. For the ones that are ready, have them find a certain numeral on the flannel board and bring it to you. Do not expect all of the children to be able to master this skill. The purpose of this unit is to expose the children to counting concepts.

 *Donna Meiss, Sonora, CA*

How Time Flies!

Learning Objectives   The children will:
1. Practice telling time by the hour.
2. Develop their small and large motor skills.

Circle or Group Time Activity

- Ahead of time, use masking tape to make a large (8'–10') circle on the rug.
- Show the children an analog clock face. Explain that each numeral represents a time to do something, such as eat breakfast, go outside, have lunch, come home, and other things families do.
- Discuss routine times the children are familiar with at school.
- Display several other time-telling devices, like alarm clocks, sundials, watches, and hourglasses, and explain how they work.
- Choose 12 children to sit around the masking tape circle on the rug. Give each child a numeral-card necklace and ask these children to sit in the places marking the hours facing toward the center of the circle, holding the numeral cards so others can see them.
- Give one child a yardstick and ask him to stand in the center of the circle, pointing the yardstick to one of the children holding a number. Ask the rest of the children what number the yardstick is pointing at, and explain that on clocks, this would indicate what time it is.
- Repeat this several times and then ask other children to sit on the clock face. Give other children time to move the yardstick "hand" and tell the time.

Learning Centers   **Art**

Ahead of time, glue several 9" x 12" sheets of yellow paper to gray sheets the same size, making sheets of paper that are yellow on one side and gray on the other side. Invite the children to think of things people do in the daytime and color daytime events on the yellow sheet. Turn the paper over and ask them to think of things usually done at night for the gray sheet. Nighttime activities include having a bonfire, sleeping, playing flashlight tag, watching fireworks, and so on.

Literacy

Provide a set of word cards that read, "one o'clock, two o'clock" and so on. Ask the children to match them to cards of clock faces showing the numerical versions of those times.

Math

Provide several pairs of clock faces with hands pointing to the hours from 1–12 and invite the children to find the matching pairs.

Music
Use the Circle or Group Time masking tape clock on the rug with children wearing the numeral necklaces. Play some music and ask a child to walk around the numerals. When the music stops, ask the child to say what hour the clock is showing.

Sand and Water
Add funnels to the sand table so the children can simulate using hourglasses.

Small Motor
Ahead of time, draw several clock faces on sheets of paper, leaving the places for the numerals blank. Give the children numeral stickers and challenge them to complete the clock faces. Provide an actual clock for the children to use as a pattern.

Book Suggestions
I Is One by Tasha Tudor
Time Flies by Eric Rohmann

Snack
Serve snacks that must be cooked for a certain amount of time. For example, microwave popcorn, or something else fast. Have the children watch the clock as the food cooks.

Review
Distribute the numeral necklaces from Circle or Group Time. Ask children to move the yardstick "hand" and ask someone else to tell the hour. Use the sets of clock faces for the children to match, and show their day and night pictures. Ask the children to tell what hour the pictures are showing.

Assessment
Show the children several clock faces and ask them what hours the clocks are showing.

 *Susan Oldham Hill, Lakeland, FL*

Leap Frog

Learning Objectives The children will:
1. Practice using a tape measure and ruler.
2. Count and separate numbers.
3. Compare long and short.
4. Observe frogs.

Circle or Group Time Activity

- Place a blue cloth on the floor in the middle of the circle. Put five chairs around the edge of the cloth. Ask five children to sit on the chairs and be the "frogs."
- Teach the children the song "Five Little Speckled Frogs." Ask the children sitting on the chairs to act it out:
- Repeat the song until there are no "frogs" left, and say, "Shh, shh" in the final line.
- Once the children know the song, repeat it using another group of children as the "frogs."
- Show the children a ruler and tape measure. Ask if they know what they are used for.
- Measure several small objects to demonstrate how to measure using the inch markings on the ruler.
- Give each child a ruler and small object to practice measuring.
- Using the tape measure, measure a piece of furniture in the classroom. Explain that people use tape measures to measure larger objects or distances.
- Have the children work in pairs, using the tape measure to measure the size or length of different things in the classroom, such as the doorway or the children's heights.
- Tell the children that they will be learning about measurement today.

Learning Centers

Math
Provide an assortment of plastic jumping frogs and a tape measure taped onto brown butcher paper, so the children can measure the distances their plastic frogs jump. Set out a marker so they can mark the distances and compare them.

Library
Set out a recording and copy of *Jump, Frog, Jump* by Robert Kalan for the children to listen to and look through.

Sand and Water
Put several plastic frogs in the sand and water table for the children to play with. Encourage them to make sand logs for the frogs to sit on.

Science
Obtain a fish tank with real frogs in it. Encourage the children to observe the frogs as they move, and ask the children to describe what they see the frogs doing. Provide note cards and help the children write down their observations.

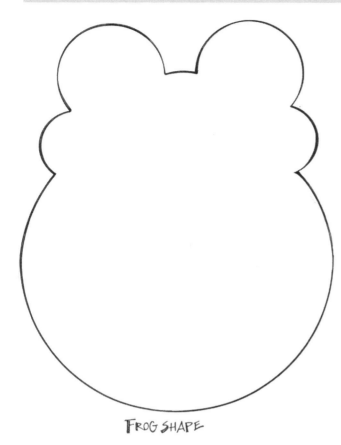

FROG SHAPE

Art

Provide several 1" x 4" and 1" x 8" strips of dark green paper and dark green paper cutouts of frog shapes. Encourage the children to draw faces on their frogs. Show the children how to make legs by folding the strips of paper over on top of themselves, making accordion shapes. Have them glue the folded paper to the bottoms of their frogs, putting the shorter pieces at the front and the longer pieces at the back, so they resemble frog legs. Encourage the children to illustrate frog habitats on construction paper and glue their frogs' legs to it. This gives the effect of the frogs leaping.

FACE DRAWN ON FROG

SHORTER STRIPS

LONGER STRIPS

Book Suggestions

The Best Bug Parade by Stuart J. Murphy
Finklehopper Frog by Irene Livingston
Inchworm and a Half by Elinor J. Pinczes
Jump, Frog, Jump by Robert Kalan

Snack

The children enjoy the frog cookie they made in the Snack and Cooking Center.

Review

Ask the children to use frog counters to compare the lengths of two objects in the room.

Assessment

Set out an assortment of objects that the children can measure. Make sure some are larger than a ruler. Can the child determine whether to use the ruler or a tape measure to measure the objects? Can the child make accurate measurements with both?

Quazonia Quarles, Newark, DE

Let's Get in the Number Line

Learning Objectives The children will:
1. Count spaces on the number line.
2. Develop their large motor skills.

Circle or Group Time Activity
- Ahead of time, make a large number line using a 10' length of bulletin board paper. Divide the 10' length of paper into equal sections, marking the divisions with the numerals 1–10. Roll it up, starting at the end with the numeral 10, so that the numeral 1 is rolled up last.
- When the children are on the rug, unroll it slowly to show the numeral 1. Reveal one numeral at a time, asking the children, "What comes next?" Use chairs to weigh down the edges of the paper to keep it flat. Ask a child to stand on the numeral 1. Ask the children to guess where the child's ending spot would be if he took two steps (the child would be at 3), then ask him to do this. Repeat this, so the child moves up the number rug.
- Continue doing this with other children, using increasingly larger numbers of steps.
- When the children are very comfortable with this concept, ask a child to stand on the 8 and take one step toward the lower end of the number line. Again, ask the children to guess where the ending spot will be.

Learning Centers

Art
Ahead of time, prepare a large number line at least 10' x 2'. Mark a horizontal line the length of the paper and mark the notches for the numerals. Lightly pencil in the numerals 1–10 so each is about 18" tall. Paint the children's hands and help them make handprints on the outlines of the penciled numeral, repeating until the handprints cover the outline. Display the number line on the bulletin board or on a long wall.

Blocks
Provide a long black piece of paper marked like a highway and wide enough for two-way block area traffic. Label the highway with markers showing "1 mile," "2 miles," and so forth. Encourage the children to build two cities and stretch the highway number line between the two cities.

Literacy
Ahead of time, cut rectangles (8" x 80") from bulletin board paper. Mark a line the length of the paper and fold it into 10 sections, back and forth, like folding a fan. In the center of each section, make a 2" vertical line. Above the line, on every section, make the outline of a numeral for the children to color in. Make outlines for the numerals 1–10.

Math

Ahead of time, fold 2' × 4'' strips of paper in half so they measure 2' × 2''. Mark a straight line the length of the strip and make 10 vertical notches, evenly spaced, to create a number line. Provide numeral cards and show the children how to copy the numerals onto their number line headbands, in the correct order. For younger children, use number stickers.

Small Motor

Ahead of time, create tactile numeral cards with tagboard and glue. Write one numeral on each card and pour a thick line of glue to outline the numerals. When they dry, the children can trace the glue to help learn the shape of each numeral. Show the children how to put the tactile numeral cards in order and provide playdough for them to make matching numerals.

Book Suggestions

Count and See by Tana Hoban
Little Rabbit's First Counting Book by Alan Baker
Moja Means One by Muriel Feelings

Snack

Make cookie dough numerals with the children. Give the children cookie dough and show them how to shape it into two or three numerals. Give them raisins and ask them to put one on the numeral 1, two raisins on the numeral 2, and so on. Bake as directed.

Review

Display the children's foldout books and discuss the order of the numerals. Ask several children to close their eyes and feel tactile numeral cards to guess which numeral they are holding. Invite several children to tell which numerals they made for snack.

Assessment

Ask each child to take a toy car and move it one step along on the number line, asking, "Where is the car now?" Repeat with directions to move one step more, two steps, and so on.

 *Susan Oldham Hill, Lakeland, FL*

Number Games

Learning Objectives The children will:
1. Play number games.
2. Count objects.
3. Develop their small and large motor skills.

Circle or Group Time Activity
- Play Find a Seat (similar to Musical Chairs) with the children.
- Place a few chairs close together. Be sure that as the game begins there are several fewer chairs out than there are children.
- Turn on some music, and ask the children to run around the chairs.
- Occasionally, stop the music, and ask the children to find chairs in which to sit.
- Ask a child who does not find a chair to count aloud the number of children sitting in the chairs.
- Unlike the game of musical chairs, increase the number of chairs with each round. If you cannot use chairs due to space constraints, replace the chairs with newspaper sheets or magazines.

Learning Centers **Blocks**

Write numerals on several large sheets of paper and challenge the children to use blocks to recreate the numerals. Challenge more advanced children to use the matching number of blocks to create the various numerals.

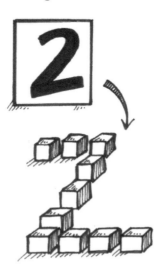
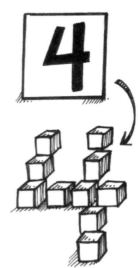

Library
Put a recording and copy of *1, 2, 3 to the Zoo* by Eric Carle in the center for the children to listen to and look through.

Math
Provide a calendar for the children to observe. Invite them to count the number of weeks in every month, and the number of days in a week.

Music
Display musical instruments. Ask the children to count the number of keys, strings, or holes in the musical instruments. Turn on music and invite the children to play drums or other simple instruments, asking them to count the number of times they tap their instruments as they play.

Sand and Water
Challenge the children to count the number of grains in a spoonful of sand.

Small Motor
Invite the children to bend chenille stems into numerical shapes.

Book Suggestions

1, 2, 3 to the Zoo by Eric Carle
Anno's Counting Book by Mitsumasa Anno

Snack

Serve oranges. Invite the children to count the slices of their oranges as they peel and eat them.

Review

Set out several magazines and newspapers and ask the children to spot numbers in the reading materials.

Assessment

Can the child count the number of legs of the tables and chairs in the classroom?

Shyamala Shanmugasundaram,
Nerul, Navi, Mumbai, India

Number Time

Learning Objectives   The children will:
1. Count from 1–10 and from 10 –1.
2. Understand one-to-one correspondence of numbers to objects.

Circle or Group Time Activity
- Teach the children the following song:

Ten Days of School by Renee Kirchner
(Tune: "The Twelve Days of Christmas")
*On the first day of school my teacher gave to me
A pencil with a big eraser.*

(Additional verses)
…two soft tissues.
…three magic markers.
…four animal crackers.
…five red blocks.
…six pieces of paper.
…seven coloring books.
…eight pretty stickers.
…nine smiley faces.
…ten big hugs.

- Tell the children that today they will learn about the numerals 1–10.
- With the children, practice counting from 1–10 and then back down from 10–1.

Learning Centers   **Art**
Help the children make homemade ring abacuses. The children choose 10 large beads, thread them onto a long chenille stem, and fold the ends of the chenille stem together.

Blocks
Give each child 10 blocks and encourage each of them to build something. Leave the structures on their tables and invite the children to walk around to see what everyone else built.

Literacy
Give each child 10 pieces of paper, each with a number on it from 1–10, and invite the children to draw corresponding numbers of objects on their sheets of paper.

Math
Play "Find the Missing Number" with the children. Give each child a piece of paper with the numbers 1–10 on it, but leave out one number and see if the children can tell what is missing (for example, "1, 2, 3, 4, 5, ___, 7, 8, 9, 10"). Challenge the children to name the missing number and write it in the empty space.

Small Motor
Set out 10 sticks and invite the children to play a game of "Pick Up Sticks."

Book Suggestions   *How Many Snails?* by Paul Giganti
Mouse Count by Ellen Stoll Walsh
Olivia Counts by Ian Falconer

Snack   Ask each child to bring 10 small food items from home, for example, 10 raisins, 10 cheerios, 10 mini marshmallows, or 10 mini pretzels. Mix all of the items in a large bowl. Give each child a small bowl of snack mix.

Review   Invite the children to wander around the classroom and look for all the places they can find numbers, such as in calendars, on number lines, on books, on rulers, and elsewhere.

Assessment   Ask the children to count from 1–10. Can they count backwards from 10–1?

Related Song   **Ten Little Puppies** by Renee Kirchner
(Tune: "Bumping Up and Down in My Little Red Wagon")
One little, two little, three little puppies.
Four little, five little, six little puppies.
Seven little, eight little, nine little puppies.
Ten little puppy dogs.

Ten little, nine little, eight little puppies.
Seven little, six little, five little puppies.
Four little, three little, two little puppies.
One little puppy dog.

(Sing other verses using kittens, hamsters, goldfish, and so on.)

 Renee Kirchner, Carrollton, TX

What Can We Do with the Number Three?

Learning Objectives   The children will:
1. Count to three.
2. Recognize the number three.
3. Learn songs, poems, and stories that are about or contain the number three.

Circle or Group Time Activity
- Play "Do as I Do" with the children.
- Make various movements, performing each three times each. Ask the children to imitate the movements.
- Some sample actions include the following:
  - Clap hands on knees
  - Tap head
  - Snap fingers
  - Touch toes
- After making the various movements, ask the children what all the actions had in common. Give hints and talk about how the children did all three movements three times.
- Invite the children to take turns making motions for the other children to copy, and encourage them to add new actions.

Learning Centers   **Art**
Use elastic bands to tie together sets of three crayons, markers, colored pencils, and regular pencils. Set out the groups, and invite the children to make designs from the sets on paper.

Dramatic Play
Invite the children to act out the story of the "Three Billy Goats Gruff." To make the bridge, provide blocks, chairs with blankets over them, or large boxes.

Literacy
Ask the children to consider what would happen if they had three eyes, three ears, or three legs. As they describe what any of these experiences would be like, and copy down what they say. After they finish, give them their sheets of paper and invite them to illustrate their descriptions.

Math
Provide a large soup bowl with 30 cutouts of the numbers 1, 2, and 4 through 10, as well as 30 cutouts of the numeral 3. Challenge the children to find and remove all the 3s from the bowl.

Sand and Water
Set out a scale and invite the children to compare the weights of one set of three objects to another set of three objects, such as weighing three blocks against three feathers, and so on.

Small Motor
Set out several small sets of three matching cutouts, such as three dogs, three bones, three bats, three balls, three cats, and three bowls. Punch holes in all the cutouts, set out strings, and invite the children to make patterns, using the matching sets of three, as well as the other sets of objects that best go with the original sets.

Book Suggestions
The Three Bears by Paul Galdone
Three Billy Goats Gruff by Stephen Carpenter
The Three Little Kittens by Paul Galdone
The Three Pigs by Patricia Seibert

Snack
Set out several various fruits, and invite the children to pick three pieces of each kind they want to eat to include in their fruit salads.

Review
Set out various objects in sets of three, and ask the children to vote for which sets of three things they like the most.

Assessment
Ask the children to count to three, find the number three in the room, and find three of their favorite toys from the room.

 *Eileen Lucas, Fort McMurray, Alberta, Canada*

Boots and Shoes

Learning Objectives   The children will:
1. Use their discussion skills.
2. Explore their design creativity.
3. Develop small and large motor skills.
4. Practice addition and subtraction.

Circle or Group Time Activity

- Before doing this activity, send home a note asking families to send in an interesting pair of their own pair of shoes or boots. Have several additional sets available for any children who forget to bring in shoes.
- Engage the children in a discussion about their family members' footwear. Explain that they will be learning about different types of boots and shoes and why people need different footwear for different occasions.
- Ask the children to take turns showing the interesting footwear they brought in. Ask them questions such as, "Who would wear these?" and "What does your (mother, father, caregiver, sister, and so on.) wear them for?" Encourage the children to try to make thoughtful guesses if they do not know.
- Discuss what you have found out about boots and shoes. Talk about what the children's families do for a living, for fun, for exercise, and so on.

Learning Centers   **Art**

Set out colorful paper, glue, markers, glitter, and other colorful items along with several milk containers (two containers per child). Cut holes into the larger sides of

the cartons and seal the edges with masking tape. Make sure the holes are big enough for the children to get their feet into them. Explain to the children that they are shoemakers, and invite them to decorate the shoes with the other avail able materials. For those children who want to add laces to their shoes, use a hole punch to make holes in the carton through which the children can thread yarn or shoelace

Library

With the children, make several recordings of various traditional fairy tales that involve boots and shoes, such as "Puss in Boots," "Cinderella," and so on. Set out copies of these stories alongside the recordings so the children can listen to them as they look through the books.

Math

Set out stacks of play $1 and $5 bills along with the various shoes the children's family members provided. Invite the children to pretend they are in a shoe store, with some children working as employees and others as customers. Have the children sell the shoes to one another for prices from $1–$5 and use the play money to pay and make change.

Small Motor

Set out several shoes with laces, as well as several thick cords so the children can practice tying laces. If available, set out buttonhooks that the children can practice buttoning.

Snack and Cooking

Set out several boot-shaped cookie cutters and a few trays with a simple cookie batter in them. Ask the children to help you spread the dough and cut the cookie shapes with the cutters, and then bake the cookies for the children.

Book Suggestions

Boots for Beth by Alex Moran
Joe Lion's Big Boots by Kara May
Sausages! by Anne Adeney
Shoes by Debbie Bailey
Shoes, Shoes, Shoes by Ann Morris

Snack

Enjoy the boot cookies the children made in the Snack and Cooking Center.

Review

Ask children which animals may need to wear footwear and why.

Assessment

Given a variety of different articles of clothing, the child will be able to identify which are boots and shoes.

 *Anne Adeney, Plymouth, United Kingdom*

Contrasts

Learning Objectives The children will:
1. Learn about opposites through observation.
2. Develop their large motor skills.

Circle or Group Time Activity
- If possible, visit a pet store with the children or arrange to have a rabbit and a turtle in the classroom for the children to observe. (You might want to contact a pet store or a local nature center to see if someone can bring these animals in.)
- Talk with the children about the two different animals.
- Read *The Tortoise and the Hare* by Janet Stevens to the children.
- Ask the children what would have happened if the rabbit did the opposite of everything he did in this story.
- Invite the children to compare the turtle and the rabbit. Write their responses on a classroom chart. Make three columns ("Characteristics," "Rabbit," and "Tortoise") and encourage the children to describe the speed, color, texture of the skin or fur, and so on of each animal.
- Show them several pictures of other animals. Ask the children to pick out animals with characteristics that are opposite of each other.

Learning Centers

Blocks
Invite the children to create block structures that are tall and short, long and short, wide and narrow, and so on.

Library
Invite the children to read books about opposites in the Library Center. Include a copy of *Archibald's Opposites* by Phil Vischer for the children to look through.

Listening
Place several small, resealable containers next to several bowls or bins containing pebbles, cotton, ice, tissues, water, and buttons. Invite the children to fill the containers with different amounts of the individual materials, and shake the containers to listen to the different sounds they make.

Sand and Water
Give the children two containers to fill with sand and then weigh them using a small kitchen scale or balance scale. After the children weigh the two containers, have them add water to one container, and reweigh the containers to compare the different results.

Small Motor
Set out several ropes and twine of various lengths. Ask the children to compare their sizes, and ask them to place them on the ground and shape them into the outlines of large and small creatures.

Snack and Cooking
Make lemonade. Cut a lemon in half and ask the children to taste the sour lemon. Tell the children the sour taste of the lemon tastes sweet when mixed with water and sugar. Squeeze the lemon into a glass of water, add three teaspoons of sugar, and stir.

Book Suggestions

Eric Carle's Opposites by Eric Carle
Exactly the Opposite by Tana Hoban
The Tortoise and the Hare by Janet Stevens

Snack

Serve tiny and large animal-shaped cookies, along with the lemonade.

Review

Ask the children to search the room and find objects that are opposite in size, such as a table and a pencil or a poster and a button.

Assessment

Can the child organize a group of objects from smallest to largest?

 *Shyamala Shanmugasundaram,*
Nerul, Navi Mumbai, India

Magnets

Learning Objectives   The children will:
1. Discover the properties of magnets.
2. Identify items that magnets push and pull.
3. Develop their small motor skills.

Circle or Group Time Activity

- Without the children seeing, place a magnet inside of a bag. Tell the children you have an item in your bag (don't tell them what it is).
- Ask the children to guess what the item in the bag is. Allow them to feel the item by putting their hands in the bag without looking.
- Provide magnetic and nonmagnetic items for the children to place against the bag one at a time. The children will see that only the metal objects and magnets stick to the bag.
- Encourage the children to guess again what may be in the bag.
- Explain that they will be learning about magnets today. Tell them that magnets push and pull other magnets as well as many types of metal.
- Give the children magnets and ask them to walk around the room finding items their magnets will push and pull.

Learning Centers   ### Literacy
Invite the children to arrange magnetic letters on a magnetic board to create words, or create a word bank of items that stick to magnets.

Math
Spread blue paper on the floor and cover it with construction paper cutouts with numbers on them. Tape a paper clip to the back of each cutout, and then add several mock fishing poles. To make a mock fishing pole, tape a small magnet to the end of a string, then attach the string to a wooden dowel. Have the children "fish" for numbers. Encourage the children to identify the numbers they "catch." Older children can add their numbers with the numbers of others at their station.

Science
Fill an activity tub with various items, including metal, nonmetal, and different types of magnets. Place magnets nearby and allow the children to detect which items will be pushed and pulled by the magnets.

Art
Give each child a shoebox lid with a piece of construction paper taped inside. Provide ball bearings (found at any local hardware store in various sizes), magnetic marbles, or any metal item that can be dipped into paint. Invite the children to choose a ball bearing or magnetic marble, dip it in paint, and put it at the edge of

their paper in the shoebox lid. They make art by guiding a magnet below the shoebox cover, dragging the painted metal items along the paper in any design they choose. Repeat on the same paper with other colors of paint.

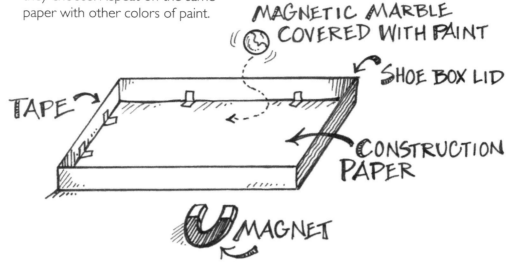

MAGNETIC MARBLE COVERED WITH PAINT

TAPE

SHOE BOX LID

CONSTRUCTION PAPER

MAGNET

Small Motor
Place magazine pictures, child-safe scissors, and glue at a working station. Give the children cutouts in the shape of horseshoe magnets and allow them to find pictures of items that stick to magnets. Direct them to cut these pictures out and glue them onto their magnets to make a collage of items that stick to magnets.

Book Suggestions
Magnets: Pulling Together, Pushing Apart by Natalie M. Rosinsky
Marta's Magnets by Wendy Pfeffer
What Makes a Magnet? by Franklyn M. Branley

Snack
Give each child a plate of pretzel sticks, peanut butter, raisins, and miniature chocolate chips. Invite the children to dip their pretzel sticks in the peanut butter making them sticky enough to pick up raisins and miniature chocolate chips at their tips.

Review
Have the children share their horseshoe magnets with the rest of the class, identifying the items that stick to their magnets.

Assessment
Given a variety of objects, can the child choose items that a magnet can push and pull?

Corrie Hornsby, Janesville, WI

Match-Ups

Learning Objectives The children will:
1. Match everyday objects that go together.
2. Develop their small and large motor skills.

Circle or Group Time Activity

- Read the story *A Chair for My Mother* by Vera B. Williams to the children several times so they know the story well.
- Gather real objects or picture cards of items from the story, such as salt and pepper, cup and saucer, shoes and socks, knife and fork, and pots and pans.
- Choose two of the pairs from the story and place them in front of the children. Ask them which two items go together. When the children choose the correct pairs, help them discover a reason the two items are related. For example, salt and pepper go together because they are both spices used on food.
- Choose two objects that do not go together, such as a knife and shoe. Ask them why they don't go together as a pair. Choose a volunteer to find the correct matches for the two objects. Continue until everyone has had a turn.
- Play "What's Missing?" Place two pairs of objects in front of the children and cover them with a dark cloth. Reach under the cloth and remove one of the four items without the children seeing. Remove the cloth and ask them which pair is still in front of them. Move the pair so that the item with its match missing remains. Ask the children to guess what the missing item is. Repeat with many different pairs.

Learning Centers **Art**

Ahead of time, scallop the edges of 7" tagboard circles to make them look like flowers and tear red, pink, fuchsia, light pink, and yellow-green tissue paper into

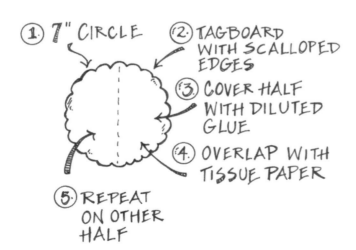

pieces about 2" long. Dilute glue with water and pour it into shallow containers, and help the children make roses like the ones on the chair in *A Chair for My Mother.*

Blocks

Talk with the children about *A Chair for My Mother* and how the characters moved the new chair with roses on it in a pickup truck. Provide doll furniture for the children to move into the Blocks Center with toy trucks.

Dramatic Play

Provide price tags, markers, and play money for the children to set up a furniture store similar to the one in the story. Give them receipt books and pens to record their sales.

Math

Provide a six-section egg carton. Put a rose sticker in the bottom of one of the sections. Place a penny, a nickel, a dime, and a quarter in the egg carton and close it. Then ask a child to shake it gently and open it to see which coin is in the rose sticker section. Ask them to name the coin, getting a friend to help if they need to. Then close the carton and play again.

Small Motor

Ahead of time, glue pictures of things that go together (such as hammer and nail, hot dog and bun, soap and water, pillow and bed, ball and bat, and so on) to 9" x 6" pieces of tagboard. Glue pairs of pictures on each piece of tagboard. When they are dry, cut them into two-piece puzzles (make sure that no two pieces have identical cuts). Spread the pieces out on the table for the children to find the matching parts.

Book Suggestions

A Chair for My Mother by Vera B. Williams
No Roses for Harry! by Gene Zion

Snack

Remind the children about the Blue Tile Diner in *A Chair for My Mother.* Give each child some play money to "buy" a snack. Give each child two vanilla wafers to represent a hamburger bun and a chocolate mint cookie to represent a hamburger — two more things that go together.

Review

Reread *A Chair for My Mother* with the children. Go back over the pages that mention pairs of matching objects and ask the children to identify them. Give them time to speculate on why the objects go together.

Assessment

Give a child 10 pictures of related items to organize into matching pairs.

 *Susan Oldham Hill, Lakeland, FL*

Opposites

Learning Objectives The children will:

1. Learn about the concept of opposites.
2. Identify opposites.
3. Develop their small motor skills.

Circle or Group Time Activity

- Read a book about opposites to the children (see the list of book suggestions below).
- Fan yourself and wipe your brow. Ask, "What's the opposite of hot?" When children respond by saying "cold," rub your arms and shiver. Smile and ask, "What's the opposite of happy?" When children respond, "sad" or "mad," make a facial expression that illustrates the emotion. Ask for more opposites and act them out.
- Play opposite charades. Write several pairs of opposites on slips of paper and put them in a container. Ask two volunteers to come up and pull a slip from the container. Whisper the names of the opposites into the children's ears and ask each of them to act out one of the two opposites. The rest of the children try to guess the opposites. Make sure everyone has a turn acting out an opposite.
- Repeat with different pairs of children.

Learning Centers ### Art

Provide white and black paper and white and black fingerpaint. Have the children experiment with making opposite paintings by painting with white paint on black paper and black paint on white paper.

Blocks

Encourage the children to make tall and small towers, long and short towers, and, if children are ready for a challenge, sturdy and weak towers. Talk about different sizes of blocks, and have children hold up a small block and large block.

Dramatic Play

Provide a bucket of soapy water, a bucket of clean water, a clothesline, clothespins, and doll clothes or washrags. Encourage the children to wet the dry clothes, wash them, and hang them on the line to dry. Talk about wet and dry.

Literacy

Invite the children to draw several pairs of opposites on different pieces of paper. Help them write the opposite underneath each picture. Assemble the pages together using a stapler or hole punch and yarn. Invite the children to make a cover for their book with the title, "My Opposites Book."

Math

Provide glue; scissors; pieces of 9" x 13" construction paper with a line drawn down the middle; and pages torn from magazines, catalogs, and newspaper inserts. Encourage the children to cut, sort, and paste pictures of items according to their likes and dislikes.

Small Motor

Provide precut octagons, craft sticks, tape, and red and green markers. Help children make signs labeled with a red "STOP" on one side and a green "GO" on the other. When finished, show the children how to use the signs when playing "Red Light, Green Light."

Book Suggestions

Black? White! Day? Night! A Book of Opposites by Laura Vaccaro Seeger
Dinosaur Roar! by Henrietta Stickland and Paul Stickland
Eric Carle's Opposites by Eric Carle
Opposites by Robert Crowther

Snack

Serve two or three of the following pairings:

- pieces of sweet pickles, sour (dill) pickles
- sweet popcorn (kettle corn), salted popcorn
- soft bananas, crunchy apples
- hot (warm) soup, cold salad
- crackers with chunky peanut butter and creamy peanut butter

Review

Ask the children to call out the opposites to the following words: "stop" ("go"), "wet" ("dry"), "yummy" ("yucky"), "yes" ("no").

Assessment

If given the first half of the following opposite pairs, can the child provide a reasonable opposite response?

Happy ⟶ _____
Hot ⟶ _____
Tall ⟶ _____

 *Cassandra Reigel Whetstone, Folsom, CA*

Same and Different

Learning Objectives The children will:
1. Identify items that belong to a particular group and those that are part of a different group.
2. Develop their small and large motor skills.

Circle or Group Time Activity
- Beforehand, collect a variety of items, such as toy cars, animals, utensils, blocks, and so on. Fill paper lunch bags or drawstring bags with three items that are alike and one different item, such as three toy cars and a small toy dog. Give each child one of the filled bags.
- Invite the children to take the items out of their bags and play with them.
- Ask the children to name the items they are playing with. Talk about how some of the items are the same and some are different.

Learning Centers **Art**
Set out watercolor paints, paintbrushes, several sheets of white construction paper, and several white crayons. Invite the children to use the crayons to draw three smiling faces and one frowning face on sheets of paper and then to paint the pages with watercolors. Watch the faces appear.

Blocks
Provide several blocks that are the same and one block that is different. Talk about what is different about the block. Invite the children to create three identical buildings using one type of block, and one differently shaped building out of the other block.

SOFT ITEMS

BREAD   COTTON BALL

TISSUE   MINI MARSHMALLOWS

FEATHER

ROUGH ITEMS

SANDPAPER   SALT

DRIED LEAF

PIECE of SCREEN

WARM ITEMS

WATER

A PLATE SITING
IN the SUN

← COOL
SETTING
ONLY

AIR FROM
a HAIRDRYER

COLD ITEMS

ICE CUBE

SNOWBALL

BOWL of SPAGHETTI or
GUMMY WORMS
(BOTH JUST REMOVED
from the FRIDGE)

Math
Put all of the items used in the Circle or Group Time activity into a large bin. Mix them up. Encourage the children to group those items that are the same, and to lay them in rows of three or five.

Sensory
Put out a variety of items with different textures and other attributes. Have the children feel all of the objects and talk about the opposites—soft and rough textures, warm and cold items, and so on.

Small Motor
Paint the children's index fingers, and help them make three prints of them on sheets of paper. Next, paint the children's big toes and make prints of them on the same pages. Help the children write their names at the bottom of their papers.

Book Suggestions　　*We're Different, We're the Same* by Bobbi Jane Kates
Whoever You Are by Mem Fox

Snack　　Serve a bowl of grapes with one banana slice on top.

Review　　Make a mark on the bottom of one of a set of paper cups. Play a variation of musical chairs in which the children pass paper cups until the music stops. The child who has the marked cup when the music stops calls out, "I've got the different cup!"

Assessment　　Show children a set of three similar items and one dissimilar item. Ask the children to identify the different item.

 *Karyn F. Everham, Fort Myers, FL*

What Goes Together

Learning Objectives   The children will:

1. Understand that many things go together.
2. Learn that some things that go together are opposites.

Circle or Group Time Activity

- Play a cat and mouse game with the children.
- Gather the children in a circle and pass one ball around. Explain to the children that this ball is "the mouse."
- Start passing a second ball, "the cat," around the circle, so it follows the "mouse." Ask the children to move the balls quickly, so that the cat does not catch the mouse.
- When the two balls meet, when one child has both at the same time, the cat caught the mouse.
- Repeat this activity with the children a few times.

Learning Centers   **Art**

Put out different colors of paint. Have the children experiment with mixing two colors to make a third color.

Blocks

Children sort blocks in shapes, sizes, and colors to show the different ways they can go together.

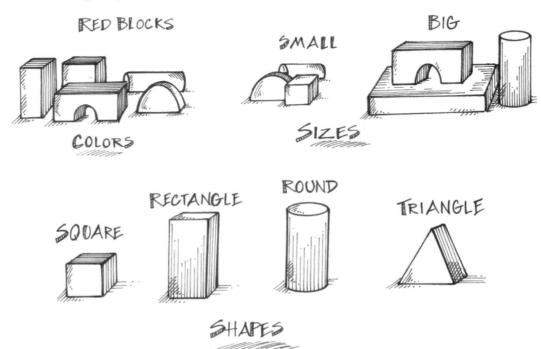

Dramatic Play

Split children into pairs and have them act out a short scene in the following roles:

- Dentist/patient
- Doctor/patient
- Teacher/student
- Mother/child

Children love this and often want to make props for their scenes. They may want to act out their scenes using puppets.

Literacy

Provide charts with upper- and lowercase letters on them and challenge the children to match the lowercase letters to the uppercase ones. This is a good time to review the letter sounds as well. Set out several sets of three objects, two of whose names start with the same letter, and a third whose name starts with a different letter. Challenge the children to determine which objects do not belong.

Math

Children use colored blocks to make a pattern, and then make a second pattern that goes together with the first one.

Book Suggestions

Cars and Trucks and Things That Go by Richard Scarry
Some Things Go Together by Charlotte Zolotow

Snack

Ask children to set their places at the table for snack, allowing them to put out what goes together for each place setting: a place mat, fork, spoon, napkin, and so on. Then the children take foods that go together for their snack, such as cheese and crackers.

Review

Children pretend to be explorers as they walk around the center looking for things that go together.

Assessment

Children play "I Spy." One child says, "I spy, with my little eye, something that goes with..." Examples include: paper goes with pencil, hat goes with head, bucket goes with shovel.

 *Eileen Lucas, Fort McMurray, Alberta, Canada*

Wow! Things Are Different

Learning Objectives The children will:
1. Identify opposites.
2. Understand that not everything is the same.
3. Learn opposite word pairs.

Circle or Group Time Activity

■ Play hide and seek with the children, but use opposite words to ask the children to hide in certain areas. For example, "Hide *behind* something or in *front* of something;" "Hide *under* something or *above* something."

■ Another way to do this is to ask half of the children to hide inside the Dramatic Play area while the other children hide outside the area.

Learning Centers

Literacy

Make pairs of word cards of opposites. For example, write the word *over* on one card and *under* on another card. Add pictures to the cards to illustrate the concept. Give each child one card from a pair and place the other card in the pair in a box. Pick out a word card and read the word. The child with the opposite word stands up and acts it out. **Note:** Some children may not want to act out the word. If this is the case, let another child act it out.

ACTING OUT

Art
Invite the children to fingerpaint. As they paint, talk about left and right, large and small, and so on. Encourage the children to paint some opposites, such as a tall person and a short person, a person with short hair and one with long hair, a long car and a short car, and so on.

Blocks
Children use blocks to show opposites; for example, over and under, in and out, up and down, left and right, more and less, and so on.

Math
Provide pieces of string and straws of different lengths and amounts. Have the children arrange them from the longest to shortest, more to less, and so on.

Sand and Water
Set several objects that either float or sink in the sand and water table. Also provide washcloths, sponges, and small towels for the children to compare what soaks up the most water.

Book Suggestions
The Foot Book by Dr. Seuss
Opposites by Sandra Boynton

Snack
Children make their own vegetable salad while discussing opposites. Give each child her own bowl and let her choose the vegetables she likes: long and short carrot sticks, celery sticks, big and little pieces of lettuce or tomato, more or less amounts of salad dressing, and so on. Use whatever vegetables are in season.

Review
Separate the children into groups. Give each group a word and ask the group to decide upon the word's opposite, and then act it out together.

Assessment
Can the children identify the opposites of various words?

 *Eileen Lucas, Fort McMurray, Alberta, Canada*

Let's Learn About
Cowboys and Cowgirls

Learning Objectives   The children will:
1. Learn some of the history of the old west.
2. Learn about cowboys and cowgirls.
3. Develop their small motor skills.

Circle or Group Time Activity
- Teach the children the words to the song "Home on the Range."
- Introduce the children to the subject of cowboys and the old west. Ask the children what they know about cowboys and cowgirls.
- Set out several images of cowboys and cowgirls for the children to look at and discuss.

Learning Centers   **Art**
Show the children how to make cowboy or cowgirl vests. Place a brown paper bag flat and draw a vest shape. Cut out the vest, leaving an opening in the front. Provide

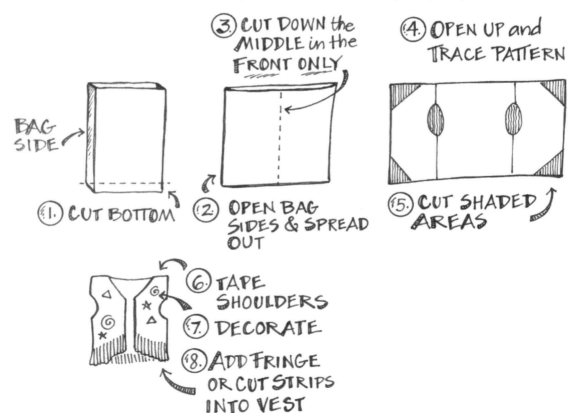

③ CUT DOWN the MIDDLE in the FRONT ONLY

④ OPEN UP and TRACE PATTERN

BAG SIDE →

①. CUT BOTTOM

②. OPEN BAG SIDES & SPREAD OUT

⑤. CUT SHADED AREAS

⑥. TAPE SHOULDERS
⑦. DECORATE
⑧. ADD FRINGE OR CUT STRIPS INTO VEST

markers, crayons, and other decorative materials so the children can decorate their vests. Help the children make "fringe" using colored construction paper.

Dramatic Play

Provide straw hats or cowboy hats. Encourage the children to act out stories of cowboys and cowgirl legends or invent their own.

Large Motor

Try your own version of a barrel race. Have children make an obstacle course using chairs, cones, trash cans, or whatever is available. Demonstrate how to run the race. Time the children to see who can finish the course first, or have team racing and add up scores from each team.

Library

Set out a recording and copy of *Yippee-Yay!: A Book About Cowboys and Cowgirls* by Gail Gibbons for the children to listen to and look through.

Music

Play square-dance music and teach the children some simple square-dance steps.

Writing

Provide paper and pencils. Let the children write (or dictate) a legend about a cowboy or cowgirl. Encourage the children to illustrate their stories, then bind them in a book and put it in the Library Center. Give it a title, such as "Legends of the _____ School Cowgirls."

Book Suggestions

The Wild West Trail Ride Maze by Roxie Munro
Yippee-Yay!: A Book About Cowboys and Cowgirls by Gail Gibbons

Snack

Serve beef jerky, cow chips (chocolate chips), and rocks (raisins) to the children.

Review

Ask the children to share what they have learned about cowboys.

Assessment

Play a game of "Now and Then." Let children call out a list of things cowboys or cowgirls would use "then" and what we use "now." Example: Then—horse, now—car.

 *Donna Alice Patton, Hillsboro, OH*

Occupations

Learning Objectives The children will:
1. Become familiar with many occupations.
2. Develop understanding of social systems in the community.
3. Increase their language and communication skills.
4. Develop their small motor skills.

Circle or Group Time Activity
- Explain that the children will be learning about different jobs.
- Place a piece of dress-up clothing at each child's place in the circle.
- Ask the children to take turns holding up the items in front of them and discussing who might wear those particular items.
- Then, as a group, discuss the kind of work this person might do.

Learning Centers

Art
Set out several magazines and child-safe scissors and ask the children to cut out pictures of people doing different jobs. Have them glue the images to pieces of construction paper to create collages.

Blocks
Provide hard hats and cardboard blocks. Encourage the children to pretend they are construction workers building a skyscraper.

Dramatic Play
Fill the dress-up area with clothes and accessories that represent different professions. Invite the children to pretend to be different workers.

Library
Invite the children to read books about different jobs, including the book *When I Grow Up...* by Peter Horn.

Writing
Write "When I grow up, I want to be a _____" on a piece of paper and make a copy for each child. Help the children complete the sentences. Provide markers and crayons and invite the children to illustrate their pages with images of them doing the jobs they described.

Book Suggestions *Career Day* by Anne Rockwell
Dreams to Grow On by Christine Hurley Deriso
Worksong by Gary Paulsen

Snack

Explain that being a chef or baker is an occupation. Bake bread with the children.

Easy Cheesy Bread

1 ¾ cups all-purpose flour
¼ cup white sugar
2 ½ teaspoons baking powder
¾ teaspoon salt
1 cup shredded cheddar
1 egg, beaten
¾ cup milk
⅓ cup vegetable oil

Preheat oven to 400 degrees. Lightly grease a 9" x 5" loaf pan. In a large bowl, mix together flour, sugar, baking powder, salt, and cheese. In another large bowl, beat together the egg, milk, and oil. Stir the flour mixture into the egg mixture until moistened. Pour batter into loaf pan and bake for 35 minutes.

Review

Invite a few family members to come in and talk a little bit about their jobs and answer questions from the children.

Assessment

Give the children the collages they made in the Art Center and ask them to identify some of the jobs represented.

Related Poem

What Will I Be? by Kimberly M. Hutmacher
Will I be a teacher?
Will I teach first grade?

Will I be a builder?
Come see what I made!

Will I be a doctor?
Will I make you well?

Will I work in a store?
Just what will I sell?

Will I be a writer?
And what will I write?

Stories that will let
My mind take flight!

 *Kimberly Hutmacher, Illiopolis, IL*

Postal Worker

Learning Objectives The children will:
1. Understand that a postal worker can have many different jobs.
2. Practice matching numbers.
3. Increase oral language skills.
4. Improve their large and small motor skills.

Circle or Group Time Activity
- Write a short note to each child and seal each in an envelope. Write each child's name on his envelope.
- Place the pieces of mail in a mailbag.
- Teach the children a song abou tthe mail, such as "Postal Worker."
- Ask three children to step forward.
- Deliver their mail to them. Give other children an opportunity to deliver and receive the mail as they sing the song several times.
- Afterwards, invite children to open the letters. Read each letter aloud.
- Share the book *Postal Workers* by Paulette Bourgeois with them. Afterwards, engage the children in a discussion about the work postal workers do.

Learning Centers

Art
Stock the center with 4" x 6" note cards. Invite each child to decorate the front of a postcard using markers, crayons, paint, and so on. Then help children write special messages to friends or family members on the other sides of their cards. Provide a rubber stamp and pad so children can "stamp" their postcards. Let them take their postcards home and "deliver" them to the appropriate people.

Blocks
Set out an assortment of letters and postcards. Invite the children to build a mailbox with blocks. Remind them to leave a space for the mail to go in near the top of the box, and a space at the bottom on the back, for mail removal. Also consider inviting the children to use other materials, such as paper, cardboard, tape, and glue to build a more sturdy mailbox.

Dramatic Play
Stock the center with postal worker clothes, pretend letters, packages, mailbags, and so on. Invite children to wear the clothing and pretend to sort, pick up, and deliver the mail.

Large Motor
Set the following items near a balance beam: a mailbox, wrapped shoebox, and three letters rubber banded together. Invite the children to pretend to be mail carriers and to walk along the balance beam. Encourage the children to balance, carry, and deliver a different item each time they walk across the beam. Challenge

the children to carry the mail high, low, behind their backs, on top of their heads, and so on.

Literacy

Provide a shoebox with a hole cut in the lid, and several note cards with simple postal worker-related words on them. Invite the children to read the various word cards and then deliver them into an "I Can Read" mailbox.

Book Suggestions

Letter Carriers: Community Workers by Alice K. Flanagan
Millie Waits for the Mail by Alexander Steffensmeier
Postal Workers by Paulette Bourgeois

Snack

Children will enjoy preparing and eating edible "mail." Invite children to set a small square of cheese (stamp) in the top right-hand corner of a saltine cracker (letter). Also, invite children to address a letter by "writing" with squirt cheese on a saltine or graham cracker.

Review

Ask the children to describe what a postal worker does for a living, and why it is important for people to receive their mail.

Assessment

Display three addressed envelopes. Invite the children to take turns picking up an envelope and sharing something they learned about postal workers as they deliver each piece of mail to you.

 Mary J. Murray, Mazomanie, WI

Way Out West

Learning Objectives The children will:
1. Demonstrate their ability to perform basic physical skills, such as running, jumping, hopping, and galloping.
2. Move with direction and beginning coordination.
3. Make several basic strokes or figures, draw some recognizable objects.

Circle or Group Time Activity
- With the children, discuss jobs that cowboys do, such as rounding up cattle, moving cattle from one place to another, and caring for cattle.
- Play a round-up game. Choose one child to be a cowboy or cowgirl. Tell the other children they will be cattle. Ask the cattle to line up on one side of the room (pasture). The cowboy or cowgirl stays in the middle of the room.
- The cattle must run to the opposite side of the room as the cowboy or cowgirl tries to tag them. The cattle that the cowboy or girl tags are considered "rounded up" and must stay with the cowboy in the pasture and help tag other cattle.
- The cattle that make it across the pasture turn around and head back to the other side.
- Continue until the cowboy or cowgirl rounds up all the cattle.

Learning Centers

Blocks
Add plastic cowboys, cows, and horses to the Blocks Center. Encourage children to make corrals with blocks.

Construction
Children build fencing by gluing craft sticks together. Cut the posts to size and glue slats perpendicular to the posts. Create a corral or a long fence. When dry, add these to the Blocks Center.

Dramatic Play
Make a western town. Use large cardboard boxes for the buildings. Cut out windows and doors from the boxes. Paint the buildings with tempera paint. Make signs for the buildings, including a barber shop, general store, and bank. Add western dress-up clothing, such as hats, boots, chaps, bandanas, and so on.

Large Motor
Put up barriers outside to simulate a corral. Children use their stick horses to race around the track, galloping and running. Put small obstacles on the track for the children to jump over. Have horse races.

Art

Help children make toy horses by cutting out two horse head shapes that are approximately 12" tall, leaving a neck at the bottom. Staple the two heads together around the edges, leaving an opening at the neck. The children stuff their horse heads with newspaper, then place wrapping paper tubes in the openings and staple the openings closed. The children then decorate their horses with markers and glue on yarn for the manes.

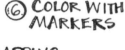

Library

Put a recording and copy of *Cowboy Camp* by Tammi Sauer in the Library Center for the children to listen to as they look through the book.

Music

Play country-western music and invite the children to two-step, square dance, and line dance.

Book Suggestions

Armadillo Rodeo by Jan Brett
Cowboy Camp by Tammi Sauer
Cowboys by Lucille Recht Penner
Cowboy Sam and Those Confounded Secrets by Kitty Griffin and Kathy Combs
How I Spent My Summer Vacation by Mark Teague
The Magic Boots by Scott Emerson and Howard Post

Snack

Serve biscuits and beans for snack. Tell the children that this is what cowboys and cowgirls commonly eat.

Review

Practice running, galloping, and jumping like horses with the children.

Assessment

When given the opportunity, can the children run, gallop, jump, and hop with direction and coordination? When given paper and pencils, can the children make several basic strokes, figures, or draw some recognizable objects?

Monica Hay Cook, Tucson, AZ

All About the Moon

Learning Objectives The children will:
1. Discover what the moon's surface is like.
2. Learn about the "man in the moon."
3. Begin to understand the concept of fractions.

Circle or Group Time Activity
- Show the children a picture of a full moon with its craters resembling a face ("man in the moon"). Ask them if they see "the man in the moon" and have volunteers come up and point out the moon's "facial features."
- Give the children paper plates and markers and ask them to draw their own men in the moon. (You may want to show a model on the board first.) Display their creations.

Learning Centers

Dramatic Play
Discuss how the moon orbits (circles around) the earth. Ask a child to stand in the center of a circle holding a large beach ball representing the earth. The other children stand in the circle and pass a smaller ball, representing the moon, from right to left, to simulate the moon's orbit. Ask the children if they could see the entire smaller ball (moon) all of the time. Explain that as the moon moves, its shape seems to change because we cannot see all of it at once, and that these different views of the moon are called "phases."

Large Motor
Cut out circles from card stock, large enough for the children to stand on. Make several more circles than there are children. Make a large masking tape circle ("moon") on the floor, large enough for all of the children's circles to fit inside. Help the children tape their circles securely to the floor, inside the masking tape circle. Explain that there are pits on the moon's surface and that the depressions (low spots) are called craters. Invite the children to explore the "moon's surface" as they walk inside the masking tape circle. Ask them to tiptoe if they are not on a circle, and bend their knees to walk at a lower height if they walk on a circle, so they can experience the irregularities of the moon's surface.

Library
Provide a recording of *On the Moon* by Anna Milbourne that the children can listen to as they look through a copy of the book.

Music
Tell the children that they would not weigh as much on the moon as they do on earth, which would enable them to take big, bouncing steps. Play music and invite the children to bounce or jump from circle to circle around the "moon's" surface. They stop when the music stops and start when the music starts again.

Snack and Cooking

Give each child four segments of a navel orange. Ask how these pieces are like the moon (four quarters). As they eat each segment, attach a construction-paper cutout of the moon to the board and use a crayon or marker to color in one quarter, two quarters, and so on until the children have eaten all four pieces.

Book Suggestions

And If the Moon Could Talk by Kate Banks
I Took the Moon for a Walk by Carolyn Curtis
Kitten's First Full Moon by Kevin Henkes

Snack

Make a "Man in the Moon" snack. Give each child a slice of circular cheese. Invite them to add raisins for eyes, a seedless grape half for the nose, and a carrot strip or curl for the mouth. Alternately, cut bread slices with a round biscuit cutter or use large round crackers. Invite the children to spread their bread or crackers with cream cheese, jelly, or peanut butter (check for allergies) and decorate with raisins, seedless grapes, and carrot strips.

Review

Give each child a picture of the full moon, showing its craters. Cut a large copy of the image into fourths. Hold up one fourth of the image and ask the children which section it is. Post it on the board and continue with the other sections. After all four pieces are up in the correct positions, ask the children what they learned about the moon.

Assessment

Ask the child the following questions, tailoring them to his age and skill level:

- Where is the moon?
- What shape is the moon?
- When do we see the moon?
- Why do people say there is a man in the moon?

 *Theresa Callahan, Easton, MD*

Blast Off

Learning Objectives The children will:
1. Recognize and count numerals from 1–10.
2. Count to 10 forward and backward.
3. Practice name recognition.
4. Practice their balancing skills.
5. Develop their oral language skills by dictating stories.

Circle or Group Time Activity
- Read *Hedgie Blasts Off* by Jan Brett to the children. Afterwards, invite the children to get ready to blast off into a space unit.
- Invite the children to stand up tall and pretend they are rockets.
- As you count down to "blast off," slowly crouch down.
- By zero, crouch all the way down to the floor. As you say, "Blast off," jump up high.

Learning Centers **Construction**
Provide tape, glue, sanded wood pieces, plastic bottles, empty paper towel rolls, paper scraps, and so on. Invite the children to use the materials to build their own rockets or spaceships.

Large Motor
Put cotton batting or pillows on the floor and cover them with a large white sheet, blanket, or shower curtain. Invite the children to pretend to walk on the moon.

LARGE
WHITE
SHEET

PILLOWS
UNDERNEATH

Literacy

Write uppercase letters on rocket die-cuts and matching lowercase letters on star die-cuts. Laminate for durability. Invite the children to match the uppercase and lowercase letters. Note: When doing this activity, keep in mind children's ability levels. Start with only five pairs at a time, and change the letters daily.

Math

Print the numbers 1–10 each on rocket die-cuts (one number per rocket) and ask the children to put them in numerical order from 1–10.

Small Motor

Print each child's name on black construction paper with white chalk (or let children do it themselves, if able). Invite the children to put star stickers on the white lines for "star-struck names."

Writing

Prepare by gluing each child's face on a rocket die-cut. Ask the children to find the rockets with their photos on them. Invite the children to glue their rockets to pieces of black construction paper and add embellishments, drawings, and sticker stars. Help them to write, "(Child's name) is going on a rocket to _____."

Book Suggestions

Hedgie Blasts Off by Jan Brett
I Am an Astronaut by Cynthia Benjamin
What's In Space? by Salina Yoon

Snack

Toast English muffins and give a half to each child. Add blue food coloring to cream cheese. Invite the children to use craft sticks to spread blue cream cheese on their muffins (to make the earth's "water"). Help the children cut lunchmeat into land shapes to place on top of the blue water.

Review

Make a class book using the children's Writing Center work. Begin the review by counting down and blasting off. Then read the book to the children and discuss their answers.

Assessment

Give each child a star shape with an alphabet letter on it (from the Literacy Center). Hold up a rocket with a letter on it. The child holding the star with the matching letter stands up and names the letter.

 *Sue Fleischmann, Sussex, WI*

Planets Move Around the Sun

Learning Objectives The children will:
1. Learn about space.
2. Learn the names of the planets.
3. Develop their small and large motor skills.

Circle or Group Time Activity
- Gather the children together in a circle.
- Place an inflatable sun or yellow ball in the middle of the circle.
- Teach the children the following song and invite them to march around the sun as they sing:

The Planets Revolve Around the Sun (author unknown)
(Tune: "The Ants Go Marching")
The planets revolve around the sun.
Hurrah! Hurrah!
The planets revolve around the sun.
Hurrah! Hurrah!
The planets revolve around the sun
And spin on their axis everyone.
And they all go spinning,
Around and around they go.

Mercury, Venus, Earth, and Mars.
Hurrah! Hurrah!
Mercury, Venus, Earth, and Mars.
Hurrah! Hurrah!
Mercury, Venus, Earth, and Mars
Are whirling and twirling around the sun.
And they all go spinning,
Around and around they go.

Jupiter and Saturn are next in line.
Hurrah! Hurrah!
Jupiter and Saturn are next in line.
Hurrah! Hurrah!!
Jupiter and Saturn are next in line.
Uranus and Neptune are the last to shine
And they all go spinning,
Around and around they go.

Learning Centers

Art

Set out orange, yellow, white, and silver paint; Styrofoam bowls (one per child); and paper lined along the bottom and blank along the top. The children choose whether they want to make suns or moons. Have them dip the bottoms of their bowls into the appropriate color of paint. When the bowls are dry, help each child staple the bowl on the top half of her paper. Each child dictates or writes at least one fact that she knows about the sun or moon to add to the bottom of the paper.

Blocks

Wrap blocks in aluminum foil for the children to use to create a working space station.

Dramatic Play

Make "oxygen tanks" by taping straps onto 2-liter bottles, so that children can slip the bottles around their shoulders. Make space helmets out of unused fried-chicken or popcorn buckets. Cut out a rectangle for eyes and spray paint the buckets silver (adult only). Attach wide elastic to sponges for children to slip around shoes for moon shoes. Encourage the children to pretend they are on the moon or exploring space.

Sand and Water

Provide red sand (if possible), small astronauts, rocks, and toy space vehicles so that the children can pretend they are exploring Mars.

Small Motor

Tape a picture of an alien to a small green soda bottle. Provide tongs and marbles. Invite the children to play Feed the Alien. Children pick up a marble with the tongs and try to drop it into the top of the bottle.

Book Suggestions

Curious George and the Rocket by H.A. Rey
Draw Me a Star by Eric Carle
I Am an Astronaut by Cynthia Benjamin and Sagasti
Papa, Please Get the Moon for Me by Eric Carle
The Planets by Gail Gibbons
Zoom! Zoom! I'm Off to the Moon by Dan Yaccarino

Snack

Serve chocolate pudding or soft ice cream in baggies and invite the children to use straws to eat it.

Review

Ask each child to name something that is in space, or ask the child to say the name of a planet. Ask the children to graph their name rockets based on the number of letters in their names.

Assessment

Show the child pictures or models of things found in space (sun, moon, stars, planet, and so on) along with pictures of everyday things. Can the child distinguish between the two groups of images?

 Wanda Guidroz, Santa Fe, TX

The Solar System

Learning Objectives The children will:
1. Learn about the parts of the solar system (sun, moon, stars, and planets).
2. Learn about the job of an astronaut.
3. Talk about rockets and how they travel to the moon.
4. Understand that the sun is a ball of gas and fire.

Circle or Group Time Activity
- Set out several balls in a variety of sizes and, using the biggest ball as the sun and the other balls as planets, show the children how the planets rotate around the sun.
- Show the children pictures of astronauts in space. Talk about the equipment that the astronauts wear. This is a great time to introduce the word "gravity" to the children. Explain that in space, gravity is diminished, and so things do not necessarily stay where they are as they would on Earth. Instead, they may float away, which is why astronauts doing space walks have tethers attaching them to their ships.
- Show the children a poster of the solar system. Encourage them to count the number of planets and talk about the characteristics of each planet.
- Show the children images that illustrate the various phases of the moon. Talk with the children about how the astronauts travel to the moon. Consider showing the children an image of a rocket and discussing the different parts of the ship.

Learning Centers **Art**

Invite the children to paint the solar system at the easel on black construction

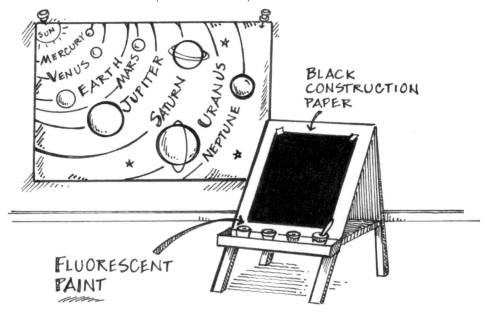

BLACK CONSTRUCTION PAPER

FLUORESCENT PAINT

paper using fluorescent paint. Next, give the children paper cutouts of circles and encourage them to paint their favorite planets or decorate the circles to look like imaginary planets. Add the planets to the solar system.

Blocks
Set out several toy astronauts among the blocks. The children can build rocket ships for the astronauts to travel in, or a solar system to which the astronauts can travel.

Math
Cut out 20 small rectangles from poster board. Write the numerals 1–10 on half of the rectangles, and place star stickers on the rest of the rectangles (one sticker on one, two stickers on another one, and so on). Turn all 20 cards over and play a memory game. **Note:** Use fewer cards for younger children.

Sand and Water
Add salt and silver glitter to the sand and water table and put plastic stars or cookie cutters in it for the children to trace around.

Science
Attach glow-in-the-dark stars and planets on the underside of a tabletop. Cover the table with a dark bed sheet on three sides. Invite the children to go under the table, lie down, and look at the stars. If desired, use a nail to punch star constellations into one end of an empty juice can (adult only step). Children hold a flashlight through the can so they can see the constellation on the table.

Writing
Set out several sheets of paper with the following statement written on them: "If I were an astronaut, I would_____." Encourage the children to finish the statement, and help them copy their responses into the blank. Give the children their papers and invite them to illustrate their answers.

Book Suggestions

If You Decide to Go to the Moon by Faith Mcnulty
If You Were an Astronaut by Dinah L. Moche
The Magic School Bus Lost in the Solar System by Joanna Cole
Our Stars by Anne Rockwell
Planets Around the Sun by Seymour Simon
The Planets in Our Solar System by Franklyn M. Branley
Spacebusters: The Race to the Moon by Philip Wilkinson
Stars! Stars! Stars! by Bob Barner

Snack

Serve the children star-shaped and round cereal.

Review

Ask the children to describe what they learned about the planets, stars, the moon, and astronauts.

Assessment

Do the children understand that the planets move around the sun?

 *Holly Dzierzanowski, Brenham, TX*

Space

Learning Objectives The children will:
1. Learn about the objects in space, including stars, planets, sun, moon, and comets.
2. Discover what astronauts do and eat.
3. Get a sense of what being weightless in space might be like.

Circle or Group Time Activity
- To prepare, cut tagboard into 4" x 6" strips. Write the name a planet, sun, moon, or stars on each strip. Punch holes at the top of each tagboard strip and string yarn through the holes. Tie knots.
- With the children, read the book *My Place in Space* by Joan Sweeney or another similar book about astronomy. After reading the book, tell the children they are going to become planets in space.
- Give the children the nametags to wear around their necks. Line up the "planets" from the one closest to the sun to the one furthest away.
- Have the moon and stars stand in appropriate spots, too.

Learning Centers ### Art
Provide several rocks, paintbrushes, and glow-in-the-dark paint. Invite the children to paint their rocks. When the rocks are dry, have the children test the rocks out in the "black hole" area (see Dramatic Play).

Blocks
Tinker toys work great for making satellites and space stations. Add cylinders and cones to the Blocks Center, too. Children can build rockets and space stations. Post some pictures in the area for children to reference.

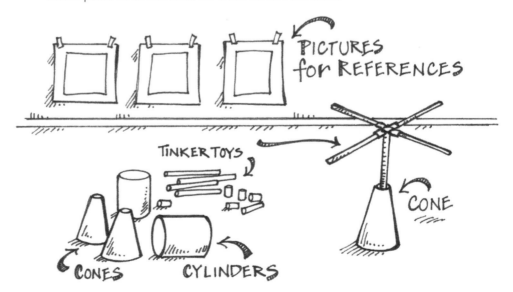

Dramatic Play

Create a "black hole" in the classroom. Put up blankets to frame a dark area. The children will have a great time pretending they are astronauts that fell into a black hole and need to be saved by their fellow astronauts. Add flashlights and moon rocks (see Art Center). Encourage the children to create alien costumes using some of the following props: swim caps, goggles, glasses, gloves, rubber shoes, shower caps, and paper grocery bags.

Music and Sound

Talk about zero gravity and being weightless in space. Play some new-age music and have the children pretend they are weightless. The children stand on one foot and try to balance. The other foot and their arms float in the air. Try a weightless free-fall, floating slowly to the ground.

Sensory

Place an air mattress on the floor and invite the children to "walk on air." Have them take off their shoes and walk or crawl across the mattress.

Small Motor

Let the children make comets. Have them crumple tissue paper into a ball and then glue strips of shiny gift bag filler onto the tissue paper. After they dry, the children can toss the comets into space and let them fall to the earth.

Book Suggestions

I Want to Be an Astronaut by Byron Barton
Me and My Place in Space by Joan Sweeney
There's No Place Like Space: All About Our Solar System by Tish Rabe
Twinkle, Twinkle, Little Star by Iza Trapani
What's Out There?: A Book About Space by Lynn Wilson

Snack

Talk about what astronauts eat in space, such as apricots, apples, cherries, pears, and so on. Other foods include granola bars, crunch bars, cookies, and brownies. Serve some of these for snack. Don't forget to clean up after yourself. Throw your garbage away or it will float around in your spaceship.

Review

Review the solar system by asking the children questions, such as:

- *What planet do we live on?*
- *What small body in the sky appears to have a tail?*
- *What shines during the day and warms the earth?*
- *What shines in the night sky?*

Assessment

When shown homemade or store-bought representations of bodies in the solar system, can the children identify stars, planets, sun, moon, and comets?

Related Songs

Sing "Twinkle, Twinkle, Little Star," or "Star Light, Star Bright" with the children.

 *Monica Hay Cook, Tucson, AZ*

Stars

Learning Objectives The children will:
1. Become familiar with comparative words.
2. Learn about stars.
3. Begin to create a representational drawing.

Circle or Group Time Activity
- Sing "Twinkle, Twinkle, Little Star" with the children.
- After singing, engage the children in a discussion about stars. Ask them what stars are. Tell children that stars are balls of gases in outer space.
- Ask the children when it is possible to see stars. Tell children that there is one star that we see in the day. Ask if anyone knows what that is (the sun).
- Tell the children that stars come in different sizes. Put a large cutout of a star on the flannel board. Say, "This is a big star." Put a slightly larger star beside it and say, "This is a bigger star," then add an even larger star. Say, "This is the biggest star." Ask children to point to big, bigger, and biggest stars.
- Repeat with small, smaller, and smallest stars.
- Give a volunteer any three stars and ask that volunteer to put them in order from smallest to largest, as the other children offer advice about the order. Repeat with other volunteers.

Learning Centers

Art
Provide dark blue or black construction paper and chalk. Encourage children to draw stars on the paper with the chalk to create a starry sky.

Dramatic Play
Help a child tape black paper to the end of a cardboard tube to make a telescope. Use a pushpin to prick holes into the paper. Encourage the child to use the telescope to pretend to see the stars.

Math
Provide an assortment of star-shaped items. Encourage each child to pick three to put in order of size. Ask the children to identify the big, bigger, and biggest or small, smaller, and smallest stars in the group.

Sand and Water
Put glitter into a tub filled with water. Encourage the children to stir the water with their hands to make the glitter swirl in the water, like stars in the sky.

Snack and Cooking
Prepare package biscuit mix. Let a child roll out a portion and use a star cutter to make a star shape. Bake per package directions and serve for snack.

Book Suggestions   *Stars! Stars! Stars!* by Bob Barner
The Sun Is My Favorite Star by Frank Asch
Twinkle, Twinkle, Little Star by Iza Trapani

Snack   Serve biscuits from the Snack and
Cooking Center along with slices of
star fruit (also called carambola).

Review   Put children into groups of three.
Help them arrange their groups
according to the heights of
the children.

Assessment   If given three stars or other similar objects, can the child put them in order by size?

 Cassandra Reigel Whetstone, Folsom, CA

The Sun, the Moon, and the Stars

Learning Objectives   The children will:

1. Understand the shapes of the sun, moon, and stars.
2. Practice classifying objects by matching and sorting.
3. Develop their scientific thinking and problem solving.
4. Increase their language and communication skills.
5. Develop their small motor skills.

Circle or Group Time Activity

- Provide Styrofoam sphere, crescent, and star shapes from a local craft store. Give one to each child.
- Begin by explaining that there are many shapes in space.
- Explain that the sun is shaped like a sphere. The moon is shaped like a sphere, too, but it can also look like a crescent. We also see stars in the sky.
- After introducing the proper names of each shape, ask the children to hold up their shapes and say which kinds they are.

Learning Centers   **Art**

Cut sponges into circle, crescent, and star shapes. Provide blue construction paper and yellow tempera paint. Show the children how to dip the shapes into the paint and press them onto the paper to create an evening sky.

Dramatic Play

Choose one child to be the sun. Choose another child to be the earth. Demonstrate how the earth revolves around the sun and invite the children to take turns acting this out.

Library

Place a variety of books about the solar system in the Library Center for the children to look through. Make sure they have lots of pictures.

Math

Cut out and laminate circles, crescents, and stars from various colors of construction paper. Place them in a basket. The children sort them by shape and then by color. Invite them to count how many of each shape there are and how many of each color.

Science
Explain to the children how the sun allows us to see our shadows. Take children outside on a sunny day. Place a piece of poster board on the ground. Hold a leaf above the paper and let each child trace the shadow on the paper. Place the leaf on the shadow. Ask the children if the leaf is larger or smaller than the shadow. Leaving the paper in the same spot, repeat this experiment later in the day. Ask the children if the shadow gets larger, smaller, or stays the same.

Book Suggestions

Comets, Stars, the Moon, and Mars: Space Poems and Paintings by Douglas Florian
Goodnight Moon by Margaret Wise Brown
How Many Stars in the Sky by Lenny Hort
Papa, Please Get the Moon for Me by Eric Carle

Snack

Let the children use cookie cutters to cut pieces of refrigerated sugar-cookie dough into crescent or star shapes. Bake the cookies. After baking the cookies, the children decorate the cookies and enjoy an out-of-this-world snack.

Review

Set several images of space-related items around the room. Ask each child to find something in the room that she would find in space.

Assessment

Ask each child to identify a sphere, a crescent, and a star.

Kimberly Hutmacher, Illiopolis, IL

Wonders in the Sky

Learning Objectives The children will:
1. Learn about the eight planets, the sun, and the moon.
2. Develop their listening skills.
3. Develop their small and large motor skills.

Circle or Group Time Activity
- Play some instrumental music.
- Occasionally, stop the music. When the music stops, give the children various instructions to perform. For instance, ask children to stand still when you say "sun," twirl slowly and walk in a circle when you say "planet" or "moon," or touch the tips of their fingers and outstretch them repeatedly when you say "star" to indicate the twinkling of stars.
- Explain to the children that the sun stays in the same place but the planets move around the sun.

Learning Centers

Art

Tape black construction paper to the wall and invite the children to use crayons to draw objects that they might see in the sky at night.

Sand and Water

Encourage the children to create craters on the sand by dropping round or oval objects from right above the sand table or sandpit (if outdoors).

Math
Show a chart of the solar system. Discuss the size of the planets. Encourage the children to use words like "small," "smaller," "smallest," "big," "bigger," and "biggest" to compare the planets. Ask the children to number the planets in order according to size.

Small Motor
Invite the children to use playdough create eight balls (eight planets) of different sizes. Hang the chart from the Math Center to help the children arrange the planets by size.

Writing
Provide cards with the name of each planet them. Invite the children to trace over the words and/or write the words on another piece of paper, depending on ability.

Book Suggestions   *I Want to Be an Astronaut* by Byron Barton
Looking into Space by Nigel Nelson

Snack   Serve two round biscuits (same size) to each child. Ask them to hold one in each hand and take 30 nibbles from the same side to finish the biscuit in the right hand. After every nibble ask them to compare the biscuit with the one in the left hand. Explain that it is similar to the waning of the moon.

Review   Ask the children to go outdoors and discuss which celestial bodies they can and cannot see.

Assessment   Display a solar system chart in the classroom. Can the children point out the sun, the moon, and the planets?

 *Shyamala Shanmugasundaram,*
Nerul, Navi, Mumbai, India

Zoom to the Moon

Learning Objectives The children will:
1. Discover information about the moon.
2. Develop their small motor skills.
3. Gain an understanding of a list.
4. Identify the smallest and largest shapes in a group.

Circle or Group Time Activity

■ Teach the children the following song:

Zoom, Zoom, Zoom (author unknown)
Zoom, zoom, zoom,
We're going to the moon.
Zoom, zoom, zoom,
We're going to the moon.
If you'd like to take a trip,
Climb aboard my rocket ship.
Zoom, zoom, zoom,
We're going to the moon.
Five, four, three, two, one, blast off!

■ Sing it again while the children jump up and down.

Learning Centers

Literacy
Write "Packing List for a Trip to the Moon" at the top of a sheet of chart paper. Ask the children what items or objects they would take on a trip to the moon. Record their items and display the list on the wall.

Math
Have the children sort plastic stars and moons in order from largest to smallest.

Sand and Water
Provide sand, golf balls, tennis balls, ping pong balls, and marbles at the sand table. The children drop the balls onto the surface of the sand to create craters, and then compare the craters to see which are the smallest and largest.

Small Motor
Have the children roll white playdough into a ball to look like the moon and then have them press their fingers into it gently to make craters.

Dramatic Play
Help the children make a space shuttle out of large cardboard boxes. Cut windows and doors into the boxes and invite the children to paint them and decorate them as desired. Provide an old computer keyboard for children to use as the shuttle's controls. Supply white clothes and plastic helmets, and encourage the children to pretend they are astronauts on a trip to the moon.

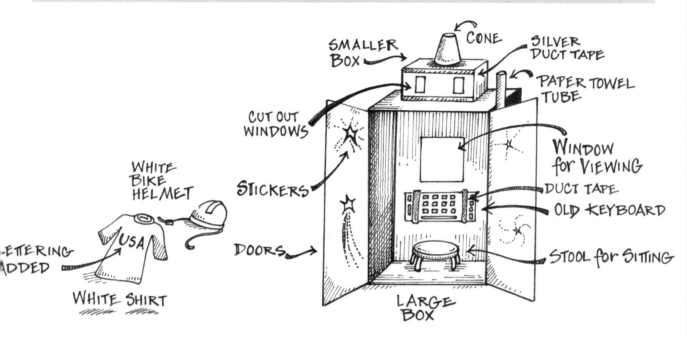

Book Suggestions

Catching the Moon by Myla Goldberg
The Moon Book by Gail Gibbons
On the Moon by Anna Milbourne
Papa, Please Get the Moon for Me by Eric Carle
So That's How the Moon Changes Shape by Allan Fowler
Zoom! Zoom! Zoom! I'm Off to the Moon by Dan Yaccarino

Snack

Make space pudding. Explain that astronauts eat certain foods in space because there is no gravity in space. Give each child a resealable sandwich bag. Pour ¼ of a box of instant pudding into each bag. Add enough milk to correspond to the directions on the pudding package. Seal the bags tightly and have the children squeeze and shake them until the pudding thickens. Cut off one corner of each bag and let the children suck the pudding out, just like real astronauts.

Review

Ask the children to describe the moon. What color is it? What shape is it? Does it always look the same, or does it change?

Assessment

Ask each child to use one word to describe the moon. Ask if the moon's surface is smooth, or if it has craters.

 *Laura D. Wynkoop, San Dimas, CA*

Caring for Pets

Learning Objectives   The children will:
1. Discover that there are different kinds of pets.
2. Help take care of a classroom pet.

Circle or Group Time Activity
- Play "Who Has My Bone?" with the children.
- Choose a volunteer to be the dog. Put a bone under a chair and ask the child to sit in the chair and close his eyes.
- Tap one child on the shoulder, or ask a child to tap another child. That child then tries to take the bone from the dog without making a sound.
- The child who took the bone goes back to her spot and hides the bone. The "dog" opens his eyes and tries to guess who took his bone.
- If the dog does not succeed with three guesses, the child who took the bone becomes the dog.
- Repeat until all the children have had a turn.

Learning Centers   ### Art
Invite the children to make pet puppets. Precut a few different animal shapes from construction paper, including a dog, cat, fish, mouse, and bird. Provide a variety of materials, such as felt, foam pieces, markers, glue, construction paper, yarn, and so on. Encourage the children to decorate their chosen pet and then glue or tape to a craft stick.

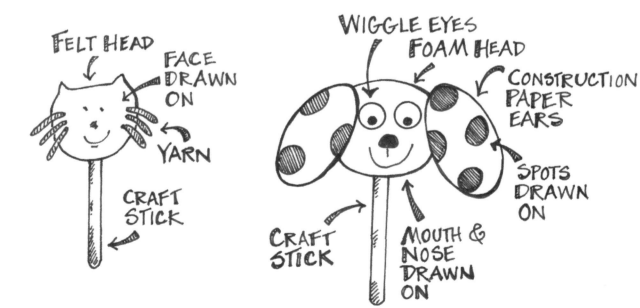

FELT HEAD
FACE DRAWN ON
YARN
CRAFT STICK

WIGGLE EYES
FOAM HEAD
CONSTRUCTION PAPER EARS
SPOTS DRAWN ON
CRAFT STICK
MOUTH & NOSE DRAWN ON

Games

Read a few riddles and have the children hold up their pet if it relates to the riddle. Some riddles are:

I have long floppy ears that hang real low.
I chew on bones that make me grow.
What am I? (dog)

I love to cuddle and purr really loud.
Sometimes I chase mice, even though it's not nice.
What am I? (cat)

Encourage the children to make up their own riddles and play with each other.

Dramatic Play

Place props such as stuffed animals, real or play pet carriers, pet dishes, pretend bones, pet beds, leash, and so on in this area. Encourage the children to pretend to run a pet store or vet office.

Science

Arrange to care for a pet (such as a fish or hamster) for a week or more in the classroom. (Some families may be willing to donate their pets for a week.) Set up an area to keep the pet. Place storybooks related to the pets you have in this area, as well as food for the animals and material for changing the cages. Let the children take turns feeding the pets, giving them water, and helping to clean the cage.

Note: Check first to be sure no children have animal allergies.

Small Motor

Cut out different body parts of different animals from magazines. Invite the children to assemble the body parts to make their own unique animal. For example, a child might put a dog's head on a snake's body and add a cat's tail.

Writing

Encourage the children to draw a picture of an animal and name it. Help them to write things about the pet (the wackier the better!). Children love this! Assemble all of their drawings and stories into a class book.

Book Suggestions

A Home for a Hermit Crab by Eric Carle
I Wanna Iguana by Karen Kaufman Orloff
"Let's Get a Pup!" Said Kate by Bob Graham

Snack

Serve blue gelatin "fishbowls." Let the children help make and pour blue gelatin into small transparent plastic cups. (**Note:** The ones used to serve wine work well.) Refrigerate to set the gelatin. When it is half set, place a few gummy fish in each cup, then put the cups back to continue setting.

Review

Graph the children's favorite pet. And they compare the results.

Assessment

Ask children what pet they would like to own and how they would care for it. Give each child an "I can care for my pet" certificate to take home. Give them pictures of their desired pet or ask them to draw their pet.

 Eileen Lucas, Fort McMurray, Alberta, Canada

Chow Time

Learning Objectives The children will:
1. Imagine themselves as pets.
2. Act out the role of pets and pet owners.
3. Develop their small and large motor skills.

Circle or Group Time Activity
- Introduce a dog puppet ("Bingo") to the children.
- Have the puppet act very excited, "jumping" on you and "licking" your face.
- Pretend to try to calm him down without success. Explain that the only thing that calms him down is the song "Bingo."
- Teach the children how to sing the song and then have the puppet act calm. Show the children how to clap the song.
- Ask if they would like Bingo to come around and lick them, or would they rather hug or pet him?

Learning Centers **Art**

Cut folded file folders into simple dog or cat shapes so that the fold is the animal's back and the pet can stand up when unfolded. Invite the children to decorate their pets using markers. Ask what the pet's name is and write it on the pet. Add a yarn leash so the children can pull their pets on a walk.

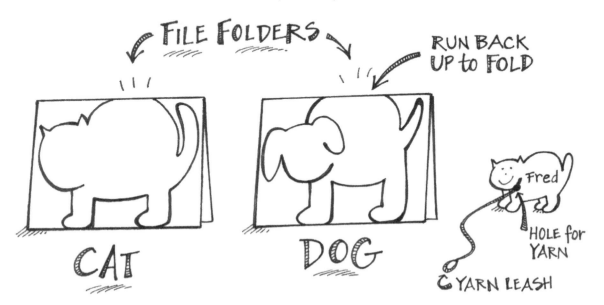

Blocks

Add stuffed animals to the Blocks Center and suggest that the children make homes for them. Ask children to bring in photos of their own pets to display in the area.

Dramatic Play

Have the children pair up and explain that one child in each pair will be a dog or cat and the other child will be the pet owner. Give the owners a paper bowl to represent pet food. The owner places the bowl on the floor and the pets pretend to eat it (on all fours) with their mouths (no paws!). The owners can pet them and talk to them until they are finished. Have them switch roles.

Literacy

Trace magnet letters to spell "Bingo" and encourage the children to match the magnets to it. Also, do the same with the words *cat* and *dog*.

Listening

Help the children record themselves singing "Bingo." Put a dog puppet in the Listening Center and invite them to listen to themselves as they hold the puppet.

Book Suggestions

Bingo by Rosemary Wells
Good Boy, Fergus by David Shannon
Kitten's First Full Moon by Kevin Henkes
Martha Speaks by Susan Meddaugh
McDuff and the Baby by Rosemary Wells
My Big Dog by Janet Stevens
Widget and the Puppy by Lyn Rossiter McFarland

Snack

Serve cereal in bowls and pretend it is "dog chow."

Review

Discuss how it felt to be the pet. Talk about and write down the names of the children's pets at home.

Assessment

Ask children about the care of pets. With their help, list different types of pets. Graph how many pets the class has at home. Clap the letters in "Bingo," and then clap the letters in their names.

 *Laura Durbrow, Lake Oswego, OR*

Different Kinds of Pets

Learning Objectives The children will:
1. Familiarize themselves with different types of animals.
2. Learn about the care and feeding of pets.

Circle or Group Time Activity
- Provide several animal puppets or stuffed animals.
- Ask the children to name the different types of animals that you have.
- Ask them questions about each one, such as, "How does the puppy sound when he barks? How does the cat sound when she meows? What does the bird like to eat for snacks?

Learning Centers

Art
Provide several old pet magazines for the children to use to cut out pictures and glue them onto paper to make a Pet Collage. If they want, children can cut out pictures of the type of pet they would like to have (horse, dog, cat).

Blocks
Add a set of small dogs and cats to the Blocks Center. Ask the children how to build houses for the animals. Ask them what other accessories they will need. Try to provide a few specific items they think they will need.

Library
Set up a "pet friendly" library. Include baskets of books about pets, large animal pillows, beds for comfy sitting while looking at books, and a few large stuffed animals to lie on or next to. Hang pictures of pets in the area too.

Sand and Water
Fill the sand and water table with bubbly water, sponges, and washcloths. Add a few plastic toy puppies and kittens and let the children give them a bath.

Science
Invite the children to bring in their small pets to keep in the classroom for a few days. Make sure the pets are in a cage or aquarium and that your program's pet policy allows this. If not, ask children to bring a photo of their pet and start a photo display of all the children and their pets. Ask other teachers to bring in their small pets (or photos) as well.

Writing
Provide rubber stamp sets of puppies and kittens in the writing area.

Book Suggestions *All About Cats & Kittens* by Emily Neye
Bad Dog, Marley by John Grogan
The Little Puppy by Judy Dunn

Snack Share goldfish crackers and encourage the children to count how many fish they have. Ask them to call out their numbers to you.

Review Take digital photos of the children throughout the day and make a small photo album of them. Display them in the room and talk about what the children are doing.

Assessment Ask the children to name all the animals that you hold up, and ask them questions about the animals. Record what the children say.

★ Sue Myhre, Bremerton, WA

Fishy Fun

Learning Objectives   The children will:
1. Gain familiarity with fish and their care.
2. Develop their small and large motor skills.

Circle or Group Time Activity
- Ask the children if anyone has a pet fish at home. If so, ask the child to describe the fish, where it lives, and what it eats. If no one has a fish, ask them if they can guess where pet fish live and what they eat.
- Make a home for a class goldfish. Let children place pebbles into a goldfish bowl.
- Add rocks, purified water, and a goldfish.
- Show the children the fish food. Invite them to touch and smell it and guess what it is made of. (Make sure they wash their hands after touching the food.)
- Ask children to guess how much food the fish will eat. Add food.

Learning Centers   **Art**
Prior to doing this activity, draw simple outlines of fish with an orange crayon on each piece of paper. Invite the children to paint with watercolor over the fish.

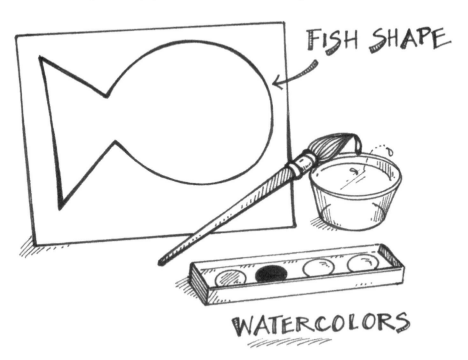

FISH SHAPE

WATERCOLORS

Dramatic Play
Invite children to pretend to be scuba divers by putting on a "scuba suit" (long underwear), flippers, and goggles. Hang posters of fish and a variety of sea life for the children to look at and pretend to photograph.

Literacy
Ask children to complete the sentence: "If I had a goldfish, I would name it _____." Then ask the children to describe their imaginary goldfish as you write their words. Invite children to illustrate their words.

Sand and Water
Place plastic fish in the water table. Invite the children to dip nets into the water and fish them out. To add math to the activity, ask them to count the fish, sort them by color, place them in order by size, and so on.

Small Motor
Encourage children to make playdough fish using fish-shaped cookie cutters, spatulas, and a rolling pin.

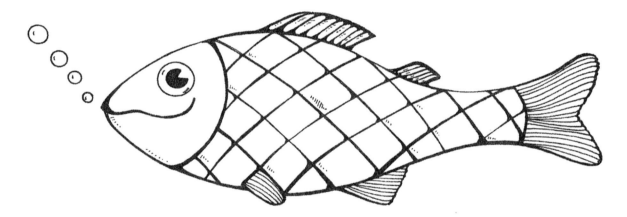

Book Suggestions *One Fish, Two Fish, Red Fish, Blue Fish* by Dr. Seuss
Rainbow Fish by Marcus Pfister
What's It Like to Be a Fish? by Wendy Pfeffer

Snack Serve goldfish crackers for snack. Add a few gummy worms, if desired.

Review Talk about keeping the goldfish healthy and strong. Make a daily chart for feeding the fish, inviting every child to participate.

Assessment Ask children to describe how a fish lives. Encourage them to use words and body movement to show this.

Karyn F. Everham, Fort Myers, FL

All Four Seasons

Learning Objectives   The children will:
1. Learn about the four seasons.
2. Name the months that belong in each season.
3. Compare weather and clothing of each season.

Circle or Group Time Activity
- Hold up a picture that illustrates one of the seasons.
- Show the children a calendar, indicating which months go with which seasons. For example, summer is June, July, and August.
- Engage the children in a discussion about the different weather in each season. **Note:** If you live in an area of the country where there isn't a lot of seasonal change, tell the children about areas that do experience seasonal changes and ask the children if they have ever experienced these seasons.
- Show them the type of clothing or accessories they would need in each season, such as mittens for winter, umbrella for spring, sunglasses for summer, and a sweater in the fall.
- Tell the children they will be learning about the four seasons today.

Learning Centers   **Art**

Read *The Seasons of Arnold's Apple Tree* by Gail Gibbons to the children. Provide paper, crayons, and markers and ask the children to draw four apple trees, one for each of the four seasons. The winter tree will have bare branches with snow on it. The spring tree will have blossoms and small green leaves. The summer tree will have big red apples. The fall tree will have orange leaves.

Library
Provide a variety of books about the seasons in the Library Center. Encourage the children to visit the center and read about the different seasons.

Literacy

Set out sheets of paper with the following statements on them:

> *The season when it snows is* _____. (winter)
> *The season when plants start to grow is* _____. (spring)
> *The season when you can go swimming is* _____. (summer)
> *The season when leaves fall off trees is* _____. (fall)

Have the children draw illustrations to complete each statement. Bind the pages together with staples or silver rings.

Math

Ask each child to name her favorite season. Graph their answers and see which seasons are the most popular. Talk about why they their favorites.

Small Motor

Talk about harvesting different foods. Explain that different fruits and vegetables are harvested at different times in the year. Provide a variety of plastic fruits and vegetables and have the children "pick" them and place them in baskets.

Book Suggestions

Caps, Hats, Socks, and Mittens: A Book About the Four Seasons by Louise W. Borden
The Little Island by Margaret Wise Brown
The Seasons of Arnold's Apple Tree by Gail Gibbons
Sunshine Makes the Seasons by Franklyn Mansfield Branley

Snack

Serve assorted fresh in-season fruit.

Review

Ask the children to describe the various seasons.

Assessment

Put pictures that go with each season on a table. Can children match each picture with the correct season?

Related Song

The Seasons of the Year by Renee Kirchner (Tune: "The Wheels on the Bus")

The seasons of the year go round and round,
Round and round, round and round.
The seasons of the year go round and round,
All through the months.

The bugs in the summer go chirp, chirp, chirp;
Chirp, chirp, chirp; chirp, chirp, chirp.
The bugs in the summer go chirp, chirp, chirp,
All through the summer months.

The leaves in the fall go crunch, crunch, crunch;
Crunch, crunch, crunch; crunch, crunch, crunch.
The leaves in the fall go crunch, crunch, crunch,
All though the fall months.

The fire in the winter goes crackle,
*   crackle, crackle;*
Crackle, crackle, crackle; crackle,
*   crackle, crackle.*
The fire in the winter goes crackle,
*   crackle, crackle,*
All through the winter months.

The wind in the spring goes whoosh,
*   whoosh, whoosh;*
Whoosh, whoosh, whoosh; whoosh,
*   whoosh, whoosh.*
The wind in the spring goes whoosh,
*   whoosh, whoosh,*
All through the spring months.

(Repeat first verse.)

 Renee Kirchner, Carrollton, TX

Autumn Leaves and Autumn Trees

Learning Objectives The children will:
1. Learn about autumn leaves and trees.
2. Improve their small and large motor skills.
3. Enhance their counting skills.

Circle or Group Time Activity

■ Before children arrive, prepare the room by cutting out trees from brown grocery bags and leaves from green, red, brown, yellow, and orange paper. Display several pictures of fall scenery around the classroom.

■ Gather the children in a circle. Sprinkle several cutout leaves around the area, letting them fall onto the children. Explain that leaves on some trees change color in the fall and then drop to the ground as the tree prepares for winter.

■ After spreading the leaves, place an empty basket in the middle of the area, and ask each child to pick up a leaf, say its color, and drop it in the basket.

■ Take the children on a color tour around the classroom. Invite the children to look for displays of fall color as you walk around the room. Talk about each fall picture as children spot the various fall images.

■ Gather the children together and remind them that fall is also a time for harvesting apples from apple trees. Have a discussion about their experiences picking and eating apples. What are their favorite types of apples?

Learning Centers

Art
Provide paper, paint, brushes, glue, and tree trunks cut from brown construction paper. The children glue four or five tree trunks to their paper, and then paint the treetops using fall colors.

Blocks
Invite the children to stand each wood block on end to represent a tree trunk and then top it off with a crumpled ball of fall-colored tissue paper.

Dramatic Play
Provide plastic apple and baskets. Invite the children to pretend to work at an apple orchard. Encourage them to pick apples and place them in bushel baskets, sell the apples, and make apple cider, pie, or caramel apples for the customers.

Large Motor
Invite the children to pour out a basket of leaves (crumpled paper balls) on the floor and then rake them up and put them in a basket.

Science

Display an assortment of autumn leaves, dry seeds, pinecones, and acorns, along with several fall-related books. The children can explore the leaves and objects by observing them with a magnifying glass, comparing their shapes, sizes, and colors, and looking through the books about autumn.

Small Motor

Provide several sheets of construction paper, child-safe scissors, and cardboard outlines of various leaves. Help the children trace the leaves on paper and cut them out. Let children punch holes in the leaves, insert craft wire through the holes and string them together. Hang these colorful displays in the classroom.

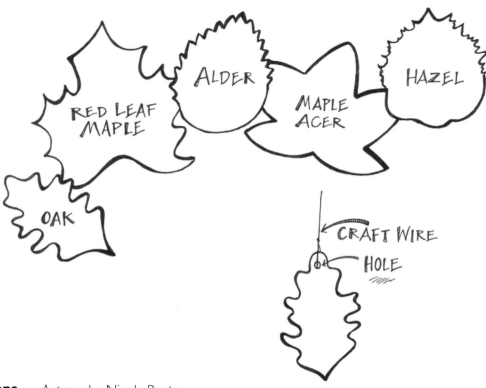

Book Suggestions

Autumn by Nicola Baxter
Autumn Is for Apples by Michelle Knudsen
Autumn Leaves by Gail Saunders-Smith
How Do Apples Grow? by Betsy Maestro

Snack

Serve apples of various colors and types, along with caramel dip.

Review

Read one of the fall-related books from the suggested book list. Invite the children to throw paper ball leaves up into the air and let them fall to the ground. Invite children to share what they learned about autumn or autumn leaves.

Assessment

Can the children describe what happens to tree leaves in the fall?

Mary J. Murray, Mazomanie, WI

Fun with Pumpkins

Learning Objectives The children will:
1. Learn about pumpkins.
2. Predict whether a pumpkin will sink or float.
3. Count to 20.
4. Taste foods made from pumpkins.

Circle or Group Time Activity
- Gather the children together in a circle and pass a small pumpkin around.
- As the children take turns holding the pumpkin, ask them to say something about the pumpkin that describes its size, shape, color, weight, and so on.
- Teach the children the following song:

Pumpkin Song (author unknown)
(Tune: "I'm a Little Teapot")
I'm a little pumpkin
Orange and round.
Here is my stem,
There is the ground.
When I get all cut up,
Don't you shout!
Just open me up
And scoop me out!

Learning Centers   **Art**
Provide paper plates, orange paint, and markers for the children to use to make jack-o-lantern paintings.

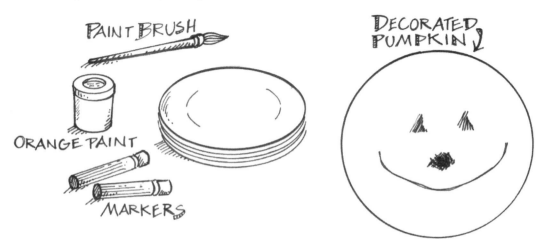

PAINT BRUSH

ORANGE PAINT

MARKERS

DECORATED PUMPKIN

Literacy

Write, "When I see a pumpkin, I think of _____" on a piece of paper. Make copies for all the children. Ask the children to finish the sentence (they can write or dictate the answer). Encourage them to illustrate their pages. Compile all the pages into a classroom book. Add a title page: "When I See a Pumpkin…"

Math

Cut out 20 pumpkin shapes from orange construction paper. Write the numerals 1–20 on them (one numeral per pumpkin) and encourage the children to put them in order. Use them to count aloud. **Note:** Make more or less depending on the age and ability of the children in your class.

Sand and Water

Encourage the children to use their fingers to draw pumpkin shapes in the sand. They can add jack-o-lantern faces, too.

Science

Set out a medium-sized pumpkin and a bucket of water and ask the children to predict whether the pumpkin will sink or float. Place the pumpkin in the bucket of water and compare the result to the children's predictions.

Book Suggestions

The Biggest Pumpkin Ever by Steven Kroll
From Seed to Pumpkin by Wendy Pfeffer
From Seed to Pumpkin by Jan Kottke
Pumpkin Pumpkin by Jeanne Titherington

Snack

Prepare pumpkin bread, pumpkin muffins, pumpkin seeds, or pumpkin pie for the children to enjoy.

Review

Ask the children to describe a pumpkin. See if they can use different sensory words to describe how it looks, smells, sounds, and feels.

Assessment

Ask each child to use one word to describe a pumpkin. Ask the children if pumpkins sink or float.

 Laura D. Wynkoop, San Dimas, CA

Harvest of Pumpkins

Learning Objectives The children will:
1. Explore the insides of pumpkins.
2. Measure the sizes of pumpkins.
3. Estimate the weight of different pumpkins.
4. Make and eat foods made with pumpkin.
5. Practice counting.

Circle or Group Time Activity
- Show the children a pumpkin and ask them if they know what is inside of it. Talk about their responses.
- Cut off the top of the pumpkin so that the children can see what is inside it. Have them take turns helping to scoop out its insides. Talk about what they find.

Learning Centers **Art**

Provide child-safe scissors, glue, construction paper, and several orange items (such as beads, fabric, paper, yarn), markers, and crayons for the children to create orange designs.

Blocks

Add small gourds and mini pumpkins to the center for the children to include in their block creations.

Large Motor

Invite the children to stand behind a throw line and toss pumpkin-shaped beanbags into a large open container.

Science

Show the children how to fold a paper towel several times, dip the towel into a container of water with red food coloring in it, and then dip it into a container of water with yellow food coloring in it. Carefully, open the towels, set them aside, and allow them to dry. Eventually, the children will see orange designs appear on the paper towel.

Sensory

Add orange scent to red and yellow playdough. Invite the children to mix it together and see if they can make orange playdough. Encourage them to smell the orange fragrance.

Snack and Cooking

Set out containers of pumpkin meat, pulp, and seeds the children can go through to separate out the seeds. Wash the pumpkin seeds, and then bake them with a little bit of oil and salt for the children to enjoy later.

Book Suggestions

Dr. Pompo's Nose by Saxton Freymann and Joost Elffers
Pumpkin Moonshine by Tasha Tudor
Pumpkin, Pumpkin by Jeanne Titherington

Snack

Provide a variety of pumpkin snacks, such as pumpkin muffins, pumpkin pie, and pumpkin seeds, along with other orange snacks such as orange slices.

Review

Ask the children to describe what is inside a pumpkin.

Assessment

Can the child count the seeds of a pumpkin?

Sandy L. Scott, Meridian, ID

It's Fall

Learning Objectives The children will:
1. Talk about the characteristics of fall weather.
2. Observe the changes that take place in the fall.
3. Develop classification skills to help sort leaves by color, type, shape, and size.

Circle or Group Time Activity
- Tell the children that you are going on a fall walk to look for signs of fall.
- Give each child a small brown lunch bag to collect fall items (leaves, acorns).
- Take photos of the children collecting fall items and looking at squirrels, trees, and so on.
- After the walk, ask the children to share specific items they found on their walk.

Learning Centers **Art**

Place a variety of leaves on the table. Children place foil over the leaves and gently rub flat chalkboard erasers back and forth over the leaves until they see imprints appear on the foil. Invite them to glue the foil imprints and the leaves they made them from beside one another on a piece of paper.

Dramatic Play

Provide several fall-related articles of clothing, such as sweaters and coats, for the children to wear and explore. Also provide football and soccer gear including uniforms, balls, helmets, and jerseys.

Literacy

Provide several outlines of fall words, such as *squirrel, leaf,* and *acorn,* as well as images of what the words describe. Give the children paper, markers, and crayons so they can copy and practice writing the words.

Math

Glue leaves of various colors and shapes down the left side of chart paper. Provide construction paper cutouts of the same leaves and ask the children to match the color and shape with the leaves on the chart paper.

Sand and Water

Provide acorns, leaves, small shovels, short-handled rakes, measuring cups, and other materials for the children to explore.

Book Suggestions

Nuts to You! by Lois Ehlert
Red Leaf, Yellow Leaf by Lois Ehlert
When Autumn Comes by Robert Maass

Snack

Make homemade applesauce using the following recipe:

- Peel and slice apples.
- Put them in a crock pot.
- Add cinnamon and a bit of sugar.
- Cook on low until it reaches the desired consistency.

Review

Ask the children to demonstrate silently an activity they did in one of the centers and challenge the other children to guess which center activity the child is mimicking.

Assessment

Can the child look at various materials that illustrate all of the seasons and pick those items that best belong to the fall?

 Kaethe Lewandowski, Centreville, VA

Leaves

Learning Objectives   The children will:
1. Learn about leaves.
2. Make leaf prints.
3. Sing and act out nursery rhymes and action rhymes.

Circle or Group Time Activity
- Show the children several leaves and engage them in a discussion about the leaves. Ask, "Do you know the parts of a leaf? Can you point to the blade, the veins, or the stem? Where can we find leaves? In which season do leaves fall? How many leaves do you see in the circle? Have you ever picked a leaf?"
- Recite the following rhyme with the children, encouraging them to act out the motions the words describe:

Three Little Leaves by Lily Erlic

Three little leaves,
Hiding in the trees,
Wondering why?
They began to cry,
"Oh my, Oh me, Oh dear,
We're going to fall, we fear!"
The wild wind said,
"It's fall,
You know,
That means,
You have to go!"

So the wind
Whooshed them away.
They fell down and down,
On a pile of hay.
"Oh what a soft landing,
I'm glad we're OK.
Let's do it again,
Some other day!"
Three little leaves,
Waving in the breeze,
Wandering around,
Without a sound.

Learning Centers   **Blocks**
Attach leaf stickers or pictures to small blocks. Challenge the children to make trees out of the blocks, using the ones with the leaf images on them as leaves and the other blocks as tree trunks.

Dramatic Play
Provide the children with a cardboard tree cutout and paper leaves for pretend play. Give them rakes so they can practice raking up the leaves.

Literacy
Give each child a sheet of construction paper and a cutout leaf shape. Ask the children to draw the outlines of the leaves on their papers. Write "My Leaf" on the tops of the papers, or challenge older children to write the phrase themselves.

Outdoors
Go outside with the children to a tree-filled area and rake up leaves with them. Let them jump in the piles!

Art

Give each child two matching paper cutouts of leaves. Explain that these will be the two sides of a puffy leaf. Have them color their leaves and staple them together, leaving enough room so they can stuff crepe paper into them. After the leaves are full, staple them once more, punch holes in their tops, and tie yarn through the holes so the children can hang them throughout the room.

① COLOR TWO CUTOUTS

④ PUNCH HOLE & ADD YARN

② STAPLE EDGES

③ LEAVE OPEN FOR STUFFING THEN STAPLE CLOSED

Small Motor

Cut out a variety of pairs of leaves in different colors, shapes, and sizes from construction paper. Be sure to cut out two matching leaves for each color, shape, or size. Place the leaf cutouts in a large basket and invite the children to search through it looking for the pairs.

Book Suggestions

Fall Leaves by Don L. Curry
It's Fall by Linda Glaser
Red Leaf, Yellow Leaf by Lois Ehlert
Why Do Leaves Change Color? by Betsy Maestro

Snack

Provide leaf-shaped cookies for the children to enjoy.

Review

Read *Why Do Leaves Change Color?* by Betsy Maestro to the children, and discuss leaves with them.

Assessment

Set out several mixed pairs of leaves and challenge them to match the pairs. Ask the children questions about leaves, such as, "Can you tell me about your leaves? What are the parts of a leaf?"

Related Fingerplay

I'm a Little Leaf by Lily Erlic
I'm a little leaf, (hold up leaf)
So warm and red, (hug self)
I like the fall, (shiver)
I like my leaf bed. (pretend to sleep)
I'm a little leaf, (hold up leaf)
I like the cold, (shiver)
I like to fly, (run around)
I like to go! (run on the spot)

 Lily Erlic, Victoria, British Columbia, Canada

Mittens and Gloves

Learning Objectives The children will:
1. Understand the difference between mittens and gloves.
2. Recognize the usefulness of mittens and gloves.
3. Practice patterning, counting, and sorting.
4. Develop large motor skills.
5. Practice oral language skills.

Circle or Group Time Activity

- Display a winter weather picture as you tell children about mittens and gloves. Ask them to comment on the usefulness of mittens and gloves.
- Have each of the children put a mitten or glove on their right hands (use pairs).
- Divide the children into two groups and have them form two concentric circles.
- Ask the outer group of children to walk in a clockwise direction and have the inner circle of children walk in a counter-clockwise direction, keeping their gloved hands extended toward the other circle of children.
- The children touch hands as they walk past each other, so they can see one another's gloves or mittens.
- After the children have walked in the circles for a short while, ring a bell, signaling the children to break from the circles and find the children wearing the gloves that match their own and give one another high fives and sit down together.
- Have the children take off their gloves, mix them up again, and repeat the activity a few more times.

Learning Centers   **Art**

Provide fingerpaint and sheets of paper with outlines of people on them, and invite the children to paint clothes onto the outlines of the people. Older children can draw their own people shapes.

Dramatic Play

Put winter clothes in the center and encourage the children to pretend to shovel snow or ski. Then have children come in and hang their mittens and gloves on the clothesline to dry.

Large Motor

Put several mittens, a laundry basket, and a few balls in the center, and invite the children to toss the balls to one another while wearing the mittens, or to try to toss the balls or even the mittens into the laundry basket.

Math

Provide a ruler and mittens of several sizes, and invite the children to measure them and determine arrange them according to size.

Small Motor

Set out modeling dough and several mitten-shaped cookie cutters, inviting the children to stamp and cut out the mitten shapes. Give the children glitter and other small decorative items with which they can decorate each glove so that they have matching pairs.

Book Suggestions

Caps, Hats, Socks, and Mittens by Louise W. Borden
Three Little Kittens by Lorianne Siomades

Snack

Give the children handprint- or mitten-shaped cookie cutouts with frosting or colored cream cheese on them, as well as several small edible fruits and seeds, and invite the children to decorate their gloves or mittens before eating them.

Review

Hand one mitten or glove to each child, keeping the matching mittens and gloves in a basket. One at a time, set the gloves on the ground, asking the children with the matching gloves to lay them beside the ones you put down. Continue until all the children set down their gloves and mittens.

Assessment

Show the children several gloves, some with the fingers cut off, and ask the children to talk about which gloves and mittens they would like to wear in the winter.

Related Fingerplay

Invite children to put on a real pair of gloves or mittens as they sing this song, then perform the actions as stated:

Gloves and Mittens by Mary J. Murray
(Tune: "Are You Sleeping?")
Gloves and mittens, gloves and mittens (put on gloves or mittens)
On my hands, on my hands. (show hands forward and show hands backward)
Keep my fingers cozy when my cheeks are rosy. (fold hands and rub cheeks)
Soft and warm, soft and warm. (rub mittens together as if keeping hands warm)

 *Mary J. Murray, Mazomanie, WI*

Mittens and Kittens

Learning Objectives The children will:
1. Learn about mittens.
2. Make mittens from paper.
3. Learn through nursery rhymes and action rhymes.

Circle or Group Time Activity

- Show the children the paper mittens. Talk about mittens. Ask, "Do you wear mittens? When do we wear mittens? When it is cold or hot? How many mittens do you see? Have you ever lost a mitten?"
- Recite the following nursery rhyme with the children:

Three Little Kittens (author unknown)

Three little kittens,
They lost their mittens,
And they began to cry,
Oh, mother dear,
We sadly fear
Our mittens we have lost.

What? Lost your mittens,
You naughty kittens!
Then you shall have no pie.
Mee-ow, mee-ow, mee-ow.
No, you shall have no pie.

The three little kittens,
They found their mittens,
And they began to cry,
Oh, mother dear,
See here, see here,
Our mittens we have found.

What? Found your mittens,
You silly kittens!
Then you shall have some pie.

Purr-r, purr-r, purr-r,
Oh, let us have some pie.

The three little kittens,
Put on their mittens,
And soon ate up the pie;
Oh, mother dear,
We greatly fear
Our mittens we have soiled.

What? Soiled your mittens,
You naughty kittens!
Then they began to sigh,
Mee-ow, mee-ow, mee-ow.
Then they began to sigh.

The three little kittens,
They washed their mittens,
And hung them out to dry;
Oh mother dear,
Look here, look here,
Our mittens we have washed.

Learning Centers **Dramatic Play**
Provide mittens, and other props related to the "Three Little Kittens" for pretend play. Invite children to act out the nursery rhyme using the props.

Literacy

Give each child a mitten cut out from construction paper. Have them dictate or write what they like to do while wearing mittens. Have them color the mittens and compile them into a classroom book.

Math

Provide a variety of mittens in a large basket. The children sort the pairs of mittens and place them in another basket. Have them count the pairs

Small Motor

Have the children put on mittens. Invite them to do a variety of small motor activities wearing the mittens, such as putting puzzles together, using writing instruments, and so on. Ask them how it feels to do these things wearing mittens.

Writing

Provide several block letters that spell "my mitten" and ask the children to trace the letters and use crayons and markers color in the outlines of the letters.

Book Suggestions

Missing Mittens by Stuart J. Murphy
One Mitten by Kristine O'Connell George

Snack

Make mitten-shaped cookies with the children. Give each child a small amount of sugar cookie dough. Let them roll out their dough and use a mitten-shaped cookie cutter to cut out a mitten shape. Bake. When cool, children can decorate the mittens as desired.

Review

Read *One Mitten* by Kristine O'Connell George to the children, and talk to them about the book.

Assessment

Show the children several mittens. Can the children place the pairs together? Ask, "Can you tell me about your mittens?"

 *Lily Erlic, Victoria, British Columbia, Canada*

The Months of Winter

Learning Objectives   The children will:
1. Learn about the weather in winter.
2. Discover fun winter activities.
3. Develop their small motor skills.

Circle or Group Time Activity

- Teach the children the following song:

Winter Has a Lot of Snow by Renee Kirchner
(Tune: "Mary Had a Little Lamb")
Winter has a lot of snow,
Lot of snow,
Lot of snow.
Winter has a lot of snow
And my hands are very cold.

Winter is very cold,
Very cold,
Very cold.
Winter is very cold.
My mittens are red and gold.

I like to ride my new sled,
My new sled,
My new sled.
I like to ride my new sled.
It is very fun.

I love to make a big snowman,
Big snowman,
Big snowman.
I love to make a big snowman
And now I am done.

- Tell the children that they are going to learn about winter today.
- Show them a calendar and tell them that winter is during the months of December, January, and February.
- Talk about how the weather is cold during winter and often there is snow and ice (depending on where they live).
- Explain that most trees do not have leaves in winter and some animals sleep through the winter. This is a great time to introduce the word *hibernate*.

Learning Centers   **Blocks**
Show the children a picture of an igloo. Invite them to try to build igloos out of white square blocks.
Library
Put books such as *The Mitten* by Jan Brett and *Three Little Kittens* in the center for the children to read.
Science
Make bird feeders with the children using empty milk and soda cartons. Cut off the tops of the cartons and let the children decorate them. When they are finished, help them label each with their names, then bring them outside and find a place to set them up so the children can observe birds eating from them. Provide birdfeed for the children put into their feeders.

Small Motor

Provide balls of yarn and several paper cutouts of mittens, with holes punched around their edges. Invite the children to put two mitten cutouts together and sew their edges together with yarn.

Art

Show the children how to make paper-plate snowmen. Help them to connect three white paper plates together with brads to resemble a snowman shape. Cut hat shapes out of black construction paper and glue on the top. Cut scarves out of red felt and glue between the top and middle paper plates. Draw a face on the snowman. Glue brown chenille stems to the side of the middle paper plate for arms.

3 PLATES

2. GLUE HAT TO TOP PLATE

4. DRAW FACE

3. GLUE SCARF BELOW FIRST PLATE

5. ADD BROWN PIPE CLEANERS

1. CONNECT PLATES WITH BRADS

PAPER PLATE SNOWMAN

Book Suggestions

Animals in Winter by Henrietta Bancroft
Dream Snow by Eric Carle
The Snowy Day by Ezra Jack Keats
The Twelve Days of Winter by Deborah Lee Rose

Snack

Serve hot cocoa and popsicles. Be sure that the cocoa is not hot enough to burn the children. Point out the difference in the temperature of each food.

Review

Set out several winter-related objects, such as mittens, scarves, ice in a cup, branches without leaves, and so on. Engage the children in a discussion of each object, and ask them how it relates to the winter season.

Assessment

Ask the children questions about winter and see if they can answer them: "How do we know when it is winter?" "What do we wear in winter?" "What do we do for fun in winter?"

 *Renee Kirchner, Carrollton, TX*

Season of Snow

Learning Objectives   The children will:
1. Talk about the winter season.
2. Experience different temperatures.
3. Explore the concept of opposites.

Circle or Group Time Activity
■ Teach the children the following song:

Snowflake, Snowflake by Ingelore Mix
Snowflake, snowflake twirling all around,
Slowly, slowly falling to the ground,
Show children how to twirl,
and dance around then gently fall to the ground.

■ Sing the song again with the children, encouraging them to spin as snowflakes and bend down to the ground at the end of the song.

Learning Centers   **Art**
Provide medium-size easel paper, blue paint, paintbrushes, and cotton balls. Have the child cover the entire sheet with blue paint. Then show them how to pull little pieces of cotton off the cotton ball and stick them onto the still-wet paint.

Blocks
Help children use large- and medium-sized blocks to construct a den or shelter to seek cover from a pretend snowstorm. (**Note:** Use a blanket for the roof.)

Dramatic Play
Provide a variety of winter-sport clothing, such as ski wear, ice skating wear, and basketball uniforms. Invite the children to explore the clothes and role-play the sports.

Large Motor
Provide a variety of sizes of paper balls, beanbags, lightweight plastic balls, and so on. Encourage the children to toss them in the air and run around in the "snow."

Science
Fill two basins with water, one with warm water and the other with ice-cold water. Provide thermometers and encourage the children to take the temperatures of each container of water, and then to graph the results. Encourage them to come back to the ice water from time to time to see if its temperature changes.

Book Suggestions   *Dream Snow* by Eric Carle
Gooseberry Goose by Claire Freedman
The Mitten by Jan Brett

Snack   Prepare a container of gelatin snack, asking the children to take turns stirring it. Pour the liquid into small paper cups and refrigerate. After two or three hours, remove the cups from the refrigerator, top each with a bit of whipped cream (snow), and have a wintry snack. Ask the children what happened to the gelatin as it got colder.

Review   Invite the children to describe ways they can tell that it is wintertime.

Assessment   Given an assortment of shoes such as snow boots, sandals, flip-flops, rubber boots, clogs, sneakers, warm slippers, can the child tell which to wear in the winter and explain why they are appropriate to wear in the winter?

Ingelore Mix, Gainesville, VA

Snow All Year Long

Learning Objectives The children will:
1. Learn about winter.
2. Participate in fun winter activities.
3. Discover that ice melts.
4. Explore size relationships.

Circle or Group Time Activity

- Show the children mittens, scarves, hats, gloves, and other similar items.
- Discuss what the items are used for. This is especially fun to do during the summer or early fall.
- Organize a relay race with the winter items. Divide the children into two teams. Place two sets of a few of the winter items on one side of the room and have the two teams line up behind them. Place two baskets at the other end of the room.
- The first child in each line puts on an item (for example, a hat) and races to the other side to take off the item and put it in the basket.
- The next child picks a different item (mittens) and does the same thing. This continues with all four items.
- The next four people in line (two for each team) have to race to the other chair to get the item, put it on, and then race to the start to take off the item.

Learning Centers **Art**

Help the children create coffee filter snowflakes by folding filters several times and cutting off portions around the edges. When they unfold their filters, they will have beautiful snowflakes. Paint on glue and add glitter for a sparkly snowflake to decorate the classroom.

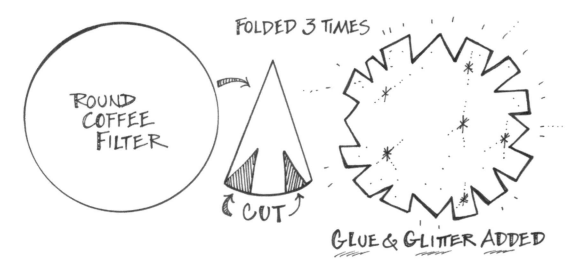

ROUND COFFEE FILTER

FOLDED 3 TIMES

CUT

GLUE & GLITTER ADDED

Games

Make a small ice hockey table by placing a small amount of water into a large, shallow plastic container for the rink. Freeze the water to make a sheet of ice. Make goals by sticking pipe cleaners into small balls of clay. Provide craft sticks for hockey sticks. Make pucks out of small balls of clay. This is a great game for two children to play.

Large Motor

Invite the children to crumple pieces of white paper to make "snowballs." Divide the children into two or three teams and give each team a basket of "snowballs" to have a snowball fight.

Math

Cut out several sizes of white circles cut from tagboard. Invite the children to compare their sizes and discuss the steps necessary to make a snowman from the circles.

Sand and Water

Fill the table with crushed ice. Add some water, shovels, scoops, spoons, bowls, and so on for the children to use to explore the ice. Have them wear smocks to keep their clothing dry. For a new dimension, add ice cubes made with food-colored water.

Small Motor

Cut out snowman parts from felt, including three white balls, a nose, eyes, scarf, hat, and two stick arms. Children can use the pieces on a felt board to retell one of the stories that you have read in class or create their own snowman story.

Book Suggestions

The Biggest Snowman Ever by Steven Kroll
Snowballs by Lois Ehlert
The Snowman by Raymond Briggs
The Snowy Day by Ezra Jack Keats
White Snow, Bright Snow by Alvin Tresselt

Snack

Make popsicles by pouring fruit juice into ice cube trays. When they are slightly frozen, add toothpicks or popsicle sticks and let them freeze.

Review

Provide several objects that relate to the summer and winter. Show the children each object and ask them to identify the season to which they belong.

Assessment

Can the children tell the difference between winter and the other seasons?

 Sandy L. Scott, Meridian, ID

Snow Is Cold!

Learning Objectives The children will:
1. Discover that snow requires cold weather.
2. Develop their small and large motor skills.

Circle or Group Time Activity
- Take the children outside on a snowy day. Give each of the children two cups and ask them to fill the cups with snow.
- Leave one set of cups outside, and bring the second set of cups into the classroom.
- Ask the children to observe cups in the classroom and watch what happens.
- Take the children outside again to look at the first set of cups.
- Talk about how and why the sets of cups differ.

Learning Centers

Art
Prepare several ice cubes by adding watercolor paint to water and freezing them in an ice cube tray. Have children wear gloves or mittens and use the colored ice to paint watercolor paper.

Dramatic Play
Turn several baskets upside down and cover with batting to make a "snow mountain." Set out several stuffed animals and invite the children to imagine that the animals live on the mountain.

Math
Set out 10–20 white clay "snowballs" and invite children to count them. Make snowballs of different sizes and challenge the children to put them in order from largest to smallest.

Small Motor
Encourage children to use playdough to make snowmen.

Science
Set out several containers filled with various amounts of snow. Ask the children to observe what happens over time. Can they guess which containers of snow will melt first and last?

Book Suggestions

All You Need for a Snowman by Alice Schertle
Snowball by Nina Crews
The Snowman by Raymond Briggs

Snack

Serve cocoa and soup to the children. Put ice cubes in each child's cup to keep the cocoa and soup from getting too hot, and so the children can feel the coolness of the ice cube, as well as observe what happens to it in hot liquids.

Review

Ask the children to describe what happens to snow. Ask the children why snow does not always melt outside.

Assessment

Ask the children to predict what would happen if they were to place snow in the freezer or on a hot stove.

Related Song

Change the words to the song, "Do You Know the Muffin Man?" to "Do You Know the Snowy Man?" or to "snowy girl" and "snowy boy."

Karyn F. Everham, Fort Myers, FL

Snowflakes and Snowballs

Learning Objectives The children will:

1. Learn about snow.
2. Improve their large and small motor skills.
3. Enhance their oral language skills.

Circle or Group Time Activity

- Invite the children to toss "snowflakes" (crumpled white tissue paper balls) up into the air and let them fall to the ground. Each time the snowflakes land, recite one of the following phrases aloud.
  - Snow is cold.
  - Snow falls from the clouds in the sky.
  - Each snowflake is different.
  - Snow is good for making a snowman.
  - It usually snows in the winter.
  - Some parts of the world never get snow because it's always warm.
  - People like snow.
  - You can ski or sled in the snow.
  - Snow creates jobs for people.
- Group the children into two teams and have a team snowball "fight."
- Place a line of string across the center of a large, uncluttered area. Invite children to toss their snowballs over the line. The goal is to have most of the snowballs on the other team's side of the game area when the bells ring.
- Ring the bells at a random time. Invite teams to count their snowballs to see which team has the most and which team has the least.

Learning Centers

Art

Invite children to create a self-portrait by gluing together an assortment of colorful paper shapes onto large colored paper. They can add details with crayons or markers. Help them use a hole punch to punch 20 holes from white paper and glue the circles randomly on the page to represent falling snow.

WHITE CIRCLES

COLORED PAPER SHAPES

DETAIL

COLORED PAPER

Blocks

Provide a bowl of packing peanuts and a toy plow. Invite children to build a small village of houses, then "let it snow" by dropping "snowflakes" (packing peanuts) all around the "neighborhood." They can use the plow to push snow into piles.

Dramatic Play

Display an assortment of winter clothing, winter sports equipment, and a snow shovel in the Dramatic Play Center. Children can put on the clothes and try on various skis, ski boots, snowshoes, and so on as they pretend to work and play in the snow.

Science

Create a small snowman from real snowballs. (Freeze one in advance for this activity if you don't often have snow available in your area.) Place the snowman in a shallow baking pan, and invite children to observe the snowman as it melts.

Small Motor

Invite the children to wrap white yarn around a 3" x 5" piece of cardboard, about 30 times. Then help them pull the card out and tie an extra piece of yarn across the center. They cut the ends of the yarn loops to create a puffy "snowball." Let the children toss their snowball up into the air and then take it home.

Writing

Supply an ample amount of shaving cream and display a set of word cards with winter-related terms on them. Invite the children to smooth out a blob of shaving cream on the table and use their finger to write the words in the shaving cream.

Book Suggestions

First Snow by Bernette Ford
Snowball by Nina Crews
Snowballs by Lois Ehlert
Snow Day by Patricia Lakin
A Snowy Day by Ezra Jack Keats

Snack

Serve mashed potatoes (or vanilla yogurt or pudding). Invite the children to use a spoon to spread their pile of "snow" around on their plate and then shovel pathways with the "shovel" as they eat each spoonful of snow.

Review

Invite children to sit in a circle. Walk around the circle and place a paper snowflake on the head or lap of five different children. The children on whom you place the snowflakes stand, hold the snowflakes high in the air, and say sentences that include the word "snow."

Assessment

Display an assortment of objects, some having to do with snow, such as a snow shovel, mittens, thermometer, and so on, as well as other objects that do not pertain to snow, such as a beach ball, leaf rake, and umbrella. Give the child a handful of paper snowballs. Invite the child to set a snowball near each item that pertains to snow.

 Mary J. Murray, Mazomanie, WI

Spring Has Come

Learning Objectives The children will:
1. Learn about spring.
2. Experience planting.
3. Gain understanding about opposites, such as *big* and *little*.

Circle or Group Time Activity
- Teach the children the following action rhyme:

  There Once Was a Little Plant by Ingelore Mix
  There once was a little plant (children kneel down on the floor)
  That was so very small,
  Along came the rain and sun
  Which made it grow real tall. (children slowly stand up and stretch both arms
      way up high)

- Repeat the rhyme with the children a few times, acting it out more quickly
  each time.

Learning Centers ### Art
Give each child a large piece of easel paper. Prepare a container of green paint and
an array of pastel color paints. Encourage children to paint several green stems all
over the paper. Then show them how to paint a blossom on top of each stem by
dipping the paintbrush into the paint, pressing down on top of the stem, and
twisting the brush around. Older children can do this with one hand, but younger
ones can use both hands.

Construction
Purchase unassembled birdhouses from a craft store. Let the children help
assemble the birdhouses and then them decorate them with grass, birdseed, sticks,
and twigs. Birds will often use the decorations as building materials, provided it
comes off easily. Hang them outside near trees or bushes. **Note:** Make sure to buy
the proper birdhouse for birds in your area or birds will not come to nest.

Literacy
Teach children the names of young animals, such as "duckling," "calf," and so on.
Show pictures of animals and their young, along with word cards with the names of
the creatures, and challenge the children to match them together. Be sure to attach
small photocopies of the images to the backs of the word cards so the children
can check their matches.

Science
Give each child a plastic cup to fill with soil about three quarters full. Provide grass
seed for the children to sprinkle in their cups and then cover the seeds with soil.
Water gently. Place cups on the windowsill. Watch the small stems of grass emerge
over time.

Small Motor

Make rainbow flags. Give each child a sheet of 9" × 12" blue construction paper. Show the children how to fold the paper in half horizontally. Cut seven slits in the paper starting at the fold line and cutting down to about 1" above the bottom of the paper. (**Note:** Encourage the children to try this step on their own using child-safe scissors. If their small motor skills are not developed enough to complete this, help the children cut these slits.) Unfold the paper. Provide precut strips, about 12" × 1 ½", in the seven colors of the rainbow (red, orange, yellow, green, blue, indigo, and violet). Show children how to weave each strip over and under. Fold excess of strips over at both ends.

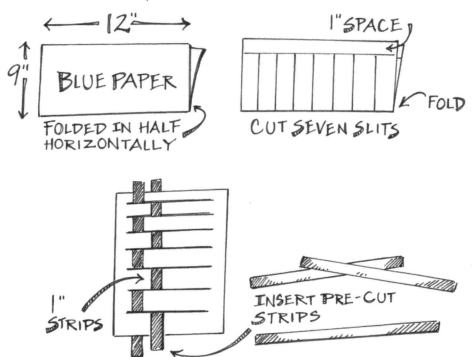

Book Suggestions	*Hurray for Spring!* by Patricia Hubbell *Planting a Rainbow* by Lois Ehlert *Splish, Splash, Spring* by Jan Carr
Snack	This is a two-day project. Bake cupcakes with the help of the children. Have children participate in measuring and mixing. Bake and store them until the next day. The next day, make pastel colored icing. Give children a choice of one of four colors. Provide children with plastic knives and let them spread the icing on top of their cupcakes.
Review	Can children tell what happens in spring?
Assessment	Can the children tell you if it is spring or not by looking around outside?

 *Ingelore Mix, Gainesville, VA*

Springtime Flowers

Learning Objectives   The children will:
1. Learn about spring.
2. Paint flowers.
3. Participate in action rhymes about flowers and bees.

Circle or Group Time Activity
- Place a tray of different kinds of flowers in front of children. Point out each flower and engage the children in a discussion about the flowers' names and appearances. Talk about spring and ask them, "What happens during the spring? Is it cold or warm? What is your favorite thing to do in the spring?"
- Play the flower game. Use four flowers to start the game. Ask the children to look at all four flowers. Then ask them to close their eyes. Place a flower under a bowl in the middle of the circle. Ask the children to guess which flower is under the bowl.
- Show the children different season pictures. Ask them to guess which scene is spring. Ask, "Why do you think this picture shows spring?"
- Recite the following action rhyme with the children:

Blossoms Are Flying by Lily Erlic
Blossoms are flying through the breeze, (stretch arms and shake hands)
Twirling and whirling through the trees, (twirl hands around)
Flying up, (jump up)
Flying down, (crouch down)
Spinning, (stand and spin)
All around, (keep spinning)
Landing softly,
On the ground. (sit on floor slowly)
Blossoms are flying through the breeze, (stretch arms and shake hands)
Blossoms are falling on me! (shake hands above head and point to self)

- Tell the children that they will be learning about spring today.

Learning Centers   **Art**
Give the children sheets of white paper cut in the shapes of flowers. Ask the children to paint the flowers. Older children can cut out their own flower shapes.
Library
Set out a recording of *It's Spring!* by Linda Glaser for the children to listen to as they look through a copy of the book.

Literacy

Ask the children to finish this sentence, "During spring, I like to _____."

Write down their answers on sheets of paper (or let them write the answer, if they can) and then encourage them to illustrate their answers.

Math

Provide a variety of matching pairs of cutout flowers, real flowers, plastic flowers, or pictures of flowers. Ask the children to match the flowers.

Sand and Water

Place a variety of flowers or blossoms in the water. Add blue food coloring to the water. Encourage the children to use their imaginations by saying, "The flowers are floating in a pond." Or ask, "Do the flowers float? Do they sink? What colors are the flowers?"

Book Suggestions

It's Spring! by Linda Glaser
Mouse's First Spring by Lauren Thompson
Read to Me Rhymes: Seasons by Lily Erlic

Snack

Serve honey and crackers for the children to enjoy. Talk about how bees pollinate flowers and make honey. **Note:** Check for allergies before serving honey.

Review

Perform the "Blossoms are Flying" action rhyme again with the children. Show the children the pictures of the seasons. Talk about the features of spring. Ask, "What happens in spring? Is it cold or warm? What do you wear during the spring?"

Assessment

Show the children pictures of the seasons. Can the child pick out the spring scene?

Related Poem

Little Bumblebee by Lily Erlic
Little bumblebee oh so round, (place arms in a circle)
Little bumblebee on the ground, (roll up like a bee on the floor)
Little bumblebee flying around, (spread arms and pretend to fly around room)
Little bumblebee on the ground. (roll up like a bee on the floor)

 Lily Erlic, Victoria, British Columbia, Canada

Staying Cool in the Heat

Learning Objectives The children will:
1. Learn about how to keep cool in the hot weather.
2. Prepare and taste foods that refresh and cool us.
3. Develop their small and large motor skills.

Circle or Group Time Activity
- During the hottest time of the school calendar, show the children pictures of a variety of warm and cool outdoor settings.
- Ask children what it is like outside today and have them point out which images resemble the season outside.
- Ask the children how they keep cool at home. Write down their answers on a large sheet of paper labeled "Keeping Cool."
- After the children name several ways to stay cool, offer a few new ideas, such as sucking on crushed ice or using a spray bottle of water to spray their face. Take out the necessary materials to let the children experience these ways of staying cool. If some children are hesitant, suggest spraying just their hands.

Learning Centers

Dramatic Play

Show the children how to fold construction paper accordion-style to make fans. The children use cooling tools such as their paper fans, small battery-operated fans, and spray bottles with water in the Dramatic Play Center. Provide sunglasses and sun hats for "staying cool in the heat" play.

Library

Begin a story about a child who went to visit a very hot country. Describe how uncomfortable the child felt in the heat. Ask the children to keep telling new parts of the story. Copy down what the children say, make a recording of it, and then put the story in the library for the children to listen to and look through.

Literacy

Read the children's "Keeping Cool" tactics back to them (from the Group activity). Invite them to illustrate the different ways to stay cool. Compile the children's drawings and comments into a book for the classroom library. Ask the children what they want to name the book, and then create a cover for it.

Outdoors

Invite the children to spray water from spray bottles outdoors. (You may have to set limits on how much water the children can spray and where.) Using spray bottles with water exercises hand and arm muscles, making this a small motor activity too.

Science

Ask children's families to help you prepare ice for ice sculptures. Collect as many cups, containers, and ice cubes as possible. Provide trays or wide basins for children to create ice sculptures in. Pieces of ice will adhere to each other as children sprinkle salt on the ice and add another layer of ice on top. The salt causes some of the ice to melt and then refreeze, connecting the pieces together. Talk about the reezing and melting process, and how salt affects ice.

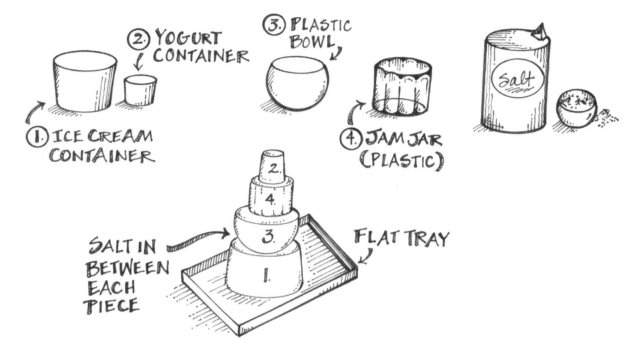

Small Motor

Make or purchase paper dolls and make sets of winter and summer clothing from scraps of appropriate fabric. Ask children if they would like to dress the dolls for summer or winter weather. Note whether children understand which types of clothing go with each season.

Book Suggestions

How I Spent My Summer Vacation by Mark Teague
Summer by Alice Low
The Summer Solstice by Ellen Jackson

Snack

Offer crushed ice or cool water to drink. Let children peel and freeze bananas, as follows:

- peel banana
- cut banana in half or quarters
- insert popsicle stick into wider end of banana and freeze

Review

Ask the children to explain some of their "Keeping Cool" drawings to the group.

Assessment

Can the children describe the differences between a summer day and the weather in other seasons?

Elisheva Leah Nadler,
Har Nof, Jerusalem, Israel

Summer at the Beach

Learning Objectives   The children will:
1. Identify items found at the beach and in the ocean.
2. Discover how colorful the ocean creatures are.
3. Taste tuna toast.
4. Experience a "day at the beach" in the classroom.

Circle or Group Time Activity
- Gather the children in a circle and provide a beach ball for them to toss around the circle.
- When each child catches the ball, she names something she would find at the beach or in the ocean. Give suggestions or clues if children can't think of anything.

Learning Centers   **Art**
Cut out (or help older children cut out) several different fish shapes from black construction paper. Show the children how to add spots of colored tempera paint

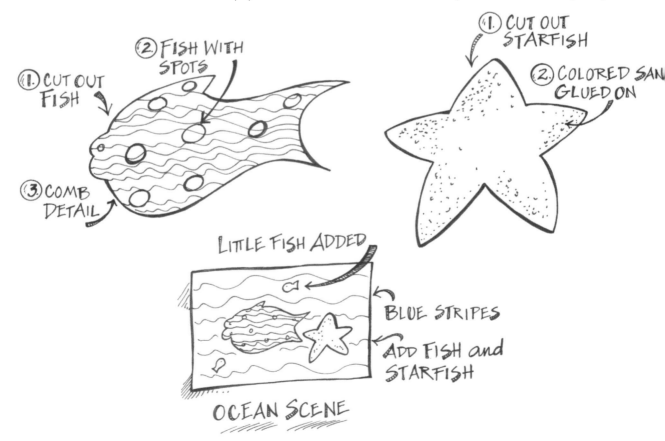

(1.) CUT OUT FISH

(2.) FISH WITH SPOTS

(3.) COMB DETAIL

(1.) CUT OUT STARFISH

(2.) COLORED SAND GLUED ON

LITTLE FISH ADDED

BLUE STRIPES

ADD FISH and STARFISH

OCEAN SCENE

and brush over it with a comb to make colorful fish scales. Provide starfish cutouts and invite the children to "paint" colored sand mixed with glue on them to create textured starfish. Invite the children to create a group ocean scene by gluing their fish cutouts to a large blue sheet or large blue butcher paper. Invite them to add additional drawings and paintings.

Blocks

Throw a beach block party. The children build "sandcastles" using the blocks. Add beach balls, shovels, sea shells, and so on. Play beach music (Beach Boys or surf music) to give the feeling of summer and the beach. Play white noise that simulates crashing waves or the gentle movement of the ocean water.

Dramatic Play

Have the children dress in beach attire and provide beach towels, sunglasses, hats, goggles, flippers, and so on. Invite them to have a "day at the beach."

Large Motor

With the children, construct a large whale out of butcher paper or a rope outline. Count the number of children that can fit inside the whale. Have them run around the outside of the whale and then try to fit inside it.

Math

Set out a variety of seashells for the children to count and sort.

Book Suggestions

Fish Is Fish by Leo Lionni
A House for Hermit Crab by Eric Carle
One Fish, Two Fish, Red Fish, Blue Fish by Dr. Seuss
Rainbow Fish and the Big Blue Whale by Marcus Pfister
Swimmy by Leo Lionni

Snack

Serve the children tuna toast. Toast a piece of bread and cut into a fish shape using a fish cookie cutter. Spread tuna fish on the toast and use a black olive for the eye.

Review

Play the beach ball game while asking the children to name items they would find in the ocean or at the beach.

Assessment

Were the children able to name more ocean and beach items then the first time the game was played earlier in the day?

 *Sandy L. Scott, Meridian, ID*

Summer Sand

Learning Objectives The children will:
1. Learn about sand.
2. Dig and discover in the sand.
3. Learn through rhymes.

Circle or Group Time Activity
- Show the children different types and colors of sand in small sealed containers.
- Engage the children in a conversation about the sand. Ask, "Do you know what sand is made from? Where can we find sand? Have you ever felt sand? Does it feel different when it is wet than when it is dry? How does it feel when it is dry? Or wet? What can you make in the sand? How many different types of sand do you see in the circle?"
- Recite the following action rhyme with the children:

One Big Sand Hill by Lily Erlic
One big sand hill, (hold up one finger and stand tall)
Hiding behind a tree, (cover face with hands)
"Look over there!" said the sand hill, (point)
"The wind is coming, see!" (move arms back and forth)
"Oh my, oh me, oh dear,
My sand will fly away, I fear!" (shiver)
The wild wind said,
"It's summer, you know,
That means, your sand has to go!"
So the wind,
Whooshing the sand away, (move arms back and forth)
Lifted it up and around. (run around room or wiggle fingers)
The sand flew through the bay.
One little sand hill, (hold one finger up and crouch)
Waving to the sea, (wave)
Swaying around, (move arms back and forth)
Without a sound. (place finger on lips)

Learning Centers **Art**
Give each child a piece of cardboard, crayons, and markers. Encourage the children to draw ocean scenes on the cardboard. Then have them add glue and sand to their pictures to make textured ocean scenes. If desired, mix silver glitter into the sand to make it sparkle.

Literacy

Give each child a piece of paper with the words *My Sand* at the top. Have them draw a beach scene. Challenge older children to print the word *sand* on their sheets. Have them dictate a sentence about their scene.

Sand and Water

Provide plastic sea creatures, rocks, or dried seaweed and invite the children to "dig and discover" in the sand.

Science

Provide containers of sand along with several magnifying glasses so the children can inspect and discuss the sand.

Small Motor

Provide a variety of colored sand in small plastic containers and put them in a large basket. Tell the children to find the pairs of sand and place them together. Also consider putting different amounts of sand in each container and challenging the children to put the containers in order from least to most sand.

Book Suggestions

Sand Castle by Brenda S. Yee
Sea, Sand, Me! by Patricia Hubbell
Warm Sun, Soft Sand by Linzi West

Snack

Provide fruit popsicles for the children to enjoy.

Review

Reread "One Little Sand Hill." Show children pictures of sand and discuss them.

Assessment

Show the child several containers of sand. Can the child place the pairs together? Ask, "Can you tell me about your sand? Where can you find sand?"

Related Song

I'm a Little Sand Grain by Lily Erlic
(Tune: "I'm a Little Teapot")
I'm a little sand grain, (pinch two fingers as though holding a grain of sand)
So warm and red, (hug self)
I like the summer, (hug self)
I like my sand bed. (pretend to sleep)
I'm a little sand grain, (pinch two fingers as though holding a grain of sand)
I like the sun, (hug self)
I like to sway, (move body back and forth)
I like to have fun! (shake around and run in place)

 Lily Erlic, Victoria, British Columbia, Canada

Eyes

Learning Objectives The children will:
1. Recognize that eyes (and seeing) help people receive information.
2. Discriminate objects by size, shape, or color.
3. Wear a blindfold to experience having no vision.
4. Develop their small motor skills.

Circle or Group Time Activity
- Gather the children together in a circle.
- Go around the circle, noting the color of each child's eyes.
- Explain that people's eyes are pretty, but they are also very important, and people must take care of their eyes. Give some examples of ways people take care of their eyes:
  - Wearing sunglasses in the bright sun.
  - Not poking their eyes.
  - Getting regular eye exams.
- Discuss how eyes are important and helpful. Talk about how eyes help people stay safe by allowing people to see where they are walking, enjoy beauty (clouds, trees, birds), recognize friends' faces, and so on. Talk about how eyes let people read books and look at pictures. (Make sure to note that people with no vision can still read by using or Braille.)
- Explain that we need light to see — either daylight or artificial light.
- Play "I Spy" with the children.

Learning Centers

Art
Provide magnifying glasses and colored cellophane so the children can see how they alter the way things look. Provide paper, markers, crayons, and so on, and invite the children to draw pictures of things as the children view the objects through the cellophane and magnifying glasses.

Dramatic Play
Provide blindfolds and encourage children to walk without seeing. **Note:** Hold onto the children's arms and make sure they walk in unobstructed, open areas. Ask, "How do you feel when you cannot see?" Provide sunglasses and binoculars for pretend play.

Library
Place a recording of *Who's Afraid of the Dark?* by Crosby Bonsall in the center for the children to listen to as they look through a copy of the book.

Literacy

Set out paper, markers, and crayons, and invite the children to make drawings that illustrate words such as *vision, eyeglasses, sunglasses,* and other eye-related terms.

Small Motor

Encourage the children to sort buttons and counters by color or size, using a muffin pan.

Book Suggestions   *The Greedy Triangle* by Marilyn Burns
Who's Afraid of the Dark? by Crosby Bonsall

Snack   Serve carrot sticks with dip. Carrots are rich in vitamin A, which helps keep eyes healthy.

Review   Ask the children to list the ways eyes help people and ways people can protect their eyes.

Assessment   Can the children name two ways people's eyes help them? Can the children name three ways people protect their eyes?

Mary Jo Shannon, Roanoke, VA

The Five Senses

Learning Objectives The children will:
1. Participate in activities that involve each of the senses.
2. Distinguish between the different senses.
3. Use each of their five senses in different centers.

Circle or Group Time Activity

- Give each child a magazine and pair of child-safe scissors.
- Ask the children to find pictures of eyes, ears, mouths, noses, hands, and feet. Ask each child to look for one particular sense-related body part (for example, a child could cut out a picture of a nose to identify smell).
- The children glue the items to construction paper.
- Use the completed projects to highlight the senses. For instance, ask the children to hold their collages in their laps. Say the name of a sense, and have the children whose collages are of body parts that relate to that sense raise their collages in their air.

Learning Centers

Art
Make scented pictures with glue and powdered gelatin. The children make a glue design on construction paper and then sprinkle flavored, scented gelatin on the glue and shake off the excess. When the glue dries, they will have scented pictures.

Blocks
Invite the children to rub or bang blocks together to make different sounds. Encourage the children to compare the sizes of various blocks. Blindfold the children so they use their sense of touch to compare the blocks.

Literacy
Trace letters onto sandpaper and cut them out. Invite the children to make words out of the letters. Provide paper and unwrapped crayons for them to rub over the letters and make crayon rubbings.

Sensory
Provide a variety of items, such as a bell (sound), real flowers (sight and smell), soft blankets (touch), and crackers (taste) in this center. Encourage the children to use all of their senses to experience the objects. Invite them to describe all of the sensations, using plenty of adjectives.

Small Motor
Make scented playdough by adding essential oils to it. Children can also add grass clippings to the playdough to create a unique texture. Blindfold the children as they try to complete a familiar task, such as a simple puzzle or playing with the playdough.

Writing

Help the children write their names or initials on card stock using glue. (You may want to write their names in pencil so that they can trace with the glue). Have a variety of materials available for the children to add to the glue, such as aquarium gravel, sand, beads, confetti, and so on.

Book Suggestions

Listening Walk by Paul Showers
Little Bunny Follows His Nose by Ken Howard
My Five Senses by Aliki
The Nose Book by Al Perkins

Snack

Anything is possible for snack. Encourage the children to describe the look, smell, and taste of the food.

Review

Make a board with the five senses listed across the top (in pictures and words). Provide several images that relate to each, and invite the children to put pictures under the correct senses.

Assessment

Can the child list the five senses and give an example of how people use each sense?

 *Sandy L. Scott, Meridian, ID*

Hearing

Learning Objectives The children will:
1. Recognize that ears (hearing) help people receive information.
2. Identify sounds, such as clapping, whistling, humming, bells, birds, cars, phones, or running water.
3. Develop their listening skills.

Circle or Group Time Activity

- Engage the children in a discussion about ears and hearing.
- Show the children a picture of an ear and explain that the outer ear catches sounds and helps bring them inside the ear to send a message to the brain. (Keep it simple!) Our brain tells us what the sound is.
- Tell them that our hearing is important for a number of reasons. In addition to helping us communicate with others, hearing helps us stay safe (by telling us a car is driving by, hearing fire drills, and so on). Ask them for some examples of how hearing keeps us safe.
- Play the game, "What Made That Sound?"
- Ask the children to close their eyes.
- Make a sound (such as clapping hands, whistling, humming, or ringing a bell) and ask them to identify it.
- After guessing, children open their eyes and watch you repeat the sound.
- As a variation, play a recording you made ahead of time and let the children find a picture that goes with the sound: a bird singing, a car starting, a phone ringing, or water running.

Learning Centers

Art
Make "musical" pictures with the children. Place paper in a box lid and add a tablespoon of tempera paint to the center of the paper. Children place jingle bells in the paint and tilt the box lid so the bells move to make an abstract design.

Dramatic Play
Encourage the children to use toy telephones to "talk" to one another.

Listening
Use film canisters to make sets of sound cylinders. Add various materials to each pair, such as paperclips, thumb tacks, marbles, and so on. Be sure to add the same amount of material to each of the two matching cylinders. Seal the cylinders with colored tape—one color for one set, another for the other set, so children can match the sounds. Encourage children to shake each cylinder and find its partner. Which sets are louder? Softer?

Music

Provide rhythm instruments for the children to explore. Encourage them to describe the sound each instrument makes, and to think of other sounds the instruments remind them of.

Science

Play the silence game. Have the children stretch out on a blanket on the floor and lie as still as they can so they can listen. Ask, "What sounds do you hear?" They may hear voices outside the classroom, cars going by, or a clock ticking. After a reasonable time, speak softly and say, "When I whisper your name, you may get up quietly and go to (whatever center or activity is next)."

Book Suggestions

Hey! What's That Sound? by Veronica Martenova Charles
My Five Senses by Aliki
Snappy Sounds, Ho, Ho, Ho! by Derek Matthews

Snack

Serve noisy, crunchy foods, such as celery, carrot sticks, and pretzels.

Review

Ask the children to list the ways that hearing helps people and ways people can protect their ears.

Assessment

Can the children name two ways ears help people? Can they name two ways people protect their ears? Can the children match sounds to the pictures of the objects that produced them?

 Mary Jo Shannon, Roanoke, VA

My Senses Are Alive

Learning Objectives The children will:
1. Learn about the five senses.
2. Express how people use their senses.
3. Name the five senses.

Circle or Group Time Activity
- Teach the children the following song:

  I Have Five Senses by Quazonia Quarles
  (Tune: "Frère Jacques")
  I have five senses. (children repeat)
  Look at me. (children repeat)
  My eyes are for seeing,
  My nose is for smelling,
  Look at me. (children repeat)

  I have five senses. (children repeat)
  Look at me. (children repeat)
  My tongue is for tasting,
  Ears are for hearing,
  Hands are for touching,
  The five senses are part of me. (children repeat)

- Show the children pictures of things people find on the beach and in the ocean, such as shells, sand, jellyfish, and water. Ask them to identify the things that people hear, see, touch, smell, and taste.

Learning Centers **Art**
Provide an assortment of paper, sand, craft shells (available at craft stores), corrugated paper, watercolor paints, glue, and child-safe scissors for the children to make their own textured beach scenes. Children can spread glue and sprinkle sand on top for the beach area and use watercolor paints for the ocean.

Dramatic Play
Provide beach chairs, a beige textured carpet for sand, inflatable palm trees, sunglasses, towels, beach umbrella, a small sandbox (or sand table) with seashells hidden under the sand, plastic sea animals, shovels, and sand toys for a "day at the beach."

Library
Make a scratch-and-sniff book with the children. In advance, collect scented advertisements found in magazines or other scented objects (flower, lemon peel, pepper, cinnamon) and place them into snack-size resealable bags. Staple the bags or advertisements onto card stock to create a book. Make a touch book using

materials such as terry cloth, wool, plastic, cellophane, sandpaper, and corrugated paper. Glue materials onto paper and use rings to make a book. Place the books in the library for children to explore.

Math
Provide several pairs of seashells and challenge the children to see if they can find which ones look alike. Ask the children to use the shells to make patterns.

Sand and Water
Put sand, sandcastle molds, shovels, spray bottles with water, sifters, sieves, sand wheels, and buckets in the sand and water table for children to explore.

Small Motor
Place seashells on a tray and invite the children to use tongs to pick up the shells and move them to a different area.

Writing
Set out several sheets of paper that have the following sentence on them: "At the beach, I _____." Ask the children to complete the statement with what they smell, see, hear, taste, or touch at the beach. Help them copy their responses onto their sheets of paper, and then have them illustrate their pages. Bind the papers together with silver rings and place in the Library Center.

Book Suggestions

Buzz by Janet S. Wong
How Do You Know? A Book About the Five Senses by Lisa Jayne
My Five Senses by Margaret Miller
My Own Five Senses by Giovanni Caviezel

Snack

Give each child a turn to crush a package of vanilla wafers using a rolling pin. Provide individual vanilla pudding cups. Each child spoons crushed wafers on top of their individual pudding cups.

Review

Ask the children to look around the room and identify one thing from the beach and ocean that uses one of their senses.

Assessment

Prepare a chart in advance by drawing a body part for each sense: an ear for hearing, an eye for sight, a nose for smell, a tongue for taste, and a hand for touch. Hold up pictures of things found at the beach and ocean. Ask the child to sort pictures by at least one sense he might use for the object.

 *Quazonia Quarles, Newark, DE*

Rhythm Instruments

Learning Objectives The children will:
1. Refine their small and large motor skills.
2. Follow directions.
3. Participate successfully in a group activity.

Circle or Group Time Activity

- Read *Thump, Thump, Rat-a-tat-tat* by Gene Baer to the children.
- Pause a short way into the book and ask the children what they think the book is about. Ask them to help with the story by clapping the "thump-thump, rat-a-tat-tat" pattern as you read.
- After the story, ask the children questions, such as "Who has been to a parade?" "What did you see?" "What did you hear?"
- Distribute rhythm instruments to the children, demonstrate how to play them, and invite the children to tap the rhythmic pattern as you reread the story.
- Talk about the sound of the instruments and the feel of the rhythm. Talk about the sense of touch.

Learning Centers

Art
Provide several sheets of blank sheet music paper and invite the children to illustrate them with notes or any images the children want to create.

Construction
Equip the center with materials for making individual drums and shakers. Demonstrate the process as necessary. Invite children to add color and decorations to their instruments.

Library
Put a recording and copy of *David Gets His Drum* by Panama Francis, Bob Reiser, and Eric Velasquez in the center for the children to listen to and enjoy. Also put out small drums the children can play while they listen.

Music
Provide an assortment of rhythm instruments and a recording of marching music. Invite children to select an instrument and play their instrument softly along with the music. For those who have motor difficulty, attach shakers or bells to elastic that can fit over a child's hand or foot.

Writing
Create charts with symbols indicating where children can play their selected instruments. Key words might be "play, play, rest, rest" or "play, play, rest, play, play, rest." Set out sheets of paper and encourage the children to create their own compositions for others to play by drawing symbols for playing and symbols for resting. Bind the pages together to form a class instrument book for your music center. Children can also create background "music" for nursery rhymes on charts.

Book Suggestions

Clifford and the Big Parade by Norman Bridwell
Parade by Donald Crews
Thump, Thump, Rat-a-tat-tat by Gene Baer

Snack

Prepare popcorn with the children. Provide them with rhythm instruments and encourage the children to play their instruments whenever they hear a popcorn kernel pop.

Review

Show the children several various instruments. Ask them to identify the instruments and explain how to play them.

Assessment

Can the child follow directions and coordinate the instrument with the words of the song or music?

Related Songs

The Marching Band by Margery Kranyik Fermino
(Tune: "When the Saints Go Marching In")
Oh, when the band goes marching by.
Oh, when the band goes marching by,
We will play, and march, and be happy,
When the band goes marching by.

The More We Play Together by Margery Kranyik Fermino
(Tune: "The More We Get Together")
The more we play together, together, together.
The more we play together, the happier we sound.
The drums and the shakers, the sticks and the bells,
The more we play together, the happier we sound!

 Margery Kranyik Fermino, West Roxbury, MA

Seeing

Learning Objectives The children will:
1. Learn that their eyes help them to see.
2. Use their eyes to look at and identify name what they see.
3. Gain understanding about the importance of sight.

Circle or Group Time Activity
- Beforehand, decorate a cardboard paper towel tube to catch the capture the children's interest.
- Read *Brown Bear, Brown Bear, What Do You See?* by Bill Martin, Jr. to the children.
- Afterwards, give each child a cardboard tube. Look around the circle through your own tube and say, "[your name], [your name], who do you see?"
- Look at the child next to you through your tube and say, "I see [child's name], looking at me." Then ask the child, "[Child's name], [child's name], who do you see?"
- The next child then looks through his tube and names a child who he sees looking at him.
- Repeat until all the children have had a chance to name someone.
- Tell the children that they will be learning about their eyes today.

Learning Centers **Art**
Provide paper, markers, and blindfolds. Place the blindfolds on children and challenge them to draw something without being able to see what they are drawing. Put older children into pairs and blindfold one child in each pair. The other child guides the blindfolded child in his drawing. Have them take off the blindfolds and look at what they drew. Ask them how they felt doing this. Have them switch roles.

Dramatic Play
Set out materials so the children can pretend they are eye doctors and patients. Hang an eye chart on the wall. Add a chair, a doctor's kit, a lab coat, and paper. Make a simple pair of glasses by twisting chenille stems into shape.

Games
Set out common objects such as a bell, crayon, and fork on a tray. Call over a small group to play this game. Give the children a minute to look at the objects on the tray with their eyes. Take the tray away. What objects did they see? Can they name and remember them all? A variation to this game is to show objects one at a time very briefly. Can the children name what they saw?

Literacy
Hang an eye chart for a print awareness enhancement. Challenge the children to use magnifying glasses to identify the letters.

Science
Put out binoculars, unbreakable mirrors, cardboard tubes, prisms, old eyeglasses without lenses, and kaleidoscopes. Talk about how all the items require sight to use them.

Small Motor
Provide liquid watercolors, eyedroppers, and paper or coffee filters. The children squeeze drops of color onto the coffee filters and observe what happens.

Book Suggestions

Arthur's Eyes by Marc Brown
Blue's Clues: Magenta Gets Glasses! by Deborah Reber
Brown Bear, Brown Bear, What Do You See? by Bill Martin, Jr.
Fish Eyes by Lois Ehlert
Look Book by Tana Hoban
Panda Bear, Panda Bear, What Do You See? by Bill Martin, Jr.

Snack

Help the children make "eye" cookies. Give each child two vanilla wafers. Have them spread white frosting over the center to make the "whites" of the eyes. They can place a chocolate chip or candy-coated chocolate in the center for the iris. The same effect can be achieved with a cracker, cream cheese, and a black olive cut in half for a less sweet snack.

Review

Play a game of "I Spy" using cardboard tubes. Give each child a tube and ask the children to use them to look at a material or object they used or made through the course of the day. Ask the children why they think seeing is important.

Assessment

Do the children use the word "see" when talking about their eyes? Can they identify their eyes and what they are used for? When shown a picture, can they point to a person's or animal's eyes? If shown a picture of a person with glasses, can they say what is different about that person and why he needs to wear glasses? Is there someone in the classroom who has glasses that they can identify?

 *Shelley Hoster, Norcross, GA*

Sight

Learning Objectives   The children will:
1. Explore their environment.
2. Use their imaginations.
3. Develop their observational skills.

Circle or Group Time Activity
- Place several objects on the floor in front of the children, such as a ball, a piece of wrapping paper, a stick, a plate, a marble, a teddy bear, and so on.
- Pick up one item, and ask the children to name and describe it.
- After the children describe one of the objects, ask the children how they know, for instance, that the ball is yellow with blue dots.
- Explain to the children that eyes help people see what is around them.
- After describing all the objects on the floor in front of the children, ask the children to close their eyes, and take one of the objects away.
- Ask the children to open their eyes and challenge them to describe and name the object that is no longer in the circle.
- Show the children the object and see how close the children's descriptions of the object were.

Learning Centers   ### Art
Place an unbreakable mirror in front of children sitting at a table. Ask them to draw their reflections or one of the objects they see in the mirror.

Dramatic Play
Before the children arrive, hide stuffed animals around the room. Encourage the children to use the binoculars they made (see Outdoors Center) to go on a search for the animals. Have them pretend they are on a safari.

Outdoors
Provide cardboard tubes for making binoculars. Tape them together, punch a hole in the outer side of each tube, and attach string to hang the binoculars around the children's necks. Provide colorful stickers for children to use to personalize their binoculars. Go outside with the children and have them look through them to find various nature items. Talk about what they see.

Sand and Water
Hide colored blocks in the sand and invite the children to use shovels to dig for the blocks. Challenge the children to sort the blocks by color, shape, and size.

Science
Provide magnifying glasses for children to use to look closely at objects (leaves, rocks, grass, crayons, fabrics, and flowers) on a large open tray. .

Book Suggestions *The Eye Book* by Dr. Seuss
Sight (the Five Senses) by Maria Rius, J.M. Paramon, and J.J. Puig

Snack Provide plastic plates to create "fruit faces." Provide sliced bananas for eyes, apple slices or orange sections for mouths, grapes for noses, and so on. Use dots of sticky icing to attach eyes, noses, and mouths.

Review Ask the children to identify the colors of their own and their friends' eyes.

Assessment From the group of objects in the "I Spy" game, ask each child what they can identify about each one.

 Sandra Saunders,
Carrum Downs, Victoria, Australia

Smell

Learning Objectives The children will:
1. Learn about the sense of smell.
2. Try to differentiate between various smells.

Circle or Group Time Activity
- Engage the children in a discussion about the five senses.
- Tell children that today they will be learning more about one of their five senses, the sense of smell.
- Ask the children to describe how they use their sense of smell.
- Pass around several scented (unlit!) candles, and ask the children if they can identify the scent of each. **Note:** Use easily identifiable scents, such as apple.

Learning Centers **Art**
Provide old magazines and ask the children to look through them and cut out pictures of anything that has a scent. Have them glue their pictures on poster board to make a collage. Hang the completed "scent collages" in the classroom.

SCENT COLLAGE

POSTER BOARD

MAGAZINE CUT OUTS

Library

Place a recording of *What's That Awful Smell?* by Heather Tekavec and Margaret Spengler in the center for the children to listen to as they look through a copy of the book. Talk about the smells.

Literacy

Ask each child to complete the following sentences: "I love the smell of _____!" "I don't like the smell of _____!" Write their responses on paper and encourage them to illustrate their pages. Compile them into a classroom book, entitled "Favorite Smells and Not-so-Favorite Smells."

Science

Place cinnamon sticks, chocolate-chip cookies, garlic, coffee, sliced lemon or oranges, and dirt in separate brown paper bags (numbered). Ask the children to smell the outsides of the bags and see if they can identify what is inside them. Record their answers. Ask the children to close their eyes, then open the bags slightly and give the children chances to smell what is inside the bags. Again, record their answers. When all the children have had turns, show the children what was inside each bag and see how many "smelled" correctly.

Small Motor

Make potpourri sachets with the children. Have the children glue two 3" fabric circles together, about two thirds of the way around. (**Note:** You might want to do this step for younger children.) Once dry, have children put small amounts of potpourri into the opening of the fabric and glue the opening shut.

Book Suggestions

Sense-Abilities: Fun Ways to Explore the Senses by Michelle O'Brien-Palmer
What's That Awful Smell? by Heather Tekavec and Margaret Spengler

Snack

Pair the children and offer them an assortment of fresh fruit and cheeses. The children place different fruit and cheese on their plates. Have one partner in each pair close his eyes, while the other partner chooses a food to smell from the other child's plate. The child smells the food and guesses what it is. Have them change positions and repeat. **Safety Note:** Be sure the children only eat foods that they touch themselves, and that partners do not feed one another.

Review

Ask children to talk about the sense of smell and how they use it.

Assessment

How accurate are the children at differentiating smells with their eyes closed as opposed to their eyes open?

 *Jane Annunziata, Sussex, NJ*

What's That I Hear?

Learning Objectives The children will:
1. Become aware of their sense of hearing.
2. Develop their listening skills.
3. Use their ears to hear different sounds.

Circle or Group Time Activity

- Prior to doing the activity, decorate a box with a lid (such as a shoebox) with drawings and images of ears. Fill it with objects from around the room that make noises, such as a bell, a shaker, a click-pen, and so on.
- Place the box on the floor in the group area. Leave the lid on.
- When children arrive, show them the box and ask what is on the outside of it.
- Engage the children in a discussion about ears and hearing. Tell them that they are going to use their ears to listen to sounds and guess what makes the sounds.
- Ask the children to close or cover their eyes. Take one object out of the box, and make a noise with it. Put it back in the box and ask the children to open their eyes and guess what made the sound. Give them clues, if needed.
- After the children name all of the objects, discuss whether the game was easy or hard and then talk about how important it is to listen.
- Tell them that today, they will learn about ears and hearing.

Learning Centers

Large Motor
Roll out a large area of bubble wrap on the floor. Invite the children to take off their shoes and dance on the bubble wrap, popping the bubbles to lively music.

HIPPOPOTAMUS

Library
Make a recording of *The Ear Book* by Al Perkins and set it out for the children to listen to as they look through a copy of the book. Have them listen closely!

Listening
Play a recording of sound effects and challenge the children to identify the various sounds.

ELEPHANT

Math

Provide animal pictures and enlargements of each animal's ears. Invite the children to match the ears with the correct animals. For added fun, encourage them to make funny pictures of their own. For example, ask them, "What would a dog look like with an elephant ear?"

CAT

GIRAFFE

Sand and Water

Line a tub or small sensory table with bubble wrap. Rub petroleum jelly on the bubble wrap and invite the children to run their hands over it and pop the bubbles.

Book Suggestions

The Ear Book by Al Perkins
The Listening Walk by Aliki
Polar Bear, Polar Bear, What Do You Hear? by Bill Martin, Jr.

Snack

Pour a small amount of crispy rice cereal in each cup. Before eating the cereal, encourage the children to listen to the sounds the cereal makes when they add milk to it.

Review

Play a game of "Silly Simon Says," reminding the children to pay more attention to what you say instead of what you do. Call out different actions and do them too, but occasionally perform an action that you do not name. For instance, run in place when you say "Simon says clap your hands." End the game by saying: "Simon says point to the part of your body that you listen and hear with."

Assessment

Can the children identify their ears or the ears of other people and animals? Can the children describe what ears are for? Can the children hear and repeat back specific directions?

Shelley Hoster, Norcross, GA

3-D Fun

Learning Objectives The children will:
1. Recognize a sphere, pyramid, and cube as well as a circle, triangle, and square and their three-dimensional counterparts.
2. Develop their small and large motor skills.

Circle or Group Time Activity
- Cut out a circle, triangle, and square (10") from card stock. Ask the children to identify the shapes.
- Review the properties of each shape. Point out that a circle has no straight sides, a triangle has three straight sides, and a square has four straight sides.
- Ahead of time, put three-dimensional shapes (sphere, pyramid, and cube) in a bag. Ask a child to close her eyes and pull out a shape. Ask questions to draw a comparison between the shapes in the bag and the two-dimensional shapes.
- Talk about how the shapes in the bag are three-dimensional (not flat) and the card stock shapes are two dimensional (flat).
- Show the children a model or picture of a pyramid (triangle or pyramid), a globe or ball (circle or sphere), and a die (square or cube).
- Put the two sets of shapes on the rug so the children can take turns choosing a two-dimensional shape and matching it with its three-dimensional counterpart.

Learning Centers
Art
Place construction paper into round cake pans. Pour red, yellow, and blue paint into shallow containers and gently place some marbles into the paint. Demonstrate how to put a marble into the pan and gently tilt the pan so that the marble rolls around on the paper, leaving a trail. Try the activity again, using a square cake pan.

Literacy
Provide spherical objects, such as beads, cotton balls, oranges, and balls. Ask the children to think about what these items are used for. Ask them to illustrate what they imagine. When they are finished, ask them to describe their picture as you write the words. Staple the pages together for a classroom book.

Music
Teach the children the following song as they roll balls in the Blocks Center or as they make rolling marble paintings in the Art Center:

Roll, Roll, Roll the Ball by Susan Oldham Hill
(Tune: "Row, Row, Row Your Boat")
Roll, roll, roll the ball
Down the tube it glides,
Watch it twirling, twisting, turn
And out the end it slides.

Blocks

Provide an assortment of small balls and varying sizes of cardboard tubes, including carpet tubes (check local hardware stores or carpet stores for these). Cut some of the tubes in half so the balls are visible when rolling down the tubes. Show the children how to raise and lower one end to make the balls roll faster or slower.

Small Motor

Provide straws cut to ½", lengths of yarn or sturdy thread, paper shapes (punch a hole in the top of each), and blunt plastic needles. Thread the needles for the children and show them how to thread a paper shape on the yarn. Demonstrate making a pattern by adding a shape, a piece of straw, a paper shape, a piece of straw, and so on. Encourage the children to try using all three shapes. Help the children tie the ends to make a necklace to wear.

LARGE BALL

CARPET TUBE

Book Suggestions

Circles, Triangles and Squares by Tana Hoban
Pancakes, Pancakes by Eric Carle
The Shape of Me and Other Stuff by Dr. Seuss
Shapes, Shapes, Shapes by Tana Hoban

Snack

Make pancakes and serve them with melon balls. Or serve triangle-shaped snacks or square cereal and miniature marshmallows (similar to a cube).

Review

Gather the children and read the book they wrote and illustrated in the Literacy Center. Take out the paper shapes and three-dimensional shapes from the Group or Circle Time Activity and review the properties of each shape, including the names of all the shapes. Ask them to make pairs of those that go together.

Assessment

Ask each child to match the two- and three-dimensional shapes used in the Group or Circle Time Activity and to name each shape.

 *Susan Oldham Hill, Lakeland, FL*

Big Circle, Small Circle

Learning Objectives   The children will:
1. Identify circles.
2. Use comparative words such as *bigger* and *smaller.*
3. Manipulate two objects at the same time.

Circle or Group Time Activity
- Before the children arrive, cut out four circles of various sizes from four different colors of felt.
- Gather the children in a circle and tell them, "I have a shape in my pocket (or behind my back). It doesn't have any corners, and it is round. What is it?"
- Hold out the first circle, and put it on a flannel board. Ask the children to name objects that are circular, such as some cereals, hula-hoops, pizza, cookies, and so on.
- Put another circle on the board, and ask the children, "Which is bigger?" "Which is smaller?"
- Put a third circle on the board and ask the children to help you put them in order from smallest to largest.
- Replace one circle with the fourth circle and ask the children to put them in order again.
- Repeat this several times with different groups of three circles.

Learning Centers   **Art**
Provide paper, paint, and circular objects for children to make circle paintings.

Library
Place a recording of *When a Line Bends… A Shape Begins* by Rhonda Gowler Greene for the children to listen to while they look through a copy of the book.

Math
Cut out five large circles and write the numerals 1 through 5 on them. Invite the children to place the circles in various arrangements, and then hop from one to the next in numerical order.

Sand and Water
Provide plastic spoons and straws and invite the children to use them to make circles in the sand.

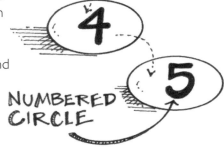

NUMBERED CIRCLE

Snack and Cooking
Using English muffin halves as bases, invite the children to use tomato sauce, grated cheese, and circle toppings to make mini pizzas.

Book Suggestions
Bear in a Square by Stella Blackstone
Brown Rabbit's Shape Book by Alan Baker
Round Is a Mooncake: A Book of Shapes by Roseanne Thong
When a Line Bends… A Shape Begins by Rhonda Gowler Greene

Snack
Serve the mini pizzas the children prepared in the Snack and Cooking Center, along with round slices of oranges.

Review
Bring the children on a "Circle Walk" around the school. Ask the children to identify the circles that they see along the way.

Assessment
If given an assortment of shapes, can the child identify the circles?

Related Song
Ring Around the Rosy (Traditional)
Ring around the rosy,
A pocket full of posies,
Ashes, ashes,
We all fall down.

The cows are in the meadow
Eating buttercups,
Ashes, ashes,
We all stand up!

 Cassandra Reigel Whetstone, Folsom, CA

Boxes, Boxes, and More Boxes

Learning Objectives The children will:
1. Sort boxes by one characteristic, such as size, shape, color, or use.
2. Use comparative words related to size, shape, texture, weight, and use.
3. Gain awareness of environmental print on boxes.

Circle or Group Time Activity

- Place several small gifts inside a box that all the children can enjoy, such as pencils, erasers, small toys, and edible treats. Make sure there is one gift for each child.
- Wrap the box with as many layers of wrapping paper as there are children.
- Play some music and ask the children to pass the box around in a circle.
- Occasionally, stop the music. Each time the music stops, the person holding the package unwraps one layer of wrapping paper.
- Keep going until all the children have had a turn to unwrap one layer of wrapping paper.
- When the children remove the last layer of paper, they open the box and enjoy the surprises inside.
- Engage the children in a discussion about the shape of the box, pointing out that it is a rectangle. Explain what a rectangle is and talk about the box's shape.

Learning Centers

Art
Set out paint and brushes and give each child a shoebox to paint. When the boxes are dry, the children can glue various decorations on them, such as glitter, pretend jewels, or foam pieces.

Blocks
Add sand or rocks to shoeboxes to weight them down. Put the lids on the boxes and tape them shut. Cover them with colored contact paper. Place the shoebox blocks in the Blocks Center for children to use to build towers and towns. Ask the children to compare the weights of the boxes.

Dramatic Play
Set out a large box, such as a refrigerator box or some other box large enough for several children to crawl inside it. Cut the flaps off one end of the box (**Safety Note:** adult-only step). Invite the children to add a blanket and turn the box into a cave. Talk about other items they might need to live in a cave, such as flashlight and helmets. Encourage them to use their imaginations and turn the box into a boat, a castle, a playhouse, or whatever else they fancy!

Large Motor
Tie a piece of rope to one end of a large box. Let the children pull the box around. They can put other boxes or items in the box to move around the room or playground.

Literacy
Collect different kinds of boxes, such as cereal boxes, tissue boxes, gift boxes, and so on. Read the labels and talk about what came in the boxes. Ask the children how items in the boxes are used.

Math
Set out a variety of boxes and challenge the children to sort them in different ways, such as by size, shape, use, and color. Challenge the children to nest the boxes from big to little and little to big. Ask the children questions to help them make comparisons between boxes.

Book Suggestions

How Many Bugs in a Box? by David Carter
Not a Box by Antoinette Portis
What's in the Box? by Richard Powell

Snack

Pack the children's snacks in the boxes the children decorated in the Art Center. Take the box lunches outside for a picnic.

Review

Challenge the children to practice sorting boxes in different ways, by size, shape, texture, weight, color, or use.

Assessment

Given various boxes, can the children sort the boxes by one property, such as by size, shape, texture, weight, color, or use?

Related Song

Stack, Stack, Stack the Boxes by Monica Hay Cook
(Tune: "Row, Row, Row Your Boat")
Stack, stack, stack, the boxes.
Stack them really high.
Watch them topple to the ground.
Start all over again.

 Monica Hay Cook, Tucson, AZ

Bubbles

Learning Objectives The children will:
1. Identify shapes.
2. Expand their oral motor skills.
3. Develop small and large motor skills.

Circle or Group Time Activity
- Teach the children the following song:

  Bubbles, Bubbles Everywhere! by Sandra Nagel
  (Tune: "Twinkle, Twinkle Little Star")
  Bubbles, bubbles, here and there. (point near and far)
  Bubbles, bubbles, everywhere. (point finger in a circle)
  Pop them with your finger here. (use pointer finger to pretend to pop bubbles)
  Pop them with your finger there.
  Bubbles, bubbles, here and there.
  Bubbles, bubbles, everywhere.

- Read the book *Bubble Trouble* by Mary Packard to the children.
- Discuss what the children think happened with the child in the story. What would they do?
- Blow bubbles and encourage the children to pop them with their pointer fingers (work on isolation of the pointer finger and eye-hand coordination).
- Talk about the circular shape of the bubbles.

Learning Centers **Art**
The children dip circular items (tops, lids, plastic cups, paper shapes) into paint and make prints of circles on paper. Talk about how bubbles are usually round and shaped like a circle. Consider either using lots of colors or using a few hues of particular colors, such as shades of blue or green. On another day, repeat the activity using items of various shapes. Ask children to identify the shapes.

Large Motor
Provide large cutouts of circles or balloons and invite the children to hold them up and pretend to float around a large space like bubbles.

Math
Make a small bubble blowing station and challenge the children to count the number of bubbles they blow. Consider blowing bubbles onto sheets of paper, and then challenging the children to count the number of circles the bubbles leave on the paper after they pop.

Sand and Water
Add mild dish soap to the water in the table. Provide whisks and egg beaters for the children to whip up as many bubbles as they can. Talk about the shape of the egg beaters and whisks.

Small Motor

The children trace cardboard circle patterns and other circular items on paper, cut them out, and glue them onto paper to create pictures. On another day, the children trace templates and items of various shapes and make pictures with a variety of shapes. Have them make a collage or build things out of the shapes.

Outdoors

Bring tins, bowls, lots of bubble mixture, and things that the children can use to make bubbles (rope tied in a ring, small hoops, hoop bracelets, plastic six-pack rings, lids, and so on) outdoors. Invite the children to try making bubbles with things that are not circular to see what happens.

Book Suggestions

Benny's Big Bubble by Jane O'Connor
Bubble Trouble by Joy N. Hulme
Bubble Trouble by Mary Packard
Double Bubble Trouble by Judy Bradbury

Snack

Serve a snack of round crackers and cookies in various sizes. Let the children add seltzer water to juice and watch the bubbles form.

Review

Ask the children to find and name things using shapes they see in the room: circle, square, triangle, and rectangle. The children name the items they use to make bubbles and the shapes of the items. (If children have difficulty naming a shape or item, ask them to find the shape or item out of a group, or point to it in a picture.)

Assessment

Can the child identify the names of the shapes of various items? Can the child use oral motor skills to blow bubbles through a bubble wand? Is the child able to use motor skills to pop bubbles using his pointer finger?

 *Sandra Nagel, White Lake, MI*

Circles

Learning Objectives The children will:
1. Explore the circle shape.
2. Develop their small motor skills.

Circle or Group Time Activity
- Tell children they will be learning about a shape called the circle.
- Teach the children the following song:

Circle Song (author unknown)
(Tune: "Bingo")
Sit right down and show your hands,
It's time to make a circle.
C, I, R, C, L, E.
C, I, R, C, L, E.
C, I, R, C, L, E.
A circle makes the shape-o. (Use index fingers to draw circles in the air, one hand
    at a time.)

Learning Centers **Art**
Provide paper, an assortment of washable paints, and various sizes of round
sponges for the children to create circle prints.

Blocks
Provide an assortment of round and cylindrical blocks. Encourage the children to
experiment with building a structure with round blocks. Talk about how they differ
from building with rectangular or square blocks.

Large Motor
Do a variety of active activities with the children that focus on circular shapes,
such as trying to get basketballs into hoops, throwing beanbags through holes,
square dancing (circular dances), running around in circles, and so on.

Literacy
Ask the children to complete the following sentence, "A _____ is a circle."
Copy down the children's responses (or help them do it), and then provide
markers and crayons so the children can illustrate their pages.

Small Motor
Place an assortment of various-shaped blocks in a basket. Encourage the children
to find all the round blocks and put them in another basket. Challenge the children
further by asking them to sort the blocks by size.

Book Suggestions
Circles by Diyan Leake
Shapes: A Book by John Reiss

Snack
Help the children mix and prepare gelatin snack according to the package directions. Pour the mixture into shallow baking trays. Refrigerate according to package directions, and after it is set cut out circular shapes with biscuit cutters and serve.

Review
Ask the children to identify round objects outdoors.

Assessment
Can the child differentiate a circle from another shape?

 *Jane Annunziata, Sussex, NJ*

Getting to Know Circles and Squares

Learning Objectives The children will:
1. Differentiate between a square and a circle.
2. Describe the differences between a square and circle.

Circle or Group Time Activity
- Prepare by drawing a circle or a square on index cards so that you have an equal number of shapes (for example, 12 squares and 12 circles). Laminate, if desired. Make enough so that each child will have one.
- Give a shape card to each child.
- Play music. When the music starts, ask the children to pass the cards to the right (tape arrows on the floor to help the children remember which way to pass) and continue passing until the music stops.
- When the music stops, hold up a card with a square on it and say, "If you are holding this card, wave your square in the air!" Demonstrate.
- Next, hold up the circle card and say, "Spin your circle 'round and 'round!" Demonstrate making a circle in the air.
- Repeat the music and corresponding body movements several times until children correctly identify cards.

Learning Centers **Blocks**
Have children use square and circle blocks to build block creations.
Large Motor
Provide blocks and a tape recording of silly instructions for the children to follow, such as:
- *touch the circle to your nose*
- *put two squares on your toes*
- *wear a circle like a hat*
- *whisper "square" and fly like a bat*
- *say "goodbye, circle, I'm leaving now"*
- *please put all shapes down*
Math
Make pattern cards by tracing square and circle blocks onto cards in various patterns (circle, square, circle, square; square, square, circle; and so on). Laminate, if possible. Challenge the children to replicate the patterns on the cards using real blocks.

Sand and Water

Hide "treasure" blocks in the sand for the children to uncover and hide again.

Art

Provide a variety of square and circular-shaped blocks. Show the children how to trace blocks on paper and then to glue yarn over the shape outlines.

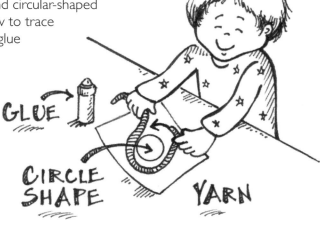

GLUE

CIRCLE SHAPE   YARN

SHAPES for TRACING

Book Suggestions   *Mouse Shapes* by Ellen Stoll Walsh
Shapes, Shapes, Shapes by Tana Hoban
So Many Circles, So Many Squares by Tana Hoban

Snack   Cut biscuits into squares and circles for the children to enjoy.

Review   Play the game from the Circle or Group Time Activity again, inviting the children to take turns holding up cards and calling out the motions that go with them.

Assessment   Give the children paper squares and circles and ask them to match them, and then ask the children to name the shapes.

Karyn F. Everham, Fort Myers, FL

Round and Round

Learning Objectives The children will:
1. Recognize the circle's shape.
2. Understand the concept of roundness.

Circle or Group Time Activity
- Sing "The Wheels on the Bus" with the children.
- Once the children learn the song, encourage them to repeat it and make motions, such as circling their hands when they sing "'round and 'round."
- Tell them they will learn about the circle shape today.

Learning Centers   **Art**
Provide strips of construction paper and tape. Show the children how to make a paper chain of circles by forming each strip into a circle and taping it shut. Form the next circle through the first circle and then tape it shut. Continue until there are several circles on each chain. Connect all the chains and hang them up in the room, straight across or in a giant circle.

GIANT CIRCLE

TAPE

Library
Place a variety of books about shapes, especially circles, in the center for children to explore.

Sand and Water
Put several objects, such as cups, plates, blocks, toys, and so on, in the center, inviting the children to press them into the sand. Discuss which items make circle shapes.

Science
Provide children with bubble solution (purchased or made with the children) and bubble wands so the children can blow bubbles and watch the circles float away. Talk about the circular shape of the bubbles.

Small Motor
Provide various sizes of construction paper circles and a paper plate. Encourage the children to use their imaginations to create a "Circle Person," such as a snowman. The children glue circles together to make bodies, arms, legs, feet, faces, and so on.

Book Suggestions

Circles by Dana Meachen Rau
Circles by Diyan Leake
Circles Around Town by Nathan Olson
So Many Circles by Elena Martin

Snack

Serve circular cereal, banana slices, mini bagels, or round crackers.

Review

Ask the children to look around the room and find circles or round shapes.

Assessment

Hold up different items and ask the children if they make circle shapes or other shapes. Ask the children to identify the shapes.

 *Donna Alice Patton, Hillsboro, OH*

Shape Party

Learning Objectives The children will:
1. Learn and recognize the four basic shapes (circle, triangle, square, and rectangle).
2. Learn common objects that have these shapes.

Circle or Group Time Activity
- Make Shape Mobiles with the children.
- Help the children cut out four shapes (circle, triangle, square, and rectangle) from construction paper.
- Help the children punch holes in each shape.
- Tie yarn through the hole in each shape and tie the other end of the yarn to a clothes hanger.
- Hang the mobiles up in the classroom.

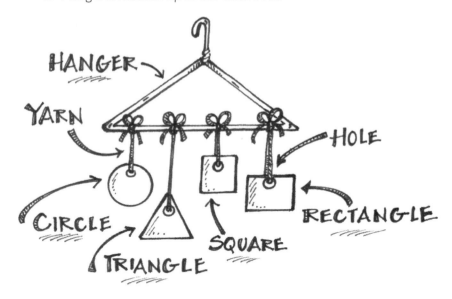

- Teach the children the following song:

Can You Name What Shape This Is? by Renee Kirchner
(Tune: "The Muffin Man")
Can you name what shape this is?
Shape this is? Shape this is?
Can you name what shape this is?
I'm holding in the air.

- Show the children different cutout shapes and challenge them to say the names of each.

Learning Centers

Art
Cut colored paper into various shapes. Give each child a large sheet of poster board per child. Challenge the children to glue the colored shapes to the poster board, making large buildings, faces, or other images.

Blocks
Provide blocks in the shape of circles, triangles, rectangles, and squares. Encourage the children to build something that uses all four shapes.

Math
Provide several paper cutouts of shapes in various colors and challenge the children to match the different shapes by color, and then to match similar shapes that are different colors.

Small Motor
Play "Sort Shape." Place many felt cutouts of shapes on a table so the children can sort them into four piles: circle, square, triangle, and rectangle.

Writing
Make a "Shape Book." Give each child four pieces of paper and invite the children to draw one of the four basic shapes on each piece of paper. Ask the children to draw some objects that are made of similar shapes as those on the sheets of paper. Help the children write the names of the objects they drew at the tops of their pages.

Book Suggestions
The Shape of Me and Other Stuff by Dr. Seuss
The Shape of Things by Dayle Ann Dodds
Shapes, Shapes, Shapes by Tana Hoban
Shapes: Slide 'n' Seek by Chuck Murphy
When a Line Bends… A Shape Begins by Rhonda Gowler Greene

Snack
Serve round crackers, American cheese cut into rectangles, cheddar cheese cut into triangles, and cantaloupe cut into squares.

Review
Repeat the "Can You Name What Shape This Is" song from the Circle or Group Time Activity.

Assessment
Hold up each of the four shapes. Can the children name each shape? Can they name an object that has each shape?

 *Renee Kirchner, Carrollton, TX*

Shape Time

Learning Objectives The children will:

1. Recognize the four basic shapes: circle, square, triangle, and rectangle.
2. Improve their oral language skills.
3. Practice sorting shapes.

Circle or Group Time Activity

- To prepare, gather four boxes and draw a different shape on the front of each (circle, square, triangle, and rectangle). Fill each box with objects or pictures of the selected shape. Add three items to each box that do not belong. For example, place one square, circle, and triangle object in the rectangle box.
- Wrap the boxes and display them on a table.
- Give each child a hand bell or other instrument.
- Let the children help you unwrap all four boxes. Draw their attention to the shape on the front of each box.
- Remove the shapes from the first box, one by one. Invite the children to name the shape of each item as you hold it high in the air. Have them ring their bell or play their instruments if you hold up a shape that does not belong in that box.
- Raise your hand to signal the children to stop playing. Invite one child to place the shape in front of the correct box. Play until the children identify all the shapes from each box and display the shapes near the corresponding boxes.

Learning Centers ### Art

Cut out 3" shapes from various colors of tissue paper. Ask each child to select 10 tissue paper shapes. The children paint the shapes with thinned glue and attach them to paper to make a shape collage.

Dramatic Play

Draw shapes on pairs of rubber gloves, T-shirts, hats, socks, flip flops, and so on. Display the various articles of clothing and invite the children to try on the shape clothing and pretend they are shapes. Challenge the children to group together based on the shapes on their clothes.

Large Motor

Display a collection of paper or plastic shapes randomly around the floor. Invite pairs of children to remove their shoes and take turns as they play together. One child names a shape and the other child hops or steps from shape to shape across the floor. For added fun, challenge them to make shapes with their bodies!

Math

Set the materials from the Circle or Group Time Activity in the Math Center. Invite the children to mix all the objects and pictures together and then sort them into the correct boxes according to their shape. Challenge the children to display the objects for each set of shapes from smallest to largest.

Small Motor

Invite the children to flatten out pieces of modeling dough and press various objects into the clay to form an assortment of shape imprints.

Snack and Cooking

Each child mixes together 1 tablespoon of pudding mix and 2 tablespoons of cold skim milk in a bowl. Invite the children to use their pointer fingers to draw each of the four shapes in the mixture. Provide colored sprinkles for them to place in the pudding for extra fun and added texture. The children eat the pudding when done.

Book Suggestions

Food for Thought by Saxton Freymann
The Shape of Things by Dayle Ann Dodds

Snack

Make shape sandwiches with the children. Cut slices of cheese, lettuce, deli meat, and soft flour tortillas into squares, triangles, circles, and rectangles. Stack the shapes together and enjoy.

Review

Group the children in pairs. Ask one of the children in the pairs to close his eyes. Show the partners images of shapes and invite them to draw those shapes on their partners' backs, challenging the children with their eyes closed to name the shape.

Assessment

Display an assortment of paper shapes. Give the child a flashlight. Can the child shine the flashlight on the correct shape when you say the shape's name?

 *Mary J. Murray, Mazomanie, WI*

Shapes in Our World

Learning Objectives   The children will:
1. Identify various shapes.
2. Name various colors.
3. Develop their small motor skills.

Circle or Group Time Activity

- Before the children arrive, make flash cards by drawing a variety of colors of shapes. Cut out the shapes and glue them to card stock pieces. Laminate, if possible. This will give you a set of shape flash cards to use throughout the year.
- During Circle or Group Time, show the children the shape cards one at time. Ask, "What shape is this?" "What color is the shape?" "How many sides does it have?"

Learning Centers   **Art**

Draw a circle, square, rectangle, and triangle, each on a separate sheet of paper. Make enough so that each child will have all four shapes. Provide sandpaper for the circle, wrapping paper or fabric for the square, felt for the rectangle, and craft sticks for the triangle. Help the children to cut the materials into the different shapes. They glue the textured shapes to the corresponding shapes on the sheets of paper. When they are finished with their papers, staple their pages together and title it, "My Shape and Touch Book."

Blocks

Provide blocks in a variety of shapes and ask the children if they can find a square, triangle, or rectangle. Encourage the children to build different things using the blocks. Ask the children what shapes they are using in their building.

Math

Provide two sets of shapes for the children to match to one another. Extend the idea by using colors in making the shapes and challenging the children to match the shapes by color (for example, red circle to red circle).

Small Motor

Make several simple shape puzzles for the children to put together.

Writing

Draw a shape on a piece of paper and make a copy for each child in the class. Provide markers and ask children to draw pictures using their shapes. When the children finish, help them to add a caption about the shapes they drew.

Book Suggestions

Circles Around the Town by Nathan Olson
Circles, Triangles, and Squares by Tana Hoban
Shapes, Shapes, Shapes by Tana Hoban
The Silly Book of Shapes by Todd Parr

Snack

Make square sandwiches and serve with juice. Talk about the shape of the sandwich and the juice cup.

Review

Give each child a piece of paper and a red, blue, purple, and orange crayon. Have the children write their names at the top of their pages. Ask them to draw shapes using particular colors. For example, ask them to draw red squares, blue rectangles, purple circles, and orange triangles. For younger children, provide sheets of paper with the shapes already on them and ask them to color the squares red, the rec tangles blue, and so on.

Assessment

Can the child look around the classroom and name the shapes of various objects?

Related Poem

As you read the following poem, draw the shapes it describes on the blackboard.

Shapes by Sherri Lawrence
What shape is round like a ball?
A circle is round like a ball.
What shape makes a house?
A square makes a house.
What shape makes a red wagon?
A rectangle makes a red wagon with four circles as wheels.
What shape makes a kite?
A triangle makes a kite.

 Sherri Lawrence, Louisville, KY

So Many Shapes

Learning Objectives The children will:

1. Identify shapes such as a square, circle, triangle, rectangle, oval, cylinder, and cone.
2. Develop their small motor skills.
3. Follow directions.

Circle or Group Time Activity

- Make shape cards by drawing different shapes on 8 ½" x 11" cardboard.
- Introduce or review names of the desired shapes with the group.
- Read *Shapes, Shapes, Shapes* by Tana Hoban to the children.
- Distribute one set of shape cards to each child. Have them identify the shapes.
- Assemble the group in a circle and sing "The Hokey Pokey," substituting the word "circle" where the song mentions body parts.

Learning Centers

Art

Provide sponges cut into a variety of shapes, shape cookie cutters, and blocks in a variety of shapes. Invite the children to dip the sponges, cookie cutters, and/or blocks into washable paint and make prints on white paper. Encourage creativity.

Blocks

Invite the children to create structures using different shaped blocks. Add cardboard food cartons (such as milk cartons and cereal boxes) to provide additional construction shapes.

Science

Collect a variety of leaves on a nature walk outdoors. In the center, provide trays labeled with the shapes. Invite children to sort the leaves based on the shapes they most closely resemble. Ask them to count the number of leaves on each tray, and say which shape has the most or fewest number of similarly shaped leaves.

Small Motor

Make a shape chain with the children. Provide construction paper in assorted colors, markers, scissors, yarn or string, a hole punch, and shape patterns. The children trace or draw the shapes and cut or tear them out. Help them punch a hole in the tops and bottoms of their shapes and tie the shapes to one another with yarn or string, forming chains.

Writing

Set out construction paper, shape patterns, lined writing paper, and markers. The children draw or trace a picture of a shape and write what they see in the room or an object they know that is the shape of what they drew. Staple sheets together and make a shape book for children to share with their family and special friends.

Book Suggestions   *The Missing Piece* by Shel Silverstein
Shapes, Shapes, Shapes by Tana Hoban
Shape Up! by David A. Adler
So Many Circles, So Many Squares by Tana Hoban
A Star in My Orange by Dana Meachen Rau

Snack   Set out ingredients for cookie dough or dough itself, cookie cutters, and shape templates. Invite the children to roll or flatten out pieces of dough, then select shaped cookie cutters or templates to use to form their own shape cookies. Collect the shaped cookies and bake so the children can enjoy them as a snack.

Review   Repeat the "Shapey Gapey" song from the Circle and Group Time Activity with the children.

Assessment   Given an assortment of shape illustrations and objects resembling the shapes, can the child name the shape and match the illustration to an object of the same shape?

Related Poem   **Shapes** by Margery Kranyik Fermino
Point to a circle,
Point to a square,
Show me a triangle,
Shapes are everywhere!
Point to a rectangle,
A cone that's over there,
Show me an oval,
Shapes are everywhere!

(Additional verses: substitute other desired shapes)

 Margery Kranyik Fermino, West Roxbury, MA

Beginning of School

Learning Objectives The children will:

1. Familiarize themselves with the rules and routine of the classroom.
2. Learn about their classmates and friendship.

Circle or Group Time Activity

■ Teach the children the song "The More We Get Together:"

The More We Get Together (Traditional)
The more we get together,
Together, together,
The more we get together, the happier we'll be.
There's _____, and _____, and _____, and _____. (name children
   in the class)
The more we get together, the happier we'll be.

■ Repeat the song until you have sung about each child.
■ Talk to the children about the classroom rules.
■ Invite the children to brainstorm some additional classroom rules. Write them
   down on large chart paper. This makes children feel like they are part of
   the process.

Learning Centers

Blocks

Take a picture of each child from head to toe.
Print and cut the pictures out (so they look like
paper dolls). Use clear packaging tape to
attach each cutout to a block and set
the blocks out for the children to use.
Note: These can last a long time if you
use a good, strong tape.

BLOCK ↘

COPY of CUTOUT

CLEAR PACKING TAPE

Art

Take a full-length picture of each child and make several copies of each picture. Provide copies of the pictures, construction paper, child-safe scissors, glue, and other art materials. The children cut out the pictures and make new pictures by gluing images of themselves next to images of their friends on construction paper.

Dramatic Play

Provide small chalkboards, paper, crayons, alphabet magnets and a magnet board, easy-to-read or wordless books and a pointer. The children take turns being the teacher and students.

Literacy

After reading the book *If You Take a Mouse to School* by Laura Numeroff, ask the children what they would bring to school. Copy their responses onto paper and have them illustrate their responses. Bind the pages together to make a class book.

Small Motor

Provide a shallow box, a variety of papers, large envelopes, and child-safe scissors. Use string to attach a few pairs of scissors to the box. Encourage the children to practice cutting the paper. Let them store the cuttings in their own envelopes.

Book Suggestions

D.W.'s Guide to Preschool by Marc Brown
If You Take a Mouse to School by Laura Numeroff
The Kissing Hand by Audrey Penn
Mouse's First Day of School by Lauren Thompson

Snack

Ask the children to bring in small portions of their favorite fruits (ask the children's families to wash and cut the fruit into bite-size pieces). The children take turns putting their fruit into a large bowl. Mix the cut pieces of fruit together and enjoy a friendship fruit salad.

Review

Set out a small, light ball. Gather the children together in a circle. Throw the ball to one child. Ask her to say her name, say the name of a new friend she made that day, and then throw the ball to another classmate. Repeat until everyone has a turn.

Assessment

Can the child name some of the children in the classroom? Can the child name some of the class's rules?

 *Gail Morris, Kemah, TX*

Beginning of the Year

Learning Objectives The children will:

1. Learn the names of classmates and staff.
2. Familiarize themselves with the classroom space and school environment.
3. Adjust to the classroom routine.

Circle or Group Time Activity

- Provide all the staff and children with nametags for the first week of school.
- Teach the children the following original chant:

Roll the ball,
Play the game,
When you get the ball,
You say your name.

- Ask the children to sit in a circle or a horseshoe formation. Show them a large ball. Explain that when they have the ball they say their names, then roll the ball to another person. Begin by saying your name and then roll the ball to a child.
- Make sure everyone in the class gets a turn. This is a fun way to learn everyone's names, and the children enjoy using the ball.
- After repeating the activity a couple of times, consider asking the children to write their names on sentence strips that read, for example, "My name is _____, and I like _____." Write the information for younger children.

Learning Centers

Art
Set out paints, brushes, and paper. Invite the children to paint images of things that remind them of their homes. Have them share the paintings with the class.

Blocks
Invite the children to build structures together in small groups. Model appropriate sharing behavior. "Can I have the square block, please?"

Large Motor
Separate the children into two groups. One group begins by reciting the following chant:

Red Rover, Red Rover,
Have ____ ____ over.

In the second line, the children name another child and a movement; for instance, they would say, "Have Billy jump over." The child then jumps from one group to the next.

Literacy

Provide paper, pictures of the school and your classroom, glue, markers, and so on, and invite the children to make a book about school. Each child makes a page of the book, and then explains the page to you. On a separate sheet of paper, copy the children's explanations. When putting the book together, be sure to put the children's explanations opposite the pictures they created.

Writing

Provide several sheets of paper with the outlines of the children's names on them. Invite the children to illustrate the names of other children they met earlier in the day, and then to give the illustrations to those children.

Book Suggestions

Clifford's First School Day by Norman Bridwell
Curious George's First Day of School by H. A. Rey
I Love School! by Philemon Sturges
Mouse's First Day of School by Lauren Thompson
School Bus by Donald Crews
Vera's First Day of School by Vera Rosenberry
The Wheels on the Bus by Paul O. Zelinsky

Snack

The children wash their hands and do helper jobs, such as passing out napkins, cups, and placemats. Provide cheese, crackers, and other foods, but ask that they use language to communicate what they want. For example, ask that the children say, "I want crackers, please. Thank you." or "I need a cup, please. Thank you." Model and encourage appropriate table conversation.

Review

Gather the children together and review what happened throughout the day. Explain to the children which things they will also do tomorrow, and that some things will be slightly different. Ask the children to repeat what you say.

Assessment

Does the child use the names of peers and staff? Is the child able to find materials and places in the classroom? Does the child follow the routine with a minimum of assistance? Does the child participate in the various learning activities and centers?

 Sandra Nagel, White Lake, MI

Kindergarten Bound

Learning Objectives
The children will:
1. Learn that kindergarten is "a place where children can grow."
2. Discover that kindergarten is a fun and happy place.
3. Develop their letter recognition and matching beginning sounds skills.

Circle or Group Time Activity
- Engage the children in a discussion about the origin of the word *kindergarten*.
- Show them a sentence strip with *kindergarten* written on it and ask them if they know what the word means.
- Explain that the word comes from two German words, the first, *kinder*, which means *children*, and the second word, *garten*, which means *garden*. Put the two words on a sentence strip and point to the words as you say them.
- After talking about the meaning of the two words, talk about how the meanings of the two separate words combine to describe a kindergarten (a place where young children come to grow).
- Read the children a book about kindergarten (see the list below for options).

Learning Centers

Art
Set out art materials and invite the children to make pictures that show different parts of what they think they will do at kindergarten during the day.

Dramatic Play
Create a play kindergarten. Hang a whiteboard, create two or three desks by adding single chairs and standing TV trays, and arrange the desks so they face the whiteboard. Add dry-erase markers and erasers, white copy paper, pencils, small boxes of crayons, and other typical kindergarten supplies. Invite the children to role-play what they think happens in a typical day at kindergarten.

Literacy
Ask the children to finish this sentence: "When I go to kindergarten, I will _____." Help the children print their complete sentences on sentence strips and then draw a picture to illustrate their thoughts. Tape the sentence strips to the bottoms of their pictures. Gather the pages together, punch holes on the left side of each page, and add heavy yarn to bind the pages into a class book.

Math
Create a countdown calendar for each child who will soon start kindergarten. Consider personalizing the calendars with photos of the children.

Small Motor
Invite the children to cut out pictures from magazines of things one would find in typical kindergarten classrooms, such as books, pencils, crayons, erasers, chairs, and desks. Use the pictures to create a kindergarten collage on a large piece of poster board.

Writing
Provide sentence strips covered with laminate or adhesive paper with the children's names on them. Give the children dry-erase markers to use as they practice tracing over the letters in their names.

Book Suggestions
Miss Bindergarten Gets Ready for Kindergarten by Joseph Slate
The Night Before Kindergarten by Natasha Wing
Off to School, Baby Duck! by Amy Hest
Welcome to Kindergarten by Anne Rockwell

Snack
Fill one bowl with letter-shaped cereal, one with cheddar snack crackers, and one with mini pretzels. The children use small spoons to spoon their choice of snacks into small bowls.

Review
Ask the children if they remember what they learned about the word *kindergarten*. Ask the children to tell you what they learned in their own words.

Assessment
Observe the children as they play in the Dramatic Play Center set up like a kindergarten and listen to how they refer to kindergarten in their conversations. Do they make positive comments? Do they seem excited about going to kindergarten? Place magnetic letters on a tray and ask the children to find the letters they know, to name them, and say words that begin with those letters.

Related Poem
Five Little Children by Virginia Jean Herrod
Five little children sitting under a tree.
The first one said, "It's a learning place for me!"
The second one said, "It's a place where I can run!"
The third one said, "It's a place to have fun!"
The fourth one said, "It's a place where I can grow like a seed!"
The fifth one said, "It's a place to learn to read!"
Then the teacher rang the bell
And the kindergarten doors opened wide,
And the five little children
Happily skipped inside.

 Virginia Jean Herrod, Columbia, SC

Off to School

Learning Objectives The children will:
1. Gain awareness of the physical surroundings within the classroom.
2. Learn the classroom rules and routines.

Circle or Group Time Activity
- Teach the children the song "The Wheels on the Bus."
- Once the children know the song, ask them to board a pretend school bus and sing "The Wheels on the Bus" as they take a trip around the classroom.
- While singing the song and walking around the classroom, stop at each center. Label the centers in front of the children, explaining the activity at each center and the rules for each center that they visit.
- Continue the ride until the bus has stopped at all the centers.
- Once the children are back at the circle area, ask specific questions about each center, for example, "What is the name of the center where you use a paintbrush, and what are the rules when painting?"
- Go on a walking tour of the inside and outside of the school and take photos of different things the children notice. After the tour, print out the photos and invite the children to dictate what they saw. Copy down what the children say, and attach the photos to the pages of text, creating a classroom book of the school.

Learning Centers

Art
Provide smocks, paint, brushes, and paper, and invite the children to paint. Show the children how to wipe their brushes on the paint container so there is not too much paint on them as they work. When they finish painting, place their paintings on a drying rack.

Blocks
Show the children how high they should build with the blocks. Show them where blocks are stored when not in use. Point out the labels or traced block symbols that indicate where the blocks go (if applicable to your classroom). Encourage the children to build classrooms out of the blocks.

Library
Place a recording of *First Day, Hooray!* by Nancy Poydar in the center for the children to listen to as they look through a copy of the book. Provide other books about starting school for them to explore. Model appropriate behavior for this center, including looking at books quietly, sharing, and taking good care of books.

Sand and Water
Each day, show the children the different materials at the Sand and Water Center and show them how they can best use the materials.

Small Motor
Set out several small school-related objects, such as erasers, bells, and other materials. Invite the children to use all the objects. Label all of the manipulatives with a picture and words. Demonstrate how to use the manipulatives and show children where to put them when they finish using them.

Book Suggestions

David Goes to School by David Shannon
First Day, Hooray! by Nancy Poydar
School Bus by Donald Crews
This Is the Way We Go to School by Edith Baer
Timothy Goes To School by Rosemary Wells

Snack

Ask a snack helper to set the table and pass out the snack.

Review

Play "I'm Thinking of a Center." Give the children clues and ask them to name a center. For instance, ask, "In which center do you pretend to cook a meal?" "At which center do you use a paint brush?" or "What center has sand in it?"

Assessment

Can the children identify various centers by name and based on the activities they do in the centers?

Related Songs

Sing "The More We Get Together" and "The Wheels on the Bus" with the children.

Kaethe Lewandowski, Centreville, VA

Teddy Bear Time

Learning Objectives
The children will:
1. Talk about and learn about real bears.
2. Learn about hibernation and why bears hibernate in winter.
3. Hear about the history of teddy bears.

Circle or Group Time Activity
- The day before doing this activity, send home a note asking family members to send in teddy bears with their children. Have extra teddy bears on hand in case anyone forgets.
- When the children arrive, lead them on a teddy-bear parade. The children hold their favorite teddy bears and march through the school. Provide small American flags for the children to wave with one hand while they hold their bears with their other hands.
- Play marching music so they can step in time to the music.
- Tell the children that today they will learn about real bears and teddy bears. Talk about behaviors of real bears. Explain that bears eat both meat and plants. They like to eat berries, grasses, insects, deer, elk, and moose.
- Ask them if they know about hibernation. Explain that bears sleep through the winter (hibernate) because it is difficult for them to find food during the winter.
- Explain that the teddy bear is named after President Teddy Roosevelt. He once saved a bear, and a toymaker heard about this and made a toy called a "teddy" bear.

Learning Centers

Dramatic Play
Read the story "Goldilocks and the Three Bears" to the children. Afterwards, invite the children to act out the story using small, medium, and large teddy bears.

Literacy
Give each child a piece of white paper. Ask them to draw a picture of a teddy bear and name it. Help the children write the names for their teddy bears on the bottom of the papers. Bind the pages together with staples or silver rings to make a book.

Math
Fill a glass jar with either teddy bear-shaped crackers or teddy bear counters. Ask the children to guess how many are in the jar, then count the bears and give a prize to the child whose guess is closest to the actual number.

Science
Set out teddy bear counters and a scale, and invite the children to practice balancing the two sides of the scale.

Art

Give each child a brown paper lunch bag to make bear puppets. Help them cut brown construction paper into bear-like ear shapes and glue the ears to the bottoms of their flat lunch bags. Children then trace and cut out round circles from black construction paper and glue them to bags for eyes. Finish by drawing mouth using black crayons.

① GLUE EARS to BAG

EAR SHAPES

② BLACK CIRCLES (EYES)

BOTTOM of BAG

BROWN BAG

③ DRAW MOUTH

Book Suggestions

Bear Snores On by Karma Wilson
Brown Bear, Brown Bear, What Do You See? by Bill Martin, Jr.
Corduroy by Don Freeman
Sam's Teddy Bear by Barbara Lindgren
The Teddy Bears' Picnic by Jimmy Kennedy
We're Going on a Bear Hunt by Michael Rosen

Snack

Make trail mix by combining the following ingredients into a large bowl. Serve a handful of each to the children. Use the following recipe to make trail mix for the children to enjoy:

- 1 cup raisins
- 1 cup chocolate chips
- 1 cup cereal
- 1 cup sunflower seeds
- 1 cup peanuts

Review

Ask the children to draw pictures of the type of food that bears eat.

Assessment

Ask the children why bears hibernate in the winter? Can children tell you what bears like to eat? Do children know where the name for teddy bears came from?

 Renee Kirchner, Carrollton, TX

Teddy Bears and Other Bears

Learning Objectives The children will:
1. Learn about real bears.
2. Develop language skills.
3. Engage in pretend play.
4. Increase their motor skills.
5. Count and sort.

Circle or Group Time Activity

■ Teach the children the following song:

Bears Are Sleeping by Sandra Nagel
(Tune: "Brother John")
Bears are sleeping, (tip head to side on hands pretend to be sleeping)
Bears are sleeping,
In their dens,
In their dens.
Soon it will be spring time.
Soon it will be spring time.
Wake up bears. (open eyes wide, spread hands as if surprised)
Wake up bears.

Note: Consider substituting the word "hibernating" for the phrase "bears are sleeping" in a second verse, as a way to introduce children to this new vocabulary word and concept.

Learning Centers

Art
Provide construction-paper cutouts of a bear and containers of black, brown, and white paint. Invite children to paint their bear cutouts and, when dry, glue on buttons, fur pieces, foam shapes, yarn pieces, and so on to decorate the bears. Have them name their bears. Ask them what their bears like to eat, where they live, and what they like to do.

Dramatic Play
Provide teddy bears, dolls, a table, tea sets, and pretend food for a teddy-bear tea party.

Math
Place different colors and sizes of teddy bear counters and three different colored bowls of various sizes on a table. Challenge the children to sort the bears by color and size by placing them in the correct bowls.

Sensory
Provide fabric pieces, fake fur (preferably in different "bear" colors), polar-bear cutouts (from fingerpaint paper), and shaving cream. Invite the children to fingerpaint with shaving cream on the bear-shaped white paper and add fur and fabric. Talk about the texture of the shaving cream and the fur.

Science

Set out a box of fabric and paper scraps, glue, markers, and small bear figures. Invite the children to create habitat areas, such as cardboard tube trees, blue paper ponds, and white foam ice.

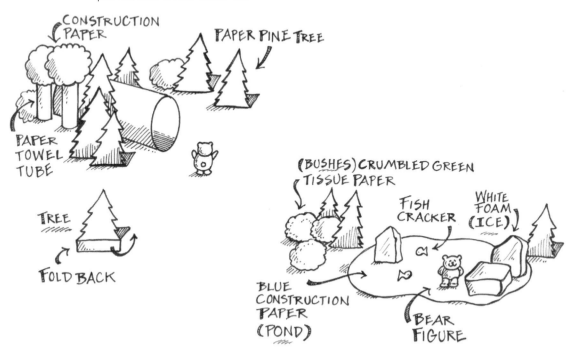

Small Motor

Draw an outline of a bear on paper and make a copy for each child (it can be an outline of a real bear or a cookie cutter-type shape of a teddy bear). Provide round-edged toothpicks and invite the children to poke holes along the outlines of the bears. Have them thread yarn through the holes.

Book Suggestions

Alaska's Three Bears by Shannon Cartwright
Bear by John Schoenherr
The Fascinating World of...Bears by Maria Angels Julivert
Golden Bear by Ruth Young

Snack

Set out mini plastic teacups. The children help make cucumber sandwiches with white bread and thinly sliced cucumbers. Cut the crust off and cut into triangles. Also serve teddy bear graham crackers. Bring the teddy bears for a teddy bear picnic!

Review

While reading books with the children, discuss the stories' real and pretend aspects.

Assessment

Set out several images of real bears, teddy bears, and other similar images of real and toy creatures. Can the child point out the bears, and say which images are of real creatures and which are of toy creatures?

 Sandra Nagel, White Lake, MI

Teddy Bears Are Terrific

Learning Objectives   The children will:

1. Identify a bear.
2. List facts about bears.

Circle or Group Time Activity

- Tell the children that they will be learning about bears today.
- Ask them to list things that they know about bears. Record their responses.
- Show the children pictures of different kinds of bears. Engage the children in a discussion about the differences between the different kinds of bears.
- Teach the children the following song:

Time for Sleeping (author unknown)
(Tune: "Sing a Song of Sixpence")
Now it's time for sleeping,
The bears go in their caves.
Keeping warm and cozy,
Time for lazy days.
When the snow is gone
And the sun comes out to play,
The bears will wake up
From their sleep and then
Go on their way.

Learning Centers

Dramatic Play

Go on a bear hunt! Tape bear prints around the classroom and hide small bags of honey-flavored cereal throughout the room. Tell the children that a bear is sleeping somewhere nearby and they have to find it's honey before it wakes up. Help the children follow the bear prints to find the "honey." The children may take backpacks, binoculars, maps, compasses, and other supplies on the bear hunt.

Library

Set out a recording of *The Teddy Bears' Picnic* by Jerry Garcia for the children to listen to as they look through a copy of the book.

Literacy

Make a classroom "Brown Bear, Brown Bear" book with the children. Assign each child a different type of bear, such as a polar bear, black bear, baby bear, grizzly bear, and so on. The children draw picture of their bears. Add the following sentence to each page: "_____ bear, _____ bear, what do you see? I see a _____ looking at me." Alter the statement so that it identifies each child's kind of bear, and ask the children what they think their bears see look at them. Gather the children's drawings together in a book. Laminate each page before binding them.

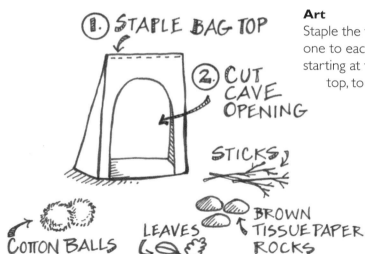

1. STAPLE BAG TOP

2. CUT CAVE OPENING

STICKS

COTTON BALLS (SNOW)

LEAVES

BROWN TISSUE PAPER ROCKS

BEAR

3. DECORATE WITH ABOVE ITEMS

Art

Staple the tops of small paper bags closed and give one to each child. Help the children cut out a square starting at the bottom of the bag and ending near the top, to represent the opening of a cave. Provide materials for the children to use to decorate their bags. For example, the children can glue on brown tissue paper "rocks," fake green leaves, cotton "snow," sticks, and so on. Invite the children to make small bears from modeling dough to include in their cave scenes.

Sand and Water

Add ice cubes to the water in the sand and water table. Tell the children that polar bears live in cold areas and swim in very cold water. Explain that polar bears have heavy coats of fur and a large amount of body fat to help keep them warm. Cover each child's hand (one hand for each child) in vegetable shortening and then have them place that hand in a small resealable bag. Ask them to put their hand into the icy water. Explain that the shortening and bag functions like the polar bear's blubber, keeping their hands warm. Ask the children to list ways that they keep warm.

Book Suggestions

The Teddy Bears' Picnic by Jerry Garcia
Wake Up Baby Bear! A First Book About Opposites by Tiphanie Beeke
We're Going on a Bear Hunt by Michael Rosen and Helen Oxenbury

Snack

On a nice day, have a teddy bear picnic! Ask the children to bring in a favorite teddy bear from home. (Have extra teddy bears for children who forget.) Ask families to supply picnic food, paper plates, tablecloths, and so on. Take the teddy bears outside and enjoy the picnic. End the picnic with an award ceremony for the softest bear, biggest bear, oldest bear, and so on.

Review

Ask the children to list facts they have learned about bears. Record their responses.

Assessment

Provide the children with several plastic animals, including a bear. Can the children identify the bear? Show the children different places that animals could live. Can the children identify which are good potential bear homes?

 Jodi Kelley, North Versailles, PA

Airplane Trip!

Learning Objectives   The children will:
1. Pretend to take a plane trip.
2. Learn about airplanes and airplane travel.
3. Fly toy airplanes and paper airplanes outdoors.

Circle or Group Time Activity
- Talk about airplanes with the children. Ask them if they have ever been on a plane or to an airport.
- Read *Miss Mouse Takes Off* by Jan Omerod to the children. In this story, a girl and her plush mouse, Miss Mouse, take a plane trip.
- Encourage the children to pretend they are taking the plane trip with the characters in the story.
- Pretend to fasten seatbelts, look out the plane windows, and eat airline food.

Learning Centers   **Art**

Invite the children to paint designs with watercolors on white paper. After they are dry, help the children fold their papers into airplanes to fly outside.

Dramatic Play

Provide airline props, suitcases, travel items, and so on. Arrange chairs into two rows and encourage the children to pretend to take a trip on a plane. Provide cafeteria trays for "meal service."

Large Motor

If outdoors, use chalk on the blacktop to draw several "runways"; if indoors, create runways using markers on long strips of butcher paper or masking tape on the floor in a large area. Encourage the children to pretend to be airplanes taking off and flying.

Literary

Pretend to be an airline representative selling airline tickets. Invite the children to purchase tickets to fly to New York, Colorado, Grandma's house, or wherever else they want to go. Help the children write their names and destinations on strips of paper that will serve as their "tickets."

Math

Provide several construction paper cutouts of airplanes with different numbers of seats drawn on them, as well as several cutouts of people, so the children can match the number of passengers to the numbers of seats.

Book Suggestions

Airplane Alphabet Book by Jerry Pallotta
Miss Mouse Takes Off by Jan Omerod
Plane Song by Diane Siebert

Snack

Set up the children's chairs like the inside of an airplane. Choose a few of the children to be flight attendants and have them serve pretzels and cheese crackers to the "passengers."

Review

Encourage the children to talk about the destinations they chose to fly to in the Literary Center. Ask them why they picked those particular destinations.

Assessment

Can the child pick out airplanes from a box of transportation toys? Can they differentiate airplanes from helicopters?

 *Karyn F. Everham, Fort Myers, FL*

Away We Go

Learning Objectives The children will:
1. Learn what transportation means.
2. Learn about the different types of transportation.
3. Find out how everyone gets to school each day.

Circle or Group Time Activity
- Teach the children the following song:

  Drive, Drive, Drive Your Bus by Renee Kirchner
  (Tune: "Row, Row, Row Your Boat")
  Drive, drive, drive your bus
  Quickly down the street.
  Bumpity, bumpity, bumpity, bumpity,
  The road is full of holes.
  Ride, ride, ride your motorcycle.
  Safely down the road.
  Safely, safely, safely, safely,
  Keep your helmet on.

- Encourage the children to make up additional verses for cars and other vehicles.
- Talk to the children about different types of transportation, such as cars, buses, trucks, motorcycles, airplanes, helicopters, trains, bikes, and boats.
- Hold up a picture of each type of transportation.
- Ask the children to tell how they got to school today.

Learning Centers

Dramatic Play
If possible, purchase a play mat or rug that looks like a road. If you do not have a commercial play mat, make your own using large paper and markers. Invite the children to pretend they are driving on the road with toy cars and trucks.

Literacy
Make individual transportation books with the children. Provide magazines for them to cut out pictures of different types of transportation. Have them glue one picture of a mode of transportation on a separate piece of paper and then help them to write the name of the mode of transportation at the bottom of the paper. Bind the pages of their books together with staples or silver rings.

Math
Ask the children how they got to school today. Did they ride in a car, a truck, or on a bus? Maybe they walked to school. Encourage the children to cut out or draw pictures that show how they came to school, and use them to create a simple bar graph. Count how many children came to school each way.

PAINT

PAINT TRAY

Art

Draw roads on large sheets of paper. Invite the children to draw traffic signals, stop signs, and other road signs on or near the roads. Provide shallow pans of paint and let the children dip the wheels of toy cars, trucks, buses, and so on in paint and drive them on the roads.

Writing

Write the words *car, bus,* and *truck* on pieces of paper, with the letters in the shapes of roads. Set out small toy versions of those vehicles and invite the children to use the matching vehicles to trace the letters of the words.

Book Suggestions

Berenstain Bears and Too Much Car Trip by Stan and Jan Berenstain
Bus-A-Saurus Bop by Diane Z. Shore
Cars and Trucks and Things that Go by Richard Scarry
Don't Let the Pigeon Drive the Bus! by Mo Willems
If I Built a Car by Chris Van Dusen
My Truck Is Stuck! by Kevin Lewis

Snack

Make edible stoplights with the children. Children spread cream cheese on a rectangular graham cracker and then place red, yellow, and green M&M's in the correct order on the cream cheese. Show them a picture of a stoplight to help them.

Review

Ask the children draw pictures of the types of transportation they use to get to school each day.

Assessment

Hold up pictures of different types of transportation. Can the child name them all? Can the child name three different ways that children in the class get to school each morning?

 Renee Kirchner, Carrollton, TX

Exploring Transportation

Learning Objectives The children will:
1. Identify different modes of transportation.
2. Sort different modes of transportation by land, air, and water.

Circle or Group Time Activity
- Ask the children to list ways that they travel. Record their responses on chart paper.
- Sing "The Wheels on the Bus" with the children.
- Encourage the children to invent their own verses to the song, including other modes of transportation, such as "the wings on the plane."
- Tell the children they will be learning about modes of transportation today.
- Show the children pictures of different types of transportation or toy cars, trains, airplanes, boats, and so on.

Learning Centers **Art**

Cut off the top halves of several egg cartons. Give one top to each child. Invite the children to paint the tops with yellow paint. Help them cut out wheels from black paper and glue them to the bottoms of the egg cartons. Write your school's name on the sides or tops of the cartons, so they look like buses. The children cut out pictures of children from magazines to glue in the windows of the "bus."

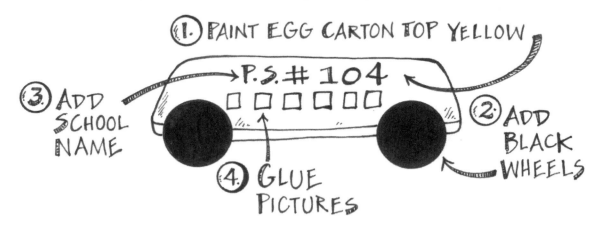

Blocks
Encourage the children to build ramps using different blocks. Provide a variety of transportation toys for the children to race down the ramps. Ask the children to predict which types of transportation they think will go the fastest and why.

Dramatic Play

Pretend to go on a train ride with the children. Line up chairs to form two rows of seats. Give each child a ticket and climb aboard! Hang paper on the wall next to the chairs and have children draw pictures of what they "see" out the windows (mountains, water, city scenes, houses). Sing "Down by the Station."

Sensory

Make mud pits with the children by adding dirt and water to a large tub. Invite the children to stir the dirt and water to make mud. Invite the children to drive different types of plastic transportation toys around in the "mud pit." Let the children explore the mud with their hands and fingers, and ask them to describe what it feels like, smells like, and so on.

Sand and Water

Take the cars from the mud pit and place them containers of water so the children can give them a "car wash." Encourage the children to wash the mud off their cars and dry them with towels when they finish.

Book Suggestions

I Spy Little Wheels by Jean Marzollo
Maisy Drives the Bus by Lucy Cousins

Snack

Supply each child with a banana (bus). Show them how to use cream cheese to attach round crackers to the banana to represent wheels. Also, add dabs of cream cheese to individual squares of a graham cracker and add them to the sides of the banana to represent windows. Add a red cherry for the stop sign on the side of the bus.

Review

Ask the children to list different types of transportation. Record their responses. Ask them how they arrive at school each morning.

Assessment

Can the child sort different images of modes of transportation by land, air, and water? Once a child finishes sorting the different types of transportation, ask him to identify each toy in the sorting activity.

Related Song

Little Airplane by Jodi Kelley
(Tune: "Frere Jacques")
Little airplane, little airplane,
In the sky, in the sky.
I can see you soaring,
I can see you soaring
Up so high, up so high.

 Jodi Kelley, North Versailles, PA

How Do I Get from Here to There?

Learning Objectives The children will:
1. Learn there are different ways to travel (using air, water, and land).
2. Explore the different modes of transportation in their environment.
3. Identify different signs.

Circle or Group Time Activity
- Engage the children in a discussion about various modes of transportation.
- Show the children pictures of different types of transportation, and ask them to name each one.
- Invite the children to pretend to be different modes of transportation as they move around the room and make different sounds such as brakes squealing, horns blowing, and so on.
- After the children are familiar with the vehicles' various sounds and ways of moving, play a game of Simon Says, in which the children imitate the sounds as well as the movements of various modes of transportation.

Learning Centers

Art
Invite the children to make signs for taxi pick-up and other road signs to use in the Dramatic Play Center. Provide a poster or pictures of signs for them to copy onto paper and cut out. Show the children pictures of taxis and invite them to make their own taxis out of large cardboard box. Provide yellow, black, and white paint for them to use to decorate the boxes. Add paper plate "steering wheels."

Blocks
Encourage the children to make an airport with blocks. Add toy ramps, airplanes, helicopters, and so on to the center. Provide passport booklets, a ticket booth and tickets, a small suitcase, and travel brochures on a little table.

Dramatic Play
Turn the center into a taxi service. Add the "taxis" and signs made in the Art Center, a few toy phones for dispatchers to use, pretend meters for the cars, and any other available props. Also have some business cards, note pads for messages, and writing tools. If possible, provide a few uniforms and hats, play money, old license plates to put on the taxis, and maps of the area. The children really enjoy this center and it leads to a lot of imagination and conversation.

Literacy
Choose a mode of transportation, for example, trains. Talk with the children about how the word train begins with the letter T. Gather several objects together in the center, and challenge the children to separate the objects into two groups, based on whether or not the objects' names start with the letter T.

Writing
Set out several sheets of paper with photocopies of various modes of transportation on them, and the names of those modes of transportation written in large bubble letters below the images. Set out markers and crayons and invite the children to color in the images as well as the letters on the pages.

Book Suggestions

I Read Signs by Tana Hoban
My Truck Is Stuck by Kevin Lewis
Planes by Byron Barton
Taxi Dog by Debra Barracca

Snack

Cut bread into square, cylindrical, and rectangular shapes, and encourage the children to use them to make edible vehicle shapes. Provide cream cheese, cheese slices, peanut butter (**Note:** check for peanut allergies), and other bread toppings. Cut up fruit or vegetables for the children to add to their edible vehicles.

Review

Separate the children into groups of four, and give each group a picture of a different mode of transportation. Ask each group to discuss how they are going to use the transportation, and where they are going to use it to go. If a group has a car, for example, they may decide that they want to use it to go to a movie.

Assessment

Can the child differentiate between various modes of transportation? Can the child suggest which mode of transportation is best for getting from one specific point to another, such as from their homes to another country, or from school to the grocery store?

 Eileen Lucas, Fort McMurray, Alberta, Canada

Trains

Learning Objectives The children will:
1. Understand that a train is an important part of transportation.
2. Identify the characteristics of a train.
3. Compare and contrast trains with other types of transportation.

Circle or Group Time Activity
- If available, wear a conductor's hat and show the children a train set.
- With the children, discuss the uses of the cars on the train and the importance of trains.
- Ask the children to tell what they know about trains. Has anyone ever seen a train or ridden on a train?

Learning Centers
Art
Cut construction paper into a variety of sizes and colors of rectangular shapes. Have the children make trains by gluing rectangular shapes on paper. They may use markers to add train features, tracks, and a landscape for the train to move through.

Blocks
Add toys trains to the center. Ask the children to make train tracks out of blocks and run the trains on the tracks. Add conductor's hats for the children to wear.

Dramatic Play
Set up a play train station. Include a toy cash register and play money to sell tickets. The children pretend to be passengers as well as railroad employees.

Library
Provide a variety of books about trains for the children to explore.

Writing
Write railroad- and train-related words on several sheets of paper. Write the words to look like train tracks. Provide small toy train engines and invite the children to trace the engines over the letters of the words. Have them say the words as they trace them.

Book Suggestions

Freight Train by Donald Crews
The Goodnight Train by June Sobel
I Love Trains by Philemon Sturges

Snack

Serve square and rectangular cracker "train cars" with slices of carrot or cheese "wheels" for children to add underneath the crackers.

Review

Ask the children to name something they should remember when they are around trains. Ask the children what kinds of things trains carry, who "drives" the train, and so on.

Assessment

Can the child describe the uses of a train? Can the child name the first and last cars of a train?

Related Poem

Train (author unknown)
This is a choo-choo train (bend elbows)
Puffing down the track. (move arms forward)
Now it's going forward, (push arms forward)
Now it's going back, (push arms back)
Now the bell is ringing, (pretend to ring bell)
Now the whistle blows. (hold fist near mouth and pretend to blow)
What a lot of noise it makes (cover ears with hands)
Everywhere it goes.

 *Jean Potter, Greensburg, PA*

Vehicle Wheels

Learning Objectives   The children will:
1. Learn about the importance of wheels.
2. Explore the types of wheels that vehicles have.
3. Develop their small and large motor skills.

Circle or Group Time Activity

■ Show the children toy versions of a car, a bus, and a truck. Ask the children to identify the similarities among the vehicles.

■ Discuss wheels and their significance for movement. Ask open-ended questions such as, "Where do we see wheels?" "What types of wheels does a truck have? What about a bus, a car, or a bicycle?" Compare and contrast the types of wheels on each vehicle. Ask, "How would these vehicles move without wheels?"

■ Sing the following song with the children:

I Love Wheels (author unknown)
(Tune: "Frere Jacques")
I love wheels, I love wheels,
'Round they go, 'round they go.
We use them to go places,
And see smiling faces,
Everywhere, everywhere.

■ Once the children learn the song, sing it again, encouraging them to make circular motions with their hands and smile at the appropriate moments.

Learning Centers   **Art**
Provide paper, stamp pads, and small wheeled toys (trucks and cars). Encourage each child to run the wheels of the cars and trucks over the stamp pad. Then run the car across the paper, making tracks.

Blocks
Place wheeled objects in the Blocks Center so children can use the blocks to make roads and neighborhoods for the vehicles.

Dramatic Play
Provide engineer and truck driver hats, reading glasses, road maps, coffee mugs, chairs to place in areas for seats and a steering wheel attached to a wooden box in the dress-up area for children to use in their pretend play.

Literacy

Give the children old magazines and ask them to cut out pictures of vehicles with wheels vehicles. Have them glue the images to paper. Ask the children about the images they cut out, and copy their responses below the images. Collect the pages together in a book and place it in the classroom library. Ask the children what they want to call the book, such as "Wild About Wheels."

Small Motor

Provide the children with small-wheeled cars on large mats with highways and neighborhoods drawn on them. Challenge them to follow the road paths to increase their eye-hand coordination.

Book Suggestions

How Willy Got His Wheels by Deborah Turner
Hubert Invents the Wheel by Claire Montgomery and Monte Montgomery
What Do Wheels Do All Day? by April Jones Prince
The Wheels on the Bus by Paul O. Zelinsky

Snack

Serve wheel-shaped pasta mixed with butter.

Review

Ask the children to name a vehicle that uses wheels and then to describe what that vehicle transports.

Assessment

Can the child name three types of wheeled transportation? Can the child say what the different modes of transportation most often carry?

 *Jean Potter, Greensburg, PA*

Cloud Shapes

Learning Objectives   The children will:

1. Learn about different types of clouds.
2. Look at clouds and their shapes.
3. Learn how water evaporates and reenters the atmosphere.
4. Develop their small motor skills.

Circle or Group Time Activity

- Before the children arrive, loosely ball up several pieces of butcher paper and attach them to the ceiling.
- Gather the children together and read them *It Looked Like Spilt Milk* by Charles G. Shaw.
- Engage the children in a discussion about the things they have seen in clouds.
- Have them lie on a rug or blanket under the butcher paper "clouds" and describe the shapes and things they see in the "clouds."
- ❖ Tell the children that they will be learning about clouds today.

Learning Centers   **Art**

Provide white paper, blue and white paint, brushes, glue, and cotton balls. Encourage the children to paint images of the sky and then glue on cotton balls for clouds after the paint is dry.

Science

Show the children pictures of the three different types of clouds: stratified, nimbus, and cumulous. Talk about each type of cloud. Provide chalk and dark paper, and

TYPES of CLOUDS

stratified   nimbus   cumulous

DARK PAPER
WHITE CHALK

challenge the children to make drawings that resemble each of these particular types of clouds.

Blocks

Attach white terrycloth to one side of a few blocks. Have the children feel the new texture and discuss what clouds might feel like as they build a cloudy scene with the blocks.

Large Motor

Place large circular blue paper ("puddles") to a large area. Add lots of pillows or polyester fill inside white pillowcases to represent clouds. Invite the children to jump around, ride on the "clouds," and jump over "puddles."

Writing

Set out several sheets of paper with the word "clouds" written on them in large outlined letters. Invite the children to use white chalk to fill in the letters, so they look like puffy clouds.

Book Suggestions

Elsina's Clouds by Jeanette Winter
It Looked Like Spilt Milk by Charles G. Shaw
Little Cloud by Eric Carle

Snack

Serve cotton candy, if available. If not, try marshmallow fluff on graham crackers.

Review

Teach the children the names of different types of clouds: cumulous, cirrus, and stratified. Show them pictures of the different types of clouds and explain the differences between them to the children.

Assessment

Show the children the cloud pictures again, and challenge them to name the types of clouds. Can the child name the characteristics of clouds? Can the child classify the clouds based on these characteristics?

 *Anna Granger, Washington, DC*

Cumulus, Cirrus, and Stratus Clouds

Learning Objectives The children will:
1. Recognize stratus, cumulus, and cirrus clouds. (For younger children, use the terms *low, middle* and *high*.
2. Develop their small and large motor skills

Circle or Group Time Activity
- Before doing this activity, draw a large circle ("earth") on a piece of blue poster board and cut out a stratus, cumulus, and cirrus cloud from white paper.
- Engage the children in a discussion about clouds. Ask them what shapes they have seen in the sky when looking into the clouds.
- Shape cotton batting into simple forms for the children to recognize, such as a butterfly, a ball, a heart, an egg, or a fish.
- Explain that there are three main types of clouds in the sky: *stratus, cumulus,* and *cirrus*. Show them photographs of each cloud. Explain that some clouds are close to the earth, some are higher, and some are very high in the sky.
- Show the children a poster of the earth and place a stratus cloud cutout on the poster, close to the earth. Explain that stratus clouds are close to the earth, lowest in the sky, like a blanket over us.
- Place a cumulus cloud cutout above the stratus cloud. Explain that these clouds are in the middle of the sky, above stratus clouds, and they are white and puffy.
- Finally, put the cirrus cloud cutout above the cumulus cloud. Explain that these are the highest of all clouds, and they are wispy and feathery.
- Play "What's Missing?" by asking the children to close their eyes. Remove one of the clouds, have the children open their eyes, and name the missing cloud.
- Repeat this activity several times, letting the child who names the missing cloud come up and remove a cloud for the others to guess.

Learning Centers **Art**
Make cloud mobiles with the children. Provide paper and chalk and ask the children to draw and cut out big cirrus (feathery and wispy) clouds. Provide patterns for the younger children. Repeat with white cumulus (puffy) clouds and gray stratus (wide, blanket-like) clouds. Help them punch holes in each and run a string through them, connecting them in order: cirrus on top, cumulus in the middle, stratus lowest.
Dramatic Play
Provide a flannel board and weather symbols, such as white clouds, dark clouds, raindrops, and sun. Also, provide a microphone and weather badge or vest, and invite the children to pretend to make weather forecasts.

Literacy

Provide white paint, small brushes, and several 9" × 12" sheets of dark blue construction paper. Ask the children to imagine clouds that make familiar shapes, and then to paint those images on the paper. When their paintings dry, talk about their images, writing down what they say. Add this text to the images and bind them together in a classroom cloud book.

Music

Write the lyrics to the following song on a piece of poster board and sing it with the children:

Cloud Song by Susan Oldham Hill
(Tune: "Baa, Baa, Black Sheep")
Stratus clouds are wide and gray
Close to earth, not far away.
Cumulus are puffy white
Above the stratus, quite a sight
Cirrus clouds are highest of all
Feathery, wispy, oh so tall.

Writing

Set out several cotton balls, as well as sheets of construction paper with the words cumulus, cirrus, and stratus written on them in puffy letters, and invite the children to use the cotton to trace the letters that spell the words.

Book Suggestions

Cloud Book by Tomie DePaola
Little Cloud by Eric Carle
Weather Forecasting by Gail Gibbons

Snack

Ahead of time, make cookie dough. Tint one half of it green, and the other half blue. Show the children a globe with blue water and green land. Give each child a small spoonful of each color, asking them to make the earth by pushing the colors together like our globe. Encourage them to keep the colors separate rather than blending the blue and green into one solid color. Show them how to flatten the ball into a round cookie shape. Bake as directed. Allow to cool and top with whipped topping for clouds.

Review

Bring out the cotton batting used in the Circle and Group Time activity and shape it into some different forms, challenging the children to guess what the shapes represent. With the children, review the names, shapes, and positions of the three types of clouds. Play "What's Missing?" to help the children remember.

Assessment

Using the three cutouts of the different types of clouds, can the child identify them and put them in order?

 *Susan Oldham Hill, Lakeland, FL*

Fluffy Clouds

Learning Objectives The children will:
1. Learn how clouds change shape.
2. Use words to name things that clouds can look like.
3. Use visual skills to guess what cloud shapes look like.
4. Use sensory skills to discover what clouds might feel like.

Circle or Group Time Activity
■ Gather the children and recite the following poem:

Drifting by Shelley Hoster
Drifting, drifting near or far,
Children, children wherever you are,
It's time to float over here so free.
Come and read a story with me!

■ Give each child a cotton ball and discuss how the cotton balls feel. Encourage the children to rub the cotton on their faces, and to squeeze and touch the cotton.
■ Ask them what the cotton reminds them of, guiding them toward connecting the look of cotton to the look of clouds.
■ Challenge the children to come up with words that describe the cotton clouds they are holding, and write their responses on the chart paper.
■ Challenge the children to change the shapes of their cotton balls and tell them that clouds also change their shapes.
■ Sing the following song with the children, encouraging them to dance with their cotton balls:

Fluffy Clouds by Shelley Hoster
(Tune: "Twinkle, Twinkle, Little Star")
Fluffy clouds up in the sky, (float hands back and forth)
Changing shapes as you float by. (turn hands over one another)
We look up and we see (look up with hand over eyes)
All the things that you can be. (open arms wide)
Fluffy clouds up in the sky,
Changing shapes as you float by.

Learning Centers   **Art**
Place cotton balls and white paint on the art table. Mix shaving cream into the paint and invite the children to paint cloud pictures. Ask them what their cloud shapes look like. Also, consider providing white dough or clay to make 3-D clouds. Display the clouds on a shelf labeled: "Our Little Clouds."

Dramatic Play

Provide decorative materials so the children can make a large box look like an airplane. Add suit coats and pilot hats, magazines, blankets, trays of play food, and paper for tickets, and the children are ready for an adventure in the clouds.

Library

Gather the illustrations the children made in the Art Center to make a class book like *It Looked like Spilt Milk* by Charles Shaw.

Literacy

Trace the shapes in *It Looked like Spilt Milk* by Charles Shaw onto pieces of Pellon, place the pieces next to a flannel board, and invite the children to put the shapes in order as they were in the book, retelling the story as they go.

Sensory

Fill the sensory table with cotton balls, scoops, and white bags so the children can scoop out the cotton balls and fill the bags to make clouds. Fill the table with shaving cream and invite the children to make and mold their own clouds. For even more fun, mix the two ingredients for some sensational contrast! Fill another table or pan with water. Give children sponges and have them absorb and squeeze water out to simulate the process of rain.

Small Motor

Have children use rolling pins and cookie cutters to cut out cloud shapes from clay. The children then use toothpicks or paintbrushes to write and draw on their clouds.

Book Suggestions

The Cloud Book by Tomie dePaola
Cloud Dance by Thomas Locker
It Looked like Spilt Milk by Charles G. Shaw
Little Cloud by Eric Carle

Snack

Serve pieces of bread and encourage the children to rip their pieces of bread into the shapes of different objects before eating them.

Review

Gather the children together and give each another cotton ball. If real clouds are visible outside, consider bringing the children outside. Invite the children to float around like clouds. Ask each child to share one thing about clouds as they float.

Assessment

Can the child point out clouds in the sky? Given a weather chart, can the child point to the image that shows what kind of clouds are in the sky that day?

 Shelley Hoster, Norcross, GA

It's Raining, It's Pouring

Learning Objectives   The children will:
1. Discover that rain falls from clouds in the sky.
2. Discuss different things people do when it rains.
3. Use their bodies to express sound.
4. Develop their small motor skills.

Circle or Group Time Activity

■ If it is a rainy day, engage the children in a discussion about what they see happening outside. Ask them what people do when it rains, such as wear raincoats, use umbrellas, turn on their windshield wipers, and splash in puddles.

■ Tell the children that they are going to help make a "rainstorm." Have them stand up, and act out the following steps:
  ■ Sway body back and forth and blow air out to make the sound of wind
  ■ Rub hands together to make a light rain sound
  ■ Clap hands together slowly, then faster and faster to make raindrops
  ■ Stomp feet to make thunder noises

■ Reverse the order of the sounds: stomp, clap, rub, blow, and then sway to slow and stop the rain.

Learning Centers   ### Art
Provide paper, cotton balls, glitter, and glue. Show the children how to stretch the cotton to make clouds, and then glue the clouds onto the paper. Have them drip glue under their clouds and sprinkle the glue with glitter. Shake off excess.

Dramatic Play
Put raincoats, rain hats, and boots in the dress-up area and invite the children to pretend they are out in a rainstorm. Have them pretend to jump in puddles.

Literacy
Ask each child to complete the following statement: "When it rains, I like to_____." Copy the children's responses onto sheets of paper, and then have them illustrate it. Help older children fill in the words themselves.

Sand and Water
Fill the table with water and add sieves, cups, and watering cans. Ask children if they can use these materials to make it rain.

Science
Pour a small amount of water into a pie tin and place a bag of cotton balls ("clouds") next to it. Fill another pie tin with sand and a few rocks ("mountains"). The children soak cotton balls in the water, and then pick them up and squeeze them over the second pie tin. Talk with the children about what they see happening. Challenge them to make the clouds rain until a river starts to form in the second tin.

Book Suggestions

Come On, Rain by Karen Hesse
It's Raining, It's Pouring by Kin Eagle
Rain by Robert Kalan
Umbrella by Taro Yashima

Snack

Serve hot cocoa and toast with butter and jam for a rainy day treat.

Review

Ask the children to name things that people use in the rain. If time permits, repeat the Circle or Group Time rainstorm activity.

Assessment

Can the child look at images of the sun, a tree, and a cloud, and pick which image shows where rain comes from?

Related Songs

It's Raining, It's Pouring (Traditional)
It's raining, it's pouring,
The old man is snoring.
He went to bed and he bumped his head,
And he couldn't get up 'til morning.

Rain, Rain (Traditional)
Rain, rain, go away,
Come again another day,
Little Johnny wants to play.

 *Cassandra Reigel Whetstone, Folsom, CA*

Rain

Learning Objectives   The children will:
1. Learn about rain.
2. Make a rain collage.
3. Perform action rhymes about rain.

Circle or Group Time Activity

■ Place a bowl of water in front of children. Demonstrate how to draw water out of the bowl with a dropper.

■ Show the children what a raindrop looks like, and show them how it falls back into the bowl by squeezing the dropper.

■ Have a discussion about rain, asking them, "How does rain feel? Is it dry or wet? What is your favorite thing to do in the rain? Where does rain come from?"

■ Pass the bowl around and encourage each child to make a "drop of rain" by squeezing water from the eyedropper.

■ Teach the children the following action rhyme:

Itsy Bitsy Raindrop by Lily Erlic
(Tune: "Itsy, Bitsy Spider")
The itsy bitsy raindrop
Went up the water spout, (wiggle fingers and lift hand up)
Down came the rain (wiggle fingers and move hand down)
And washed the raindrop out
Out came the sun (make a circle with arms)
And dried up all the rain (wiggle fingers)
And the itsy bitsy raindrop,
Flew up the spout again. (wiggle fingers and lift hand up)

■ Tell the children that they will be learning about rain today.

Learning Centers   **Art**
Give each child a white piece of paper. Ask the children to glue 1" pieces of yarn on the paper to form a rain collage.

GLUE

YARN PIECES

WHITE PAPER

Literacy

Ask the children to finish this sentence: "After the rain, I see _____." Copy the children's answers on pieces of paper. Older children may write their own response, with help. Encourage them to illustrate their responses.

Math

Provide a variety of colored, plastic, raindrop-shaped counters (decorative small discs from craft stores). Ask the children to sort the "raindrops" by color.

Music

Provide several rainmakers for the children to play with and explore.

Sand and Water

Provide the children with droppers and containers of water. Add blue food coloring to the water and invite the children to squirt small raindrop-sized drops.

Book Suggestions

Come On, Rain by Karen Hesse
Listen to the Rain by Bill Martin
Who Likes Rain? by Wong Herbert Yee

Snack

Serve small fruit snacks cut in the shapes of raindrops.

Review

Sing "The Itsy Bitsy Spider" with the children. Show the children pictures of rain. Talk about the features of rain. Ask, "What does rain sound like? Where does rain come from? How does rain help plants?"

Assessment

Can the child pick out an image of rain from pictures of various weather-related images?

Lily Erlic, Victoria, British Columbia, Canada

Rain Day Fun

Learning Objectives The children will:
1. Learn that rain comes from clouds in the sky.
2. Improve their oral language skills.
3. Develop their small and large motor skills.

Circle or Group Time Activity
- Gather the children together in a circle.
- Stand in the middle of the circle holding an opened umbrella.
- Give each child a balled piece of blue tissue paper ("raindrop"). Invite each child to hold the "raindrop" and spread out around the room. Tell them that when you put up the umbrella, the music will begin a pitter-pat sound. (Enlist a parent or child helper to play a pitter-pat tune on a xylophone or woodblock.)
- At that time, the children make it "rain" by tossing their raindrops into the air and catching them several times.
- When you close your umbrella, stop the music, and the children catch their raindrops and sit quietly.
- Repeat this several times, having it rain gently and slowly, or hard and fast, according to the sound of the music.
- Read *Why Does it Rain?* by Chris Arvetis to the children.

Learning Centers
Dramatic Play
Stock the center with raincoats, rain boots, rain hats, umbrellas, and so on. Invite pairs of children to put on the raincoats, hats, and boots, and then hold up the umbrellas as they pretend to go for a walk in the rain.

Large Motor
Provide several balls of blue paper ("raindrops"). Place an open umbrella on the floor, pointing upward. The children stand a few feet from the umbrella and toss their "raindrops" at the umbrella and watch them splash off.

Library
Invite the children to sit quietly and listen to a "rain sounds" CD as they look through books about rain.

Literacy
Display the book *Rain* by Donald Crews. Help the children become familiar with the text using word cards that correspond to the story line. Invite children to "read" and manipulate the various word cards as they recite the familiar text from the book. Have them draw a "rainy day" picture that includes the many colorful parts of the story so they can recite the text at home.

Sand and Water
Provide pitchers, sieves, strainers, and plastic toy people and animals. Children pour water into a sieve as they hold it over the various figures, causing it to rain on the animals and people. Encourage children to verbalize as they explore.

Small Motor
Set out blue paper, markers, crayons, hole punches, and plastic raindrop shapes. Invite the children to trace the outlines of the raindrop shapes onto blue paper, punch two holes in the top of each raindrop, and string them together.

Book Suggestions

Rain by Robert Kalan
The Rainy Day by Anna Milbourne
Why Does It Rain? by Judith Jengo-Cohen

Snack

Insert a small toothpick umbrella into healthy bran muffins and serve up these fun rainy day snacks. Add blue food coloring to the milk or water.

Review

Hold the umbrella high in the air and display five pictures to represent the five senses (a nose for smell, a tongue for taste, and so on). Invite each child to stand under the umbrella and look at the five senses cards. Ask the child to say how she can use her five senses to experience and describe rain.

Assessment

Sit beneath an umbrella with a child. Ask questions about rain, such as, "How does rain help people?" "How is rain good for plants?" "How does rain feel?" "What does rain sound like?"

Related Song

Rain on Me by Mary J. Murray
Rain on my face,
Rain on my toes,
Rain on my tongue,
Rain on my nose,
Rain on the rabbit,
Rain on the squirrel,
Rain on the boy,
Rain on the girl,
Rain on the flowers,
Rain on the trees,
Rain on you, and
Rain on me!

 *Mary J. Murray, Mazomanie, WI*

Snow

Learning Objectives The children will:
1. Talk about snow.
2. Develop their small motor skills while making crafts.
3. Do a scientific experiment to study snow.

Circle or Group Time Activity
■ Teach children the following song:

Snowflakes, Snowflakes by Donna Alice Patton
(Tune: "Twinkle, Twinkle, Little Star")
Snowflakes, snowflakes falling down, (move fingers and hands down like snow falling)
Snowflakes falling to the ground. (sink to sitting position)
When they pile up you'll see (begin to stand up slowly)
Mountains of snowflakes higher than me. (lift hands and jump into the air)

■ Once the children learn the song, have them stand up and repeat the song, while doing all of the actions.
■ Tell the children they will be learning about snow today.

Learning Centers

Art
Give the children coffee filters and child-safe scissors. Show them how to fold the filters in half (half-moon shapes) and then into fourths (like wedges of pie.) Demonstrate how to cut designs in the folded edges of their filters. When the children open the filters, they will have "snowflakes." This is a good time to look at the many designs and remind them that no two snowflakes are exactly alike. Provide glue and glitter for the children to use to make their snowflakes sparkle.

Construction
If time and situation permit (snowy day), invite the children to make a snow fort, house, or snowman during outdoor time. Provide plastic cups, boxes, and other materials to mold the creations. To do this inside, roll playdough into snowmen. Provide small twigs, scraps of cloth, and buttons for clothing and arms.

Library
Place a recording of *The First Snowfall* by Anna and Harlow Rockwell Katy in the center for the children to listen to as they look through a copy of the book.

Snack and Cooking
Make snow ice cream. During a snowfall, leave a plastic bowl outside to collect clean snow. Mix one cup of condensed milk with one cup of evaporated milk, add half a teaspoon of vanilla, and add it all to the snow. Mix rapidly and eat.

Writing

Ask each child to complete the following sentence, "One day it snowed so much _____." Use a blue marker to copy the children's responses onto one large sheet of paper, making a story out of the children's responses. Title it: "The Giant Snowfall" and read it aloud to the children. In addition, you might give each child a sheet of paper with their response written on it to illustrate. Collect these pages together to make a book version of "The Giant Snowfall."

Book Suggestions

The Big Snow by Virginia Lee Burton
The First Snowfall by Anne Rockwell and Harlow Rockwell
Millions of Snowflakes by Mary McKenna Sidddals
Snowflake Bentley by Jacqueline Briggs Martin
The Snowy Day by Ezra Jack Keats

Snack

Serve white foods, such as marshmallows, popcorn, or celery sticks with cream cheese and sprinkles of coconut flakes.

Review

Ask each child to remember one fact about snow or snowflakes.

Assessment

Can the child describe snow, using descriptive words, such as *cold, freezing, shiny, wet, white,* and so on?

Donna Alice Patton, Hillsboro, OH

Warming Up!

Learning Objectives   The children will:
1. Develop self-care skills, such as figuring out how to stay warm.
2. Match items using one-to-one correspondence.

Circle or Group Time Activity
- Invite the children to look through magazines and newspapers for pictures of things that help keep them warm in cold weather.
- Have them cut out the pictures and glue onto sheets of construction paper.
- Ask the children to explain why they chose the various images and encourage them to talk to each other about their collages.

Learning Centers   ### Art
Give each child a piece of colored construction paper and a container of glue. Have them use the glue to make the outlines of three circles in the shape of a snowman on the paper. Have them add glitter to the circles. When dry, invite them to decorate their snowmen using markers, fabric scraps, and so on.

Blocks
After reading *Katy and the Big Snow* by Virginia Lee Burton, invite the children to act out the story in the Block Center. Provide small toy snowplows, bulldozers, and steam shovels. Add cotton balls for pretend snow. The children scatter the cotton balls around and use the small toys to move the snow like Katy did.

Math
Use large index cards to make a set of five counting cards. Draw one dot on the first card, two dots on the second card, and so on. Place the cards and 15 cotton balls on the table. The children take turns counting and placing the cotton balls on the dots on the cards.

Sand and Water
Place a container of real snow or crushed ice in the sand and water table. Provide aprons and gloves. Help them put on aprons and invite them to play in the snow with and without gloves. Ask them how their hands feel when playing in the snow without gloves and with gloves.

Science
Provide a large container of snow or crushed ice. Help the children make snowballs. Place each snowball in a small bowl and put one of each child's snowballs inside and one outside where children can see them easily. Let the children observe both snowballs throughout the day. Talk about what they see. "What's happening to the snowballs inside?" "What about the snowballs outside? Why aren't they melting?" Give them time to work through the thought process and deductive reasoning instead of providing an answer for them.

Snack and Cooking
Make Polar Bear Salad. Place a cottage cheese or vanilla yogurt and black olives or raisins on a low table. Ask the children to create a polar bear head shape by placing a spoonful of cottage cheese on a small plate and using a spoon to press it into a round shape. Add two smaller dabs of cottage cheese at the top of the head for the ears and use the black olives for eyes and a nose.

Book Suggestions
Katy and the Big Snow by Virginia Lee Burton
Snow Day by Betsy Maestro
The Snowman by Raymond Briggs

Snack
Serve the Polar Bear Salad made in the Snack and Cooking Center, or serve cottage cheese or yogurt and mixed fruit.

Review
Ask the children to look around the room and identify items that help them stay warm. Ask the children to explain how the various items help keep people warm.

Assessment
Can the child look at photos of gloves, hats, swimsuit, shorts, and coats and say which will help a person stay warm?

Related Songs
Snowflakes Song by Virginia Jean Herrod
(Tune: "Twinkle, Twinkle, Little Star")
Snowflakes, snowflakes dance around.
Snowflakes, snowflakes touch the ground.
Snowflakes, snowflakes in the air.
Snowflakes, snowflakes everywhere.
Snowflakes, snowflakes dance around.
Snowflakes, snowflakes touch the ground.

 Virginia Jean Herrod, Columbia, SC

What's the Weather Today?

Learning Objectives The children will:
1. Explore the different types of weather (sunny, rainy, snowy, and windy).
2. Discuss what type of clothing to wear for different weather conditions.
3. Talk about fun activities to do in each type of weather.

Circle or Group Time Activity

■ Teach the children the following song:

The Snow Is on the Roof by Renee Kirchner
(Tune: "The Farmer in the Dell")
The snow is on the roof.
The snow is on the street.
I put on my hat and boots,
And crunch it with my feet.

■ Tell children that they are going to learn about weather today.
■ Talk about the different types of weather in each of the four seasons.
■ Hold up a calendar and look at the current month. Ask the children to tell you how the weather has been over the last month. Has it rained? Snowed? Been windy? Sunny? Warm or cold?
■ Talk with the children about different activities they can do in different kinds of weather. For example, they can swim in warm, sunny weather, sled in snowy weather, and so on.

Learning Centers ### Art
Provide fingerpaint and paper, and invite the children to fingerpaint images of different kinds of skies: rainy skies, snowy skies, sunny skies, and so on. Ask the children which pictures are their favorites and why.
Dramatic Play
Provide clothing and materials for different types of weather, such as umbrellas, scarves, mittens, sweaters, jackets, sunglasses, and so on. Invite the children to pretend that it is winter, spring, summer, or fall, and wear the appropriate attire.
Science
Have the children observe the weather every day for a week. Make a class chart together. Ask the children to predict what the weather will be like the next week.
Literacy
Cut out cloud-shaped letters from construction paper. Write different weather-related words on cloud cutouts, such as *cloud, wind, rain, sunny,*

and so on. Encourage the children to match the letter cutouts to the letters in the words.

Math
Cut out 10 cloud shapes from blue paper. On the back of each cloud, write a numeral from 1–10 using a black marker. Ask the children to put the cloud shapes in order from lowest to highest number, and then in order from highest to lowest number.

Book Suggestions

Maisy's Wonderful Weather Book by Lucy Cousins
Oh Say Can You Say What's the Weather Today? by Tish Rabe
The Snowy Day by Ezra Jack Keats
Spot's Windy Day by Eric Hill
Sun Song by Jean Marzollo
Whatever the Weather by Karen Wallace

Snack

Make Sunshine gelatin snacks. Make yellow gelatin in a 9" × 13" pan and allow it to set. Provide round cookie cutters for the children to use to cut out the gelatin. Provide thin red licorice cut into 2" pieces for the children to use to make rays coming from the round gelatin "sun." Provide round candies or grape halves for them to make smiley faces!

Review

Ask the children to look outside and describe the weather. Ask them what kind of activities they would want to do and what kind of clothes they would wear in such weather.

Assessment

Can the child say what to wear on a rainy day, as opposed to a hot day or a snowy day?

Renee Kirchner, Carrollton, TX

Going to the Zoo

Learning Objectives The children will:
1. Learn about the job of various zoo workers.
2. Role-play the parts of animals and zoo workers.
3. Develop their large and small motor skills.
4. Increase their oral language skills.

Circle or Group Time Activity
- Place several towels around the border of the Circle or Group Time area.
- Display animal pictures behind each towel to represent zoo animals in enclosures.
- Invite the children to look around the room and guess the topic of the day.
- Ask for volunteers to play "zoo" with you. Have the volunteers stand inside the "enclosures" and play the parts of the animals pictured. Invite the remaining children to watch.
- Give the other children chances to be animals.
- Discuss what might be involved in taking care of zoo animals. Read *I Want to Be a Zookeeper* by Dan Liebman as a way of extending the discussion.
- Play the song "Goin' to the Zoo" by Raffi and invite the children to sing along.

Learning Centers **Art**

Invite the children to fold paper in half, and then in half again, and then open the paper, creating four spaces. Have the children tear colored construction paper or

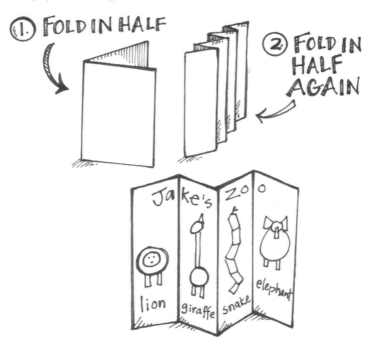

tissue paper scraps and glue to their pages to create animal figures in each space. Have them use markers to add detail to each animal picture. Help the children add titles to their papers, such as: "_____'s Zoo."

Blocks
Provide pattern blocks for the children to use to create an assortment of animal sculptures.

Dramatic Play
Put animal puppets in the center and ask the children to use them to talk about how to feed and care for different animals. For example, the elephant might say, "I need lots of room to walk. If you give me a ball to push around with my trunk, I will enjoy playing."

Large Motor
Use yarn to mark off a large area for this activity. Display the animal pictures from the Circle and Group Time activity nearby. Invite the children to select animals and then move around as if they were those animals, hopping, running, roaring, waddling, slithering, and so on within the marked area.

Math
Create Zoo Animal Counting Books. Provide animal stamps and 5" x 7" note cards. Invite the children to stamp between one and seven images of animals on various note cards. Punch holes in the sides of the cards and challenge the children to string the cards along in ascending or descending numerical order.

Book Suggestions

Hippo! No, Rhino by Jeff Newman
I Want to Be a Zookeeper by Dan Liebman
My Visit to the Zoo by Aliki
Zoo by Gail Gibbons

Snack

Serve the snack by calling out "feeding time." Encourage children to pretend they are various animals as they eat. Serve any animal snack you want, such as animal-shaped crackers or cookies, animal fruit snacks, and so on.

Review

Divide the children into two or three groups. Give each child a plastic or stuffed toy zoo animal to feel. Have them close their eyes as they feel these animals and try to guess what they are. After two guesses, children open their eyes to check if they were right. Encourage them to try this activity several times, as they share what they know about each zoo animal they identify.

Assessment

Display the materials from the Dramatic Play Center. Can the child name some of the jobs that a zoo worker might have?

 *Mary J. Murray, Mazomanie, WI*

Guess Who Lives at the Zoo?

Learning Objectives The children will:
1. Discover what animals often live in the zoo.
2. Develop their large motor skills.
3. Make a snack.

Circle or Group Time Activity

■ Play a guessing game with the children. Tell the children some of the following riddles and see if they can guess which zoo animals the riddles are about.

I'm clever and sly.
My den is made from rocks.
I have red fur and a bushy tail.
I am a _____. (fox)

The baby in my pouch
Is looking straight at you.
I hop on my hind legs.
I'm a mother _____. (kangaroo)

I can fly very high
And am the size of a beagle.
My eyesight is great
Because I am an _____. (eagle)

■ Let the children make up their own riddles, if they are developmentally ready.

Learning Centers
Art
Provide animal stamps, paint, and paper and encourage the children to draw illustrations of zoo animals. Also, provide playdough for them to use to create different zoo animals.

Dramatic Play
Have the children pretend they are visiting a zoo. Some of the children pretend to be zoo animals and others pretend to be the visitors. Make sure the zoo animals make plenty of animal noises. Occasionally, ask the children to trade roles.

Literacy
Ask each child to finish the following sentence: "At the zoo I saw a _____."
Write down the children's answers on pieces of white paper and ask them to illustrate the pages. Bind the pages together with staples. Place the "Zoo Animal Book" in the classroom library.

Math

Ask each of the children to name their favorite zoo animals. Provide cutouts of the various animals and encourage the children to use them to make a graph of their answers.

Snack and Cooking

Prepare Animals in Cages with the children. Provide peanut butter (or another spread if anyone has peanut allergies) and honey for the children to spread on graham crackers. The children place animal crackers in the middle of each graham cracker, then add licorice strips for cage bars.

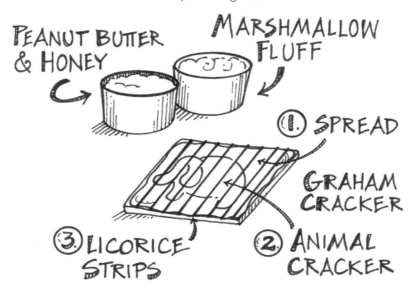

Book Suggestions	*1, 2, 3 to the Zoo* by Eric Carle
	If I Ran the Zoo by Dr. Seuss
	My Visit to the Zoo by Aliki
	There's a Zoo in Room 22 by Judy Sierra
	Zoo-Looking by Mem Fox
Snack	Serve the "Animals in Cages" snack the children prepared in the Snack and Cooking Center.
Review	Make zoo animal noises and ask the children to name the animals that make the noises.
Assessment	Place plastic zoo animals and farm animals on a table. Can the child pick out the zoo animals?

 *Renee Kirchner, Carrollton, TX*

Polar Bears

Learning Objectives The children will:
1. Learn about polar bears.
2. Create polar-bear crafts.
3. Do action rhymes about polar bears.

Circle or Group Time Activity

- Show the children pictures of polar bears and talk about polar bears. Talk about the environment in which polar bears live. "What color is the polar bear?" "Is it hot or cold where the polar bear lives?" Point out the ice in the picture.
- Show the children a stuffed polar bear toy and pass it around so they may feel the item. Ask, "How does it feel?"
- Recite the following original rhyme with the children, inviting them to perform the actions as indicated.

Two Polar Bears Swimming by Lily Erlic
Two polar bears swimming, (hold up two fingers and pretend to swim with arms)
Swimming and diving all day, (pretend to swim and dive)
"Look over there!" said one polar bear, (point)
The cubs are on their way!" (clap loudly)
"Oh my, oh me, oh dear,
They're fighting, I fear!" (shiver)
The cubs said, "We're just playing this way!
We've been play fighting all day! "

Two polar bears diving, (hold up two fingers and pretend to dive with arms)
Fishing under the ice, (pretend to fish)
"Let's have our lunch, (pretend to eat)
Maybe we'll eat twice!" (put two fingers up)
Two polar bears swimming, (pretend to swim with arms)
Eating seals and fish all day, (pretend to eat)
Climbing and jumping on ice, (pretend to climb and jump)
Sliding all the way! (open and close hands quickly)

Learning Centers **Art**
Give each child a polar bear cutout, cotton balls, and glue. Ask the children to create their own "furry" polar bears by gluing pieces of the cotton to their cutouts.
Dramatic Play
Make a sign that reads "Polar Bear Sea Ice." Give each child a stuffed polar bear, if available. Ask the children to put their cubs to sleep. Provide small laminated polar bear cutouts on craft sticks (stick puppets) and invite the children to make up a polar bear puppet show.

Literacy

Give each child a piece of paper. Invite them to draw a polar bear habitat (show them pictures of real polar bear habitats). Title their pages "My Polar Bear's Home" and have them say a sentence about their picture as you write it down. (Challenge older children to print the words *polar bear* on their paper.)

Math

Place a variety of polar bear pictures or cutouts in a basket. Ask the children to count the polar bear pictures. Ask them, "How many polar bears are there?" "Can you count by twos?" "How many groups of twos can you make?"

Music

Sing the following song with the children and do the actions:

If You Can Hear the Polar Bear by Lily Erlic
(Tune: "If You're Happy and You Know It")
If you can hear the polar bear, clap your hands. (clap twice)
If you can hear the polar bear, clap your hands. (clap twice)
If you can hear the polar bear, then your ears will surely show it! (put hands behind
   ears and shout "hooray")
If you can hear the polar bear, (place hand behind ear)
Clap your hands. (clap twice)

If you can hear the cubs playing, stomp your feet, (stomp twice)
If you can hear the cubs playing, stomp your feet, (stomp twice)
If you can hear the cubs playing, then your ears will surely show it! (put hands
   behind ears and shout "hooray")
If you can hear the cubs playing, stomp your feet. (stomp twice)

Book Suggestions

A Polar Bear Journey by Debbie S. Miller
Polar Bear, Polar Bear, What Do You Hear? by Bill Martin Jr. and Eric Carle
The Three Snow Bears by Jan Brett

Snack

Cut bread into polar bear shapes and have the children spread cream cheese on top. Provide raisins for eyes and noses.

Review

Repeat the "Two Polar Bears Swimming" rhyme from the Circle or Group Time Activity. Talk some more about some polar bears.

Assessment

Can the child pick out a polar bear from pictures of several different kinds of bears? Can the child explain the differences between the bears?

 Lily Erlic, Victoria, British Columbia, Canada

Tigers

Learning Objectives The children will:
1. Learn about tigers.
2. Identify and continue a pattern.
3. Write the letters T, I, G, E, and R.

Circle or Group Time Activity

■ Teach the children the following song:

Tiger (author unknown)
(Tune "Bingo")
There is a cat who is orange and black,
And it is called a tiger.
T-I-G-E-R,
T-I-G-E-R,
T-I-G-E-R,
And it is called a tiger.

■ Continue singing the song, replacing each letter with a clap (like "Bingo").
■ Tell the children that they will be learning about tigers today.

Learning Centers

Math

Provide each child with a sheet of white construction paper, along with six 1" × 9" strips of black paper, six 1" × 9" strips of orange paper, and glue. The children glue

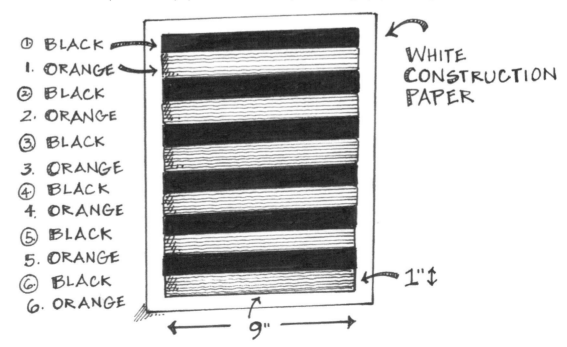

① BLACK
1. ORANGE
② BLACK
2. ORANGE
③ BLACK
3. ORANGE
④ BLACK
4. ORANGE
⑤ BLACK
5. ORANGE
⑥ BLACK
6. ORANGE

WHITE
CONSTRUCTION
PAPER

1"↕

9"

black strips along the shorter edges of their papers, and then glue orange strips, continuing the alternating pattern until they cover their papers completely in black and orange stripes. Challenge them to draw tigers on their stripes.

Art

Invite the children to draw pictures of tigers on white construction paper using crayons and markers. Have them draw the tiger's habitat too.

Dramatic Play

Provide masks in the shapes of tigers' faces and the faces of other jungle animals. Encourage the children to pretend they are animals living in the jungle.

Literacy

Give the children paper with the following statement on it: "If I were a tiger, I would _____." Ask the children to complete the statements. Copy the children's answers on their papers and invite them to illustrate their ideas. Punch holes in the papers and bind them together with yarn or silver rings to make a book for the classroom library.

Science

Provide photos of tigers in their natural habitats for the children to explore and discuss.

Book Suggestions

Close Your Eyes by Kate Banks
The Loudest Roar by Thomas Taylor
Who Is the Beast? by Keith Baker
Why Do Tigers Have Stripes? by Helen Edom

Snack

Serve animal crackers and see if the children can find the tiger-shaped crackers before eating them.

Review

Ask the children to share what they learned about tigers today.

Assessment

Show each child pictures of a lion, a tiger, and a cheetah. Can the child pick out the tiger? Ask the child where tigers live.

 Laura D. Wynkoop, San Dimas, CA

What Lives in the Zoo?

Learning Objectives   The children will:
1. Learn what type of animals live at the zoo.
2. Talk about what zookeepers do.
3. Discover what a zoo does for endangered animals.

Circle or Group Time Activity

- Ask the children if any of them have visited a zoo. Brainstorm a list of animals that live at the zoo. If most of the children have not visited a zoo, show them a book about zoos, and add each animal the book names to the list. When the children finish naming animals, count how many animals are on the list.
- Engage the children in a discussion of the word *endangered*. Explain that zoos help endangered animals by keeping them safe and having them reproduce.
- Talk about the jobs of the people who work at the zoo (such as ticket takers, concession-stand workers, zookeepers, and veterinarians).
- Talk about where animals typically found in zoos live in the wild. Show the children a globe and point out the parts of the world where these animals would live if they were not in the zoo.

Learning Centers   **Art**

Make a classroom zoo with artwork. Provide paper and paint for the children paint pictures of their favorite zoo animals. Have them make paper-plate lions by gluing yarn or strips of yellow and brown paper to make eyes, a nose, whiskers, and a mane. Show them how to make snakes by painting a paper plate and then cutting it into a spiral shape (you may need to help with the cutting). Display the animals in a designated area of the room.

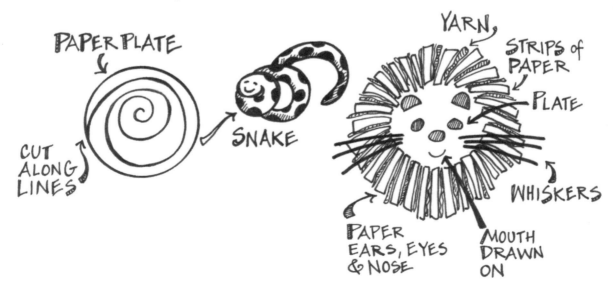

PAPER PLATE

CUT ALONG LINES

SNAKE

YARN

STRIPS of PAPER

PLATE

WHISKERS

PAPER EARS, EYES & NOSE

MOUTH DRAWN ON

Blocks

Challenge the children to use blocks to build a zoo for various plastic animals.

Dramatic Play

Invite the children to role-play different zoo jobs. Place stuffed zoo animals in the center with toy veterinary tools, such as stethoscopes, lab coats, syringes, bandages, and splints.

Math

Using chart paper, write down the names of four zoo animals. Let the children vote for their favorite animal and then count the results. Talk about the animal that received the most votes, the animal that received the fewest, and so on. Set out several photocopied images of the animals and challenge the children to put one photocopy image beneath the original image for every vote each animal received.

Sensory

Provide different real objects that might be found at a zoo, such as a turtle shell, feathers from different birds, and fur pieces for the children to touch and explore.

Book Suggestions

Amazing Gorillas by Sarah L. Thomson
Animal Dads by Sneed B. Collard III
If I Ran the Zoo by Dr. Seuss
Panda Bear, Panda Bear, What Do You See? by Bill Martin Jr.
Put Me in the Zoo by Robert Lopshire

Snack

Serve food animals might eat, such as bananas, berries, and melon.

Review

At the end of the day, ask the children a few zoo-related questions, such as: "What does a zookeeper do?" "Who takes care of the animals?" "What does *endangered* mean?"

Assessment

Designate different parts of the room the "ape house," the "lizard house," and so on. Can the child put images of various zoo animals in the correct locations?

 *Holly Dzierzanowski, Brenham, TX*

Who's at the Zoo?

Learning Objectives The children will:
1. Sequence parts of a story.
2. Talk about zoo animals.
3. Classify animals.
4. Identify animal sounds.

Circle or Group Time Activity
- Beforehand, draw or make a copy of each animal in the book, *Polar Bear, Polar Bear, What Do You Hear?* by Bill Martin, Jr. and Eric Carle. Punch holes in the top of each page and loop string through to make animal necklaces. (You may want to make more than one of   each animal so that there are enough for each child to have one.) Be sure to make one or two zookeepers. **Note:** If you prefer, make stick puppets instead of the necklace signs.
- Gather the children in a circle and hand out the animal (and zookeeper) necklaces.
- Ask the children if they know their animals' names and habitats. Tell them they are going to listen to a story about zoo animals and when they see their animals in the story, they should stand up and make those animals' sounds.
- Read *Polar Bear, Polar Bear, What Do You Hear?* to the children. Afterwards, have the children with the zookeeper cards come up to the front.
- Challenge the zookeepers to place all the animals in the order they appeared in the book. Give them clues, if necessary, or let them look in the book.
- The other children can also help; they can place themselves in the correct order if the zookeepers need help.
- Talk about the animals in a zoo and how zookeepers take care of the animals.

Learning Centers

Art
Set out playdough and invite the children to use it to make zoo animal shapes. Encourage the children to work together to put their animals in the different areas of the zoo.

Games
Cut out several pictures of animals, photocopy them, and attach them to 3" x 5" index cards. Put the cards in various patterns, and challenge the children to repeat the patterns with additional animal cards. Invite the children to create their own patterns and challenge other children to continue the patterns they make.

Literacy
Place a recording of animal sounds, along with photocopied pictures of those animals in the center. Write the name of each animal at the bottom of the picture. Play the recordings, and invite the children to hold up the images of the animals as they hear them. Encourage the children to illustrate the animals and then copy the words on the pictures to write them on their illustrations.

Blocks

Stack three large blocks, attach butcher paper to them, draw zoo animals on the paper, then cut the zoo animals out and attach each piece to a block. Encourage the children to build "crazy animals," and to use other blocks to create cages.

Math

Place two hoops on the floor, each with one these sentence strip labels attached: "Lives in the zoo," and, "Does not live in the zoo." Place a picture of a zoo on both hoops, crossing out the one that goes in the "Does not live in the zoo." Provide plastic sorting animals for the children to place in the correct hoops.

Book Suggestions

A Children's Zoo by Tana Hoban
Curious George Visits the Zoo by H.A. Rey
Goodnight, Gorilla by Peggy Rathman
Zoo-Looking by Mem Fox

Snack

Provide green-tinted frosting for the children to spread on graham crackers. Have them attach zoo-animal cookies on the frosting-covered graham crackers.

Review

Play animal charades. See if the children can act out their favorite zoo animals by action, sound, or both. The children guess and see how many zoo animals they remember.

Assessment

When given a group of animals, can the child identify those who live in a zoo? Can the child make the sounds of various zoo animals?

Shelley Hoster, Norcross, GA

Index of Children's Books

Index

Index

Index

Index

Index

Index

Index

Index

Index

Index

Index

Index